International Series in Operations Research & Management Science

Volume 210

For further volumes:
http://www.springer.com/series/6161

Yasar A. Ozcan

Health Care Benchmarking and Performance Evaluation

An Assessment using Data Envelopment Analysis (DEA)

Second Edition

with contribution by Kaoru Tone

 Springer

Yasar A. Ozcan
Department of Health Administration
Virginia Commonwealth University
Richmond, VA, USA

ISSN 0884-8289   ISSN 2214-7934 (electronic)
ISBN 978-1-4899-7471-6 ISBN 978-1-4899-7472-3 (eBook)
DOI 10.1007/978-1-4899-7472-3
Springer New York Heidelberg Dordrecht London

Library of Congress Control Number: 2014940286

Printed on acid-free paper

Springer is part of Springer Science+Business Media (www.springer.com)

To my wife Gulperi Ozcan

Acknowledgments

Writing this book could not have been achieved without the help and encouragement of many individuals. I take this opportunity to thank them; if I miss anyone, it is through authorial oversight only, as all the help received was deeply appreciated. First of all, I thank my colleague Liam O'Neil, who provided valuable insights and edits for the method chapters for the first edition. Many thanks go to my doctoral students, who received the early draft of the manuscript and pointed out many corrections. Especially, I thank Drs. Nailya DeLellis and Cynthia Childress (former doctoral students) who lent their class projects to become part of this book in Chaps. 11 and 13, respectively.

I would like to acknowledge Anne Doherty Renz for her diligent editing of the second edition of the manuscript from cover to cover. For their encouragement and cooperativeness in the production of this manuscript, I also extend my sincere thanks to Springer publishing editors Nicholas Philipson, Neil Levine, and Matthew Amboy and International Series in Operations Research and Management Science editors Frederick S. Hiller and Camille C. Price. Special thanks go to Professor Kaoru Tone who graciously lent a learning version of DEA Solver software to be distributed with the second edition of this book.

No book can be written without the support and encouragement of loved ones. I am indebted to my wife Gulperi Ozcan, who served as my sounding board for every aspect of this text. Moreover, she extended her support throughout the development and revision of the manuscript even as I deprived her of my time in favor of this manuscript. I thank her for the sustained support she has given me throughout my academic career and our personal lives.

Richmond, VA, USA   Yasar A. Ozcan
January, 2014

Contents

List of Figures

List of Tables

Foreword

Improving the efficiency of health care, the primary focus of this book, is one of the most important management challenges of this century. The US health care spending exceeded $3.6 trillion in 2013, and credible estimates suggest that this amount will exceed $4 trillion by 2016. Over one of every seven dollars (16 %) of gross domestic product is devoted to health care. In addition to spending more on health care than other countries by some measure, this weakens the US-based business' global competitiveness. Globally, on average, over 10 % of gross domestic product is spent on health care, and the national health systems are feeling the stress of high costs and seeking ways to improve efficiency, contain costs, and maintain quality of care. The value and relevance of this book are significant and can benefit government policy makers, health care managers, and students of management, public health, and medicine; and of course the value and relevance apply around the globe to wherever there are organized health care systems.

Professor Yasar Ozcan is literally one of a handful of academics that has the background, experience, and acumen to develop this book focusing on improving health care productivity using data envelopment analysis (DEA) and related methods. He has been actively researching and publishing on issues of health care management, use of operations research methods in health care to improve delivery and quality of care, and specifically DEA for over 20 years. A study in *Socio-Economic Planning Sciences* (by Gattoufi, Oral, Kumar, and Reisman—vol. 38—2004) notes that Prof. Ozcan is one of the 15 most prolific DEA contributors as of 2001, measured in volume of academic journal publications. More importantly, I believe that Prof. Ozcan is distinguished as the only one of these major DEA contributors that is a widely recognized expert in health care management. In addition to his significant body of work in health care operations research and DEA, Prof. Ozcan is the founder and editor of *Health Care Management Science*. Professor Ozcan's work on health systems in several countries around the globe makes the perspective of his writing sensitive to and applicable to health system issues throughout the globe.

While Professor Ozcan's volume of work is substantial and impressive, the element that makes this book particularly valuable is that Prof. Ozcan's work focuses on applications to a broad set of health care fields and organizations. The focus on field studies and the quality of that work will allow managers and policy makers to gain new insights into ways to enhance the productivity of their health care services or to understand the way alternative initiatives will impact efficiency and cost of care. After offering a perspective on health care productivity management, a primer on DEA, and alternative models, this book provides field examples that speak directly to every significant facet of health care services that I can think of. Included are major providers: hospitals, managed care (health maintenance—HMO) organizations, nursing homes, home health agencies, dialysis centers, mental health centers, dental clinics, aging programs, and other specialized activities. The focus also extends both to managing the organization and its method of delivering health services and the providers' practice patterns (physicians, nurses) in their delivery of general care and in specialized disease treatments.

This book offers a perspective on the unique strengths of DEA in addressing the types of service management issues common to most health care services. Specifically, DEA is particularly powerful in managing services where there are multiple outputs (types of patients, diverse severity of patients, etc.) and multiple inputs used to provide these services. At the same time, Prof. Ozcan identifies the boundaries of DEA and also describes related methods that are used for health care productivity analysis such as regression analysis and total factor productivity. The result is that the reader is encouraged, challenged, and energized to apply these concepts to their research or directly to their organization, as has occurred with many students that have worked with Prof. Ozcan over the years.

Managers, government policy makers, consultants, students, and academics can all gain new insights into the quest to improve productivity of health care services, manage costs of care, and develop methods to tackle related problems from this book. *HEALTH CARE BENCHMARKING AND PERFORMANCE EVALUATION: An Assessment using Data Envelopment Analysis* is, in my view, a welcome and needed addition to the DEA literature and health care management literature.

College of Business Administration   H. David Sherman DBA, CPA
Northeastern University
Boston, MA, USA

Preface

The second edition of this book, as in the first edition, places emphasis on the application of contemporary performance and efficiency evaluation methods, using data envelopment analysis (DEA), to create optimization-based benchmarks including, but not limited to, hospitals, physician group practices, health maintenance organizations, nursing homes, and other health care delivery organizations. Hence, this book will not only be useful for graduate students to learn DEA applications in health care but will also be an excellent reference and "how-to book" for practicing administrators.

There are various evaluation methods to assess performance in health care. Each method comes with its strengths and weaknesses. The key to performance evaluation is how to conceptualize the service production in various health care settings as well as appropriately measure the variables that would define this process. The research papers published in various health care and operations research journals provide insight into conceptualization of service production processes in various health care organizations. Also many research papers delineate methods that can be used for this purpose. Depending upon when and where the research was conducted, and the availability of the measures for inputs and outputs or their proxies, researchers can determine which variables they should employ in conceptualization of the health service production process. The nature of data availability further implies that some research findings on performance may produce sensitive results; thus, a comparison of the results using different variables, if possible, is prudent.

Part 1 of this book has eight chapters that are designed to introduce the performance concepts and DEA models of efficiency most frequently used in health care. An example consisting of ten hospitals is used throughout these eight chapters to illustrate the various DEA models. This example includes only two output and two input variables. The intent for the example is to create understanding of the methodology with a small number of variables and observations. In practice, measurement of efficiency in hospitals or in other health care organizations using DEA goes beyond the presented example and requires appropriate conceptualization of service production in these organizations. The extensive health care provider applications are left to the second section of this book, where DEA models with appropriate output and input variables for various health care providers and the like are presented.

In this first section of the book, Chap. 1 provides a brief survey of performance evaluation methods for health care and discusses their strengths and weaknesses for performance evaluation. These methods include ratio analysis, the least-square regression analysis, total factor productivity (TFP) including the Malmquist Index, stochastic frontier analysis (SFA), and DEA.

Efficiency measures and efficiency evaluations using DEA are the subject of Chap. 2. This chapter explains the most commonly used concepts of efficiency, such as technical, scale, price, and allocative efficiency. Other sections of Chap. 2 provide more detail on DEA techniques, including model orientation (input versus output), and various frontier models such as constant returns to scale (CRS). The hospital example and software illustration on how to run these models provide enhanced understanding to readers.

Chapter 3 further develops the returns to scale concept and introduces the variable returns to scale (VRS) model with software illustration. Weight-restricted (multiplier) models (cone ratio or assurance region models) are presented and illustrated in Chap. 4. Chapter 5 discusses non-oriented or slack-based models and shows how and under what circumstances they can be used. The second edition includes two versions of non-controllable variable models and adds categorical variable models.

Longitudinal (panel) evaluations are illustrated in Chap. 6 using the Malmquist Index and Windows analysis. This chapter not only illustrates an efficiency change between two or more time periods but also accounts for technological changes.

Chapter 7 is dedicated to the effectiveness dimension of performance evaluation. This chapter introduces effectiveness in a performance model and shows the potential misuse of quality variables in DEA models. Furthermore, it suggests a procedure to evaluate both efficiency and effectiveness. The second edition provides extended examples of using quality variables in DEA models and provides sensitivity testing.

Chapter 8, a new addition to this section, is where new and advanced models of DEA are discussed and illustrated. These include super-efficiency, congestion DEA, network DEA, and dynamic network DEA models. The chapter also provides discussion of two-stage DEA where researchers conduct post hoc analysis of DEA scores to evaluate determinants of efficiency. Discussion includes logistic regression and Tobit regression and it provides guidance in using these techniques in conjunction with bootstrapping to obtain bias-corrected estimates.

The aim of this book is to reduce the anxiety about complex mathematics and promote the use of DEA for health care managers and researchers. Thus, the mathematical formulations of various DEA models used in this book are purposefully placed in the appendices at the end of appropriate chapters for interested readers.

Part 2 includes the health care applications. In this section, DEA is applied to health care organizational settings to determine which providers are functioning efficiently when compared to a homogenous group of providers in their respective services.

The most frequently evaluated health care providers are hospitals, physician practices, nursing homes, and health maintenance organizations (HMOs). The DEA models for these providers are discussed in Chaps. 9 through 12, respectively.

Many DEA studies defined hospital service production and delineated the variations in hospital production by suggesting models that provide conceptualization of inputs and outputs in this process. Hollingsworth, Dawson, and Maniadakis (1999) and Hollingsworth (2003) provided extensive review of nonparametric and parametric performance evaluation applications in the health care arena. In these reviews, the focus was on health care issues conducted in both the USA and abroad. Hollingsworth (2003) shows that about 50 % of the 168 DEA health care applications are for hospitals. Chapter 9 develops a robust hospital DEA model based on these previous studies, where we also provide a synopsis of some of these studies and suggest a model that can serve as a standard for future hospital performance evaluations.

The scope of physician studies is varied based on different categorization methods. These different categories are workplace, diseases, and type of physician. The workplace-related studies assess physicians in independent practice association (IPA)-type HMOs, physicians in hospitals, and physicians in a general group practice. The studies based on disease encompass heart failure and shock, otitis media, sinusitis, stroke, and so on. Other studies focused on generalists or specialists.

Due to different scopes of these studies, the inputs and outputs selected to assess efficiency via DEA are not consistent. In those studies that focused on diseases and primary care, the variables of primary care provider (PCP) visits, specialist visits, emergency visits, laboratory tests, and prescriptions were usually selected to be input variables; patient episodes with different degrees of severity of disease were usually selected to be output variables. In the studies that focused on diseases and hospitals or in HMOs, the length of stay was added to the input group. The output variables were almost the same as the variables in the primary care studies. Chapter 10 provides an in-depth look at DEA-based physician evaluations. Few studies focused on dental services, but they are discussed in Chap. 14.

The nursing home studies are more consistent and provide a more focused scope. Common observations for nursing homes are the type of outputs used and definition of the decision-making units (DMUs) as intermediate care and skilled nursing facilities. Another consistency is in the overall theme of the inputs such as staff numbers and financial issues. Chapter 11 specifies the DEA-based nursing home models.

Chapter 12 introduces a few studies on HMOs and DEA models associated with them. Chapter 13 explores home health care and introduces DEA models for home health agencies.

Other types of health care providers covered include dialysis centers, community mental health centers, community-based youth services, organ procurement organizations, aging agencies, and dental providers. DEA models for these providers are shown in Chap. 14.

Chapter 15 provides an insight into other DEA models designed to evaluate health care provider performance for specific treatments including stroke, mechanical ventilation, and perioperative services. This chapter also includes DEA models for physicians at hospital settings, hospital mergers, hospital closures, hospital labor markets, hospital services in local markets, and sensitivity analysis for hospital service production.

A new chapter in this section, Chap. 16, examines international-country-based applications of DEA in health care. There are 16 countries, plus OECD and multi-country studies are examined, almost half of which had significant health care reforms during the past decade, while other countries have interesting applications of DEA where often cultural and other country-specific structural factors may need attention.

A learning version of DEA Solver (DEA-Solver-LV) software written by Professor Kaoru Tone accompanies this text and can be accessed at http://link.springer.com/10.1007/978-1-4899-7472-3. This learning version of DEA Solver can solve up to 50 DMUs for various DEA models listed in the User's Guide at the end of the book. For the full professional version of the software, the reader is advised to visit www.saitech-inc.com. The reader should examine the section on "User's Guide to DEA-Solver-Learning Version," especially the data format for the Excel worksheet.

Developing examples for the techniques explained in each chapter has been a consuming task. Any errors and oversights in that process are solely mine. I will appreciate reader comments to improve or correct the mistakes as well as suggestions for incorporating additional materials in future editions. Please e-mail your comments to ozcan@vcu.edu.

Richmond, VA, USA   Yasar A. Ozcan

Section I
Methods

The next eight chapters introduce performance concepts and models of efficiency that can be solved using data envelopment analysis (DEA) and that incorporate effectiveness into a performance model. Chapter 1 provides a brief survey of performance evaluation methods for health care and discusses their strengths and weaknesses for performance evaluation. Efficiency measures and efficiency evaluations using DEA are the subject of Chap. 2. Later sections of the Chap. 2 provide more detail on DEA techniques, including model orientation (input versus output) and various frontier models such as constant returns to scale (CRS). Chapter 3 introduces variable returns to scale (VRS) models with software illustration. Chapter 4 presents weight-restricted (multiplier) models (cone ratio or assurance region models). Chapter 5 discusses non-oriented or slack-based models and shows how and under what circumstances they can be used. Chapter 6 illustrates longitudinal (panel) evaluations using Windows analysis and the Malmquist Index. Chapter 7 introduces effectiveness in a performance model and shows the potential misuse of quality variables in DEA models. Finally, Chap. 8 discusses the newer DEA methods and shows how they can be used in health care.

Chapter 1
Evaluation of Performance in Health Care

1.1 Introduction

The health care industry faces new challenges every day, and comprises one-seventh of the gross national product (GNP) in the United States. New regulations, new technologies, and new organizations are being created continuously as a result of public policy. Managers of health care need to respond to these challenges with sound performance evaluation and decision making. This book will offer state-of-the-art performance evaluation methods as well as relevant and current examples to aid practicing managers, researchers new to this discipline, and students studying in this field.

Management in all industries is moving toward more objective performance evaluation and decision making. The health care industry, however, has lagged behind many other industries in this respect. In the United States, when the prospective payment system first began in 1983, the health care industry had to scramble to meet the needs of their clients due to significant decreases in reimbursements for Medicare patients. The initial reaction to this was to cut costs or avoid cases that would likely lose money, but later most administrators realized that the only way to keep their institutions financially viable was to improve their performance. In addition, more recent health care reforms—not only in the United States but also in many other countries with further tightened reimbursement systems—require better performance from the providers. In particular, the Centers for Medicare & Medicaid Services' (CMS) Hospital Value-Based Purchasing (HVPB) program demands higher performance and quality of care. Hence, benchmarking became the latest tool to evaluate performance. Unfortunately, the benchmarks established using old analytical schemes based on various multiple ratios created more dilemmas than solutions. Performance evaluation is based on optimization techniques and their normative structure and not only creates benchmarks, but also provides information for lacking organizations and illustrates how to improve performance. This is what is needed in the health care industry today.

Y.A. Ozcan, *Health Care Benchmarking and Performance Evaluation*,
International Series in Operations Research & Management Science 210,
DOI 10.1007/978-1-4899-7472-3_1, © Springer Science+Business Media New York 2014

This book places emphasis on the application of contemporary performance and efficiency evaluation methods, using Data Envelopment Analysis (DEA), to create optimization-based benchmarks including, but not limited to, hospitals, physician group practices, health maintenance organizations, nursing homes, and other health care delivery organizations. Hence, this book will not only be useful for students to learn DEA applications in health care, but will also be an excellent reference and "how to book" for practicing administrators as well as for those researchers who are new to this field.

1.2 Performance Measurement

During the past few decades, parametric and non-parametric methods have been employed increasingly to measure and analyze the performance of health care services. This section reviews the issues in performance measurement for health services.

Health care managers must adapt new methods to use the resources at their disposal in order to achieve high performance, namely effective and high-quality medical outcomes. Performance, as in other service industries, can be defined as an appropriate combination of efficiency and effectiveness. However, those frequently used terms, efficiency and effectiveness, are often used with a somewhat vague sense of meaning in the health care context. *Efficiency* generally refers to using the minimum number of inputs for a given number of outputs. Efficient care, therefore, means a health care facility produces a given level of care or quantity that meets an acceptable standard of quality, using the minimum combination of resources. In performance literature, *efficiency* and *productivity* are often used interchangeably. While productivity generally connotes a broader meaning, both terms are considered a component of performance. As conceptualized in Fig. 1.1, research studies suggest that improving efficiency should lead to greater health service performance, while holding constant the quality, staff skill-mix, and case-mix. *Effectiveness*, more specifically, evaluates the outcomes of medical care and can be affected by efficiency or can influence efficiency as well as have an impact on the health service performance. For instance, *effectiveness* encourages us to ask if the necessary

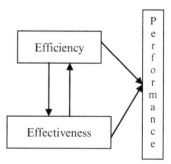

Fig. 1.1 Components of performance

Table 1.1 Multi-facility and multi-time performance comparison

Health care organization	Efficiency Time 1	Efficiency Time 2	Effectiveness Time 1	Effectiveness Time 2
Hospital 1	0.81	0.88	0.86	0.93
Hospital 2	1.00	0.84	0.84	0.91
Hospital 3	1.00	1.00	1.00	1.00
Hospital 4	0.78	0.94	0.86	0.96
Hospital 5	0.62	0.55	0.71	0.62

inputs are being used in order to produce the best possible outcomes. A hospital can be efficient, but not effective; it can also be effective, but not efficient. The aim is to be both.

Health care organizations will continue to face turbulent times and more intense competition. Health care managers must address promoting and improving performance within their institutions if they and their organizations are to continue to exist. There is not a standard formula for improving performance. Each health care organization, service, and/or procedure must be examined individually. In some contexts, the organization may have to increase the inputs used to improve quality. In other situations, more must be done with fewer resources while holding quality constant. Health care managers will always be challenged with one of the most difficult tasks, determining the proper mix of inputs and outputs.

The relationship between efficiency and quality of care has had mixed results in prior studies. Singaroyan et al. (2006) concluded that improving quality of health care may not always lead to efficient operations. On the other hand, Helling et al. (2006) found that increasing efficiency will result in quality. Mobley and Magnussen (2002) indicated that poor quality outcomes are associated with less efficiency. Ferrando et al. (2005) stated that with proper guidelines, hospitals can increase efficiency without affecting the quality of care. Ozcan (2009, pp. 222–3) illustrates how efficiency and quality can be improved simultaneously.

Performance needs to be measured and compared across health care providers for several purposes, including:

- detecting changes from one time period to another
- determining how organizations are functioning relative to others in a given competitive market (benchmarking or peer review)
- adjusting to public policy mandates
- responding to reimbursement changes

Performance in this context should be viewed as a *relative* phenomenon across health care organizations. Thus it can be compared across different providers at one point in time, or it can be compared for the same provider across multiple points in time.

Table 1.1 illustrates the measurements of performance where efficiency and effectiveness are measured in time as well as across health care organizations, using

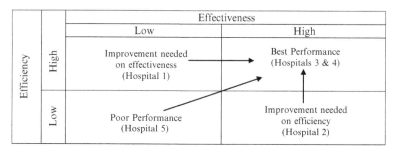

Fig. 1.2 Performance classification schema

efficiency and effectiveness scores (these will be explained later in Chap. 2). Performance scores range from 0.0 to 1.0, where 1.0 is the highest achievable. For the time being, let us assume that 0.90 is an acceptable performance criterion for either high efficiency or effectiveness.

In this example there is no question about the performance of Hospital 3, which held its efficiency and effectiveness score at the top for both periods. *Relative* to other hospitals, this particular hospital would be considered a *benchmark* health care organization. Conversely, the other hospitals relative to Hospital 3 had some performance issues. Hospital 4, although relatively inefficient and ineffective in Time 1, closed this gap and became a high performer in Time 2. The trend for Hospital 1 is also promising. Both efficiency and effectiveness improved over time; however, this hospital needs more improvement on its efficiency to become as high a performer as Hospitals 3 and 4. Hospital 2 exhibits a mixed performance from Time 1 to Time 2, since its efficiency went down while effectiveness reached an acceptably high standard. In the past, many health care managers argued this point, suggesting that to improve quality (effectiveness) something has to be taken away from efficiency. Of course, the performance of Hospital 4 argues against this point, since both efficiency and effectiveness increased over time. Lastly, Hospital 5 was a poor performer in Time 1, and this poor performance was amplified in Time 2. Given these scenarios, one can classify the health care performance of these organizations into four groups based on their efficiency and effectiveness scores using Time 2 scores as shown in Fig. 1.2. Hospitals exhibiting less than high performance in either measure should aim toward the upper-right quadrant of the performance classification schema.

The challenge of performance improvement planning is in determining the values that yield efficiency and effectiveness scores; namely, what should health care managers do to improve the performance situation of the health care organization? This brings us to the methodologies that are used to calculate efficiency and effectiveness measures.

1.3 Performance Evaluation Methods

Comparative performance analysis can be undertaken by various methods, including:

- Ratio analysis,
- Least-squares regression (LSR),
- Total factor productivity (TFP),
- Stochastic frontier analysis (SFA), and
- Data envelopment analysis (DEA).

1.3.1 Ratio Analysis

The ratio analysis approach is the simplest of the methods for calculating performance, especially productivity/efficiency. It produces information on the relationship between *one input* and *one output*. That is, efficiency is defined as the number of output units per unit of input:

$$Efficiency \ (Productivity) = \frac{Output}{Input} \tag{1.1}$$

Often, however, many ratios have to be calculated to capture various dimensions of performance among compatible units, or of a given unit over different time periods. This is especially true for the hospital sector, where various data warehouse and analytics organizations provide comparative benchmark and performance statistics.

The hospital industry reports, through these organizations' publications, many inpatient as well as outpatient statistics displaying crude and adjusted patient volume for a given facility. These reports also characterize hospital operational information from labor, supply, and cost points of view across the peer groups of hospitals. The peer groups often are organized by region, hospital size, specialty, and so on.

Similarly, physician group practice performance statistics are reported by departmental and group levels for subscribing groups by various organizations such as Medical Group Management Association (MGMA). Either hospital or group practices receive these thick volumes of quarterly reports, or online versions containing several hundred ratios to be monitored for benchmarking by health care managers.

Using multiple ratios often produces mixed results that confuse health care managers in comparative performance analysis. To illustrate this, let us examine the situation presented in Table 1.2, where we compare ten hospitals.

For simplicity, let us assume there are two inputs, nursing hours and medical supplies, and two outputs, inpatient admissions and outpatient visits. Using this

Table 1.2 Hospital inputs and outputs

Provider ID	Inputs		Outputs	
	Nursing hours	Medical supplies ($)	Inpatient admissions	Outpatient visits
H1	567	2,678	409	211
H2	350	1,200	90	85
H3	445	1,616	295	186
H4	2,200	1,450	560	71
H5	450	890	195	94
H6	399	1,660	209	100
H7	156	3,102	108	57
H8	2,314	3,456	877	252
H9	560	4,000	189	310
H10	1,669	4,500	530	390

Table 1.3 Hospital performance ratios (bold numbers indicate best performance)

Provider ID	Nursing hours/ inpatient admissions	Medical supplies/ inpatient admissions	Nursing hours/ outpatient visits	Medical supplies/ outpatient visits
H1	**1.39**	6.55	2.69	12.69
H2	3.89	13.33	4.12	14.12
H3	1.51	5.48	2.39	**8.69**
H4	3.93	**2.59**	30.99	20.42
H5	2.31	4.56	4.79	9.47
H6	1.91	7.94	3.99	16.60
H7	1.44	28.72	2.74	54.42
H8	2.64	3.94	9.18	13.71
H9	2.96	21.16	**1.81**	12.90
H10	3.15	8.49	4.28	11.54

information, one can calculate four possible performance ratios as illustrated in Table 1.3.

These ratios are analogous to what is being reported in hospital performance statistics by data warehousing and analytics organizations.

Please note that all ratios presented in Table 1.3 reflect input/output, the reverse of what is indicated with formula (1.1); thus, the lowest ratio reflects the best value. In order to identify benchmarks (i.e., best performers), one can standardize each of these performance ratios across the hospitals by identifying the best score in each ratio, then dividing this into the particular ratio of each hospital. For example, Hospital 1 (H1) has the best ratio for the nursing hours per inpatient admission, which is 1.39. By dividing this into other hospitals' nursing hours per inpatient admissions, we can obtain a relative value compared to H1, which is considered a benchmark hospital for this particular ratio. We can label this relative benchmarking score as the standardized efficiency ratio. Table 1.4 depicts the standardized efficiency ratios for four categories. Based on the relative scores of each hospital, one can

Table 1.4 Standardized efficiency ratios and ranking of the hospitals (bold numbers indicate best performance)

Provider ID	Nursing hours/ inpatient admissions	Medical supplies/ inpatient admissions	Nursing hours/ outpatient visits	Medical supplies/ outpatient visits
H1	**1.00 [1]**	0.40 [5]	0.67 [3]	0.68 [4]
H2	0.36 [9]	0.19 [8]	0.44 [6]	0.62 [7]
H3	0.92 [3]	0.47 [4]	0.76 [2]	**1.00 [1]**
H4	0.35 [10]	**1.00 [1]**	0.06 [10]	0.43 [9]
H5	0.60 [5]	0.57 [3]	0.38 [8]	0.92 [2]
H6	0.73 [4]	0.33 [6]	0.45 [5]	0.52 [8]
H7	0.96 [2]	0.09 [10]	0.66 [4]	0.16 [10]
H8	0.53 [6]	0.66 [2]	0.20 [9]	0.63 [6]
H9	0.47 [7]	0.12 [9]	**1.00 [1]**	0.67 [5]
H10	0.44 [8]	0.30 [7]	0.42 [7]	0.75 [3]

rank the hospitals (shown in brackets in Table 1.4). This case further illustrates the dilemma for the health care managers when benchmark performance rankings vary depending upon which ratio is under consideration.

For example, H1 is considered a benchmark hospital for nursing hours per inpatient admissions; however, H1 ranks fifth on "medical supplies per inpatient admissions," third on "nursing hours per outpatient visit," and fourth on "medical supplies per outpatient visit." On the other hand, H4 displays more dramatic results: while ranking first on "medical supplies per inpatient admissions," H4 ranks tenth on "nursing hours per inpatient admissions" as well as "nursing hours per outpatient visits," and ninth on "medical supplies per outpatient visits." Similar mixed results can be observed from Table 1.4 for H9, which is a benchmark hospital on "nursing hours per outpatient visits," and for H3, which ranks highest on "medical supplies per outpatient visits."

This illustrates the weakness of ratio-based analysis, where health care managers often cannot pinpoint a consistent benchmark incorporating all inputs and outputs of the health care organization.

1.3.2 The Least-Squares Regression

The least-squares regression (LSR) is a very popular parametric technique and, by its formulation, it assumes that all health care organizations are efficient. While it can accommodate multiple inputs and outputs, it can also account for noise, using an error term (see "e" in formula (1.2)). A general formula for a least-squares regression is:

$$y = \beta_0 + \beta_1 x_1 + \beta_2 x_2 + \dots \beta_n x_n + e \qquad (1.2)$$

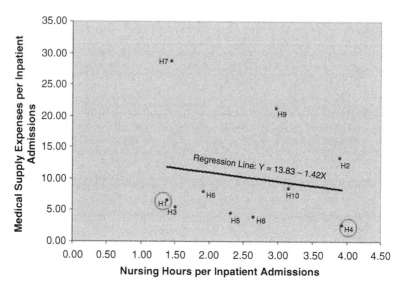

Fig. 1.3 Hospital performance I

For this model, it is further assumed that:

- for any fixed value of x, y is a random variable $(y|x) = \beta_0 + \beta_1 x$,
- the y values are independent of one another
- the mean value of y is a straight-line function of x, $y = \beta_0 + \beta_1 x_1 + e$,
- the variance of y is the same for any x, and
- y has a normal distribution for any fixed value of x.

The least-squares regression has some benefits. It can be used to measure technical change if time-series data are used. In addition, scale economies can be calculated. However, its drawbacks are greater.

Using least-squares regression in performance analysis poses many weaknesses. Firstly, the least-squares regression uses central tendency measures (averaging techniques), which are not necessarily efficient relationships. Furthermore, LSR does not identify the individual inefficient units, and it requires a pre-specified production function due to its parametric formulation.

Let us illustrate these weaknesses using the example developed in Sect. 1.3.1. Consider the first two ratios, in which nursing hours and medical supplies per inpatient admissions were calculated. Using these two ratios one can map the hospitals on a scatter diagram, as shown in Fig. 1.3, to analyze the hospital performance from an inpatient admissions perspective (let us label this "Hospital Performance I").

We established earlier that H1 was the best hospital in terms of nursing hours per inpatient admissions, while H4 was the best based on medical supplies per inpatient admissions. Using regression analysis, an estimate of hospital performance from the inpatient admissions perspective (Hospital Performance I) is described by line

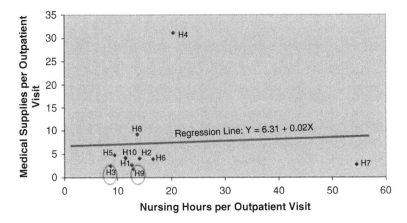

Fig. 1.4 Hospital performance II

$y = 13.83 - 1.42\times$, as shown in Fig. 1.3. This average line best predicts efficiency relationships when observations in a scatter diagram are closer to the estimated line. Hence, H2, H6, and H10 are the closest hospitals to this line while H1 and H4 are at a further distance. Thus, according to regression analysis, for better performance H1 and H4 should move closer to the average, as illustrated by the regression line. In reality, this means H1 and H4 should give up their benchmark status with respect to these ratios and actually become more inefficient.

We can replicate the same evaluation for the second dimension of the performance using a regression estimate of hospital performance from the outpatient visits perspective (Hospital Performance II). This case is described by line $y = 6.31 + 0.02\times$, as shown in Fig. 1.4. As can be interpreted from this figure, H3 and H9, which were considered benchmark hospitals for this dimension of the hospital performance, are not good examples of performance based on the regression line because they are further away from the average performance with respect to H2, H5, H6, H8, and H10.

As these two examples illustrate, the regression analysis does not necessarily predict the best performance or the most efficient relationships. Hence, we must explore other methodologies that would describe more robust performance measures.

1.3.3 Total Factor Productivity (TFP)

Total factor productivity overcomes the weakness of single ratio analysis and incorporates multiple inputs/outputs into a single performance ratio. More specifically, total factor productivity is measured using index numbers. Index numbers can be used to measure price and quantity changes over time, and also measure differences across health care organizations.

$$TFP_{ab} = \frac{\displaystyle\sum_{i=1}^{N} p_{ib}q_{ib}}{\displaystyle\sum_{i=1}^{N} p_{ia}q_{ia}} \tag{1.3}$$

In formula (1.3) TFP_{ab} index measures the change in the value of selected quantities of N outputs from period "a" to "b," where p represents the prices of these outputs. The most commonly used indices are: Laspeyres index, Pasche index, Fisher index, Tornqvist index, and Malmquist index. The difference between the Laspeyres and Pasche indices is whether the base period or current period quantities are used as weights. To overcome this difference, the Fisher index uses a geometric mean of the Laspeyres and Pasche indices. Similarly, the Tornqvist index uses various geometric averages for price and quantity, and finally the Malmquist index is further described below.

The Laspeyres, Pasche, Fisher, and Tornqvist indices are non-parametric techniques that can be used with panel or cross-sectional data to measure the performance of two health care organizations in one time period or the performance of one health care organization in two time periods. However, when more than two health care organizations need to be compared at the same time or over time, these methodologies are not useful. Since TFP is not commonly used by the health care industry, we will not elaborate on these four indices any further. Of the TFP measures, the most frequently used method in health care is the Malmquist index.

The Malmquist index overcomes some of the shortcomings of the other indices discussed above. With the Malmquist index, health care managers can compare many organizations across two time periods. The Malmquist index can be obtained through frontier approaches such as stochastic frontier analysis or data envelopment analysis (DEA). The Malmquist index does not assume that all firms are efficient or require price data.

Malmquist index numbers can be defined using either the output-oriented approach or the input-oriented approach. An important feature of the DEA Malmquist index is that it can decompose the overall efficiency measure into two mutually exclusive components, one measuring change in technical efficiency (catching-up effect) and the other measuring change in technology (innovation). In Chap. 6, we will illustrate the use of the Malmquist index for hospital performance in multiple periods.

1.3.4   Stochastic Frontier Analysis (SFA)

Stochastic frontier analysis is also a parametric technique. SFA assumes that all firms are not efficient (this is an improvement over LSR) and accounts for noise.

A general stochastic frontier model can be formulated as:

$$TC = TC(Y, W) + V + U \qquad (1.4)$$

where

TC = total cost
Y = output
W = input prices
V = random error assumed normally distributed with zero mean and variance
U = the inefficiency residual

SFA can be used to conduct tests of hypotheses. It can also be used to measure technical efficiency, scale economies, allocative efficiencies, technical change, and TFP change (if panel data are available). However, SFA requires input and output quantities for empirical estimation of production functions. It can also be used to analyze panel or cross-sectional data.

SFA comes with certain shortcomings as well. For example, it requires specification of functional form and specification of a distributional form for the inefficiency term, U in formula (1.4). With the use of price information as well as quantity information, additional measurement errors may be added to the results (Kooreman 1994). The resulting inefficiency may be due to technical or allocative inefficiency or a combination of both. These two sources of inefficiencies cannot be separated, which is prudent since such knowledge might illustrate the need for different policy actions (Kooreman 1994).

1.3.5 Data Envelopment Analysis (DEA)

Data envelopment analysis (DEA) is a non-parametric technique. DEA assumes that not all firms are efficient. It allows multiple inputs and outputs to be used in a linear programming model that develops a single score of efficiency for *each* observation used to measure technical efficiency, scale efficiency, allocative efficiency, congestion efficiency, technical change, and TFP change (if panel data are available and Malmquist indices are calculated). DEA requires input and output quantities if production efficiency is examined and can be used with both cross-sectional and panel data.

DEA does not account for noise due to its deterministic nature (deviation from the frontier is a result of inefficient operations). However, by using bootstrapping techniques with DEA, one can build confidence intervals for the efficiency measures; thus stochastic and other variants of DEA models may account for a random error.

Since the DEA is the main performance evaluation methodology considered in this book, the remaining chapters will illustrate the various DEA models and their applications.

1.4 Measurement Difficulties in Health Care

Measurement of the variables that describe the true nature of service production is an important prerequisite for performance measurement. In health care, due to the nature of the services provided, it is often difficult to find the appropriate variables and their measurements. Of course this depends on the level of analysis and whether it is carried out at the hospital level or the departmental level. Often, the departmental-level measurements cannot be aggregated to the hospital level. For example, unit measures in a laboratory are different than in radiology or in nursing units. Thus, when hospital-level measures are considered, what has been included in service production measures might be considerably different if these evaluations are carried out at the departmental level. For instance, performance of laboratories or radiology services across hospitals can be carried out as long as the measurements are consistent for each department.

Defining and measuring the output at the hospital level varies considerably across providers by the volume and scope of services provided, and also by patients' severity. Thus appropriate adjustments such as case-mix adjustment should be undertaken. In addition, outputs such as education, research, and certain community services may not be available in all hospitals. Lack of homogeneity in outputs produced and scale of operations may force one to conduct the performance analysis on those facilities that are considered peer-group organizations. Similarly, defining and measuring the inputs may pose difficulties as well. For example, differences may arise in pricing of input units, supply and materials, or labor costs across facilities depending upon region. Likewise, capital assets valuation, depending upon when these are acquired and what type of depreciation rate is used, may render great variations in inputs. These issues will be further explored as various performance measurement applications are presented in ensuing chapters.

1.5 Summary

This chapter has introduced concepts of performance measurement in health care organizations. These included two dimensions of performance: efficiency and effectiveness (quality). To evaluate the performance, we provided a survey of methods including their strengths and weaknesses. These methods include: ratio analysis, the least-squares regression, total productivity factor indices including the Malmquist index, stochastic frontier analysis, and data envelopment analysis (DEA). In what follows, we describe the various DEA models and their extensive use for performance evaluation in health care.

Chapter 2
Performance Measurement Using Data Envelopment Analysis (DEA)

2.1 DEA in Health Care

The 1980s brought many challenges to hospitals as they attempted to improve the efficiency of health care delivery through the fixed pricing mechanism of Diagnostic Related Groupings (DRGs). In the 1990s, the federal government extended the fixed pricing mechanism to physicians' services through Resource-Based Relative Value Scale (RBRVS). Enacted more recently, the Hospital Value-Based Purchasing (HVPB) program demands higher performance and quality of care and reduces payments for those providers that cannot achieve certain performance levels. Although these pricing mechanisms attempted to influence the utilization and quality of services by controlling the amount paid to hospitals and professionals, effective cost control must also be accompanied by a greater understanding of variation in physician practice behavior and development of treatment protocols for various diseases.

Although the origins of efficiency or benchmarking trace back to Farrell's (1957) study, theoretical development of the Data Envelopment Analysis (DEA) approach was started in 1978 by Charnes et al., who produced a measure of efficiency for decision making units (DMU). DEA is a nonparametric linear programming based technique that develops an efficiency frontier by optimizing the weighted output/input ratio of each provider, subject to the condition that this ratio can equal, but never exceed, unity for any other provider in the data set (Charnes et al. 1978). In health care, the first application of DEA dates to 1983, in the work of Nunamaker and Lewin, who measured routine nursing service efficiency. Since then DEA has been used widely in the assessment of hospital technical efficiency in the United States as well as around the world at different levels of decision making units. For example, Sherman (1984) was first in using DEA to evaluate overall hospital efficiency.

Y.A. Ozcan, *Health Care Benchmarking and Performance Evaluation*,
International Series in Operations Research & Management Science 210,
DOI 10.1007/978-1-4899-7472-3_2, © Springer Science+Business Media New York 2014

2.2   Efficiency and Effectiveness Models

In order to understand the nature of the models that will be shown throughout the book, expanding on the definitions of the efficiency and effectiveness measures presented in Chap. 1 is in order. This will help not only in understanding the models developed here, but will also be useful for the curious reader examining other research in this area.

2.2.1   Efficiency Measures

As shown in formula (1.1), basic efficiency is a ratio of output over input. To improve efficiency one has to either increase the outputs or decrease the inputs. If both outputs and inputs increase, the rate of increase for outputs should be greater than the rate of increase for inputs. Conversely, if both outputs and inputs are decreasing, the rate of decrease for outputs should be lower than the rate of decrease for inputs. Another way to achieve higher efficiency is to introduce technological changes, or to reengineer service processes—lean management—which in turn may reduce inputs or increase the ability to produce more outputs (Ozcan 2009; pp. 121–123 and 222–224).

DEA models can generate new alternatives to improve performance compared to other techniques. Linear programming is the backbone methodology that is based on optimization platform. Hence, what differentiates the DEA from other methods is that it identifies the optimal ways of performance rather than the averages. In today's world, no health care institution can afford to be an average performer in a competitive health market.

Identification of optimal performance leads to benchmarking in a normative way. Using DEA, health care managers can not only identify top performers, but also discover the alternative ways to spur their health care organizations into becoming one of the best performers.

Since the seminal work of Charnes et al. (1978), DEA has been subject to countless research publications, conferences, dissertations, and applications within both the non-profit and for-profit sectors. Until now, the use of DEA within health care has been limited to conference sessions and research publications. Thus health care managers have not adopted DEA as a standard tool for benchmarking and decision-making. Part of this is due to its complicated formulation and to the failure of DEA specialists to adequately bridge the theory–practice gap. The aim of this book is to present DEA from a practical perspective, leaving the black box of sophisticated formulations in the background, so that health care managers, or those who are not trained in mathematical fields, can use Excel spreadsheet-based software, which they are familiar with, to analyze the performance of their organizations. The practical approach shown in this book will not only ease the fears of managers towards a new technique, but will also enable them to understand the pitfalls of the performed evaluations so they will feel confident in presenting, validating, and making decisions based on DEA results.

DEA is a comparative approach for identifying performance or its components by considering multiple resources that are used to achieve outputs or outcomes in health care organizations. These evaluations can be conducted not only at the organization level, but also in sub-units, such as departmental comparisons, where many areas of improvement in savings of particular input resources or strategies to augment the outputs can be identified.

In summary, DEA can help health care managers to:

1) assess their organization's relative performance,
2) identify top performance in the health care market, and
3) identify ways to improve their performance, if their organization is not one of the top performing organizations.

2.2.2   Efficiency Evaluations Using DEA

As described in Chap. 1, one of the major components of performance is efficiency. Efficiency is defined as the ratio of output(s) to input(s). Efficiency calculated by DEA is relative to these health organizations analyzed in a particular evaluation. The efficiency score for best performing (benchmark) health organizations in this evaluation would only represent the set of organizations considered in the analysis. Health care organizations identified as top performers in 1 year may not achieve this status if evaluations are repeated in subsequent years. Additionally, if more health organizations are included in another evaluation, their status may change since the relative performance will consider the newcomers. Although DEA can clearly identify improvement strategies for those non-top-performing health care organizations, further improvement of top performers depends on other factors, such as new technologies and other changes in the health service production process.

Efficiency attainment of health care organizations may also be the result of various factors, such as the price of the inputs or scope of the production process (scale) and other factors. Thus, it is prudent to understand types and components of efficiency in more depth. Major efficiency concepts can be described as technical, scale, price and allocative efficiency.

2.2.2.1   Technical Efficiency

Consider Hospital A treating brain tumors using the Gamma Knife technology. Hospital A can provide 80 procedures per month with 120 h of neurosurgeon time. Last month Hospital A produced 60 procedures while neurosurgeons were on the premises for 120 h. As shown in Table 2.1, the best achievable efficiency score for Hospital A is 0.667 (80/120), while due to their output of 60 procedures, their current efficiency score is 0.5 (60/120). We assess that Hospital A is operating at

Table 2.1 Technical efficiency

Hospital	Treatment capacity per month	Neurosurgeon time in hours	Current treatments per month	Best achievable efficiency	Efficiency
A	80	120	60	0.667	0.500

Table 2.2 Technical and scale efficiency

Hospital	Treatment capacity per month	Neurosurgeon time in hours	Current treatments per month	Best achievable efficiency	Efficiency	Scale efficiency
A	80	120	60	0.667	0.500	–
B	30	180	30	0.167	0.167	0.333

75 % (0.75 = 0.5/0.667) efficiency. This is called technical efficiency. In order for Hospital A to become technically efficient, it would have to increase its current output by 20 procedures per month.

2.2.2.2 Scale Efficiency

Also consider Hospital B, which does not have the Gamma Knife. Hence neurosurgeons at Hospital B remove tumors using the standard surgical technique (i.e., resection); to conduct 30 procedures a month, a neurosurgeon spends 180 h. The efficiency score of Hospital B is 0.167 (30/180). Compared to what Hospital A could ideally provide, Hospital B is at 25 % efficiency (0.25 = 0.167/0.667) in utilizing the neurosurgeon's time. If we consider only what Hospital A was able to achieve, Hospital B is operating at 33.3 % (0.333 = 0.167/0.5) relative efficiency in this comparison. If Hospital B used similar technology as Hospital A, then it could have produced 90 additional procedures given 180 h of neurosurgeon time; it would need to produce an additional 60 treatments to achieve the same efficiency level as Hospital A. The total difference between Hospital B's efficiency score and Hospital A's best achievable efficiency score is 0.5 (0.667 − 0.167). The difference between Hospital B's efficiency score and Hospital A's current efficiency score is 0.333 (0.5 − 0.167). Thus, we make the following observations (Table 2.2):

1) Hospital B is technically inefficient, illustrated by the component 0.167.
2) Hospital B is also scale inefficient, illustrated by the difference of 0.333.

The scale inefficiency can only be overcome by adopting the new technology or new service production processes. By contrast, the technical inefficiency is a managerial problem, where more outputs are required for a given level of resources.

We should also add that even though Hospital A produced 80 procedures a month, we cannot say that Hospital A is absolutely efficient unless it is compared to other hospitals with similar technology. However, at this point we know that differences in technology can create economies of scale in the health service production process. Using various DEA methods, health care managers can calculate both technical and scale efficiencies.

2.2.2.3 Price Efficiency

Efficiency evaluations can be assessed using price or cost information for inputs and/or outputs. For example, if the charge for the Gamma Knife procedure is $18,000 and for traditional surgery is $35,000, the resulting efficiency for Hospital A and Hospital B would be as follows:

Efficiency (A) = (60*18,000)/120 = $9,000.00
Efficiency (B) = (30*35,000)/180 = $5,833.33

Assuming that a neurosurgeon's time is reimbursed at the same rate for either traditional surgery or Gamma Knife procedures, Hospital A appears more efficient than Hospital B; however, the difference in this case is due to price of the output. If Hospital B used 120 h to produce half as many procedures (30) as Hospital A, its price efficiency score would have been $8,750, which clearly indicates the effect of the output price. If health care managers use the cost information in inputs or charge/revenue values for outputs, DEA can provide useful information for those inefficient health care organizations about potential reductions in input costs and needed revenue/charges for their outputs. In health care, although charges/revenues are generally negotiated with third-party payers, these evaluations would provide valuable information to health care managers while providing a basis for their negotiations.

2.2.2.4 Allocative Efficiency

When more than one input (and/or output) is part of health services delivery, health care managers are interested in the appropriate mix of the inputs to serve patients so the organization can achieve efficiency. Let us consider three group practices—A, B and C—where two types of professionals, physicians (P) and nurse practitioners (NP), provide health services. Furthermore assume that a physician's time costs $100/h, whereas a nurse practitioner's time costs $60/h. Let us suppose that Group Practice A employs three physicians and one nurse practitioner, that Group Practice B employs two physicians and two nurse practitioners, and that Group Practice C employs three physicians and three nurse practitioners. Assume that all group practices produce 500 equivalent patient visits during a week. Further assume that the practices are open for 8 h a day for 5 days a week (40 h). Input prices for the group practices are:

Inputs for Group Practice A = [(3*100) + (1*60)]*40 = $14,400
Inputs for Group Practice B = [(2*100) + (2*60)]*40 = $12,800
Inputs for Group Practice C = [(3*100) + (3*60)]*40 = $19,200

Table 2.3 Allocative efficiency

Group practice	Physicians ($100/h)	Nurse practitioners ($60/h)	Input: prices ($)	Output: visits	Efficiency	Allocative efficiency
A	3	1	14,400	500	$28.80	0.889
B	2	2	12,800	500	$25.60	1.000
C	3	3	19,200	500	$38.40	0.667

Fig. 2.1 Allocative efficiency

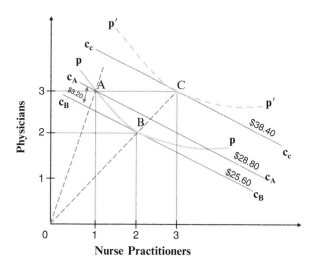

Since the output is the same, evaluating the input mix for these three group practices per visit yields the following ratios:

Group Practice A = 14,400/500 = $28.80
Group Practice B = 12,800/500 = $25.60
Group Practice C = 19,200/500 = $38.40

Table 2.3 summarizes these calculations as follows:

We can also illustrate these three group practices graphically on a production possibilities curves [pp] and [p'p'] shown in Fig. 2.1. Group Practices A and B lie on production possibilities curve [pp]. Because Group Practice C operates with a higher number of physicians and nurse practitioners when compared to Practices A and B, the production possibilities curve [p'p'] is in a higher position. Further-more, the cost per case is shown using cost lines c_A ($28.80), c_B ($25.60), and c_C ($38.40), where Group Practice B is producing the services for $3.20 less per case compared to Group Practice A, as shown by cost line c_A. Furthermore, Group Practice B is producing the services for $12.80 less per case when compared to Group Practice C.

Comparing these costs, one can conclude that Group Practice A is 88.9 % (25.60/28.80) efficient compared to Group Practice B. Similarly, Group Practice C is

66.7 % (25.60/38.40) efficient compared to Group Practice B. In addition, Group Practice C is not only allocatively inefficient, but it is also technically inefficient, since it operates on a less efficient production possibilities curve [p'p']. This example illustrates the concept of allocative efficiency, where various combinations (mixes) of inputs and their prices will yield different efficiencies.

We should also note that the contribution to outputs from each input might be different. In this example, while physicians can provide a full spectrum of services to the patients, nurse practitioners may be able to provide only a percentage, say, 70 %, due to their limited scope of practice. This raises the concern of whether using physicians and nurse practitioners as equal professions (e.g., substitutes for each other) in efficiency calculations is appropriate, or if a weighting scheme should be imposed to correctly assess the nurse practitioners' contributions to the total output. These weights are not readily available in most instances; however, DEA can estimate these weights in comparative evaluations.

2.2.3 *Effectiveness Measures*

Effectiveness in health care measured by outcomes or quality is of prime importance to many constituencies including patients, clinicians, administrators, and policy makers. Measuring the outcomes and quality is more problematic than efficiency measures. While inputs and outputs of the processes are relatively known to health care managers, multiple perspectives on outcomes and quality introduce additional practical difficulties in measurement. Although most hospitals report their inputs and outputs, until recently most outcome measures and quality measures, aside from mortality and morbidity statistics, were not reported on a systematic basis. The current quality reports from hospitals will be discussed in Chap. 7, and appropriate models will be developed to evaluate performance using both efficiency and effectiveness components.

2.3 Data Envelopment Analysis (DEA)

DEA essentially forms a frontier using the efficient organizations. To illustrate the conceptualization of the DEA frontier, consider the performance ratios of the first five hospitals from the example in Chap. 1. Here we consider two inputs, nursing hours and medical supplies, by dividing them by inpatient admissions; thus we obtain standardized usage of each input per inpatient admission.

As we observed before, H1 and H4 are efficient providers with their respective mix of use on these two inputs. We also know that H3 was an efficient provider from other dimensions of the performance. Graphically, as shown in Fig. 2.2 below, we can draw lines connecting these three efficient providers. As can be observed, there are two more hospitals, H5 and H8, that fall on the boundaries drawn by these

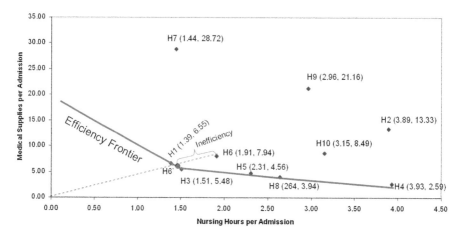

Fig. 2.2 Efficiency frontier

	Nursing hours/	Medical supplies/
Provider ID	inpatient admissions	inpatient admissions
H1	**1.39**	6.55
H2	3.89	13.33
H3	1.51	5.48
H4	3.93	**2.59**
H5	2.31	4.56
H6	1.91	7.94
H7	1.44	28.72
H8	2.64	3.94
H9	2.96	21.16
H10	3.15	8.49

Table 2.4 Hospital performance ratios (bold numbers indicate best performance)

lines between H1 and H4. Hence, these lines connecting H1, H3, H4, H5, and H8 represent the efficiency frontier for this example; they are among the benchmark hospitals because these hospitals have the lowest combinations of the inputs when both ratios are taken into account (Table 2.4).

If we go back to the logic used to create the Table 1.4, where standardized efficiency ratios were calculated, we can observe that H1 and H4 received a standardized efficiency score of 1, and the other hospitals' standardized efficiency scores were somewhere between 0 and less than 1 from one dimension of the performance. Here also in DEA, the efficient hospitals will receive a score of 1 and those that are not on the efficiency frontier line will be less than 1 but greater than 0. Although we cannot explain why H5 and H8 are on the frontier line based on the graphic (due to its two dimensions), it suffices to say that they also have the lowest combinations of the inputs when both ratios are taken into account. Later when we employ all inputs and outputs into the model, we will demonstrate with DEA why H5 and H8 receive a score of 1 and are efficient.

Hospital 6 compared to H1 and H3 is considered inefficient using these input combinations. The amount of inefficiency can be understood by examining the dashed line from the origin to H6. In this dashed line, the amount of inefficiency exists from the point it crosses the efficiency frontier to H6. So, for H6 to become efficient, it must reduce usage of both inputs proportionately to reach point H6'. This is the normative power of DEA, where it can suggest how much improvement by each inefficient hospital is needed in each dimension of the resources.

2.4   Model Orientation

As in ratio analysis, when we calculate efficiency output over input and place emphasis on reduction of inputs to improve efficiency, in DEA analysis this is called *input orientation*. Input orientation assumes health care managers have more control over the inputs than over the number of patients arriving either for outpatient visit or admissions. Figure 2.2 is an example of an input-oriented model, where H2 must reduce its inputs to achieve efficiency.

However, the reverse argument can be made: that the health care managers, through marketing, referrals, or by other means (such as reputation on quality of services), can attract patients to their facilities. This means they can augment their outputs given their capacity of inputs to increase their organization's efficiency. Output augmentation to achieve efficiency in DEA is called *output orientation*. Output orientation will be further discussed in Sect. 2.11 below.

Various DEA models have been developed to use either the input or output orientation, and these models emphasize proportional reduction of excessive inputs (input slacks) or proportional augmentation of lacking outputs (output slacks). However, there are also models where health care managers can place emphasis on both output augmentation and input reduction at the same time by improving output slacks and decreasing input slacks. These slack-based models are also called the additive model or non-oriented models in DEA literature and software.

2.5   Basic Frontier Models

This book will consider various models that would be needed by health care managers. In this chapter, the basic frontier models will be presented. The subsequent chapters will introduce the extensions to these basic models for those specific management needs in evaluation of health care organizational performance.

There are various types of DEA models that may be used depending on the conditions of the problem on hand. Types of DEA models concerning a situation can be identified based on scale and orientation of the model. If one can assume that

Fig. 2.3 DEA model classifications—basic envelopment models

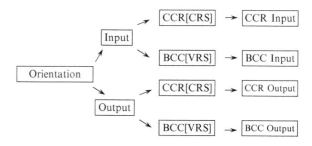

economies of scale do not change as size of the service facility increases, then constant returns to scale (CRS) type DEA models are an appropriate choice.

The initial basic frontier model was developed by Charnes et al. (1978), known as the CCR model, using the initials of the developers' last names, but now is widely known as the *constant returns to scale* (CRS) model. The other basic frontier model, known as BCC (Banker, Charnes and Cooper), followed CCR as the *variable returns to scale* (VRS) model, though in this model one cannot assume that economies of scale do not change as size of the service facility increases. Figure 2.3 shows the basic DEA models based on returns to scale and model orientation. These models will be referred as "Basic Envelopment Models."

2.6 Decision Making Unit (DMU)

Organizations subject to evaluation in the DEA literature are called Decision Making Units (DMUs). For example, the hospitals, nursing homes, group practices, and other facilities that are evaluated for performance using DEA are considered as DMUs by many popular DEA software programs.

2.7 Constant Returns to Scale CCR [CRS] Model

The essence of the constant returns to scale model is the maximization of the ratio of weighted multiple outputs to weighted multiple inputs. Any health care organization compared to others should have an efficiency score of 1 or less, with either 0 or positive weights assigned to the inputs and outputs.

Here, the calculation of DEA efficiency scores are briefly explained using mathematical notations (adapted from Cooper et al. 2007, p. 23). The efficiency scores (θ_o) for a group of peer DMUs ($j = 1 \ldots n$) are computed for the selected outputs ($y_{rj}, r = 1, \ldots, s$) and inputs ($x_{ij}, i = 1, \ldots, m$) using the following fractional programming formula:

$$Maximize \ \theta_o = \frac{\displaystyle\sum_{r=1}^{s} u_r y_{ro}}{\displaystyle\sum_{i=1}^{m} v_i x_{io}} \qquad (2.1)$$

$$subject \ to \ \frac{\displaystyle\sum_{r=1}^{s} u_r y_{rj}}{\displaystyle\sum_{i=1}^{m} v_i x_{ij}} \leq 1 \qquad (2.2)$$

$$u_r, v_i \geq 0 \quad for \ all \ r \ and \ i.$$

In this formulation, the weights for the outputs and inputs, respectively, are u_r and v_i, and "o" denotes a focal DMU (i.e., each hospital, in turn, becomes a focal hospital when its efficiency score is being computed relative to others). Note that the input and output values, as well as all weights, are assumed by the formulation to be greater than zero. The weights u_r and v_i for each DMU are determined entirely from the output and input data of all DMUs in the peer group of data. Therefore, the weights used for each DMU are those that maximize the focal DMU's efficiency score. In order to solve the fractional program described above, it needs to be converted to a linear programming formulation for easier solution.

Since the focus of this book is not on the mathematical aspects of DEA, an interested reader is referred to the appendix at the end of this chapter for more detail on how the above equations are algebraically converted to a linear programming formulation. Other DEA books listed in the references may also be consulted for an in-depth exposure.

In summary, the DEA identifies a group of optimally performing hospitals that are defined as efficient and assigns them a score of one. These efficient hospitals are then used to create an "efficiency frontier" or "data envelope" against which all other hospitals are compared. In sum, hospitals that require relatively more weighted inputs to produce weighted outputs or, alternatively, produce less weighted output per weighted inputs than do hospitals on the efficiency frontier, are considered technically inefficient. They are given efficiency scores of strictly less than 1, but greater than zero.

Although DEA is a powerful optimization technique to assess the performance of each hospital, it has certain limitations which need to be addressed. When one has to deal with significantly large numbers of inputs and outputs in the service production process and a small number of organizations are under evaluation, discriminatory power of the DEA will be limited. However, the analyst could overcome this limitation by only including those factors (input and output) which provide the essential components of the service production process, thus not distorting the outcome of the DEA results. This is generally done by eliminating one of pair of factors that are strongly positively correlated with each other.

Cooper et al. (2007, p. 116) suggest that in order to have adequate numbers of degrees of freedom (adequate discriminatory power for the DEA model), the "n"

(number of DMUs) should exceed the number of inputs (m) and outputs (s) by several times. More specifically, they suggest a rule of thumb formula that "n" should be greater than $max\{m*s, 3*(m+s)\}$.

2.8 Example for Input-Oriented CCR [CRS] DEA Model

Consider again the sample data presented in Chap. 1 with ten hospitals, two inputs, and two outputs. Table 2.5 depicts the inputs and outputs according to formulation discussions presented above. As one can observe, peer hospitals ($j = 1, \ldots, 10$) are listed for the selected inputs (x_{ij}, $i = 1, 2$) and outputs (y_{rj}, $r = 1, 2$).

The next step is to enter this information into the DEA Solver software, which runs on an Excel macro-based platform. For information regarding installation of the learning version (LV) of the software and other relevant details, readers are referred to the "Running the DEA Solver-LV" section of the book at the end. The Excel sheet containing the data for DEA analysis is named "Data" and is shown in Fig. 2.4 below.

Please note that the first column is recognized as the DMU identifier (e.g., hospital), followed by two columns of inputs and two columns of outputs. Also note that the top row identifies input and output names, and designation of either "(I)" for input or "(O)" for output precedes the variable names to identify their type (in this case either input or output, however, this will be expanded to other type of variables in ensuing chapters). Before running the model, the Excel file shown in Fig. 2.4 should be saved in a directory on the hard drive.

To run the model, double click on DEA Solver-LV (from hard drive directory), which should bring an empty Excel sheet, as shown in Fig. 2.5 Part A, where the user should activate the macro by clicking on "Options" in the Security Warning

Table 2.5 Hospital inputs and outputs

| Hospitals j | Inputs | | Outputs | |
	Nursing hours x_{1j}	Medical supplies (\$) x_{2j}	Inpatient admissions y_{1j}	Outpatient visits y_{2j}
1	567	2,678	409	211
2	350	1,200	90	85
3	445	1,616	295	186
4	2,200	1,450	560	71
5	450	890	195	94
6	399	1,660	209	100
7	156	3,102	108	57
8	2,314	3,456	877	252
9	560	4,000	189	310
10	1,669	4,500	530	390

	A	B	C	D	E
1	Hospital	(I)Nursing Hours	(I)Medical Supply	(O)Inpatient	(O)Outpatient
2	H1	567	2678	409	211
3	H2	350	1200	90	85
4	H3	445	1616	295	186
5	H4	2200	1450	560	71
6	H5	450	890	195	94
7	H6	399	1660	209	100
8	H7	156	3102	108	57
9	H8	2314	3456	877	252
10	H9	560	4000	189	310
11	H10	1669	4500	530	390
12					
13					

Fig. 2.4 DEA solver-LV data setup

Part A   Part B   Part C

Fig. 2.5 DEA solver-LV macro activation

banner (shown in a circle). When the "Security Alert – Macro" warning pops up, select the radio button "Enable the content" and click "OK" to activate the "DEA Solver-LV" software, Fig. 2.5 Part B.

Once the "DEA Solver" is clicked to start, Fig. 2.5 Part C, a new popup menu appears with four-step instructions as depicted in Fig. 2.6 Part A. To run the CRS model, choose the "CCR Model" option, Fig. 2.6 Part B. This will prompt another instruction to select either CCR-I (input orientation) or CCR-O (output orientation),

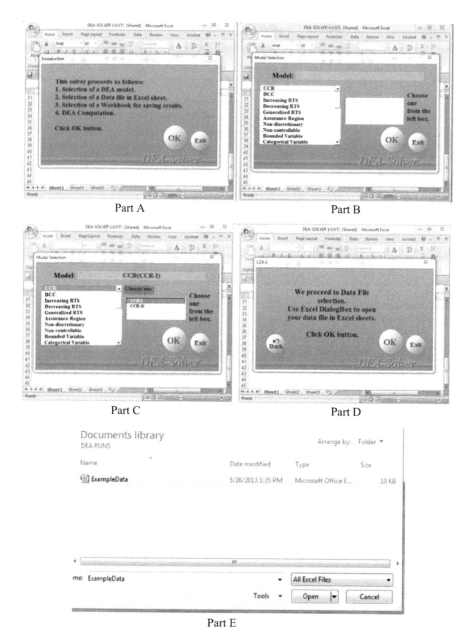

Part A

Part B

Part C

Part D

Part E

Fig. 2.6 Illustration of DEA solver-LV CCR-I model example run

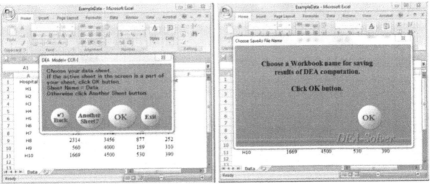

Part F   Part G

Part H

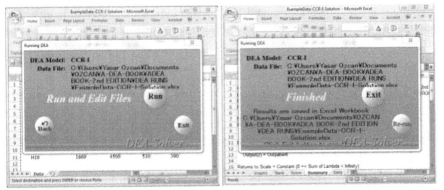

Part I   Part J

Fig. 2.6 (continued)

Documents library
DEA RUNS

Arrange by: Folder ▼

Name ⌄	Date modified	Type	Size
ExampleData	5/26/2013 1:35 PM	Microsoft Office E...	10 KB
ExampleData-CCR-I-Solution	5/26/2013 2:34 PM	Microsoft Office E...	28 KB

Part K

Fig. 2.6 (continued)

Fig. 2.6 Part C. After selecting the CCR-I option, another popup menu will guide the user for the data file selection, Fig. 2.6 Part D. In this illustration, a file named "ExampleData," which was previously saved on "Documents Library," is selected and clicked "open," Fig. 2.6 Part E. Next, the data file will appear in an Excel sheet and a new popup menu will instruct the user to check whether this is the data set that was intended for use in the analysis, Fig. 2.6 Part F. If the data set is the correct one, click "OK" to move to the next menu, which will guide the user to select a workbook name to save the results of DEA computations, Fig. 2.6 Part G. It is recommended that the user save the results file (containing DEA computations) in the same directory where the raw data file is stored and include in the file name the same startup with extension indicating the model type and orientation. For the example shown in Fig. 2.6 Part H, "ExampleData-CCR-I-Solutions" was used as the name to differentiate the solutions from raw data as well as from potential other model runs. Clicking "Save" to create results files will prompt yet another popup menu requiring a click on the "Run" button, Fig. 2.6 Part I. After the program runs, a final popup menu will indicate the "Finish" of the program, as depicted in Part J of Fig. 2.6.

If any of the steps are not followed correctly, the user should start from the beginning of the process to complete computations without any difficulty. The results of the computations will be active on screen for observations, or can be examined later by opening the saved result file (in this case, "ExampleData-CCR-I-Solution") as shown in Fig. 2.6 Part K.

At this stage the user or health care manager can observe many results of the model to identify not only the benchmark hospitals, but also improvement strategies for those hospitals that are currently inefficient.

The results are organized in various Excel worksheets (tabs), as shown at the bottom banner in Fig. 2.7. These worksheets include results of efficiency analysis in the "Score" worksheet, target inputs and outputs in the "Projection" worksheet, and the amount of inefficiencies (slacks) in the "Slack" worksheet. Next we will discuss the results from each of these worksheets.

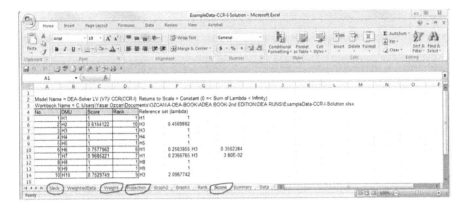

Fig. 2.7 Results of CCR input-oriented model solution

Fig. 2.8 Efficiency report
for input-oriented CCR
model

CCR-I

DMU	Score
H1	1
H2	0.6154122
H3	1
H4	1
H5	1
H6	0.7577962
H7	0.9685221
H8	1
H9	1
H10	0.7529749

2.9   Interpretation of the Results

Figure 2.8 depicts the abridged version of the efficiency report, where efficiency
scores of all ten hospitals are reported. This two-input and two-output model shows
that six of the ten hospitals are efficient using these four dimensions. There is no
surprise that H1, H3, H4, and H9 all received a score of 1 and are considered
efficient. Furthermore, we observe that the efficiency of two additional hospitals,
H5 and H8, could not be determined in ratio-based analysis shown in Chap. 1.
However, with DEA using multiple inputs and outputs at the same time, we are able
to discover them.

	A	B	C	D	E	F	G
1							
2	Model Name = DEA-Solver LV (V7)/ CCR(CCR-I) Returns to Scale = Constant (0 =< Sum of Lambda < Inf						
3	Workbook Name = C:\Users\Yasar Ozcan\Documents\OZCAN\A-DEA-BOOK\ADEA BOOK-2nd EDITION\						
4				Excess	Excess	Shortage	Shortage
5	No.	DMU	Score	Nursing Hours	Medical Supply	Inpatient	Outpatient
6				S-(1)	S-(2)	S+(1)	S+(2)
7	1	H1	1	0	0	0	0
8	2	H2	0.6154122	12.03405018	0	44.81182796	0
9	3	H3	1	0	0	0	0
10	4	H4	1	0	0	0	0
11	5	H5	1	0	0	0	0
12	6	H6	0.7577962	0	0	0	19.663685
13	7	H7	0.9685221	0	2309.186459	0	0
14	8	H8	1	0	0	0	0
15	9	H9	1	0	0	0	0
16	10	H10	0.7529749	323.6506093	0	88.5483871	0
17							

I◄ ◄ ► ►I   Slack / WeightedData / Weight / Projection / Graph2 / Graph1 / Rank / Score / Summary

Fig. 2.9 Input and output slacks for input-oriented CCR model

2.9.1 Efficiency and Inefficiency

Hospitals H2, H6, H7, and H10 have scores of less than 1 but greater than 0, and thus they are identified as inefficient. These hospitals can improve their efficiency, or reduce their inefficiencies proportionately, by reducing their inputs (since we run an input-oriented model). For example, H2 can improve its efficiency by reducing certain inputs up to 38.5 % $(1.0 - 0.6154122)$. Similarly, H6 and H10 can do so with approximately 25 % input reduction. However, H7 is closer to an efficiency frontier and needs only a 3.2 % reduction in resources.

This raises the question: which inputs need to be reduced by calculated proportions? These input reductions (or output augmentations in some cases) are called total inefficiencies which comprise not only the amount of proportional reductions, but also an amount called "Slack" for those hospitals that cannot reach their efficiency targets (at frontier) despite the proportional reductions.

2.9.2 Slacks

Figure 2.9 comes from the "Slack" worksheet of the DEA computation results. Mathematical derivation of these slacks is presented in Appendix B of this chapter. Here, we observe that none of the efficient hospitals have any slacks. Slacks exist only for those hospitals identified as inefficient. However, slacks represent only the leftover portions of inefficiencies; after proportional reductions in inputs or increases in outputs, if a DMU cannot reach the efficiency frontier (to its efficient target), slacks are needed to push the DMU to the frontier (target).

It is interesting to note that H2 would be required to reduce its nursing hours by approximately 12 h. However, despite the reduction in this input, it would not achieve efficiency. No other input can be reduced, thus to achieve efficiency, H2 should also augment its inpatient admission by 44.8 %. A similar situation in a different magnitude exists for H10. On the other hand, H6 cannot reduce any inputs, but must augment outpatient visits by 19.7 % or 20 visits. Lastly, H7 should spend $2,309.19 less for medical supplies. Please note that these calculations are the results of Models 2 and 4 executed in succession or Model 5, as explained in the appendices at the end of the chapter.

2.9.3 Efficiency Targets for Inputs and Outputs

We can summarize the efficiency targets by examining the "Projection" worksheet. Here, for each hospital, target input and output levels are prescribed. These targets are the results of respective slack values added to proportional reduction amounts. To calculate the target values for inputs, the input value is multiplied with an optimal efficiency score, and then slack amounts are subtracted from this amount. For detailed formulations of these calculations, the reader is referred to Appendix B, Part 3. Figure 2.10 displays these target values. As the reader can observe, the target values for efficient hospitals are equivalent to their original input and output values.

However, for the inefficient DMUs, the targets for input variables $(\widehat{x}_{io})$ in the CCR input-oriented DEA model will comprise proportional reduction in the input variables by the efficiency score of the DMU minus the slack value, if any, given by the formula:

$$\widehat{x}_{io} = \theta^* x_{io} - s_i^{-*} \quad i = 1, ...m \tag{2.3}$$

For example, the target calculations for Nursing Hours (NH) and Medical Supply (MS) inputs of Hospital 2 are calculated as follows:

$$\widehat{x}_{NH,H2} = \theta^* x_{NH,H2} - s_{NH}^{-*}$$

$$\widehat{x}_{NH,H2} = 0.61541 * 350 - 12.03405$$

$$\widehat{x}_{NH,H2} = 203.36022$$

where 0.61541 comes from Fig. 2.8, 350 from Fig. 2.4, and 12.03405 from Fig. 2.9. The reader can confirm the results with Fig. 2.10. Similarly, target calculation of Medical Supply for H2 is:

$$\widehat{x}_{MS,H2} = \theta^* x_{MS,H2} - s_{MS}^{-*}$$

	A	B	C	D	E	F
4	No.	DMU	Score			
5		I/O	Data	Projection	Difference	%
6	1	H1	1			
7		Nursing Hours	567	567	0	0.00%
8		Medical Supply	2678	2678	0	0.00%
9		Inpatient	409	409	0	0.00%
10		Outpatient	211	211	0	0.00%
11	2	H2	0.6154122			
12		Nursing Hours	350	203.36022	-146.6398	-41.90%
13		Medical Supply	1200	738.49462	-461.5054	-38.46%
14		Inpatient	90	134.81183	44.811828	49.79%
15		Outpatient	85	85	0	0.00%
16	3	H3	1			
17		Nursing Hours	445	445	0	0.00%
18		Medical Supply	1616	1616	0	0.00%
19		Inpatient	295	295	0	0.00%
20		Outpatient	186	186	0	0.00%
21	4	H4	1			
22		Nursing Hours	2200	2200	0	0.00%
23		Medical Supply	1450	1450	0	0.00%
24		Inpatient	560	560	0	0.00%
25		Outpatient	71	71	0	0.00%
26	5	H5	1			
27		Nursing Hours	450	450	0	0.00%
28		Medical Supply	890	890	0	0.00%
29		Inpatient	195	195	0	0.00%
30		Outpatient	94	94	0	0.00%
31	6	H6	0.7577962			
32		Nursing Hours	399	302.36067	-96.63933	-24.22%
33		Medical Supply	1660	1257.9416	-402.0584	-24.22%
34		Inpatient	209	209	0	0.00%
35		Outpatient	100	119.66368	19.663685	19.66%
36	7	H7	0.9685221			
37		Nursing Hours	156	151.08945	-4.91055	-3.15%
38		Medical Supply	3102	695.16914	-2406.831	-77.59%
39		Inpatient	108	108	0	0.00%
40		Outpatient	57	57	0	0.00%
41	8	H8	1			
42		Nursing Hours	2314	2314	0	0.00%
43		Medical Supply	3456	3456	0	0.00%
44		Inpatient	877	877	0	0.00%
45		Outpatient	252	252	0	0.00%
46	9	H9	1			
47		Nursing Hours	560	560	0	0.00%
48		Medical Supply	4000	4000	0	0.00%
49		Inpatient	189	189	0	0.00%
50		Outpatient	310	310	0	0.00%
51	10	H10	0.7529749			
52		Nursing Hours	1669	933.06452	-735.9355	-44.09%
53		Medical Supply	4500	3388.3871	-1111.613	-24.70%
54		Inpatient	530	618.54839	88.548387	16.71%
55		Outpatient	390	390	0	0.00%
56						

H ◄ ► H | Slack / WeightedData / Weight / **Projection** / Graph2 / Graph1

Fig. 2.10 Input and output efficient targets for input-oriented CCR model

$$\widehat{x}_{MS,H2} = 0.61541 * 1200 - 0$$

$$\widehat{x}_{MS,H2} = 738.49462$$

Again, the reader can confirm the result from Fig. 2.10.

In an input-oriented model, efficient output targets are calculated as:

$$\widehat{y}_{ro} = y_{ro} + s_i^{+*} \quad r = 1,....s \tag{2.4}$$

In our ongoing example with H2, Inpatient Admissions (IA) and Outpatient Visits (OV) can be calculated as:

$$\widehat{y}_{IA,H2} = y_{IA,H2} + s_{IA}^{+*} \qquad \widehat{y}_{OV,H2} = y_{OV,H2} + s_{OV}^{+*}$$

$$\widehat{y}_{IA,H2} = 90 + 44.81183 \qquad \widehat{y}_{OV,H2} = 85 + 0$$

$$\widehat{y}_{IA,H2} = 134.81183 \qquad \widehat{y}_{OV,H2} = 85.00$$

The reader can confirm these results from Fig. 2.10 for Hospital 2. The other inefficient hospitals' targets are calculated in the same manner.

2.10   Input-Oriented Model Benchmarks

The "Score" worksheet in Fig. 2.11 provides benchmark results shown in columns E through H. In Chap. 4 we will discuss the use of the information presented here in more detail when more foundational material has been presented. However, here

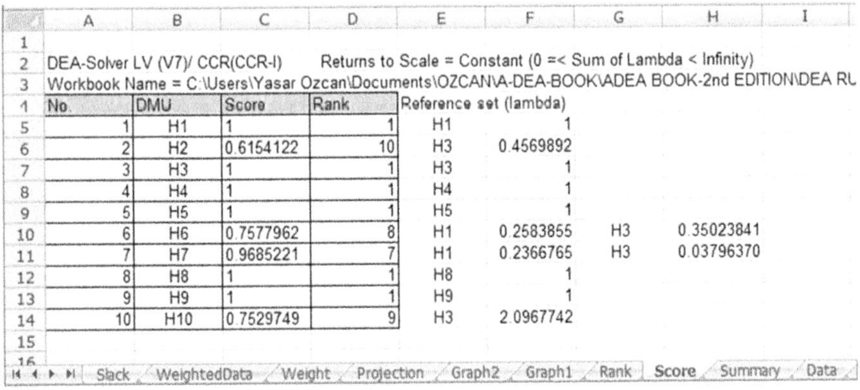

	A	B	C	D	E	F	G	H	I
1									
2	DEA-Solver LV (V7)/ CCR(CCR-I)			Returns to Scale = Constant (0 =< Sum of Lambda < Infinity)					
3	Workbook Name = C:\Users\Yasar Ozcan\Documents\OZCAN\A-DEA-BOOK\ADEA BOOK-2nd EDITION\DEA RL								
4	No.	DMU	Score	Rank	Reference set (lambda)				
5	1	H1	1	1	H1	1			
6	2	H2	0.6154122	10	H3	0.4569892			
7	3	H3	1	1	H3	1			
8	4	H4	1	1	H4	1			
9	5	H5	1	1	H5	1			
10	6	H6	0.7577962	8	H1	0.2583855	H3	0.35023841	
11	7	H7	0.9685221	7	H1	0.2366765	H3	0.03796370	
12	8	H8	1	1	H8	1			
13	9	H9	1	1	H9	1			
14	10	H10	0.7529749	9	H3	2.0967742			
15									
16									

H ◄ ► H   Slack   WeightedData   Weight   Projection   Graph2   Graph1   Rank   Score   Summary   Data

Fig. 2.11 Benchmarks for input-oriented CCR model

we will explain the benchmark portion of the information presented. The "benchmarks" are created through the DEA computations.

Here, health care managers whose hospital is inefficient can observe the benchmark hospitals to which they need to catch up.

Of course, efficient hospitals may consider themselves to be their own "benchmarks." So, the benchmark for H1 is H1, for H3 is H3, and so on. However, for inefficient hospitals, their benchmarks are one or many of the efficient hospitals. For example, a benchmark for H2 and H10 is H3 (observe that H3 is efficient). A benchmark for H6 and H7 are two hospitals, H1 and H3. This means, to become efficient, H6 and H7 must use a combination from both H1 and H3 in this case (a virtual hospital) to become efficient. How much of H1 and how much of H3 (what combination) are calculated to achieve efficiency and reported next to each benchmark hospital? These are λ (lambda) weights obtained from the dual version of the linear program that is solved to estimate these values. Further formulation details are provided in Appendix A at the end of this chapter. For example, H7 will attempt to become like H1 more than H3 as observed from respective λ weights of H1 and H3 ($\lambda_1 = 0.237$ vs. $\lambda_3 = 0.038$).

2.11   Output-Oriented Models

The essence of output orientation comes from how we look at the efficiency ratios. When we illustrated the input orientation we used the ratios in which inputs were divided by outputs. Hence we can do the opposite by dividing outputs by inputs to create reciprocal ratios. Using the same inputs and outputs from Table 1.2 from Chap. 1, we can calculate these mirror ratios as shown in Table 2.6 below. The first two columns show two different outputs, inpatient admissions and outpatient visits, being divided by the same input, nursing hours. The higher ratio values here would mean better performance for the hospitals.

Table 2.6 Hospital performance ratios

Provider ID	Inpatient admissions/ nursing hours	Outpatient visit/ nursing hours
H1	0.72	0.37
H2	0.26	0.24
H3	0.66	0.42
H4	0.25	0.03
H5	0.43	0.21
H6	0.52	0.25
H7	0.69	0.37
H8	0.38	0.11
H9	0.34	0.55
H10	0.32	0.23

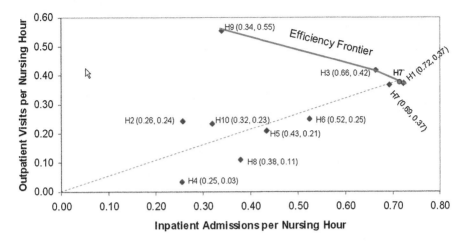

Fig. 2.12 Efficiency frontier for output-oriented model

As can be observed from the first column, H1 has the highest inpatient admissions per nursing hour compared to other providers. However, H9 has the highest outpatient visits per nursing hour as displayed in the second column.

A graphical view of these measures is shown in Fig. 2.12, where H1, H3, and H9 have the highest combination of these ratios when considered together. Here, no other hospital can generate more outputs using the nursing hours as input. However, when other inputs are included in the model using DEA, we may discover other hospitals joining the efficiency frontier.

The reader should also note that H7, an inefficient hospital, can reach this output-oriented frontier by increasing its inpatient admissions and outpatient visits along the direction of the dashed line to H7'. The distance given by H7'–H7 defines the amount of inefficiency for H7.

2.12   Output-Oriented CCR [CRS] DEA Model

Using the similar steps in Sect. 2.8, this time we will select "CCR-O" Output-Oriented model from the popup menu as shown in Fig. 2.13.

Again following the similar steps in Sect. 2.8, we get the results shown in Fig. 2.14, which is similar to Fig. 2.7; however, the results are reported as output orientation.

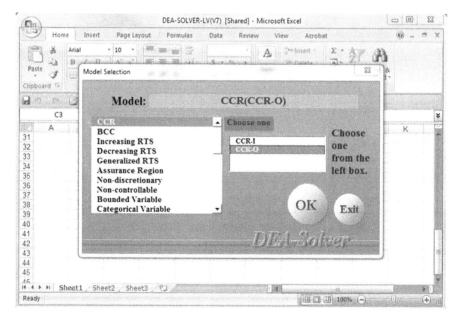

Fig. 2.13 Output-oriented CCR model

	A	B	C	D	E	F	G	H	I
1									
2	Model Name = DEA-Solver LV (V7)/ CCR(CCR-O) Returns to Scale = Constant (0 =< Sum of Lambda < Infinity)								
3	Workbook Name = C.\Users\Yasar Ozcan\Documents\OZCAN\A-DEA-BOOK\ADEA BOOK-2nd EDITION\DEA RUNS\								
4	No	DMU	Score	Rank	1/Score	Reference set (lambda)			
5	1	H1	1	1	1	H1	1		
6	2	H2	0.6154122	10	1.6249272	H3	0.7425743		
7	3	H3	1	1	1	H3	1		
8	4	H4	1	1	1	H4	1		
9	5	H5	1	1	1	H5	1		
10	6	H6	0.7577962	8	1.3196161	H1	0.3409697	H3	0.4621802
11	7	H7	0.9685221	7	1.0325009	H1	0.2443688	H3	0.0391976
12	8	H8	1	1	1	H8	1		
13	9	H9	1	1	1	H9	1		
14	10	H10	0.7529749	9	1.3280655	H3	2.7846535		
15									

Fig. 2.14 Results of output-oriented CCR model

2.13 Interpretation of Output-Oriented CCR [CRS] Results

Figure 2.15 depicts the abridged version of the efficiency report, where efficiency scores of all ten hospitals are reported. This two-input and two-output model shows six of the ten hospitals are efficient using these four dimensions in an output-oriented model.

Fig. 2.15 Efficiency report
for output-oriented CCR
model

CCR-O

DMU	Score	Rank	1/Score
H1	1	1	1
H2	0.6154122	10	1.6249272
H3	1	1	1
H4	1	1	1
H5	1	1	1
H6	0.7577962	8	1.3196161
H7	0.9685221	7	1.0325009
H8	1	1	1
H9	1	1	1
H10	0.7529749	9	1.3280655

2.13.1   Efficiency and Inefficiency

Observing the "1/Score" column, hospitals H2, H6, H7, and H10 have scores greater than 1; thus they are identified as inefficient in the output-oriented model. These hospitals can improve their efficiency, or reduce their inefficiencies proportionately, by augmenting their outputs (since we run an output-oriented model). For example, H2 can improve its efficiency by augmenting certain outputs up to 62.5 % (1.6249272 − 1.0). Similarly, H6 and H10 can do so with approximately 33 % increases. However, H7 is closer to the efficiency frontier and needs only a 3.3 % increase in outputs.

2.13.2   Slacks

Figure 2.16 comes from the "Slack" worksheet of the DEA run results. Here again we observe that the efficient hospitals have zero ("0") slacks. Slacks exist only for those hospitals identified as inefficient.

It is interesting to note that H2 is required to increase its inpatient admissions by 72.8 patients, after having proportionately increased this output by its efficiency score. However, despite the augmentation in this output, it still would not achieve efficiency. No other output can be increased. Thus, H2 should also reduce its nursing hours by 19.5 h. A similar situation in a different magnitude exists for H10. On the other hand, H6 can augment its outpatient visits by 26. Lastly, H7 cannot augment its outputs at all, but should decrease its medical supplies cost by $2,384.24.

	A	B	C	D	E	F	G	H	I
1									
2	Model Name = DEA-Solver LV (V7)/ CCR(CCR-O) Returns to Scale = Constant (0 =< Sum of Lambda < Infinity)								
3	Workbook Name = C \Users\Yasar Ozcan\Documents\OZCAN\A-DEA-BOOK\ADEA BOOK-2nd EDITION\DEA RUNS'								
4				Excess	Excess	Shortage	Shortage		
5	No.	DMU	Score	Nursing Hours	Medical Supply	Inpatient	Outpatient		
6				S-(1)	S-(2)	S+(1)	S+(2)		
7	1	H1	1	0		0	0	0	
8	2	H2	0.6154122	19.55445545		0	72.81595807	0	
9	3	H3	1	0		0	0	0	
10	4	H4	1	0		0	0	0	
11	5	H5	1	0		0	0	0	
12	6	H6	0.7577962	0		0	0	25.9485142	
13	7	H7	0.9685221	0	2384.237207	0	0		
14	8	H8	1	0		0	0	0	
15	9	H9	1	0		0	0	0	
16	10	H10	0.7529749	429.8292079		0	117.5980579	0	
17									

H ◀ ▶ H **Slack** / WeightedData / Weight / Projection / Graph2 / Graph1 / Rank / Score / Summary / Data

Fig. 2.16 Slacks of output-oriented CCR model

2.13.3 Efficient Targets for Inputs and Outputs

Again, we can summarize these finding further by examining the "Projection" worksheet. For each hospital, target input and output levels are prescribed. These targets are the results of respective slack values added onto original outputs, and subtracted from original inputs. To calculate the target values for inputs, the input slacks are subtracted from the inputs. Targets for outputs are calculated by multiplying optimal efficiency scores by the outputs and then adding the slack values to that value. For a detailed formulation of these calculations, the reader is referred to Appendix C, Part 2. Figure 2.17 displays these target values. As the reader can observe, the target values for efficient hospitals are equivalent to their original input and output values.

Health care managers should be cautioned that some of these efficiency improvement options (and the target values) may not be practical. Health care managers can opt to implement only some of these potential improvements at the present time due to their contracts with labor and supply chains and insurance companies.

2.14 Output-Oriented Model Benchmarks

Figure 2.18 displays the results from the initial "Score" worksheet. Here health care managers whose hospital is inefficient can observe the benchmark hospitals.

As in the input-oriented model, the efficient hospitals in the output-oriented model will consider themselves as their own "benchmark." Thus, the benchmark for H1 is H1, for H3 is H3, and so on. On the other hand, for those inefficient hospitals the benchmarks are one or many of the efficient hospitals. For example, the benchmark for H2 and H10 is H3 (observe that H3 is efficient). The benchmark

No.	DMU I/O	1/Score Data	Projection	Difference	%
1	H1	1			
	Nursing Ho	567	567	0	0.00%
	Medical Sup	2678	2678	0	0.00%
	Inpatient	409	409	0	0.00%
	Outpatient	211	211	0	0.00%
2	H2	1.624927			
	Nursing Ho	350	330.4455	-19.55446	-5.59%
	Medical Sup	1200	1200	0	0.00%
	Inpatient	90	219.0594	129.0594	143.40%
	Outpatient	85	138.1188	53.11881	62.49%
3	H3	1			
	Nursing Ho	445	445	0	0.00%
	Medical Sup	1616	1616	0	0.00%
	Inpatient	295	295	0	0.00%
	Outpatient	186	186	0	0.00%
4	H4	1			
	Nursing Ho	2200	2200	0	0.00%
	Medical Sup	1450	1450	0	0.00%
	Inpatient	560	560	0	0.00%
	Outpatient	71	71	0	0.00%
5	H5	1			
	Nursing Ho	450	450	0	0.00%
	Medical Sup	890	890	0	0.00%
	Inpatient	195	195	0	0.00%
	Outpatient	94	94	0	0.00%
6	H6	1.319616			
	Nursing Ho	399	399	0	0.00%
	Medical Sup	1660	1660	0	0.00%
	Inpatient	209	275.7998	66.79976	31.96%
	Outpatient	100	157.9101	57.91012	57.91%
7	H7	1.032501			
	Nursing Ho	156	156	0	0.00%
	Medical Sup	3102	717.7628	-2384.237	-76.86%
	Inpatient	108	111.5101	3.510102	3.25%
	Outpatient	57	58.85255	1.852554	3.25%
8	H8	1			
	Nursing Ho	2314	2314	0	0.00%
	Medical Sup	3456	3456	0	0.00%
	Inpatient	877	877	0	0.00%
	Outpatient	252	252	0	0.00%
9	H9	1			
	Nursing Ho	560	560	0	0.00%
	Medical Sup	4000	4000	0	0.00%
	Inpatient	189	189	0	0.00%
	Outpatient	310	310	0	0.00%
10	H10	1.328065			
	Nursing Ho	1669	1239.171	-429.8292	-25.75%
	Medical Sup	4500	4500	0	0.00%
	Inpatient	530	821.4728	291.4728	54.99%
	Outpatient	390	517.9455	127.9455	32.81%

H ◀ ▶ H   Slack ╱ WeightedData ╱ Weight ╲ **Projection** ╱ Graph2 ╱ Gr

Fig. 2.17 Efficient targets for inputs and outputs for output-oriented CCR model

	A	B	C	D	E	F	G	H	I
1									
2	Model Name = DEA-Solver LV (V7)/ CCR(CCR-O) Returns to Scale = Constant (0 =< Sum of Lambda < Infinity)								
3	Workbook Name = C:\Users\Yasar Ozcan\Documents\OZCAN\A-DEA-BOOK\ADEA BOOK-2nd EDITION\DEA RUNS								
4	No.	DMU	Score	Rank	1/Score	Reference set (lambda)			
5	1	H1	1	1	1	H1	1		
6	2	H2	0.6154122	10	1.6249272	H3	0.7425743		
7	3	H3	1	1	1	H3	1		
8	4	H4	1	1	1	H4	1		
9	5	H5	1	1	1	H5	1		
10	6	H6	0.7577962	8	1.3196161	H1	0.3409697	H3	0.4621802
11	7	H7	0.9685221	7	1.0325009	H1	0.2443688	H3	0.0391976
12	8	H8	1	1	1	H8	1		
13	9	H9	1	1	1	H9	1		
14	10	H10	0.7529749	9	1.3280655	H3	2.7846535		
15									

H ◄ ► H   Slack / WeightedData / Weight / Projection / Graph2 / Graph1 / Rank / Score / Summary / Data /

Fig. 2.18 Benchmarks for output-oriented CCR model

for H6 and H7 are two hospitals: H1 and H3. This means, to become efficient, H6 and H7 must use a combination of H1 and H3 (a virtual hospital) to become efficient. How much of H1 and how much of H3 are calculated and reported next to each benchmark hospital? These are λ (lambda) weights obtained from the dual version of the linear program that is solved to estimate these values. Further formulation details are provided in the Appendix A. For example, H7 will attempt to become like H1 more than H3, as observed from respective λ weights of H1 and H3 ($\lambda_1 = 0.244$ vs. $\lambda_3 = 0.039$).

2.15   Summary

This chapter introduced the basic efficiency concepts and DEA technique. The model orientation and returns to scale are basic concepts that help health care managers to identify what type of DEA model they should use. We discussed only input- and output-oriented CRS models in this chapter.

Appendix A

A.1 Mathematical Details

Fractional formulation of CCR [CRS] model is presented below:

Model 1

$$\text{Maximize } \theta_o = \frac{\sum\limits_{r=1}^{s} u_r y_{ro}}{\sum\limits_{i=1}^{m} v_i x_{io}}$$

$$\text{subject to } \frac{\sum\limits_{r=1}^{s} u_r y_{rj}}{\sum\limits_{i=1}^{m} v_i x_{ij}} \leq 1$$

$$u_r, v_i \geq 0 \quad \text{for all } r \text{ and } i.$$

This model can be algebraically rewritten as:

$$\text{Maximize } \theta_o = \sum_{r=1}^{s} u_r y_{ro}$$

$$\text{subject to } \sum_{r=1}^{s} u_r y_{rj} \leq \sum_{i=1}^{m} v_i x_{ij}$$

With further manipulations we obtain the following linear programming formulation:

Model 2

$$\text{Maximize } \theta_o = \sum_{r=1}^{s} u_r y_{ro}$$

subject to:

$$\sum_{r=1}^{s} u_r y_{rj} - \sum_{i=1}^{m} v_i x_{ij} \leq 0 \quad j = 1, \dots n$$

$$\sum_{i=1}^{m} v_i x_{io} = 1$$

$$u_r, v_i \geq 0$$

A.2 Assessment of the Weights

To observe the detailed information provided in Fig. 2.7, such as benchmarks and their weights (λ), as well as $\Sigma\lambda$ leading to returns to scale (RTS) assessments, a dual version of Model 2 is needed. The dual model can be formulated as:

Model 3

Minimize θ_o

subject to:

$$\sum_{j=1}^{n} \lambda_j x_{ij} \leq \theta x_{io} \quad i = 1, ...m$$

$$\sum_{j=1}^{n} \lambda_j y_{rj} \geq y_{ro} \quad r = 1, ...s$$

$$\lambda_j \geq 0 \quad j = 1, ...n.$$

In this dual formulation, Model 3, the linear program, seeks efficiency by minimizing (dual) efficiency of a focal DMU ("o") subject to two sets of inequality. The first inequality emphasizes that the weighted sum of inputs of the DMUs should be less than or equal to the inputs of focal DMU being evaluated. The second inequality similarly asserts that the weighted sum of the outputs of the non-focal DMUs should be greater than or equal to the focal DMU. The weights are the λ values. When a DMU is efficient, the λ values would be equal to 1. For those DMUs that are inefficient, the λ values will be expressed in their efficiency reference set (ERS). For example, observing Fig. 2.7, H7 has two hospitals in its ERS, namely H1 and H3. Their respective λ weights are reported as $\lambda_1 = 0.237$ and $\lambda_3 = 0.038$.

Appendix B

B.1 Mathematical Details for Slacks

In order to obtain the slacks in DEA analysis, a second stage linear programming model is required to be solved after the dual linear programming model, presented in Appendix A, is solved. The second stage of the linear program is formulated for slack values as follows as:

Model 4

$$Maximize \sum_{i=1}^{m} s_i^- + \sum_{r=1}^{s} s_r^+$$

$$\sum_{j=1}^{n} \lambda_j x_{ij} + s_i^- = \theta^* x_{io} \quad i = 1, ...m$$

$$\sum_{j=1}^{n} \lambda_j y_{rj} - s_r^+ = y_{ro} \quad r = 1, ...s$$

$$\lambda_j \geq 0 \quad j = 1, ...n$$

Here, θ^* is the DEA efficiency score resulting from the initial run, Model 2, of the DEA model. Here, s_i^- and s_r^+ represent input and output slacks, respectively. Please note that the superscripted minus sign on input slacks indicates reduction, while the superscripted positive sign on output slacks requires augmentation of outputs.

In fact, Model 2 and Model 4 can be combined and rewritten as:

Model 5: Input-Oriented CCR [CRS] Model

$$Minimize \ \theta - \varepsilon \left(\sum_{i=1}^{m} s_i^- + \sum_{r=1}^{s} s_r^+ \right)$$

$$\sum_{j=1}^{n} \lambda_j x_{ij} + s_i^- = \theta x_{io} \quad i = 1, ...m$$

$$\sum_{j=1}^{n} \lambda_j y_{rj} - s_r^+ = y_{ro} \quad r = 1, ...s$$

$$\lambda_j \geq 0 \quad j = 1, ...n$$

The ε in the objective function is called the non-Archimedean, which is defined as infinitely small, or less than any real positive number. The presence of ε allows a minimization over efficiency score (θ) to preempt the optimization of slacks, s_i^- and s_r^+. Model 5 first obtains optimal efficiency scores (θ^*) from Model 2 and calculates them, and then obtains slack values and optimizes them to achieve the efficiency frontier.

B.2 Determination of Fully Efficient and Weakly Efficient DMUs

According to the DEA literature, the performance of DMUs can be assessed either as fully efficient or weakly efficient. The following conditions on efficiency scores and slack values determine the full and weak efficiency status of DMU:

Condition	θ	θ^*	All s_i^-	All s_r^+
Fully efficient	1.0	1.0	0	0
Weakly efficient	1.0	1.0	At least one $s_i^- \neq 0$	At least one $s_r^+ \neq 0$

When Models 2 and 4 run sequentially (Model 5), weakly efficient DMUs cannot be in the efficient reference set (ERS) of other inefficient DMUs. However, if only Model 2 is executed, then weakly efficient DMUs can appear in the ERS of inefficient DMUs. The removal of weakly inefficient DMUs from the analysis would not affect the frontier or the analytical results.

B.3 Efficient Target Calculations for Input-Oriented CCR [CRS] Model

In input-oriented CCR [CRS] models, levels of efficient targets for inputs and outputs can be calculated as follows:

Inputs: $\widehat{x}_{io} = \theta^* x_{io} - s_i^{-*} \quad i = 1, ...m$

Outputs: $\widehat{y}_{ro} = y_{ro} + s_i^{+*} \quad r = 1, ...s$

Appendix C

C.1 CCR [CRS] Output-Oriented Model Formulation

Since Model 5, as defined in Appendix B, combines the needed calculations for the input-oriented CRS model, we can adapt the output-oriented CRS model formulation using this fully developed version of the model.

Model 6: Output-Oriented CCR [CRS] Model

$$Maximize\ \phi - \varepsilon \left(\sum_{i=1}^{m} s_i^- + \sum_{r=1}^{s} s_r^+ \right)$$

$$\sum_{j=1}^{n} \lambda_j x_{ij} + s_i^- = x_{io} \quad i = 1, \dots m$$

$$\sum_{j=1}^{n} \lambda_j y_{rj} - s_r^+ = \phi y_{ro} \quad i = 1, \dots s$$

$$\lambda_j \geq 0 \quad j = 1, \dots n$$

The output efficiency is defined by ϕ. Another change in the formula is that the efficiency emphasis is removed from input (first constraint) and placed into output (second constraint).

C.2 Efficient Target Calculations for Output-Oriented CCR [CRS] Model

In output-oriented CCR models, levels of efficient targets for inputs and outputs can be calculated as follows:

Inputs: $\widehat{x}_{io} = x_{io} - s_i^{-*} \quad i = 1, \dots m$

Outputs: $\widehat{y}_{ro} = \phi^* y_{ro} + s_i^{+*} \quad r = 1, \dots s.$

Chapter 3
Returns to Scale Models

3.1 Constant Returns Frontier

Health care managers can seek alternative evaluations to assess which components of their organization are contributing to the inefficiency of their organization, such as the size of their operation, poor organizational factors, flow processes, or other related factors. For example, a small hospital, in certain instances, may appear less efficient compared to larger ones, and this may be due to its scale size. On the other hand, the reverse can be seen as well, due to diseconomies of scale, which occur when larger hospitals may be operating inefficiently due to other reasons, such as poor management or a lack of strategic focus.

The Charnes, Cooper and Rhodes (Constant Returns to Scale) CCR [CRS] models assume a constant rate of substitution between inputs and outputs. Figure 3.1 depicts the CCR efficiency frontier for the sample hospital data we have been familiar with. Considering one output and one input, Hospital 1 defines the CCR [CRS] frontier. To reach this frontier, all the hospitals must move their positions proportionately either to the left or toward the top, wherever they can reach toward this target line, which is constant.

On the other hand, when economies of scale exist, and for various other reasons, the frontier may be defined differently. For instance, if a proportional increase in one or more inputs can cause greater than proportional increase in outputs, then constant returns are not present. Similarly, a proportional increase in inputs may yield less than a proportional increase in outputs. These situations raise the notion of varying returns; in DEA literature this is identified as variable returns to scale and calculated through Banker et al. (1984) or BCC models in DEA Solver-LV.

Y.A. Ozcan, *Health Care Benchmarking and Performance Evaluation*,   49
International Series in Operations Research & Management Science 210,
DOI 10.1007/978-1-4899-7472-3_3, © Springer Science+Business Media New York 2014

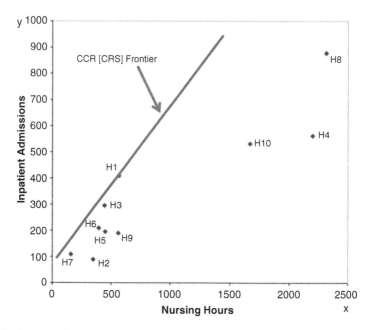

Fig. 3.1 Conceptualization of CCR [CRS] frontier

3.2   Variable Returns Frontier

Let us consider the health care managers in our sample facilities, and assume that they are planning to increase nursing hours by 25 % to satisfy the 25 % increase in inpatient admissions. Some of these facilities may reach this goal and exceed it, while others may not realize the expected levels of inpatient admissions. Those hospitals that realize more than 25 % inpatient admissions achieved an increasing rate of return, while others that have an increase in inpatient admission of less than 25 % rate have achieved a decreasing rate of return.

Figure 3.2 shows conceptualization of variable returns and the associated frontier. Here, H7, H1, and H8 define the different parts of the frontier. Close examination of the line segment between H7 and H1 shows a sharp increase (the slope of the line is steep in this segment), and the segment between H1 and H8 also displays an increase, but in a decreasing pattern (slope of the line segment is less steep compared to H7 vs. H1). While the hospitals on the frontier exhibit these varying returns, the cluster of the hospitals in the region between H7 and H1, namely H2, H3, H5, H6, and H9, would expect increasing returns as well, since they are closer to the frontier defined by H7 and H1. The remaining hospitals H4 and H10 may exhibit decreasing returns.

Although returns to scale (RTS) discussions may be more meaningful for those hospitals that comprise the BCC [VRS] frontier, the efficient targets are less obvious

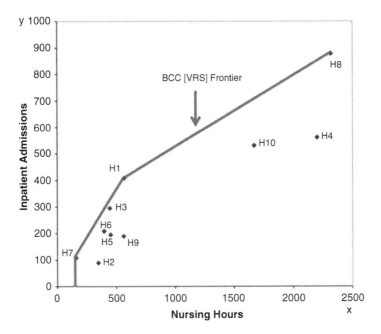

Fig. 3.2 Conceptualization of BCC [VRS] production frontier

for non-frontier hospitals. The orientation of the model, input versus output, further plays a role in how inefficient hospitals would move toward the VRS frontier.

To illustrate, consider Fig. 3.3, in which both CCR [CRS] and BCC [VRS] frontiers are displayed. In addition, we know which segments of the BCC [VRS] frontier are either increasing or decreasing. H1 is at a point where CRS and VRS are tangent to each other, indicating that H1 is both CCR [CRS] and BCC [VRS] efficient, and that thus H1's returns are constant. Hence, H1 would be considered the "optimal" scale size, as described below.

Let us investigate the position of H9 ($x = 560$, $y = 189$), a non-frontier hospital. If an input-oriented VRS model is used, to reach efficiency H9 must reduce its nursing hours by moving horizontally to $H9^{iv}$ ($x = 250$, $y = 189$), where it becomes BCC [VRS] efficient. Since $H9^{iv}$ is located at the increasing returns to scale (IRS), H9 can reduce its nursing hours further to the point $H9^{ic}$ ($x = 175$, $y = 189$), where it becomes CCR [CRS] efficient.

If H9 wishes to reach the efficiency frontier via output augmentation, the nearest point it can reach vertically is $H9^{ov}$ ($x = 560$, $y = 420$). It should be noted that point $H9^{ov}$ is at a decreasing returns to scale (DRS) section of the BCC [VRS] frontier. Similarly, H9 can further augment its outputs to $H9^{oc}$ ($x = 560$, $y = 460$), where it can reach output-oriented CCR [CRS] efficiency. A summary of these potential efficiency points and their coordinates for H9 are summarized in Table 3.1.

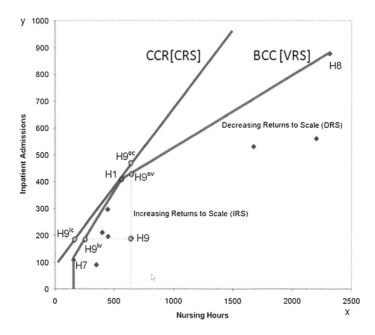

Fig. 3.3 CCR [CRS], BCC [VRS] models and RTS

Table 3.1 Potential efficiency coordinates for H9

	Original	Input CCR	CCR	Output BCC	BCC
		H9^{iv}	H9^{ic}	H9^{ov}	H9^{oc}
Coordinates	H9				
Nursing hours (x)	560	250	175	560	560
Inpatient admissions (y)	189	189	189	420	460

Using the values from these coordinates, the efficiency scores of H9 based on different orientations and returns to scale assumptions can be calculated. Using the input orientation we get:

BCC [VRS] efficiency through input reduction (x): H9^v ÷ H9 or $250 \div 560 = 0.4464$.

CCR [CRS] efficiency through input reduction (x): H9^c ÷ H9 or $175 \div 560 = 0.3125$.

Here the CCR [CRS] efficiency score generally does not exceed BCC [VRS] efficiency score. Similarly, for output orientation we get:

BCC [VRS] efficiency through output augmentation (y): H9^o ÷ H9 or $420 \div 189 = 2.2222$.

CCR [CRS] efficiency through output augmentation (y): H9^o ÷ H9 or $460 \div 189 = 2.4339$.

Here, conversely, the CCR [CRS] output efficiency score will generally be greater than the BCC [VRS] output efficiency score, as shown in Fig. 3.3.

3.3   Assessment of RTS

In order to calculate and assess the RTS—whether it is increasing, constant, or decreasing—we need to sum the lambda (λ_j) weight values. If the summation of lambda weights $\Sigma\lambda < 1.0$, then such DMU exhibits increasing rates of return. If $\Sigma\lambda > 1.0$, then the DMU exhibits decreasing rates of return. The efficient DMUs are considered as having constant returns to scale, and they will have $\Sigma\lambda = 1.0$. Using the "Score" worksheet from the original CCR-I solution, we placed the formula for the $\Sigma\lambda$ calculations on column I and determined the RTS on column J. The reader can verify these from Fig. 3.4, which displays $\Sigma\lambda$ and RTS for the sample hospitals. For those "maverick" hospitals that have only one benchmark in their reference set, $\Sigma\lambda$ is equal to λ weight of that reference hospital. However, for those with more than one hospital in their benchmark set (i.e., H6 and H7), $\Sigma\lambda$ is an addition of their respective λ weights. For example, $\Sigma\lambda$ value of H7, 0.275, is calculated by adding λ weight of H1 and λ weight of H3 ($0.237 + 0.038 = 0.275$).

3.4   Input-Oriented BCC [VRS] Model Example

As before, we will leave the mathematical details for the curious reader at the end of this chapter. Mathematical formulation of the BCC [VRS] DEA model is presented in Appendix D for input orientation and Appendix E for output orientation. Consider again the sample data presented in Chap. 1 with ten hospitals, two inputs, and two outputs. Now, we can employ the DEA Solver-LV software to calculate BCC [VRS] input- and output-oriented models using the same data presented in Table 2.5, which depicts the inputs and outputs according to required formulations.

	A	B	C	D	E	F	G	H	I	J
2	Model Name = DEA-Solver LV (V7)/ CCR(CCR-I) Returns to Scale = Constant (0 =< Sum of Lambda < Infinity)									
3	Workbook Name = C:\Users\Yasar Ozcan\Documents\OZCAN\A-DEA-BOOK\ADEA BOOK-2nd EDITION\DEA RUNS\ExampleData-									
4	No.	DMU	Score	Rank	Reference set	λ_j	Reference set	λ_j	$\Sigma\lambda$	RTS
5	1	H1	1	1	H1	1			1	Constant
6	2	H2	0.6154122	10	H3	0.4569892			0.456989	Increasing
7	3	H3	1	1	H3	1			1	Constant
8	4	H4	1	1	H4	1			1	Constant
9	5	H5	1	1	H5	1			1	Constant
10	6	H6	0.7577962	8	H1	0.2583855	H3	0.3502384	0.608624	Increasing
11	7	H7	0.9685221	7	H1	0.2366765	H3	0.0379637	0.27464	Increasing
12	8	H8	1	1	H8	1			1	Constant
13	9	H9	1	1	H9	1			1	Constant
14	10	H10	0.7529749	9	H3	2.0967742			2.096774	Decreasing
15										
16										
	Slack WeightedData Weight Projection Graph2 Graph1 Rank Score Summary Data									

Fig. 3.4 Increasing, constant, and decreasing returns

3.5   Input-Oriented BCC [VRS] DEA Model Results

In order to run an input-oriented BCC [VRS] model, we will select BCC, then choose the BCC-I option, and then click OK, as shown in Fig. 3.5.

The resulting efficiency scores are displayed in Fig. 3.6. Now, all but one hospital are efficient. As demonstrated in an earlier section of this chapter, this is not surprising.

In BCC [VRS] models, more DMUs can find their way to the frontier. Additionally, BCC [VRS] efficiency scores are generally higher than CCR [CRS] efficiency scores (for input-oriented models). Thus, more hospitals are considered to be efficient using this approach.

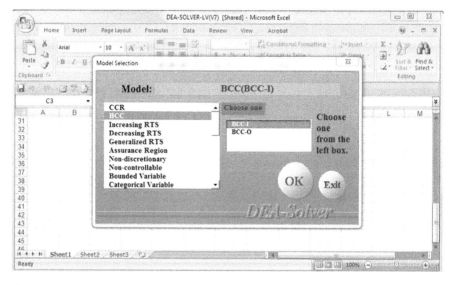

Fig. 3.5 Model selections for BCC [VRS] input orientation

DMU	Score
H1	1
H2	1
H3	1
H4	1
H5	1
H6	0.9654066
H7	1
H8	1
H9	1
H10	1

Fig. 3.6 Efficiency scores for BCC [VRS] input-oriented model

3.6 Slacks and Efficient Targets for Input-Oriented BCC [VRS] Model

Figures 3.7 and 3.8 display the slacks and targets for the input-oriented BCC [VRS] model. The calculation of targets is the same as for the CCR [CRS] model, and they can be found in Sect. D.2 of Appendix D.

Only one hospital, H6, is inefficient, and this hospital cannot reach the BCC frontier through input reduction only; output augmentation of approximately 16 outpatient visits is needed. The reader should recall the inputs and outputs of H6 as shown in Table 3.2

Using these values and the target formulations from Appendix D, for inputs we get:

$$\widehat{x}_{io} = \theta^* x_{io} - s_i^{-*} \quad i = 1, ...m, \text{ more specifically for this case}$$
$$\widehat{x}_{16} = \theta^* x_{16} - s_1^{-*} \text{ and}$$
$$\widehat{x}_{26} = \theta^* x_{26} - s_2^{-*}$$

By substituting the efficiency score (see Fig. 3.6), actual inputs (Table 3.2) and optimal slack values (Fig. 3.7) in these formulas, we get:

$$\widehat{x}_{16} = 0.96541 * 399 - 0 = 385.200 \text{ and}$$
$$\widehat{x}_{26} = 0.96541 * 1660 - 0 = 1602.587$$

Similarly for outputs, we get:

$$\widehat{y}_{ro} = y_{ro} + s_i^{+*} \quad r = 1, ...s, \text{ more specifically for H6:}$$
$$\widehat{y}_{16} = y_{16} + s_1^{+*} \text{ and}$$
$$\widehat{y}_{26} = y_{26} + s_2^{+*}$$

	A	B	C	D	E	F	G	H
1								
2	Model Name = DEA-Solver LV (V7)/ BCC(BCC-I) Returns to Scale = Variable (Sum of Lambda = 1)							
3	Workbook Name = C:\Users\Yasar Ozcan\Documents\OZCAN\A-DEA-BOOK\ADEA BOOK-2nd EDITION'							
4				Excess	Excess	Shortage	Shortage	
5	No.	DMU	Score	Nursing Hours	Medical Supply	Inpatient	Outpatient	
6				S-(1)	S-(2)	S+(1)	S+(2)	
7	1	H1	1	0	0	0	0	
8	2	H2	1	0	0	9.25E-04	0	
9	3	H3	1	0	0	0	0	
10	4	H4	1	0	0	0	0	
11	5	H5	1	0	0	0	0	
12	6	H6	0.9654066	0	0	0	16.127664	
13	7	H7	1	0	3.18E-02	0	0	
14	8	H8	1	0	0	0	0	
15	9	H9	1	0	0	0	0	
16	10	H10	1	0	0	0	0	

RTS | **Slack** | WeightedData | Weight | Projection | Graph2 | Graph1 | Rank | Score | Sum

Fig. 3.7 Slack report for input-oriented BCC [VRS] model

	A	B	C	D	E	F
4	No.	DMU	Score			
5		I/O	Data	Projection	Difference	%
6	1	H1	1			
7		Nursing Hours	567	567	0	0.00%
8		Medical Supply	2678	2678	0	0.00%
9		Inpatient	409	409	0	0.00%
10		Outpatient	211	211	0	0.00%
11	2	H2	1			
12		Nursing Hours	350	350	0	0.00%
13		Medical Supply	1200	1200	0	0.00%
14		Inpatient	90	90	0	0.00%
15		Outpatient	85	85	0	0.00%
16	3	H3	1			
17		Nursing Hours	445	445	0	0.00%
18		Medical Supply	1616	1616	0	0.00%
19		Inpatient	295	295	0	0.00%
20		Outpatient	186	186	0	0.00%
21	4	H4	1			
22		Nursing Hours	2200	2200	0	0.00%
23		Medical Supply	1450	1450	0	0.00%
24		Inpatient	560	560	0	0.00%
25		Outpatient	71	71	0	0.00%
26	5	H5	1			
27		Nursing Hours	450	450	0	0.00%
28		Medical Supply	890	890	0	0.00%
29		Inpatient	195	195	0	0.00%
30		Outpatient	94	94	0	0.00%
31	6	H6	0.9654066			
32		Nursing Hours	399	385.19722	-13.80278	-3.46%
33		Medical Supply	1660	1602.5749	-57.42508	-3.46%
34		Inpatient	209	209	0	0.00%
35		Outpatient	100	116.12766	16.127664	16.13%
36	7	H7	1			
37		Nursing Hours	156	156	0	0.00%
38		Medical Supply	3102	3102	0	0.00%
39		Inpatient	108	108	0	0.00%
40		Outpatient	57	57	0	0.00%
41	8	H8	1			
42		Nursing Hours	2314	2314	0	0.00%
43		Medical Supply	3456	3456	0	0.00%
44		Inpatient	877	877	0	0.00%
45		Outpatient	252	252	0	0.00%
46	9	H9	1			
47		Nursing Hours	560	560	0	0.00%
48		Medical Supply	4000	4000	0	0.00%
49		Inpatient	189	189	0	0.00%
50		Outpatient	310	310	0	0.00%
51	10	H10	1			
52		Nursing Hours	1669	1669	0	0.00%
53		Medical Supply	4500	4500	0	0.00%
54		Inpatient	530	530	0	0.00%
55		Outpatient	390	390	0	0.00%
56						
57						

⏮ ◀ ▶ ⏭   RTS / Slack / WeightedData / Weight | **Projection** / Graph2 / Gr

Fig. 3.8 Target report for input-oriented BCC [VRS] model

Table 3.2 Inputs and outputs for H6

	Inputs		Outputs	
Hospitals j	Nursing hours x_{1j}	Medical supplies ($) X_{2j}	Inpatient admissions y_{1j}	Outpatient visits Y_{2j}
6	399	1,660	209	100

By substituting actual output values and optimal slack scores in these formulas, we get:

$$\widehat{y}_{16} = 209 + 0 = 209 \text{ and}$$
$$\widehat{y}_{26} = 100 + 16.127 = 116.127$$

The reader can verify the results of these calculations by comparing the target values of H6 from Fig. 3.8.

3.7 Benchmarks for Input-Oriented BCC [VRS] Model

Since the BCC [VRS] model forms a different frontier, the benchmarks for a two-input and two-output model are certainly different than the CCR [CRS] frontier. Here, the only inefficient hospital, H6, has three benchmark hospitals. That is, H6 can reach the BCC [VRS] frontier by any combination of H3, H5, and H7, a virtual hospital. The λ weights corresponding to these reference hospitals are shown in Fig. 3.9.

3.8 Output-Oriented BCC [VRS] Model Example

In order to run the output-oriented BCC [VRS] model, this time we will select BCC Model and BCC-O as "Output-Oriented" from the dropdown options, and then click OK as shown in Fig. 3.10.

3.9 Output-Oriented BCC [VRS] Model Results

At this point readers are familiar with the presentation of the results; thus, we will only show the calculation of targets using Figs. 3.11, 3.12, and 3.13.

Using the values from Table 3.2 and the target formulations from Appendix D, we get the following inputs:

$$\widehat{x}_{io} = x_{io} - s_i^{-*} \quad i = 1, \ldots m, \text{ more specifically for this case}$$
$$\widehat{x}_{16} = x_{16} - s_1^{-*} \text{ and}$$
$$\widehat{x}_{26} = x_{26} - s_2^{-*}$$

	A	B	C	D	E	F	G	H	I	J
1										
2	Model Name = DEA-Solver LV (V7)/ BCC(BCC-I) Returns to Scale = Variable (Sum of Lambda = 1)									
3	Workbook Name = C:\Users\Yasar Ozcan\Documents\OZCAN\A-DEA-BOOK\ADEA BOOK-2nd EDITION\DEA RUNS\ExampleData-									
4	No.	DMU	Score	Rank	Reference set	λ_j	Reference set	λ_j	Reference set	λ_j
5	1	H1	1	1	H1	1				
6	2	H2	1	1	H2	1				
7	3	H3	1	1	H3	1				
8	4	H4	1	1	H4	1				
9	5	H5	1	1	H5	1				
10	6	H6	0.9654066	10	H3	0.3269322	H5	0.4582155	H7	0.2148422
11	7	H7	1	1	H7	1				
12	8	H8	1	1	H8	1				
13	9	H9	1	1	H9	1				
14	10	H10	1	1	H10	1				

Fig. 3.9 Benchmarks for input-oriented BCC [VRS] model

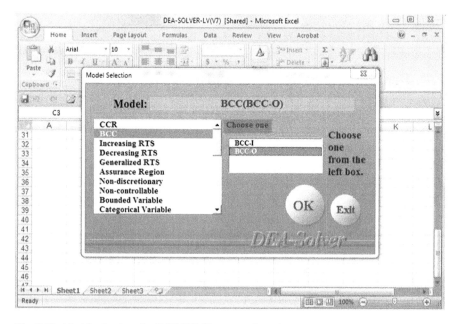

Fig. 3.10 Model selections for BCC [VRS] output orientation

By substituting actual output values (Table 3.2) and optimal slack scores (Fig. 3.12) in these we get:

$$\widehat{x}_{16} = 399 - 0 = 399 \text{ and}$$
$$\widehat{x}_{26} = 1660 - 0 = 1660$$

Similarly for outputs we get:

$$\widehat{y}_{ro} = \phi^* y_{ro} + s_i^{+*} \quad r = 1, ...s, \text{ more specifically for H6:}$$
$$\widehat{y}_{16} = \phi^* y_{16} + s_1^{+*} \text{ and}$$
$$\widehat{y}_{26} = \phi^* y_{26} + s_2^{+*}$$

Fig. 3.11 Efficiency results for output-oriented BCC [VRS] model

DMU	Score	Rank	1/Score
H1	1	1	1
H2	1	1	1
H3	1	1	1
H4	1	1	1
H5	1	1	1
H6	0.8823806	10	1.1332978
H7	1	1	1
H8	1	1	1
H9	1	1	1
H10	1	1	1

	A	B	C	D	E	F	G
1							
2	Model Name = DEA-Solver LV (V7)/ BCC(BCC-O) Returns to Scale = Variable (Sum of Lambo						
3	Workbook Name = C:\Users\Yasar Ozcan\Documents\OZCAN\A-DEA-BOOK\ADEA BOOK-2						
4				Excess	Excess	Shortage	Shortage
5	No.	DMU	Score	Nursing Hours	Medical Supply	Inpatient	Outpatient
6				S-(1)	S-(2)	S+(1)	S+(2)
7	1	H1	1	0	0	0	0
8	2	H2	1	0	0	0	0
9	3	H3	1	0	0	0	0
10	4	H4	1	0	0	0	0
11	5	H5	1	0	0	0	0
12	6	H6	0.8823806	0	0	0	26.236242
13	7	H7	1	0	0	0	0
14	8	H8	1	0	0	0	0
15	9	H9	1	0	0	0	0
16	10	H10	1	0	0	0	0

RTS Slack WeightedData Weight Projection Graph2

Fig. 3.12 Slack report for output-oriented BCC [VRS] model

By substituting the efficiency score (see Fig. 3.11), actual outputs (Table 3.2) and optimal slack values (Fig. 3.12) to these formulas, we get:

$\widehat{y}_{16} = 1.1332978 * 209 + 0 = 236.85923$ and
$\widehat{y}_{26} = 1.1332978 * 100 + 26.236242 = 139.56602$

The reader can verify the results of these calculations by comparing the target values of H6 from the abridged version of the "Projection" worksheet in Fig. 3.13.

Benchmarks are the same reference set hospitals as for the input orientation. However, the λ weights corresponding to these reference hospitals are different in output orientation, as shown in Fig. 3.14, in which inefficient H6 has three benchmark hospitals (H3, H5, and H7) in its reference set.

DMU I/O	1/Score Data	Projection	Difference	%
H5	1			
Nursing Hours	450	450	0	0.00%
Medical Supply	890	890	0	0.00%
Inpatient	195	195	0	0.00%
Outpatient	94	94	0	0.00%
H6	1.1332978			
Nursing Hours	399	399	0	0.00%
Medical Supply	1660	1660	0	0.00%
Inpatient	209	236.85923	27.859231	13.33%
Outpatient	100	139.56602	39.566017	39.57%
H7	1			
Nursing Hours	156	156	0	0.00%
Medical Supply	3102	3102	0	0.00%
Inpatient	108	108	0	0.00%
Outpatient	57	57	0	0.00%

Fig. 3.13 Target report for the output-oriented BCC [VRS] model

Fig. 3.14 Benchmarks for output-oriented BCC [VRS] model

3.10   Comparison of CCR and BCC Models, and Scale Efficiency

In this section we will provide a brief overview of basic envelopment models and compare efficiency results. Figure 3.15 summarizes the results that were generated using input and output orientation on CCR and BCC models. As the reader can verify, input- and output-oriented models identify the same exact DMUs as efficient. Furthermore, the reciprocals of the efficiency scores for the output-oriented models are equal to the efficiency scores of the input-oriented models. Average efficiency scores for input-oriented BCC models will generally be greater than

DMU Name	Input - Oriented CCR[CRS] Efficiency	Output - Oriented CCR[CRS] Efficiency	Input - Oriented BCC[VRS] Efficiency	Output - Oriented BCC[VRS] Efficiency
H1	1.00000	1.00000	1.00000	1.00000
H2	0.61541	1.62493	1.00000	1.00000
H3	1.00000	1.00000	1.00000	1.00000
H4	1.00000	1.00000	1.00000	1.00000
H5	1.00000	1.00000	1.00000	1.00000
H6	0.75780	1.31962	0.96541	1.13327
H7	0.96852	1.03250	1.00000	1.00000
H8	1.00000	1.00000	1.00000	1.00000
H9	1.00000	1.00000	1.00000	1.00000
H10	0.75297	1.32807	1.00000	1.00000
Average	0.90947	1.13051	0.99654	1.01333

Fig. 3.15 Comparison of efficiency scores in basic envelopment models

DMU Name	Input - Oriented CCR Efficiency	Input - Oriented BCC Efficiency	SE=C CR/BCC	θ^*_{BCC} PURE TE	θ^*_{CCR} TE
H1	1.00000	1.00000	1	1.00000	1.0000
H2	0.61541	1.00000	0.615412186	1.00000	0.6154
H3	1.00000	1.00000	1	1.00000	1.0000
H4	1.00000	1.00000	1	1.00000	1.0000
H5	1.00000	1.00000	1	1.00000	1.0000
H6	0.75780	0.96541	0.784944545	0.96541	0.7578
H7	0.96852	1.00000	0.968522114	1.00000	0.9685
H8	1.00000	1.00000	1	1.00000	1.0000
H9	1.00000	1.00000	1	1.00000	1.0000
H10	0.75297	1.00000	0.75297491	1.00000	0.7530
Average	0.90947	0.99654			

Fig. 3.16 Scale efficiency

those for an input-oriented CCR model. The reverse can be shown for the output-oriented models (see Fig. 3.15).

In comparing CCR and BCC models, health care managers can depict another important aspect of efficiency briefly discussed in Chap. 2. Cooper et al. (2007) show (pp. 152–153) that the scale efficiency (SE) can be calculated by dividing the optimal CRS efficiency score by the optimal VRS efficiency score. Hence, it can be written as:

$$ScaleEfficiency \ (SE) = \frac{\theta^*_{CCR}}{\theta^*_{BCC}}.$$

The BCC efficiency scores, θ^*_{BCC}, are considered pure technical efficiency, while CCR efficiency scores, θ^*_{CCR}, are considered technical efficiency. Thus, the formula above can be used to decompose the technical efficiency into pure technical efficiency and scale efficiency, as in: $\theta^*_{CCR} = SE * \theta^*_{BCC}$. Applying this formula to our results, we obtain the SE scores shown in Fig. 3.16.

This also relates to the concepts introduced earlier in Sect. 3.2. The conceptual distances from CCR and BCC fronts to an inefficient hospital were shown in Fig. 3.3. Once the distances are calculated, one would have the respective CCR and BCC efficiency scores. By substituting these values into the above ratio, scale efficiency can be obtained.

3.11   Summary

In this chapter, we examined the concept of returns to scale (RTS) and demonstrated the increasing, constant, and decreasing returns to scale. In addition, variable returns to scale (BCC) models were introduced. Finally, we showed how to obtain the scale efficiency scores from the results of CCR and BCC models.

Appendix D

D.1 BCC [VRS] Input-Oriented Model Formulation

Adopting from the input-oriented Model 5 defined in Chap. 2, Appendix B, the VRS input model formulation requires an additional set of constraints, in which summation of λ values are set equal to 1.

Model 7: Input-Oriented BCC [VRS] Model

$$Minimize \quad \theta - \varepsilon \left(\sum_{i=1}^{m} s_i^- + \sum_{r=1}^{s} s_r^+ \right)$$

$$\sum_{j=1}^{n} \lambda_j x_{ij} + s_i^- = \theta x_{io} \quad i = 1, \ldots m$$

$$\sum_{j=1}^{n} \lambda_j y_{rj} - s_r^+ = y_{ro} \quad r = 1, \ldots s$$

$$\sum_{j=1}^{n} \lambda_j = 1 \quad j = 1, \ldots n$$

$$\lambda_j \geq 0 \quad j = 1, \ldots n$$

D.2 Efficient Target Calculations for Input-Oriented BCC [VRS] Model

The efficiency targets in the input-oriented BCC model are calculated in the same way as in the CCR model, and the levels of efficient targets for inputs and outputs can be obtained as follows:

Inputs: $\widehat{x}_{io} = \theta^* x_{io} - s_i^{-*}$ $i = 1, ...m$

Outputs: $\widehat{y}_{ro} = y_{ro} + s_i^{+*}$ $r = 1, ...s$

Appendix E

E.1 BCC [VRS] Output-Oriented Model Formulation

Adopting from output-oriented Model 6 defined in Chap. 2, Appendix C, the VRS output orientation model formulation requires an additional set of constraints, in which summation of λ values are set equal to 1.

Model 8: Output-Oriented BCC [VRS] Model

$$Maximize \;\; \phi - \varepsilon \left(\sum_{i=1}^{m} s_i^- + \sum_{r=1}^{s} s_r^+ \right)$$

$$\sum_{j=1}^{n} \lambda_j x_{ij} + s_i^- = x_{io} \quad i = 1, ...m$$

$$\sum_{j=1}^{n} \lambda_j y_{rj} - s_r^+ = \phi y_{ro} \quad i = 1, ...s$$

$$\sum_{j=1}^{n} \lambda_j = 1 \quad j = 1, ...n$$

$$\lambda_j \geq 0 \quad j = 1, ...n$$

The output efficiency is defined by ϕ. Another change in the formula is that the efficiency emphasis is removed from input (first constraint) and placed into output (second constraint).

E.2 Efficient Target Calculations for Output-Oriented BCC [VRS] Model

Efficient targets in the output-oriented BCC model are calculated in the same way as in the CCR model, and the levels of efficient targets for inputs and outputs can be obtained as follows:

Inputs: $\widehat{x}_{io} = x_{io} - s_i^{-*}$ $i = 1, ...m$

Outputs: $\widehat{y}_{ro} = \phi^* y_{ro} + s_i^{+*}$ $r = 1, ...s.$

Chapter 4
Weight Restricted (Multiplier) Models

4.1 Introduction

When considering various inputs and outputs in the basic DEA models discussed in earlier chapters, we made no judgment about the importance of one input versus another, and we assumed that all outputs had the same importance. In fact, in our example data, we assumed outpatient visits would consume the resources at the same level as inpatient admissions. Similarly, in producing the patient outputs, we valued the contribution of nursing hours the same as the contribution of medical supplies. Beside these assumptions, DMUs in a DEA can become efficient by simply taking advantage of a particular input or output variable. Simply, a hospital can become efficient by emphasizing a favorable input or output. For instance, observing from the example data, Hospital 9 has relatively low nursing hours but a high amount of medical supplies. The low nursing hours may be the reason this hospital is at the efficiency frontier (see Fig. 2.7). In the DEA literature, these DMUs that take advantage of these weak assumptions are sometimes called maverick DMUs.

To address this issue, health care managers can alter their models using prior information regarding inputs and outputs. For example, if one average inpatient admission is equivalent to four outpatient visits, then inpatient admissions can be weighted accordingly. On the other hand, if health care managers do not have a priori information on such weights, the relative weights can be estimated from the data using the DEA models. In any case, imposing restrictions based on weights (in DEA literature also called "multipliers") should be done based on known and reliable substitution among either inputs or outputs. Furthermore, health care researchers can test the impact of substitution among inputs (and/or outputs) to answer various policy or managerial questions. For example, practice patterns for physicians versus nurse practitioners as shown in Fig. 2.1 can be evaluated so that efficient practices using extreme values on either of these inputs can be constrained

Y.A. Ozcan, *Health Care Benchmarking and Performance Evaluation*,
International Series in Operations Research & Management Science 210,
DOI 10.1007/978-1-4899-7472-3_4, © Springer Science+Business Media New York 2014

to balanced or acceptable practice patterns. Ozcan (1998) showed how various substitutions among inputs or outputs can impact physician practice patterns from the managed care perspective. The study demonstrated how using reasonable weight restrictions can result in more balanced models of physician practice, and the economic impact of these models can be estimated. In Chap. 10, we discuss more detailed applications of weight restricted models.

4.2   Determination of Weights

Optimal input and output weights, v_i and u_r, shown in formulas in Sect. 2.7, are derived by solving the DEA based on relative evaluation of all DMUs in the data. To observe these weights, health care managers and researchers can click on the "Weight" worksheet of the solutions. Figure 4.1 shows the weights for the CCR [CRS] Input-Orientation solution.

Here, one can observe the optimal weights (multipliers) for each input, v_1 (nursing hours) and v_2 (medical supplies), and each output, u_1 (inpatient admissions) and u_2 (outpatient visits).

These weights also yield information on how efficiency improvements can be achieved for the inefficient hospitals. For example, Hospital 7 has an efficiency ratio of 0.969. This means that this hospital must increase its rating by 3.15 % $(1.00 - 0.969 = 0.031)$ to become relatively efficient among the other nine hospitals. Using the weights reported in Fig. 4.1, the hospital can decrease its nursing hours by $(0.031)/0.00641 = 4.92$ h, to an efficient target of 151.08, as reported in Fig. 2.10. Our aim in this chapter is to use this weight information to assure a better practice pattern for the group of hospitals in the data set.

No.	DMU	Score	V(1) Nursing Hours	V(2) Medical Supply	U(1) Inpatient	U(2) Outpatient
1	H1	1	0.001763668	0	0.002444988	0
2	H2	0.6154122	0	0.000833333	0	0.007240143
3	H3	1	0.001588422	0.000181406	0.003389831	0
4	H4	1	0.000279008	0.000266333	0.001785714	0
5	H5	1	0.000597393	0.000821643	0.00424068	0.001841143
6	H6	0.7577962	0.001699003	0.000194035	0.003625819	0
7	H7	0.9685221	0.006410256	0	0.005361735	0.006832539
8	H8	1	0.000205992	0.000151428	0.001140251	0
9	H9	1	0.001785714	0	0.001071822	0.002572341
10	H10	0.7529749	0	0.000222222	0	0.001930705

Model Name = DEA-Solver LV (V7)/ CCR(CCR-I) Returns to Scale = Constant (0 =< Sum of Lambda < Infinity)
Workbook Name = C:\Users\Yasar Ozcan\Documents\OZCAN\A-DEA-BOOK\ADEA BOOK-2nd EDITION\DEA RUNS\ExampleD

Slack   WeightedData   Weight   Projection   Graph2   Graph1

Fig. 4.1 Input and output weights

4.3   Assurance Regions and Cone Ratio Models

Also called assurance region (AR) models as developed by Thompson et al. (1990) or cone ratio models, a more generalized version developed by Charnes et al. (1990) can impose restrictions (constraints) on weights to control how much a DMU can freely use the weights to become efficient. This means that lower and upper bounds can be established on a weight ratio of a given pair of inputs or outputs to assure that no DMU can freely choose to become efficient through using excessive outputs or insufficient inputs. Thus, the DMUs will reassess their input usage and output production within given limits (constraints) that are equivalent to policy or managerial restrictions.

Figure 4.2 illustrates the conceptualization of assurance regions for the ongoing example data, where three styles of input usage are identified. These styles are identified by drawing lines from the origin to the extreme use of either input. For example, the line from the origin passing through H7 represents a practice that proportionately uses more medical supplies and very few nursing hours. On the

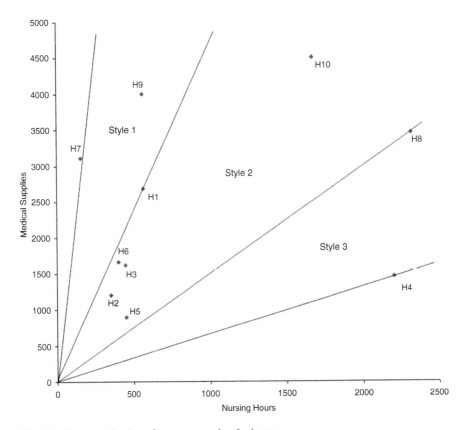

Fig. 4.2   Conceptualization of assurance region for inputs

other extreme, the line passing through H4 represents a high usage of nursing hours with a proportionately lower usage of medical supplies. The other two lines going through H1 and H8 show more balanced usages of either input. This way, three styles of input usage patterns can be identified. Each style can be shown in a cone, in which the tip of the cone is in the origin, and thus the name of *cone ratio* originates. Once the health care manager/researcher decides that style one and style three are not acceptable practice, then he or she can impose restrictions on weights so that any efficient hospital in style one or style three would become inefficient and advised to practice input usage represented in style two. We can also call style two, for practical purposes, an assurance region.

In order to impose the restrictions on input or output weights, we can define the following ratios with upper and lower bound restrictions for inputs:

$$L_{i,k} \leq \frac{v_i}{v_k} \leq U_{i,k} \quad i = 1, \ldots, m \tag{4.1}$$

v_i and v_k represent the weights for two different inputs, and $L_{i,k}$ and $U_{i,k}$ denote the lower and upper bounds on this ratio, respectively. This implies that many such ratios can be calculated and their lower and upper bounds can be determined. For example, if there are three inputs, one can calculate six such ratios (v_1/v_2, v_2/v_1, v_1/v_3, v_3/v_1, v_2/v_3, v_3/v_2). The number of ratios that can be calculated is n! Of course, it does not make sense to calculate a complete set of these ratios to impose the restrictions on input weights. This can also be complicated by the presence of zeroes in the input data. Health care managers/researchers should therefore use prudent judgment and practical vision in proper selection of these ratios so that managerial and policy implications can be tested appropriately.

We can imagine similar restrictions to output production as well. This means that a hospital cannot become efficient by only producing high levels of inpatient admissions or outpatient visits. Figure 4.3 illustrates the conceptualization of assurance region for outputs, in which three styles of output usage are identified.

Restrictions to outputs via weights can be imposed using the following formula:

$$L_{r,z} \leq \frac{\mu_r}{\mu_z} \leq U_{r,z} \quad r = 1, \ldots, s \tag{4.2}$$

where μ_r and μ_z represent the weights for two different outputs, and $L_{r,z}$ and $U_{r,z}$ denote the lower and upper bounds on this ratio, respectively.

4.4 Assessment of Upper and Lower Bound Weights

Although health care managers and researchers can impose their own estimates for lower and upper bounds on input and output weight ratios, we suggest a practical statistical approach to obtain the limits placed on these ratios. Once the multiplier

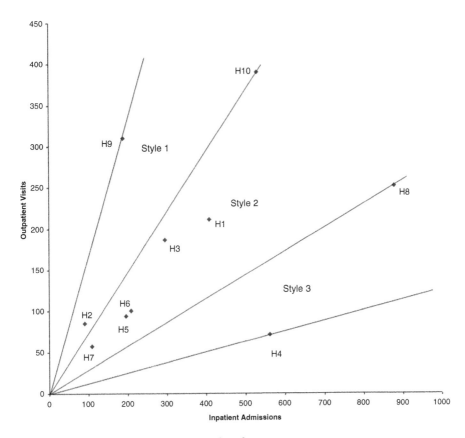

Fig. 4.3 Conceptualization of assurance regions for outputs

model has run and optimal multipliers are obtained, as shown in Fig. 4.1, various distributional values of each weight can be calculated. For example, first, second (median), and third quartiles of the distribution for each weight can be easily obtained using the Excel function "Quartile" to obtain these values. For example, "=QUARTILE(E9:E14, 1)" would yield the first quartile of the data identified in an array (cells in a column E9 to E14). Although quartiles are suggested in this example, one can easily examine various weight percentiles of the distributions on each variable as well.

Imposing upper bound restrictions, for example, at the third quartile, and lower bound restrictions at the median, would provide a tightening of the assurance region closer to style two. However, for further tightening, one can choose the first quartile as a lower bound and the median as an upper bound. These decisions should be assessed case by case, depending upon the distributional values of the weights.

Let us demonstrate this with our example data set. Using the values from Fig. 4.1, median and third quartile values of input and output weights are shown in Table 4.1.

The next step would be to assess substitutability of inputs to each other, as well as the outputs. In terms of policy, we can test the substitution of outpatient care for

Table 4.1 Median and third quartile values

	Nursing hours	Medical supply	Inpatient	Outpatient
Median	0.001092908	0.00018772	0.002115351	0.000920571
Quartile 3	0.001747502	0.00025530	0.003566822	0.002411932

inpatient. This is in line with the developments that occurred within the past two decades. For example, due to advances in technology, such as interventional radiology for hysterectomies, many surgical procedures can now be done on an outpatient basis.

This means that we prefer the outpatient treatment to inpatient, or that the second output variable is preferred to the first output variable, μ_2/μ_1. Thus, we need to divide outpatient weights by inpatient weights to impose restrictions; however, these restrictions should have lower and upper bound values. Having calculated median and third quartile values on weights of each output variable (Table 4.1), we can use median values for lower bounds, as follows:

$$L_{2,1} \leq \frac{\mu_2}{\mu_1} \leq U_{2,1}$$

or

$$L_{2,1} \leq \frac{Outpatient}{Inpatient} \leq U_{2,1}$$

Outpatient/Inpatient $= 0.000920571/0.002115351 = 0.435186132\ (L_{2,1})$. Similarly we can use the third quartile for the upper bound, as shown: Outpatient/Inpatient $= 0.002411932/0.003566822 = 0.676213153\ (U_{2,1})$. Hence we have the restriction ratio for output weights, as shown:

$$0.435186132 \leq \frac{Outpatient}{Inpatient} \leq 0.676213153 \qquad (4.3)$$

Again, in this formula, health care managers and researchers are implying their preference of outpatient treatment to inpatient.

Using a similar analogy, we can write a preference ratio stating that nursing hours are a preferred input to medical supplies (the first input is preferred to the second input):

$$L_{1,2} \leq \frac{v_1}{v_2} \leq U_{1,2}$$

or

$$L_{1,2} \leq \frac{Nur\sin g\ Hours}{Medical\ Supplies} \leq U_{1,2}$$

Since median and third quartile values on weights of each input variable are available from Table 4.1, we can use median values for the lower bound, as shown:

Nursing Hours/Medical Supplies $= 0.001092908/0.00018772 = 5.821996871$ $(L_{1,2})$.

Similarly we can use the third quartile for an upper bound, as shown:

Nursing Hours/Medical Supplies $= 0.001747502/0.00025531 = 6.844748469$ $(U_{1,2})$.

Hence we have the restriction ratio for input weights, as shown:

$$5.8219966871 \leq \frac{Nur\sin g\ Hours}{Medical\ Supplies} \leq 6.844748469 \qquad (4.4)$$

Once these lower and upper bounds on input and output weights are determined, we can impose these as constraints in a subsequent run in a multiplier restricted model.

4.5 Weight Restricted (Multiplier) Model Example

Weight (multiplier) restrictions can be imposed in stages or all at once. However, to see the impact of different policies or managerial preferences [outpatient preferred to inpatient or more nursing hours (human contact) preferred to medical supplies], one may want to test each policy independently or in succession.

In order to implement the first preference, outpatient to inpatient, we need to include the constraint in the model. In DEA Solver-LV software, this is done by adding a row after leaving one blank row. The top part of the Fig. 4.4 shows the original data, and the bottom part shows the added constraint. More specifically, row 12 is left blank, and the weight restriction constraint defined by formula (4.3) is entered on row 13. In row 13, outpatient and inpatient variables shown in columns B and C indicate the ratio of weights for these two variables, whereas column A shows the lower bound and column D shows the upper bound value calculated earlier.

	A	B	C	D	E
1	Hospital	(I)Nursing Hours	(I)Medical Supply	(O)Inpatient	(O)Outpatient
2	H1	567	2678	409	211
3	H2	350	1200	90	85
4	H3	445	1616	295	186
5	H4	2200	1450	560	71
6	H5	450	890	195	94
7	H6	399	1660	209	100
8	H7	156	3102	108	57
9	H8	2314	3456	877	252
10	H9	560	4000	189	310
11	H10	1669	4500	530	390
12					
13	0.435186	(O)Outpatient	(O)Inpatient	0.676213	

Fig. 4.4 Data setup for weight restricted model

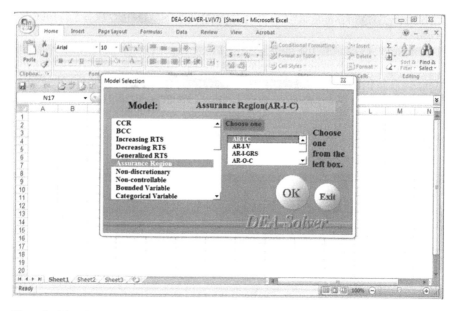

Fig. 4.5 CCR [CRS] input-oriented assurance region model selection

With these set up, we are now ready to run the weight restricted model. Figure 4.5 depicts the model selection platform from DEA Solver-LV. We select the "Assurance Region" model; to run the input-oriented CCR [CRS] based version of the model, we must choose AR-I-C, where "AR" stands for assurance region, "I" for input orientation, and "C" for CCR.

The result of the CCR [CRS] input-oriented weight restricted model is shown in Fig. 4.6. One can clearly observe that the number of efficient hospitals (compare to Fig. 2.7) was reduced from six to four hospitals. Hospitals H8 and H9 are no longer at the efficiency frontier due to restrictions imposed on output weights.

After seeing the impact of the outpatient preference to inpatient treatment policy, we can enter an additional constraint to measure the impact of input preferences, namely by restricting the weights on the ratio for nursing hours to medical supplies.

In this second stage, we add the second constraint defined by formula (4.4) into the "Data" worksheet as shown in Fig. 4.7. Now we have both output and input restrictions in place. Running the model in a similar way, using the "Data" worksheet shown in Fig. 4.7, we obtain the results where both ratios are in effect. These results are shown in Fig. 4.8.

It is interesting to observe that, after imposing restrictions on input weights in addition to the output weights, an additional three hospitals dropped from the efficiency frontier. These hospitals are H1, H4, and H5. Only H3 remains on the efficiency frontier.

Figure 4.9 provides a comparison of three models. The first one is the basic input-oriented CCR model, with no restrictions on input or output weights. The second model is the first stage weight restricted model, where we imposed

	A	B	C	D	E	F	G	H
1								
2	Model Name = DEA-Solver LV (V7)/ Assurance Region(AR-I-C) Returns to Scale = Constant (0 =<							
3	Workbook Name = C:\Users\Yasar Ozcan\Documents\OZCAN\A-DEA-BOOK\ADEA BOOK-2nd ED							
4	No.	DMU	Score	Rank	Reference set (lambda)			
5	1	H1	1	1	H1	1		
6	2	H2	0.4681593	10	H3	0.3230391	H5	0.0446741
7	3	H3	1	1	H3	1		
8	4	H4	1	1	H4	1		
9	5	H5	1	1	H5	1		
10	6	H6	0.7329577	7	H1	0.2499163	H3	0.3387585
11	7	H7	0.9654703	6	H1	0.2656321		
12	8	H8	0.9907902	5	H3	1.4463402	H4	0.749576
13	9	H9	0.7315983	8	H1	0.7225662		
14	10	H10	0.6470262	9	H3	1.6631639	H4	0.1544449

Fig. 4.6 Weight restricted CCR input-oriented solution—with Ratio 1

	A	B	C	D	E
1	Hospital	(I)Nursing Hours	(I)Medical Supply	(O)Inpatient	(O)Outpatient
2	H1	567	2678	409	211
3	H2	350	1200	90	85
4	H3	445	1616	295	186
5	H4	2200	1450	560	71
6	H5	450	890	195	94
7	H6	399	1660	209	100
8	H7	156	3102	108	57
9	H8	2314	3456	877	252
10	H9	560	4000	189	310
11	H10	1669	4500	530	390
12					
13	0.435186	(O)Outpatient	(O)Inpatient	0.676213	
14	5.821997	(I)Nursing Hours	(I)Medical Supply	6.844748	

Fig. 4.7 Weight restrictions for both outputs and inputs

outpatient to inpatient weight restriction with formula (4.3), Ratio 1. The final model is the weight restricted model, which includes both the first stage and the second stage weight restriction, imposed by nursing hours to medical supplies with formula (4.4), Ratio 2.

It should be further noted that the efficiency scores of individual hospitals can only decrease as more restrictions are imposed on them. The average efficiency

	A	B	C	D	E	F
1						
2	Model Name = DEA-Solver LV (V7)/ Assurance Region(AR-I-C) Returns to					
3	Workbook Name = C:\Users\Yasar Ozcan\Documents\OZCAN\A-DEA-BO					
4	No.	DMU	Score	Rank	Reference set (lambda)	
5	1	H1	0.9468689	2	H3	1.3321757
6	2	H2	0.4553981	9	H3	0.3504911
7	3	H3	1	1	H3	1
8	4	H4	0.463734	8	H3	1.5717694
9	5	H5	0.7520972	3	H3	0.627506
10	6	H6	0.7131237	4	H3	0.671691
11	7	H7	0.3949512	10	H3	0.3532584
12	8	H8	0.6522126	5	H3	2.6245007
13	9	H9	0.5638296	6	H3	0.9473601
14	10	H10	0.5581666	7	H3	1.8863333

Fig. 4.8 Weight restricted solutions: Ratio 1 and Ratio 2

Hospital	CCR-I	Weight Restricted Models with	
		Ratio 1	Ratios 1 & 2
		AR-I-C	AR-I-C
H1	1.00000	1.00000	0.94687
H2	0.61541	0.46816	0.45540
H3	1.00000	1.00000	1.00000
H4	1.00000	1.00000	0.46373
H5	1.00000	1.00000	0.75210
H6	0.75780	0.73296	0.71312
H7	0.96852	0.96547	0.39495
H8	1.00000	0.99079	0.65221
H9	1.00000	0.73160	0.56383
H10	0.75297	0.64703	0.55817
Average	0.90947	0.85360	0.65004

Ratio 1	0.435186	>= Outpatient /	Inpatient <=	0.676213
Ratio 2	5.821997	>= Nursing Hours /	Medical Supply <=	6.844748

Fig. 4.9 Comparison of basic and weight (multiplier) restricted models

score of the unrestricted model, in which there were six efficient hospitals, was 0.91. With output weight restrictions (Ratio 1), this average was reduced by 6.1 %. However, imposing both output and input weight restrictions reduced the efficiency by 28.5 % compared to the basic model. Thus, in this case, the weight restricted model provides 28.5 % more pure efficiency evaluation when compared to the basic model, or the impact of weight restrictions shifts the efficiency frontier by 28.5 %.

4.6 Summary

In this chapter, we introduced the weight restricted models, also known as multiplier models; these models are also known as assurance region models, or cone ratio models in DEA literature. The assurance region models provide additional discrimination compared to the standard DEA models by reducing the number of hospitals that make up the best-practice frontier. The impact of these models in determining truly efficient health care organizations is extremely valuable. In addition, using these models, health care managers and researchers can test the impact of various managerial decisions or policies, as discussed in more detail in Chap. 10.

Appendix F

F.1 Input-Oriented Weight Restricted (Assurance Region) Model Formulation

---

Model 9

$$Maximize \sum_{r=1}^{s} \mu_r y_{ro} + \mu$$

Subject to:

$$\sum_{r=1}^{s} \mu_r y_{rj} - \sum_{i=1}^{m} v_i x_{ij} + \mu \leq 0 \quad j = 1, ... n$$

$$\sum_{i=1}^{m} v_i x_{io} = 1$$

$\mu_r, v_i \geq 0(\varepsilon)$, in CCR $\mu = 0$, and in BCC μ is free.

F.2 Output-Oriented Weight Restricted (Assurance Region) Model Formulation

---

Model 10

$$Maximize \ m\sum_{i=1}^{m} v_i x_{io} + v$$

Subject to:

$$\sum_{i=1}^{m} v_r x_{ij} - \sum_{r=1}^{s} \mu_r y_{rj} + v \geq 0 \quad j = 1,....n$$

$$\sum_{i=1}^{m} \mu_r y_{ro} = 1$$

$\mu_r, v_i \geq 0(\varepsilon)$, in CCR $v = 0$, and in BCC v is free.

Chapter 5
Non-oriented and Measure Specific Models

5.1 Non-oriented (Slack-Based) Models

When the health care manager is able to both reduce inputs and augment outputs simultaneously, a non-oriented model is of great use. The non-oriented model is formulated based on input and output slacks and, in the DEA literature, is called an *additive model* or a *slack-based* model. The illustrated slack-based model (SBM) assumes equal weights (e.g., 1) for all non-zero input and output slacks. However, there are weighted SBM models when a priori information on the relative importance of the slacks is available (in terms of reducing inputs or augmenting outputs). The weighted SBM models will not be pursued as DEA Solver-LV does not include this specific model.

Figure 5.1 shows the setup for the non-oriented slack-based model (SBM), and the choice of "SBM-C," the CCR version. Figure 5.1 displays the selection options for other choices for this model as well. For example, one can run the BCC [VRS] version by selecting "SBM-V" or assurance region versions by selecting "SBM-AR-C" or "SBM-AR-V." Continuing our example from previous chapters, we select the CCR model to demonstrate the slack-based model.

Figure 5.2 provides the solution for the setup shown in Fig. 5.1. Columns B and E of the Excel worksheet named "Slack Report" showing the solution provides this information.

"Slack Report" in Fig. 5.3 displays the input and output slacks as well as other pertinent information relating to the DEA solution. Examining the DEA score in this *non-oriented* model, we can determine that Hospitals 1, 3, 4, 5, 8, and 9 are efficient, as they were in an *input-oriented* CCR model. However, it is interesting to observe that the magnitude of slacks between these two models is different. Figure 5.4 depicts the slacks from an input-oriented CCR model, a non-oriented SBM CCR model, and the differences in slack values from the non-oriented model and the input-oriented model.

Y.A. Ozcan, *Health Care Benchmarking and Performance Evaluation*,
International Series in Operations Research & Management Science 210,
DOI 10.1007/978-1-4899-7472-3_5, © Springer Science+Business Media New York 2014

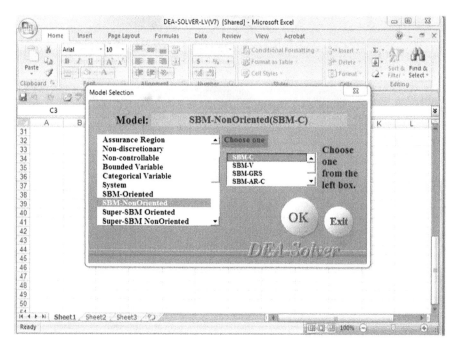

Fig. 5.1 Slack-based model setup

Fig. 5.2 Non-oriented slack-based model: CCR solution

For example, examining H2 and H10 for the nursing hours input, we observe that the slack-based model produced significantly higher values for these hospitals, where nursing hours slack increased from 12.03 to 19.55 (by 7.52) for H2, and from 323.65 to 429.83 (by 106.18) for H10. For the medical supply input, H6 needs to reduce by 211.05, and H7 has to reduce this input to 2,449.83 compared to 2,309.19 (by 140.64). On output slacks, H2, H6, and H10 had some slacks in the input-oriented model, but with SBM the magnitude and composition of these slacks changed as well; H7 was added to the slack list to increase its outpatient visits by 4.6.

	A	B	C	D	E	F	G	H	I	J
1										
2	Model Name = DEA-Solver LV (V7)/ SBM-NonOriented(SBM-C) Returns to Scale = Constant (0 =< Sum of Lambda < Infinity)									
3	Workbook Name = C:\Users\Yasar Ozcan\Documents\OZCAN\A-DEA-BOOK\ADEA BOOK-2nd EDITION\DEA RUNS\ExampleData-s									
4				Excess	Excess	Shortage	Shortage			
5	No.	DMU	Score	Nursing Hours	Medical Supply	Inpatient	Outpatient			
6				S-(1)	S-(2)	S+(1)	S+(2)			
7	1	H1	1	0	0	0	0			
8	2	H2	0.4789771	19.55445545	0	129.05941	53.118812			
9	3	H3	1	0	0	0	0			
10	4	H4	1	0	0	0	0			
11	5	H5	1	0	0	0	0			
12	6	H6	0.6384817	0	211.047191	55.505618	66.773034			
13	7	H7	0.5816164	0	2449.828494	0	4.6070556			
14	8	H8	1	0	0	0	0			
15	9	H9	1	0	0	0	0			
16	10	H10	0.6054394	429.8292079	0	291.47277	127.94554			
17										

Decomposition **Slack** WeightedData Weight Projection Graph2 Graph1 Rank Score Summary Data

Fig. 5.3 Slack report for non-oriented SBM-CCR solution

Comparisons for solution targets are displayed in Fig. 5.5. Input-oriented and non-oriented (slack-based) solution targets, as well as the differences between the oriented and non-oriented models, are shown in this figure. It is interesting to note that the differences on targets show change on inefficient hospitals 2, 6, 7, and 10. Most of the adjustments are done through simultaneous input reduction and output augmentation based on efficiency scores plus slacks.

An interested reader can find the mathematical formulations of the non-oriented SBM CCR [CRS] model (Model 11) in Appendix G.

5.2   Measure Specific Models

Health care managers and researchers often find variables that are not at their discretion or over which they have little control. However, inclusion of these variables into the DEA model is often essential to capture the health service production process. The measure specific DEA models incorporate the uncontrollable nature of such variables into the formulation. That is, even in the model, health care managers will not be able to exercise input reduction or output augmentation over these variables. In the DEA literature, the measure specific models are also called models with non-controllable variables or models with non-discretionary variables.

Depending upon input or output orientation, one can designate the variables that we have no control over (or variables that are not at our discretion). If the non-controllable variables constitute a group (set) of inputs then they will be identified by I, which is a set of such inputs. Similarly, if the controllable variables constitute a group (set) of outputs then they will be identified by O, which is a set of such outputs. Although both envelopment models and measure specific models will produce the same frontier, the measure specific models will result in different efficient targets.

Slacks - Input Oriented CCR [CRS] Model

DMU	Score	Excess Nursing Hours S-(1)	Excess Medical Supply S-(2)	Shortage Inpatient S+(1)	Shortage Outpatient S+(2)
H1	1	0	0	0	0
H2	0.6154122	12.03405018	0	44.811828	0
H3	1	0	0	0	0
H4	1	0	0	0	0
H5	1	0	0	0	0
H6	0.7577962	0	0	0	19.663685
H7	0.9685221	0	2309.186459	0	0
H8	1	0	0	0	0
H9	1	0	0	0	0
H10	0.7529749	323.6506093	0	88.548387	0

Slacks - Non-Oriented SBM- CCR [CRS] Model

DMU	Score	Excess Nursing Hours S-(1)	Excess Medical Supply S-(2)	Shortage Inpatient S+(1)	Shortage Outpatient S+(2)
H1	1	0	0	0	0
H2	0.4789771	19.55445545	0	129.05941	53.118812
H3	1	0	0	0	0
H4	1	0	0	0	0
H5	1	0	0	0	0
H6	0.6384817	0	211.047191	55.505618	66.773034
H7	0.5816164	0	2449.828494	0	4.6070556
H8	1	0	0	0	0
H9	1	0	0	0	0
H10	0.6054394	429.8292079	0	291.47277	127.94554

Differences Between Oriented and Non-Oriented Models

DMU	Score	Excess Nursing Hours S-(1)	Excess Medical Supply S-(2)	Shortage Inpatient S+(1)	Shortage Outpatient S+(2)
H1	0	0	0	0	0
H2	0.136435	7.52040527	0	84.24758	53.11881
H3	0	0	0	0	0
H4	0	0	0	0	0
H5	0	0	0	0	0
H6	0.119314	0	211.047191	55.50562	47.10935
H7	0.386906	0	140.6420351	0	4.607056
H8	0	0	0	0	0
H9	0	0	0	0	0
H10	0.147536	106.178599	0	202.9244	127.9455

Fig. 5.4 Comparison of oriented and non-oriented models

Fig. 5.5 Solution targets compared

DMU I/O	CCR-I Projection	SBM-C Projection	Difference
H1			
Nursing Hours	567	567	0
Medical Supply	2678	2678	0
Inpatient	409	409	0
Outpatient	211	211	0
H2			
Nursing Hours	203.3602	330.4455	127.085
Medical Supply	738.4946	1200	461.505
Inpatient	134.8118	219.0594	84.2476
Outpatient	85	138.1188	53.1188
H3			
Nursing Hours	445	445	0
Medical Supply	1616	1616	0
Inpatient	295	295	0
Outpatient	186	186	0
H4			
Nursing Hours	2200	2200	0
Medical Supply	1450	1450	0
Inpatient	560	560	0
Outpatient	71	71	0
H5			
Nursing Hours	450	450	0
Medical Supply	890	890	0
Inpatient	195	195	0
Outpatient	94	94	0
H6			
Nursing Hours	302.3607	399	96.6393
Medical Supply	1257.942	1448.953	191.011
Inpatient	209	264.5056	55.5056
Outpatient	119.6637	166.773	47.1093
H7			
Nursing Hours	151.0894	156	4.91055
Medical Supply	695.1691	652.1715	-42.998
Inpatient	108	108	0
Outpatient	57	61.60706	4.60706
H8			
Nursing Hours	2314	2314	0
Medical Supply	3456	3456	0
Inpatient	877	877	0
Outpatient	252	252	0
H9			
Nursing Hours	560	560	0
Medical Supply	4000	4000	0
Inpatient	189	189	0
Outpatient	310	310	0
H10			
Nursing Hours	933.0645	1239.171	306.106
Medical Supply	3388.387	4500	1111.61
Inpatient	618.5484	821.4728	202.924
Outpatient	390	517.9455	127.946

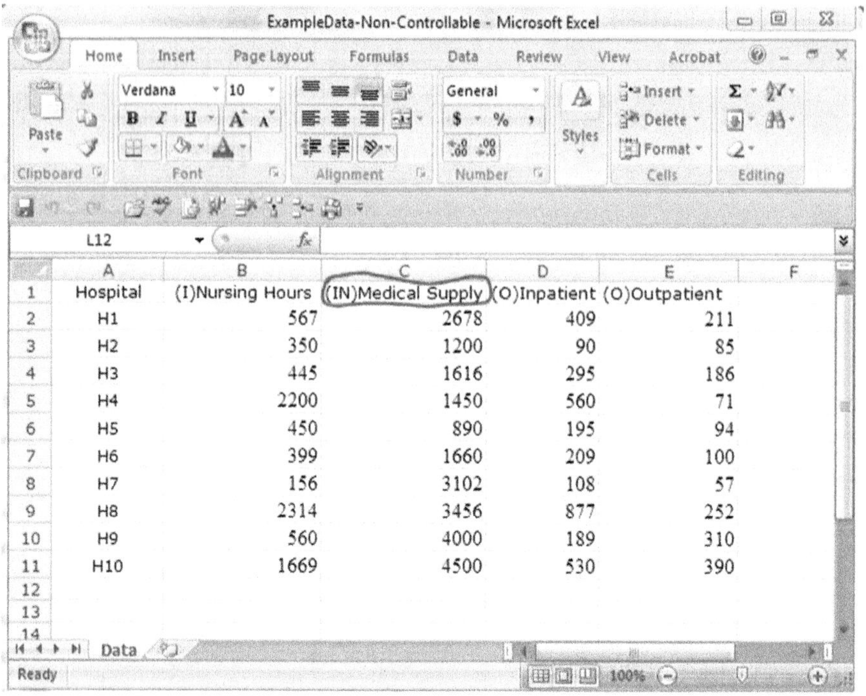

Hospital	(I)Nursing Hours	(IN)Medical Supply	(O)Inpatient	(O)Outpatient
H1	567	2678	409	211
H2	350	1200	90	85
H3	445	1616	295	186
H4	2200	1450	560	71
H5	450	890	195	94
H6	399	1660	209	100
H7	156	3102	108	57
H8	2314	3456	877	252
H9	560	4000	189	310
H10	1669	4500	530	390

Fig. 5.6 Measure specific model data setup

For the purposes of demonstration, let us assume that "Medical Supply" is a non-controllable variable. Thus, we identify "Medical Supply" as a non-controllable variable by inserting "N" next to its input designation, or coding the variable with "(IN)" designation in an Excel sheet indicating non-controllable input. Figure 5.6 displays measure specific model data setup specifications for this example. Put another way, in this selection we assume that the variable "Nursing Hours" is controllable, and "Medical Supply" is a non-controllable input in an input-oriented CCR [CRS] model. Thus, "Nursing Hours" $\in I$ and "Medical Supply" $\notin I$. Appendix H details the formulation of an input-oriented measure specific model where Model 12 specifies the CCR [CRS] version.

Figure 5.7 shows the model setup for measure specific models for our ongoing example. Once the "Non-Controllable Model" option is selected from the DEA Solver-LV menu, we choose NCN-I-C to evaluate the input-oriented CCR version.

The solution to the measure specific CCR [CRS] input-oriented model for this example is provided in Fig. 5.8. Note that the efficiency scores for inefficient hospitals H2, H6, and H10 are different than those for the input-oriented CRS model (the reader can verify this by comparing the efficiency scores reported in Fig. 5.8 to the efficiency scores in Fig. 2.8).

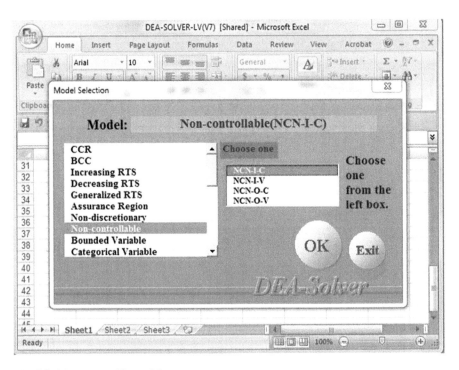

Fig. 5.7 Measure specific model setup

Fig. 5.8 Solution to measure specific model

Similarly, target values (Projections) shown in Fig. 5.9 for the measure specific input-oriented CCR [CRS] model for the inefficient hospitals are different than those reported in Fig. 2.10 for the input-oriented CCR [CRS] model. For convenience, the results from Fig. 2.10 are included in Fig. 5.9 to compare the target values of both models. Since "Nursing Hours" is the only controllable

DMU I/O	Score Data	CCR-I Projection	Score Data	Category Projection	Difference
H1	1		1	1	
Nursing Hours	567	567	567	567	0
Medical Supply	2678	2678	2678	2678	0
Inpatient	409	409	409	409	0
Outpatient	211	211	211	211	0
H2	0.615412		0.615412	2	
Nursing Hours	350	203.3602	350	203.3602	0
Medical Supply	1200	738.4946	1200	738.4946	0
Inpatient	90	134.8118	90	134.8118	0
Outpatient	85	85	85	85	0
H3	1		1	2	
Nursing Hours	445	445	445	445	0
Medical Supply	1616	1616	1616	1616	0
Inpatient	295	295	295	295	0
Outpatient	186	186	186	186	0
H4	1		1	1	
Nursing Hours	2200	2200	2200	2200	0
Medical Supply	1450	1450	1450	1450	0
Inpatient	560	560	560	560	0
Outpatient	71	71	71	71	0
H5	1		1	2	
Nursing Hours	450	450	450	450	0
Medical Supply	890	890	890	890	0
Inpatient	195	195	195	195	0
Outpatient	94	94	94	94	0
H6	0.757796		0.757796	2	
Nursing Hours	399	302.3607	399	302.3607	0
Medical Supply	1660	1257.942	1660	1257.942	0
Inpatient	209	209	209	209	0
Outpatient	100	119.6637	100	119.6637	0
H7	0.968522		0.968522	2	
Nursing Hours	156	151.0894	156	151.0894	0
Medical Supply	3102	695.1691	3102	695.1691	0
Inpatient	108	108	108	108	0
Outpatient	57	57	57	57	0
H8	1		1	1	
Nursing Hours	2314	2314	2314	2314	0
Medical Supply	3456	3456	3456	3456	0
Inpatient	877	877	877	877	0
Outpatient	252	252	252	252	0
H9	1		1	2	
Nursing Hours	560	560	560	560	0
Medical Supply	4000	4000	4000	4000	0
Inpatient	189	189	189	189	0
Outpatient	310	310	310	310	0
H10	0.752975		1	1	
Nursing Hours	1669	933.0645	1669	1669	-735.9354839
Medical Supply	4500	3388.387	4500	4500	-1111.612903
Inpatient	530	618.5484	530	530	88.5483871
Outpatient	390	390	390	390	0

Fig. 5.9   Comparison of efficient targets for basic CCR and non-controllable variable model

(discretionary) input variable, the health care manager has to reduce its use. Examining inefficient hospitals H2, H6, and H10, the reader can verify the amount of Nursing Hours reduction compared to the basic model is more dramatic in the measure specific model. Of course, this is for demonstration purposes only; in reality, reducing the nursing hours so dramatically might be impractical.

Efficient targets for measure specific models are calculated by taking the controllable nature of the variable (see Appendix H, Part 2).

The formulation of an output-oriented version of this model is shown as Model 13 in Appendix I. The BCC [VRS] version of both input-oriented and output-oriented models can be easily solved as shown in Appendices H and I by adding the following constraint to either formulation:

$$\sum_{j=1}^{n} \lambda_j = 1 \quad j = 1, ...n.$$

5.3   Non-discretionary Variable Models

A special case of the non-controllable model is a non-discretionary model. In the non-controllable variable model, the constraining variable should be compared with the similar magnitude (e.g., size of medical supply use). However, if this is not the right assumption, and the researcher would like to account for the variation on the non-controllable variable, then a non-discretionary (ND) variable model can be used. The non-discretionary variable models may generate different efficiency scores. DEA Solver-LV provides this option, and since model setup is the same as non-controllable variable models, the illustration of this model will not be carried.

5.4   Categorical Models

It is sometimes necessary to categorize the health care organizations based on certain characteristics so that evaluation of these can be made within their category. For example, the health care manager may want to compare academic medical centers and general hospitals within their categories. In order to evaluate efficiency for these hospitals in two categories, we would deploy a categorical DEA model. Let us assume the hospitals 1, 4, 8, and 10 in our example are academic medical centers and assign them to a category "1" as shown in Fig. 5.10. The remaining hospitals are general hospitals and are assigned to category "2."

Given the data setup for hospital categories in Fig. 5.10, we can now evaluate these hospitals with the categorical model of DEA Solver-LV. The Categorical model setup for this problem is shown in Fig. 5.11; after selecting the "Categorical Variable" model, the next selection is "CAT-I-C," which indicates the input-oriented CCR [CRS] model.

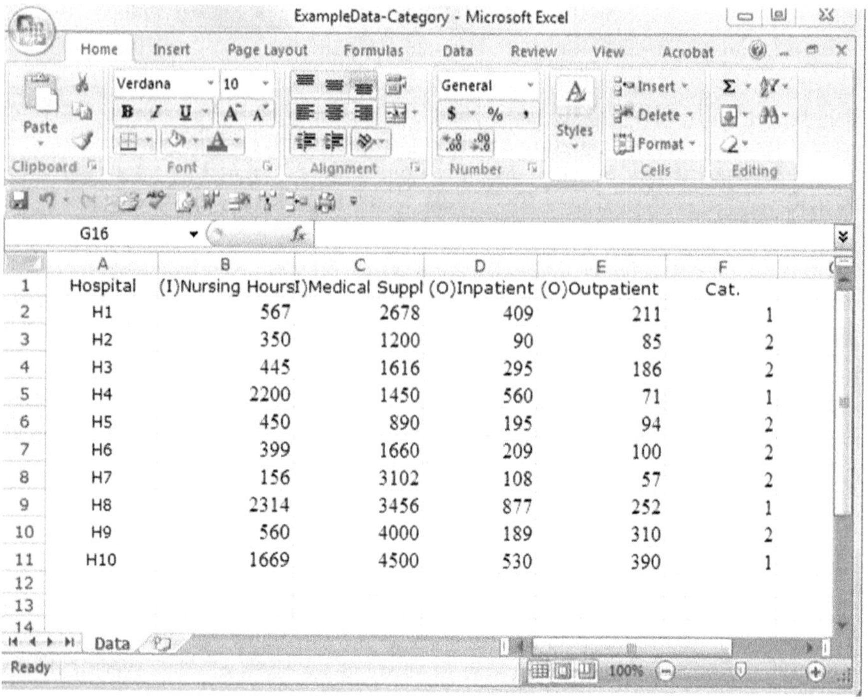

	A	B	C	D	E	F
1	Hospital	(I)Nursing Hours	I)Medical Suppl	(O)Inpatient	(O)Outpatient	Cat.
2	H1	567	2678	409	211	1
3	H2	350	1200	90	85	2
4	H3	445	1616	295	186	2
5	H4	2200	1450	560	71	1
6	H5	450	890	195	94	2
7	H6	399	1660	209	100	2
8	H7	156	3102	108	57	2
9	H8	2314	3456	877	252	1
10	H9	560	4000	189	310	2
11	H10	1669	4500	530	390	1

Fig. 5.10 Categorical model data setup

The solution to the categorical model can be observed in Fig. 5.12. It is interesting to observe that all six general hospitals (category "2") have the same efficiency scores as reported as CCR-I in Chap. 2, Fig. 2.11. Furthermore, the reference hospital for all hospitals is the same except one. Only one change occurred in academic medical center hospitals (category "1"), namely, H10 became efficient. This illustrates the importance of evaluation of hospitals within their peer groups. This way the health care manager can make more meaningful performance comparisons.

DEA Solver-LV generates a detailed report under the "Summary" sheet as shown in Fig. 5.13. The summary report breaks down the statistics by categories as well as overall. These statistics show category, number of DMUs in the category, minimum, maximum, average, and standard deviation of efficiency scores.

When DMUs are evaluated within categories, the frontier and projection calculations may change as well. To illustrate this, original targets through CCR-I and targets through categorical evaluations are placed in Fig. 5.14 side by side to compare these models. A "Difference" column is also created by subtracting Categorical model solution targets (projections) from CCR-I model targets.

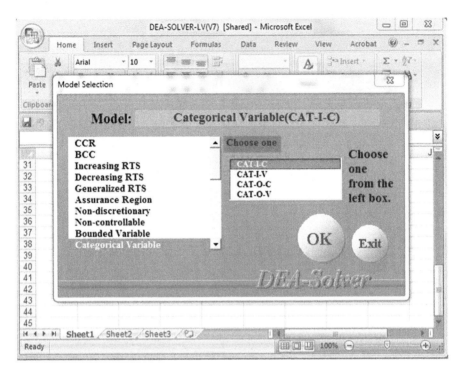

Fig. 5.11 Categorical model setup

	A	B	C	D	E	F	G	H	I
1									
2	Model Name = DEA-Solver LV (V7)/ Categorical Variable(CAT-I-C)								
3	Workbook Name = C:\Users\Yasar Ozcan\Documents\OZCAN\A-DEA-BOOK\ADEA BOOK-2nd EDITION\DEA R								
4	No.	DMU	Score	Rank	Category	Reference set (lambda)			
5	1	H1	1		1	1	H1	1		
6	2	H2	0.6154122	10	2	H3	0.4569892		
7	3	H3	1	1	2	H3	1		
8	4	H4	1	1	1	H4	1		
9	5	H5	1	1	2	H5	1		
10	6	H6	0.7577962	9	2	H1	0.2583855	H3	0.3502384
11	7	H7	0.9685221	8	2	H1	0.2366765	H3	0.0379637
12	8	H8	1	1	1	II0	1		
13	9	H9	1	1	2	H9	1		
14	10	H10	1	1	1	H10	1		
15									
16									

Fig. 5.12 Categorical model solution

Fig. 5.13 Summary for
categorical model

Statistics by Category
Category   1
No. of DMU: 4
Average   1
SD   0
Maximum   1
Minimum   1

Category   2
No. of DMU: 6
Average   0.8902884
SD   0.1501896
Maximum   1
Minimum   0.6154122

No. of DMUs in Data =   10
No. of DMUs with inappropriate Data =   0
No. of evaluated DMUs =   10

Average of scores =   0.934173
No. of efficient DMUs =   7
No. of inefficient DMUs =   3

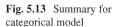
▸ ▸I   Graph1   Rank   Score   Summary   Data   🖑

For academic medical center hospitals, it can be observed that H10 has achieved efficiency, thus, the targets are not the same as the raw data. The "Difference" column shows the impact of change due to the categorical model evaluation.

5.5 Summary

This chapter introduced four additional extensions to the basic envelopment model and illustrated their use for health care managers and researchers. Non-oriented (slack-based) models allow managers and researchers to work on both inputs and outputs to achieve efficiency. On the other hand, measure specific models allow them to work only on those inputs or outputs under their control (discretion). This way, those variables that do not provide flexibility to managers can be included in the DEA model for control purposes. Two versions of the non-controllable variable models were discussed, namely, non-controllable and non-discretionary variable models. Lastly, the categorical hospital model is another valuable tool to evaluate the different categories of hospitals or health care providers in a more homogenous platform.

DMU I/O	Score Data	CCR-I Projection	Score Data	Category Projection	Difference
H1	1		1	1	
Nursing Hours	567	567	567	567	0
Medical Supply	2678	2678	2678	2678	0
Inpatient	409	409	409	409	0
Outpatient	211	211	211	211	0
H2	0.615412		0.615412	2	
Nursing Hours	350	203.3602	350	203.3602	0
Medical Supply	1200	738.4946	1200	738.4946	0
Inpatient	90	134.8118	90	134.8118	0
Outpatient	85	85	85	85	0
H3	1		1	2	
Nursing Hours	445	445	445	445	0
Medical Supply	1616	1616	1616	1616	0
Inpatient	295	295	295	295	0
Outpatient	186	186	186	186	0
H4	1		1	1	
Nursing Hours	2200	2200	2200	2200	0
Medical Supply	1450	1450	1450	1450	0
Inpatient	560	560	560	560	0
Outpatient	71	71	71	71	0
H5	1		1	2	
Nursing Hours	450	450	450	450	0
Medical Supply	890	890	890	890	0
Inpatient	195	195	195	195	0
Outpatient	94	94	94	94	0
H6	0.757796		0.757796	2	
Nursing Hours	399	302.3607	399	302.3607	0
Medical Supply	1660	1257.942	1660	1257.942	0
Inpatient	209	209	209	209	0
Outpatient	100	119.6637	100	119.6637	0
H7	0.968522		0.968522	2	
Nursing Hours	156	151.0894	156	151.0894	0
Medical Supply	3102	695.1691	3102	695.1691	0
Inpatient	108	108	108	108	0
Outpatient	57	57	57	57	0
H8	1		1	1	
Nursing Hours	2314	2314	2314	2314	0
Medical Supply	3456	3456	3456	3456	0
Inpatient	877	877	877	877	0
Outpatient	252	252	252	252	0
H9	1		1	2	
Nursing Hours	560	560	560	560	0
Medical Supply	4000	4000	4000	4000	0
Inpatient	189	189	189	189	0
Outpatient	310	310	310	310	0
H10	0.752975		1	1	
Nursing Hours	1669	933.0645	1669	1669	-735.9354839
Medical Supply	4500	3388.387	4500	4500	-1111.612903
Inpatient	530	618.5484	530	530	88.5483871
Outpatient	390	390	390	390	0

Fig. 5.14 Comparison of targets between basic and categorical CCR models

Appendix G

G.1 Non-oriented SBM CCR [CRS]: Additive Model Formulation

Model 11

$$Maximize \ \sum_{i=1}^{m} s_i^- + \sum_{r=1}^{s} s_r^+$$

subject to

$$\sum_{j=1}^{n} \lambda_j x_{ij} + s_i^- = x_{io} \quad i = 1, ...m$$

$$\sum_{j=1}^{n} \lambda_j y_{rj} - s_r^+ = y_{ro} \quad r = 1, ...s$$

$$\lambda_j, s_i^-, s_r^+ \geq 0 \quad j = 1, ...n$$

For the BCC [VRS] version of Model 11, add the following constraint:

$$\sum_{j=1}^{n} \lambda_j = 1 \quad j = 1, ...n$$

Appendix H

H.1 Input-Oriented Measure Specific Model Formulation

Model 12: Input-Oriented CCR [CRS]: Measure Specific Model

$$Minimize \ \theta - \varepsilon \left(\sum_{i=1}^{m} s_i^- + \sum_{r=1}^{s} s_r^+ \right)$$

$$\sum_{j=1}^{n} \lambda_j x_{ij} + s_i^- = \theta x_{io} \quad i \in I, \text{ where } I \text{ represents controllable inputs}$$

(continued)

Model 12: (continued)

$$\sum_{j=1}^{n} \lambda_j x_{ij} + s_i^- = x_{io} \quad i \notin I, \text{ for those non-controllable inputs}$$

$$\sum_{j=1}^{n} \lambda_j y_{rj} - s_r^+ = y_{ro} \quad r = 1, ...s$$

$$\lambda_j \geq 0 \quad j = 1, ...n$$

For the BCC [VRS] version of Model 12, add the following constraint:

$$\sum_{j=1}^{n} \lambda_j = 1 \quad j = 1, ...n.$$

H.2 Efficient Target Calculations for Input-Oriented Measure Specific Model

Inputs:

$$\widehat{x}_{io} = \theta^* x_{io} - s_i^{-*} \quad i \in I, \text{ for controllable inputs}$$
$$\widehat{x}_{io} = x_{io} - s_i^{-*} \quad i \notin I, \text{ for non-controllable inputs}$$

Outputs:
$$\widehat{y}_{ro} = y_{ro} + s_i^{+*} \quad r = 1, ...s$$

Appendix I

I.1 Output-Oriented Measure Specific Model

Model 13: Output-Oriented CCR [CRS]: Measure Specific Model

$$Minimize \quad \theta - \varepsilon \left(\sum_{i=1}^{m} s_i^- + \sum_{r=1}^{s} s_r^+ \right)$$

$$\sum_{j=1}^{n} \lambda_j x_{ij} + s_i^- = x_{io} \quad i = 1, ...m,$$

(continued)

Model 13: (continued)

$$\sum_{j=1}^{n} \lambda_j y_{rj} - s_r^+ = \phi y_{ro} \quad r \in O, \text{ where } O \text{ represents controllable outputs}$$

$$\sum_{j=1}^{n} \lambda_j y_{rj} - s_r^+ = y_{ro} \quad r \notin O, \text{ where } O \text{ represents non-controllable outputs}$$

$$\lambda_j \geq 0 \quad j = 1, ...n$$

For the BCC [VRS] version of Model 13, add the following constraint:

$$\sum_{j=1}^{n} \lambda_j = 1 \quad j = 1, ...n.$$

I.2 Efficient Target Calculation for Output-Oriented Measure Specific Model

Inputs:
$$\widehat{x}_{io} = x_{io} - s_i^{-*} \quad i = 1, ...m$$

Outputs:
$$\widehat{y}_{ro} = \phi^* y_{ro} + s_i^{+*} \quad r \in O, \text{ for controllable outputs}$$
$$\widehat{y}_{ro} = y_{ro} + s_i^{+*} \quad r \notin O, \text{ for non-controllable outputs}$$

Chapter 6
Longitudinal (Panel) Evaluations Using DEA

6.1 Introduction

Monitoring performance over time is essential in health care organizations. There are often major policy changes, new regulations, new medical technologies, adaptation of new organizational structures, and new ways of doing business that affect the performance of organizations over time. This dynamic environment of the health care industry, as well as providers who are adopting these changes, may show varying performance gains (or losses) over time depending upon how they respond to various external or sometimes system-wide internal influences. In DEA literature, there are popular techniques that enable health care managers and researchers to conduct evaluations over time through longitudinal (panel) analysis. One of these methods is the Malmquist productivity index, a method that provides an opportunity to compare the health care facility's performance from one period to another. The second method is called "Windows" analysis, which provides an opportunity to analyze and compare multiple periods of performance data.

6.2 Malmquist Index

Monitoring performance over time is essential in health care organizations. The Malmquist index is a method that provides an opportunity to compare the health care facility's performance from one period to another. Such a tool was suggested first by Malmquist in 1953, then developed as a productivity index by Caves et al. (1982), and then further developed by Fare et al. (1994) as the Malmquist-DEA performance measure.

Assessment of the performance change of a hospital between two time periods can be visualized as shown in Fig. 6.1. In this conceptualization, a hospital, "H_i", in time period "t", with "x" level input (point A) and "y" level output (point C), reduces the level of input (point B) and increases output (point D) at time $t + 1$. H_i^{t+1}

Y.A. Ozcan, *Health Care Benchmarking and Performance Evaluation*,
International Series in Operations Research & Management Science 210,
DOI 10.1007/978-1-4899-7472-3_6, © Springer Science+Business Media New York 2014

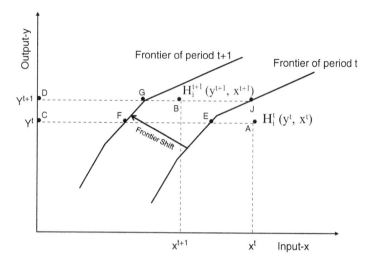

Fig. 6.1 Illustration of Frontier Shift (Catch-up). Source: Adapted from Cooper et al. 2007

(y^{t+1}, x^{t+1}) is the symbol of this hospital in time t, and $H_i^t (y^t, x^t)$ is the symbol in time t + 1. This particular hospital seems to be inefficient at time "t" as it is not on the frontier at that time period. The frontier, as defined by other efficient hospitals, shifts higher in time period t + 1; however, H_i falls behind the frontier again, despite the fact that it has reduced its input and increased the output. Although considering the frontier at time "t." H_i is in a better position with improved efficiency; however, the other hospitals, especially those who were efficient, also improved their relative position, making H_i once more inefficient. This begs the question whether H_i will ever catch up with the frontier and, if so, how? Another question is about the reasons causing this frontier to shift. The Malmquist index can assess these productivity changes by incorporating how much a hospital can improve (or worsen) its efficiency in two time periods, as well as the impact of changes for the frontier shift. The former, change in efficiency for a given DMU (hospital), is termed as catch-up or recovery in DEA literature. The latter, the frontier shift, occurs due to technological changes or innovation. Hence, the Malmquist index is calculated as a product of efficiency change and technical change.

Now, let's examine Fig. 6.1 more closely and develop the Malmquist index with its mentioned two components. If we only focus on input reduction (input orientation) to improve hospital H_i's position relative to frontiers, we can write the catch-up portion of the Malmquist index from period t to t + 1 as:

$$\text{Catch-up} = \frac{DG/DB}{CE/CA} \quad \text{or} \quad \frac{Period \ t+1}{Period \ t} \tag{6.1}$$

Here the numerator of the formula (6.1) calculates efficiency at time $t+1$ with respect to the frontier of period $t+1$. The denominator calculates efficiency for time t with respect to the frontier of period t. From Fig. 6.1 we can express this as:

$$Catch\text{-}up = \frac{\theta_0^{t+1}\left(x_o^{t+1}, y_o^{t+1}\right)}{\theta_0^t\left(x_o^t, y_o^t\right)} \tag{6.2}$$

If Catch-up > 1, efficiency is increased from period t to period $t+1$.
If *Catch-up* $= 1$, there is no change in efficiency from period t to period $t+1$.
If *Catch-up* < 1, efficiency is decreased from period t to period $t+1$.

The frontier-shift effect (innovation or technical change) portion of the Malmquist index can be constructed by measuring the distances between the respective frontiers. In our example, point E from the frontier of period t shifted to point F on the frontier of period $t+1$. Hence, the frontier-shift for $H_i^t(y^t, x^t)$ can be measured as CE/CF. More specifically:

$$\text{Frontier-shift Effect for Period t} = \left[\frac{Period\ t\ on\ Period\ t+1}{Period\ t}\right] \quad \text{or} \quad \frac{CE/CA}{CF/CA} \tag{6.3}$$

We need to measure the shift effect for period $t+1$, and this can be expressed as:

$$\text{Frontier-shift Effect for Period t}+1 = \left[\frac{Period\ t+1\ on\ Period\ t}{Period\ t+1}\right] \quad \text{or} \quad \frac{DJ/DB}{DG/DB} \tag{6.4}$$

Full frontier effect is defined as the geometric mean of both period t and period $t+1$ effects as:

$$\text{Frontier-shift} = \sqrt{\frac{Period\ t\ on\ Period\ t+1}{Period\ t} * \frac{Period\ t+1\ on\ Period\ t}{Period\ t+1}} \tag{6.5}$$

or

$$\text{Frontier-shift} = \sqrt{\frac{CE/CA}{CF/CA} * \frac{DJ/DB}{DG/DB}} \tag{6.6}$$

If Frontier-shift > 1, efficiency is increased from period t to period $t+1$.
If Frontier-shift $= 1$, there is no change in efficiency from period t to period $t+1$.
If Frontier-shift < 1, efficiency is decreased from period t to period $t+1$.

So, in summary, the Malmquist DEA calculates DEA efficiency for the following input- (or output-) oriented CCR [CRS] models:

[a] Calculating the frontier in time period $t+1$ and comparing efficiency scores, $\theta_0^{t+1} (x_0^{t+1}, y_0^{t+1})$, of health care organizations at period $t+1$,
[b] Calculating the frontier in period t and comparing efficiency scores, $\theta_0^t (x_0^t, y_0^t)$, of health care organizations at period-t,
[c] Comparing efficiency scores of period $t+1$, $\theta_0^{t+1} (x_0^t, y_0^t)$, to the frontier at period t, and,
[d] Comparing efficiency scores of time period t, $\theta_0^t (x_0^{t+1}, y_0^{t+1})$, to the frontier at time period $t+1$.

An important feature of the DEA Malmquist index is that it can decompose the overall efficiency measure into two mutually exclusive components, one measuring change in technical efficiency (catch-up effect) and the other measuring change in technology (innovation). Since the Malmquist efficiency index is the product of these two components, the decomposition can be shown as:

$$M_o = \frac{[a]Period\ t+1}{[b]Period\ t} * \sqrt{\frac{[a]Period\ t}{[d]Period\ t+1\ on\ Period\ t} * \frac{[c]Period\ t\ on\ Period\ t+1}{[b]Period\ t+1}}$$

EFFICIENCY CHANGE   (TECHNICAL CHANGE)

$$(6.7)$$

or

$$M_o = \frac{\theta_0^{t+1}\left(x_0^{t+1}, y_0^{t+1}\right)}{\theta_0^t\left(x_0^t, y_0^t\right)} * \sqrt{\frac{\theta_0^t\left(x_0^t, y_0^t\right)}{\theta_0^{t+1}\left(x_0^t, y_0^t\right)} * \frac{\theta_0^t\left(x_0^{t+1}, y_0^{t+1}\right)}{\theta_0^{t+1}\left(x_0^{t+1}, y_0^{t+1}\right)}} \quad (6.8)$$

(EFFICIENCY CHANGE)   (TECHNICAL CHANGE)

We can also write these two product terms together for more compact formulation of Malmquist index as:

$$M_o = \sqrt{\frac{\theta_0^t\left(x_0^{t+1}, y_0^{t+1}\right)}{\theta_0^t\left(x_0^t, y_0^t\right)} * \frac{\theta_0^{t+1}\left(x_0^{t+1}, y_0^{t+1}\right)}{\theta_0^{t+1}\left(x_0^t, y_0^t\right)}} \quad (6.9)$$

The efficiency component of the index (the first half) measures changes in technical efficiency from period t to period $t+1$. That is, it measures how the units being examined have managed to catch up to the frontier. On the other hand, the technical component of the index (the second half) measures changes in the production frontier (i.e., a shift in best-practice technology) from period t to period $t+1$. In an input-oriented evaluation, if the values of the Malmquist index and its components are greater than 1, equal to 1, or less than 1, they indicate progress, no change, or regress, respectively (Caves et al. 1982; Fare et al. 1994).

The CCR [CRS] output orientation can be handled similarly. However, for BCC [VRS] the following constraint should be added to the model:

$$\sum_{j=1}^{n} \lambda_j = 1 \quad j = 1, \ldots n \qquad (6.10)$$

6.3 Malmquist-DEA Efficiency Example

To illustrate the use of DEA-based Malmquist index, we will use the ongoing example, in which we will consider the existing data belonging to Period t. Additional data from the same hospitals were gathered from another time period (year) and labeled as Period t + 1. The top part of Fig. 6.2 illustrates Period t and the bottom part of Fig. 6.2 shows the data belonging Period t + 1. As the reader can observe, the data setup is similar to the cross-sectional (single time period) version; however, for each period under consideration a new Excel sheet must be present. Health care managers and researchers can include more than two periods; however, the evaluation of Malmquist-DEA will be carried by two periods at a time.

To evaluate performance over time using Malmquist-DEA, select the Malmquist-Radial option as the method from the DEA Solver-LV menu, then select "Malmquist-Radial-I-C" for CCR [CRS] version, as shown in Fig. 6.3.

Once the model runs, the health care manager or researcher can view a file containing outputs in a single spreadsheet titled "Malmquist." Naturally, "Summary" and the raw "Data" are the essential parts of this file. The Malmquist index file shown in Fig. 6.4 displays the summary information for the Malmquist-DEA. The three sets of three columns of information display the results for each hospital, as shown in the formulation earlier in Sect. 6.2. The first set of columns (A through C) displays the Catch-up, the second set of columns (E through G) depicts Frontier-shift, and the final

	A	B	C	D	E	F	G	H	I
1		Period t				Period t+1			
2	Hospital	(I)Nursing Hours	(I)Medical Supply	(O)Inpatient	(O)Outpatient	(I)Nursing Hours	(I)Medical Supply	(O)Inpatient	(O)Outpatient
3	H1	567	2678	409	211	600	2500	415	222
4	H2	350	1200	90	85	375	1250	95	95
5	H3	445	1616	295	186	475	1700	300	200
6	H4	2200	1450	560	71	2260	1500	565	80
7	H5	450	890	195	94	475	900	200	99
8	H6	399	1660	209	100	415	1600	225	111
9	H7	156	3102	108	57	175	3000	110	60
10	H8	2314	3456	877	252	2360	3500	900	245
11	H9	560	4000	189	310	590	3900	250	300
12	H10	1669	4500	530	390	1800	4200	650	450

Fig. 6.2 Malmquist data for the example problem

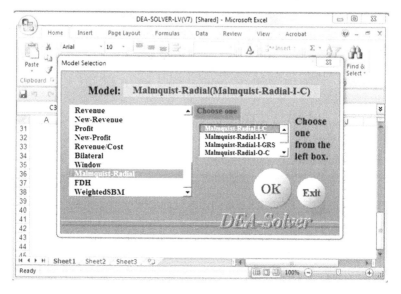

Fig. 6.3 Setup for Malmquist-DEA

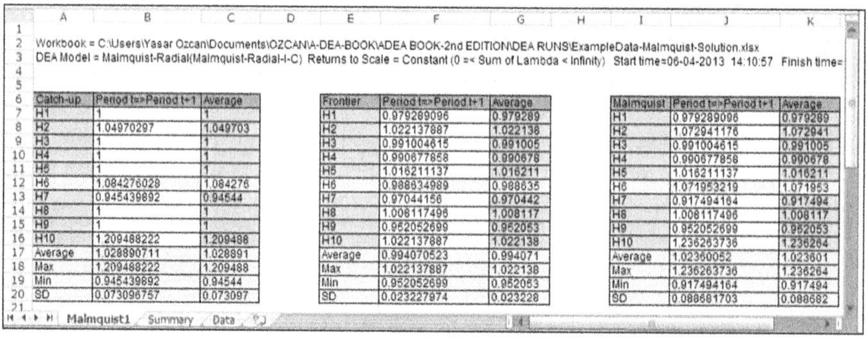

Fig. 6.4 Summary of Malmquist-DEA results for the hospital example

set of columns (I through K) shows the Malmquist index. The average column in each part does not differ from efficiency scores when only two periods are evaluated. When there are more than two periods, these averages will reflect the results of efficiency from multiple periods and will be obvious to the reader.

The reader can verify that "Malmquist Index = Efficiency Change * Frontier Shift" by multiplying the values in columns B and F of the report shown in Fig. 6.4. As discussed earlier, if $M_o > 1$, Malmquist index is increased from period t to period t + 1; hence H2, H5, H6, H8 and H10 exhibit such increase. On the other hand, if $M_o < 1$, Malmquist index is decreased from period 1 to period 2; hospitals 1, 3, 4, 7 and 9 all decreased their performance between these two periods.

Now, if we customize (rewrite) the formula (6.8) for this example, let us say for hospital 6, then we get

$$M_6 = \frac{\theta_6^{t+1}\left(x_6^{t+1}, y_6^{t+1}\right)}{\theta_6^t\left(x_6^t, y_6^t\right)} * \sqrt{\frac{\theta_6^t\left(x_6^t, y_6^t\right)}{\theta_6^{t+1}\left(x_6^t, y_6^t\right)} * \frac{\theta_6^t\left(x_6^{t+1}, y_6^{t+1}\right)}{\theta_6^{t+1}\left(x_6^{t+1}, y_6^{t+1}\right)}}$$

$$\text{(EFFICIENCY CHANGE)} \qquad \text{(TECHNICAL CHANGE)}$$

and, substituting the respective efficiency values, θ_6^*, from Fig. 6.4, we obtain:

$$M_6 = 1.084276028 * 0.988634989$$
$$M_6 = 1.071953219$$

6.4 Malmquist Index with More Than Two Periods

It should be noted that when more than two periods are involved in the evaluation, one can perform the Malmquist index for any pair of periods given that periods are identified properly on Excel worksheets. Ozgen and Ozcan (2004) demonstrated a 7-year evaluation of performance for dialysis centers using the Malmquist index (see Chap. 14, Sect. 14.2 for further information).

Figure 6.5 depicts a 3-year study of 15 hospitals to illustrate a Malmquist index approach with more than two periods. In this case, the multi-period Malmquist index is measured by four inputs and four outputs over the years 2005, 2006, and 2007. Here, we replicate the study by Chou et al. (2012) using only 15 DMUs. Inputs consist of Beds, Service-complexity, Labor, and Supplies, whereas outputs include Surgeries, Emergency visits, Outpatient visits and Case-mix adjusted discharges. Detailed development of these variables can be found in the larger study (Chou et al. 2012).

To demonstrate and explain the multi-period Malmquist, an input-oriented CCR [CRS] model (see Fig. 6.3) was selected. The "Summary" results are presented in Fig. 6.6, where the number of DMUs (hospitals), input and output names, as well as periods in evaluation are displayed. Another observation from the solution is that now instead of "Malmquist1," as also displayed in Fig. 6.4 for two-period Malmquist index, another sheet labeled "Malmquist2" is shown. Each of the

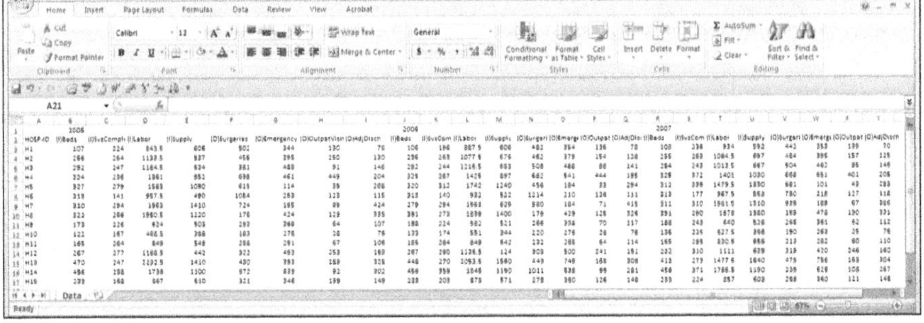

Fig. 6.5 Malmquist data for 3-period evaluation

Workbook Name = C:\Users\Yasar Ozcan\Documents\OZCAN\A-DEA-BOOK\ADEA BOOK-2nd EDITION\DE
Data File = C:\Users\Yasar Ozcan\Documents\OZCAN\A-DEA-BOOK\ADEA BOOK-2nd EDITION\DEA RUNS
DEA model = DEA-Solver LV (V7)/ Malmquist-Radial(Malmquist-Radial-I-C)
Problem =

No. of DMUs = 15
No. of Input items = 4
Input(1) = Beds
Input(2) = SvsComplx
Input(3) = Labor
Input(4) = Supply
No. of Output items = 4
Output(1) = Surgeries
Output(2) = Emergency
Output(3) = OutpatVisit
Output(4) = AdjDisch
No. of Time periods = 3
Time period(1) = 2005
Time period(2) = 2006
Time period(3) = 2007

Malmquist2 Malmquist1 Summary Data

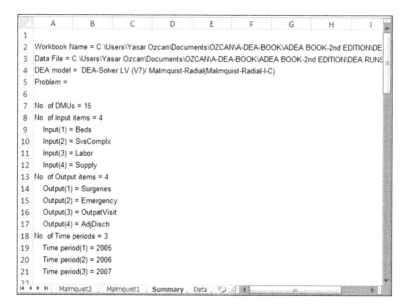

Fig. 6.6 Malmquist 3-period solution summary

Workbook = C:\Users\Yasar Ozcan\Documents\OZCAN\A-DEA-BOOK\ADEA BOOK-2nd EDITION\DEA RUNS\Malmquist-Windows-3-Preiod-Solution.xlsx
DEA Model = Malmquist-Radial(Malmquist-Radial-I-C) Returns to Scale = Constant (0 =< Sum of Lambda < Infinity) Start time=06-16-2013 11:17:35 Finish time=06-16-2013

Catch-up	2005=>200	2006=>200	Average
H1	1	1	1
H2	0.9866672	1.0230996	1.0048834
H3	1	1	1
H4	1	1	1
H5	0.9013975	1.2472575	1.0743275
H6	1	1	1
H7	1	1	1
H8	0.9819692	1.0183619	1.0001655
H9	1	1	1
H10	1	1	1
H11	1.0116822	1.020102	1.0158921
H12	1	1	1
H13	1	1	1
H14	0.9941047	0.9585758	0.9763402
H15	1	1	1
Average	0.9917214	1.0178265	1.0047739
Max	1.0116822	1.2472575	1.0743275
Min	0.9013975	0.9585758	0.9763402
SD	0.0258685	0.0651155	0.0207346

Frontier	2005=>200	2006=>200	Average
H1	1.0440102	0.9125458	0.978278
H2	0.9997488	0.9645799	0.9821644
H3	1.01018	1.0441926	1.0271863
H4	0.9168902	0.879593	0.8982416
H5	1.0143863	0.9344857	0.974436
H6	1.0321405	0.6567316	0.844436
H7	1.3799371	0.6444986	1.0122178
H8	0.9911774	0.9695207	0.980349
H9	1.0196993	0.9577737	0.9887365
H10	0.9380761	0.8964798	0.917278
H11	0.995666	0.9646579	0.980162
H12	1.8794331	0.409979	1.144706
H13	1.0714064	1.1017556	1.086581
H14	0.9198088	0.9426848	0.9312468
H15	0.9453804	0.9492464	0.9473134
Average	1.0771961	0.881915	0.9795555
Max	1.8794331	1.1017556	1.144706
Min	0.9168902	0.409979	0.844436
SD	0.2474709	0.1780282	0.0728529

Malmquist	2005=>200	2006=>200	Average
H1	1.0440102	0.9125458	0.978278
H2	0.9864194	0.9868614	0.9866404
H3	1.01018	1.0441926	1.0271863
H4	0.9168902	0.879593	0.8982416
H5	0.9143653	1.1655442	1.0399547
H6	1.0321405	0.6567316	0.844436
H7	1.3799371	0.6444986	1.0122178
H8	0.9733057	0.9873229	0.9803143
H9	1.0196993	0.9577737	0.9887365
H10	0.9380761	0.8964798	0.917278
H11	1.0072976	0.9840495	0.9956735
H12	1.8794331	0.409979	1.144706
H13	1.0714064	1.1017556	1.086581
H14	0.9143862	0.9036348	0.9090105
H15	0.9453804	0.9492464	0.9473134
Average	1.0688618	0.8986806	0.9837712
Max	1.8794331	1.1655442	1.144706
Min	0.9143653	0.409979	0.844436
SD	0.2513569	0.1936791	0.0758789

Malmquist2 Malmquist1 Summary Data

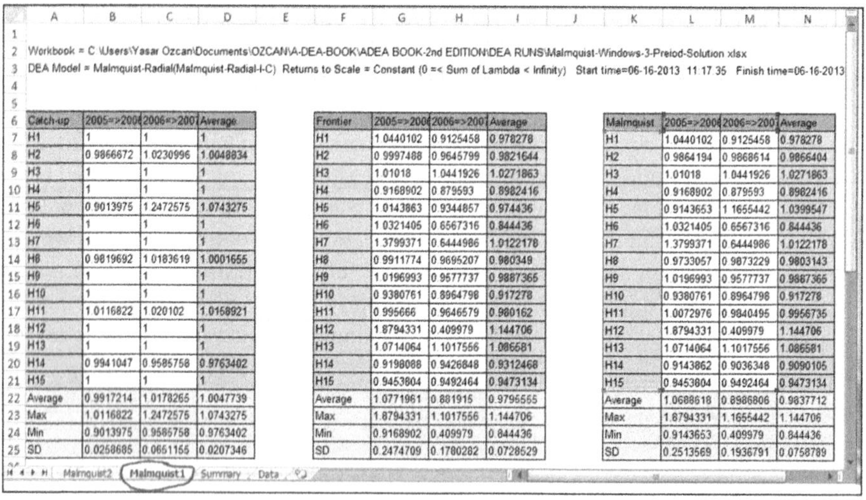

Fig. 6.7 Malmquist results for adjacent periods

Malmquist Excel tabs provides useful information for multi-period evaluations. Figure 6.7 displays the results for "Malmquist1;" the results provided here display the performance over adjacent periods in the evaluation. As in Fig. 6.4, Fig. 6.7 displays the results in three sets of columns, Catch-up, Frontier-shift, and Malmquist index, respectively. However, the only difference in Fig. 6.7 is that in each section efficiency scores are shown for a pair of adjacent years. Since the example had three periods, there are only two adjacent years to show for each component of the Malmquist index.

A quick observation shows that the first hospital (H1) was efficient in both periods in terms of technical efficiency. It had increased in technical change (innovation) during the 2005–2006 period (frontier-shift core: 1.044), however, in the ensuing years (2006–2007) there was regress in technical change (frontier-shift score: 0.912). Thus Malmquist index was in increase (1.044) in the 2005–2006 period, but in decrease (0.912) during the 2006–2007 period.

Another interesting observation is the third hospital (H3), which was efficient in both evaluation periods, and its frontier-shift was also increasing in both the 2005–2006 and 2006–2007 periods (frontier-shift scores: 1.014, 1.044, respectively); hence, Malmquist index was in an increasing direction in both periods. Hospital 11 (H11) has an increase on technical efficiency but decline in innovation (technology change), especially greater in the 2006–2007 period (frontier-shift score: 0.964), and its Malmquist index is increasing in the 2005–2006 period (1.007) but decreasing in the 2006–2007 period (0.984). Hospital 14 (H14) shows decrease in efficiency and in innovation in both adjacent pair evaluations, and its Malmquist index shows decline during these times.

Sometimes, a 1-year time lag may not be enough to see the impact of important policy, technological innovations, and other organizational changes that may impact the health care delivery organizations. Thus, observation of the results through the first and last period may provide a different picture to hospital managers and researchers. This is especially important for longer periods of evaluations. The results provided in Fig. 6.8 depict "Malmquist2," where the Malmquist index is evaluated over the periods of 2005 and 2007. Observing the same hospitals, H1 was technically efficient over 2005–2007; however, its technical change (frontier-shift core: 0.932) was in regress, thus the Malmquist index was decreasing (0.932) during the 2005–2007 period.

H11 showed an increase in technical efficiency but a little decline in frontier-shift (innovation), and the overall Malmquist index was in decline. Here one can observe the sharper impact of the Malmquist index for H11, compared to Fig. 6.7. H14 shows a decrease in efficiency and in innovation in both adjacent pair evaluations, and its Malmquist index shows decline during these times.

6.5   Window Analysis

Window analysis is an alternative way to evaluate multi-period performance. Compared to the Malmquist index, window analysis is a more straightforward approach as the efficiency of DMUs are evaluated only within their respective years, then various periodic averages are calculated to observe overall trends in performance. Early applications of window analysis can be found in Bowling (1986), who evaluated US Air Force maintenance activities over five quarterly

Workbook = C \Users\Yasar Ozcan\Documents\OZCAN\A-DEA-BOOK\ADEA BOOK-2nd EDITION\DEA RUNS\Malmquist-Windows-3-Prei

DEA Model = Malmquist-Radial(Malmquist-Radial-I-C) Returns to Scale = Constant (0 =< Sum of Lambda < Infinity) Start time=06-16-20

Catch-up	2005=>200	Average	Frontier	2005=>200	Average	Malmquist	2005=>200	Average
H1	1	1	H1	0.9316668	0.9316668	H1	0.9316668	0.9316668
H2	1.0094589	1.0094589	H2	0.870239	0.870239	H2	0.8784705	0.8784705
H3	1	1	H3	0.9972775	0.9972775	H3	0.9972775	0.9972775
H4	1	1	H4	0.8029006	0.8029006	H4	0.8029006	0.8029006
H5	1.1242747	1.1242747	H5	0.9667684	0.9667684	H5	1.0869133	1.0869133
H6	1	1	H6	0.7224618	0.7224618	H6	0.7224618	0.7224618
H7	1	1	H7	0.9660503	0.9660503	H7	0.9660503	0.9660503
H8	1	1	H8	0.9385845	0.9385845	H8	0.9385845	0.9385845
H9	1	1	H9	0.9602113	0.9602113	H9	0.9602113	0.9602113
H10	1	1	H10	0.891526	0.891526	H10	0.891526	0.891526
H11	1.032019	1.032019	H11	0.947152	0.947152	H11	0.9774789	0.9774789
H12	1	1	H12	0.7765182	0.7765182	H12	0.7765182	0.7765182
H13	1	1	H13	1.0394989	1.0394989	H13	1.0394989	1.0394989
H14	0.9529246	0.9529246	H14	0.8607844	0.8607844	H14	0.8202627	0.8202627
H15	1	1	H15	0.8857307	0.8857307	H15	0.8857307	0.8857307
Average	1.0079118	1.0079118	Average	0.9038247	0.9038247	Average	0.9117035	0.9117035
Max	1.1242747	1.1242747	Max	1.0394989	1.0394989	Max	1.0869133	1.0869133
Min	0.9529246	0.9529246	Min	0.7224618	0.7224618	Min	0.7224618	0.7224618
SD	0.0356932	0.0356932	SD	0.0865032	0.0865032	SD	0.1005628	0.1005628

Malmquist2 | Malmquist1 | Summary | Data

Fig. 6.8 Malmquist results for first and last periods

periods. Charnes et al. (1989) used two periods (years) to evaluate the economic performance of 28 key Chinese cities. Ozcan and associates used window analysis to evaluate mental health care organizations (Ozcan et al. 2004). Their study investigated the implementation and impact of a Medicaid managed care program over the 5-year period. More information about this study is provided in Chap. 14, Sect. 14.3.

The Window-DEA evaluation data file setup in DEA Solver-LV is the same as the Malmquist data setup shown in Figs. 6.2 and 6.5. We will demonstrate the Window-DEA using the 15 hospital, 3-period data example from Fig. 6.5. Using DEA Solver-LV, we select "Window" as the model and the "Window-I-C" option for the input-oriented CCR [CRS] model as shown in Fig. 6.9.

The "Summary" results are presented in Fig. 6.10, as in Fig. 6.6 for the Malmquist version. Again the number of DMUs (hospitals), input and output names, as well as periods in evaluation are displayed. Another observation from the solution is that now instead of "Malmquist1" or "Malmquist2," we observe "Window1" and "Window2." Each of the Window (1 and 2) Excel tabs provides useful information for multi-period evaluations.

The comparison of technical efficiencies between Malmquist Catch-up and Window-DEA is remarkably similar. Examining hospitals from Figs. 6.7 and 6.8 for years 2005–2006, 2006–2007, and 2005–2007, we observe hospitals 2, 5, 8, 11, and 14 were inefficient. The same hospitals in the 2005, 2006, and 2007

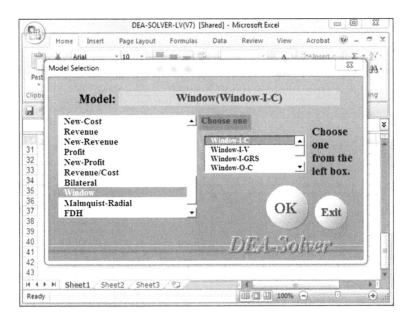

Fig. 6.9 Setup for window-DEA

Fig. 6.10 Window-DEA 3-period solution summary

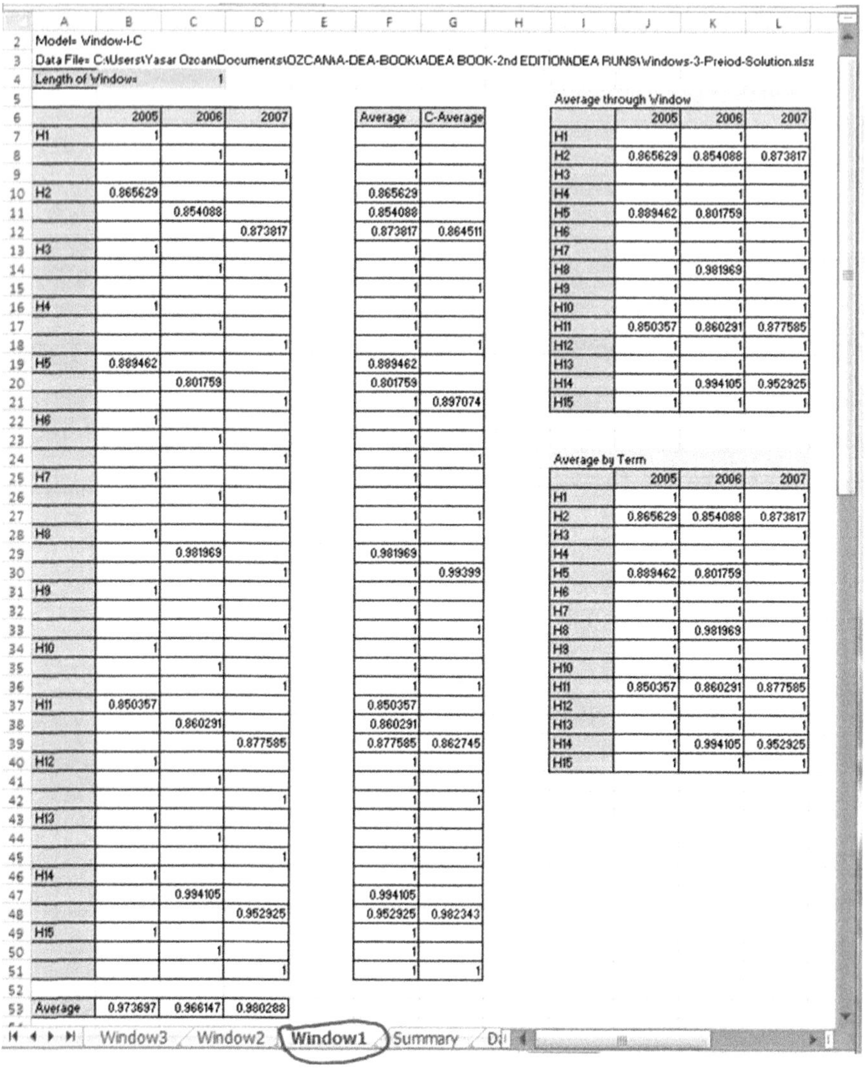

Model= Window-I-C

Data File= C:\Users\Yasar Ozcan\Documents\OZCAN\A-DEA-BOOK\ADEA BOOK-2nd EDITION\DEA RUNS\Windows-3-Preiod-Solution.xlsx

Length of Window= 1

	2005	2006	2007		Average	C-Average
H1	1				1	
		1			1	
			1		1	1
H2	0.865629				0.865629	
		0.854088			0.854088	
			0.873817		0.873817	0.864511
H3	1				1	
		1			1	
			1		1	1
H4	1				1	
		1			1	
			1		1	1
H5	0.889462				0.889462	
		0.801759			0.801759	
			1		1	0.897074
H6	1				1	
		1			1	
			1		1	1
H7	1				1	
		1			1	
			1		1	1
H8	1				1	
		0.981969			0.981969	
			1		1	0.99393
H9	1				1	
		1			1	
			1		1	1
H10	1				1	
		1			1	
			1		1	1
H11	0.850357				0.850357	
		0.860291			0.860291	
			0.877585		0.877585	0.862745
H12	1				1	
		1			1	
			1		1	1
H13	1				1	
		1			1	
			1		1	1
H14	1				1	
		0.994105			0.994105	
			0.952925		0.952925	0.982343
H15	1				1	
		1			1	
			1		1	1
Average	0.973697	0.966147	0.980288			

Average through Window

	2005	2006	2007
H1	1	1	1
H2	0.865629	0.854088	0.873817
H3	1	1	1
H4	1	1	1
H5	0.889462	0.801759	1
H6	1	1	1
H7	1	1	1
H8	1	0.981969	1
H9	1	1	1
H10	1	1	1
H11	0.850357	0.860291	0.877585
H12	1	1	1
H13	1	1	1
H14	1	0.994105	0.952925
H15	1	1	1

Average by Term

	2005	2006	2007
H1	1	1	1
H2	0.865629	0.854088	0.873817
H3	1	1	1
H4	1	1	1
H5	0.889462	0.801759	1
H6	1	1	1
H7	1	1	1
H8	1	0.981969	1
H9	1	1	1
H10	1	1	1
H11	0.850357	0.860291	0.877585
H12	1	1	1
H13	1	1	1
H14	1	0.994105	0.952925
H15	1	1	1

Window3 / Window2 / Window1 / Summary

Fig. 6.11 Solution with window Length-1

windows are also identified as inefficient by Window analysis as shown in Fig. 6.11. In this case the window length is 1 year, where each hospital is compared to its peers within that year. However, the picture is different when hospitals are compared in a 2-year window as shown in Fig. 6.12, or a 3-year window as shown in Fig. 6.13. This time hospitals are compared in 2- or 3-year

Model= Window-I-C
Data File= C:\Users\Yasar Ozcan\Documents\OZCAN\A-DEA-BOOK\ADEA BOOK-2nd EDITION\DEA RUNS\Windows-3-Preiod-Solution.xlsx
Length of Window= 2

	2005	2006	2007		Average	C-Average
H1	1	1			1	
		1	1			1
H2	0.838349	0.8357015			0.8370253	
		0.8395805	0.8331867		0.8363836	0.8367044
H3	0.9838516	0.9937157			0.9887837	
		0.9768188	1		0.9884094	0.9885966
H4	1	1			1	
		1	1			1
H5	0.8548551	0.7870759			0.8209655	
		0.8006802	0.9372046		0.8689424	0.844954
H6	1	1			1	
		1	0.8491487		0.9245743	0.9622872
H7	1	1			1	
		1	0.929043		0.9645215	0.9822608
H8	1	0.9621218			0.9810609	
		0.9567145	0.925267		0.9409907	0.9610258
H9	1	1			1	
		1	1			1
H10	1	0.9522563			0.9761282	
		1	0.8942824		0.9471412	0.9616347
H11	0.8182227	0.8396784			0.8289506	
		0.846071	0.8338731		0.839972	0.8344613
H12	1	1			1	
		1	0.9687833		0.9843916	0.9921958
H13	1	1			1	
		1	1			1
H14	1	0.9315058			0.9657529	
		0.9443298	0.816143		0.8802364	0.9229947
H15	1	0.9666948			0.9833474	
		0.94647	0.9413611		0.9439156	0.9636315
Average	0.9663519	0.9526472	0.9285529			

Average through Window

	2005-2006	2006-2007
H1	1	1
H2	0.8370253	0.8363836
H3	0.9887837	0.9884094
H4	1	1
H5	0.8209655	0.8689424
H6	1	0.9245743
H7	1	0.9645215
H8	0.9810609	0.9409907
H9	1	1
H10	0.9761282	0.9471412
H11	0.8289506	0.839972
H12	1	0.9843916
H13	1	1
H14	0.9657529	0.8802364
H15	0.9833474	0.9439156

Average by Term

	2005	2006	2007
H1	1	1	1
H2	0.838349	0.837641	0.8331867
H3	0.9838516	0.9852673	1
H4	1	1	1
H5	0.8548551	0.7938781	0.9372046
H6	1	1	0.8491487
H7	1	1	0.929043
H8	1	0.9594181	0.925267
H9	1	1	1
H10	1	0.9761282	0.8942824
H11	0.8182227	0.8428747	0.8338731
H12	1	1	0.9687833
H13	1	1	1
H14	1	0.9379178	0.816143
H15	1	0.9565824	0.9413611

Window3 / Window2 / Window1 / Summary / Data

Fig. 6.12 Solution with window Length-2

windows, meaning each hospital is considered in the analysis twice or thrice, once for first year, once for the next year, and so on. In a 3-year period there would be three such evaluations, namely 2005–2006, and 2006–2007, and 2005–2007. The results reported by window length-2 generate more inefficient hospital outcomes. This continues to be the case for window length-3, where average efficiency is less than both the window length-1 and window length-2 versions. The window analysis report provides average efficiency scores by year and by window length in Figs. 6.11, 6.12, and 6.13. C-Average provides the overall average for all terms (periods) in these reports.

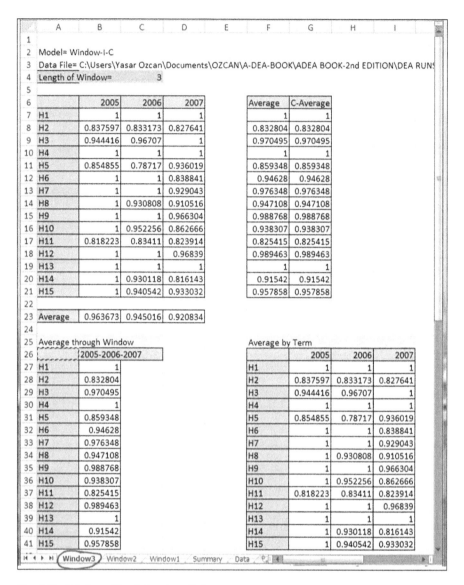

Fig. 6.13 Solution with window Length-3

6.6 Summary

This chapter demonstrated the longitudinal evaluations of performance using the Malmquist-DEA index and Window analysis. Using the Malmquist index, one can identify changes in efficiency from one period to another, but can also determine whether this change is due to pure efficiency improvement and/or due to technological changes in service delivery, such as medical innovations, which caused a shift in the efficiency frontier. As health care organizations adopt many new technologies, frontier change is expected, provided there is a sufficiently long duration lag to capture this effect. On the other hand, using Window analysis, technical efficiency can be observed for multiple periods organized by various window lengths. Average efficiencies and overall efficiency for all periods provide useful information to health care managers and researches for performance trends.

Chapter 7
Effectiveness Dimension of Performance

7.1 Incorporation of Quality into DEA Models

The two components of health care facility performance, efficiency and effectiveness (quality), were introduced in Chap. 1. In this chapter, a closer examination of the effectiveness component is provided. Sherman and Zhu (2006) introduce quality-adjusted DEA applied to bank branches. In this discussion, they incorporate quality into DEA benchmarking in two different models. The first model adds a quality variable as an additional output into the standard DEA model. They demonstrate that, using this approach, the model may exhibit a quality/efficiency tradeoff. Of course in health care, managers would not welcome such a tradeoff sacrificing quality for efficiency. The second approach, which avoids such tradeoffs, is an evaluation of quality and efficiency independently. Using the hospital example, we illustrate these concepts below.

7.2 Quality as an Additional Output

Hospital quality for this example is measured using data from the Hospital Quality Alliance (HQA) for the purpose of public reporting on the Hospital Compare website. The data include information about clinician adherence to clinical guidelines for patients with three conditions including pneumonia, acute myocardial infarction, and congestive heart failure (Hospital Quality Alliance Overview Summary 2005). The data were coded to produce a total hospital quality score by providing a dichotomous measure of whether the hospital performed above (1) or below (0) the national average for each individual measure, and then dividing this score by the number of measures the hospital reported. This resulted in the range of scores from 0 to 100, with 100 indicating perfect adherence to clinical guidelines in these measures.

Y.A. Ozcan, *Health Care Benchmarking and Performance Evaluation*,
International Series in Operations Research & Management Science 210,
DOI 10.1007/978-1-4899-7472-3_7, © Springer Science+Business Media New York 2014

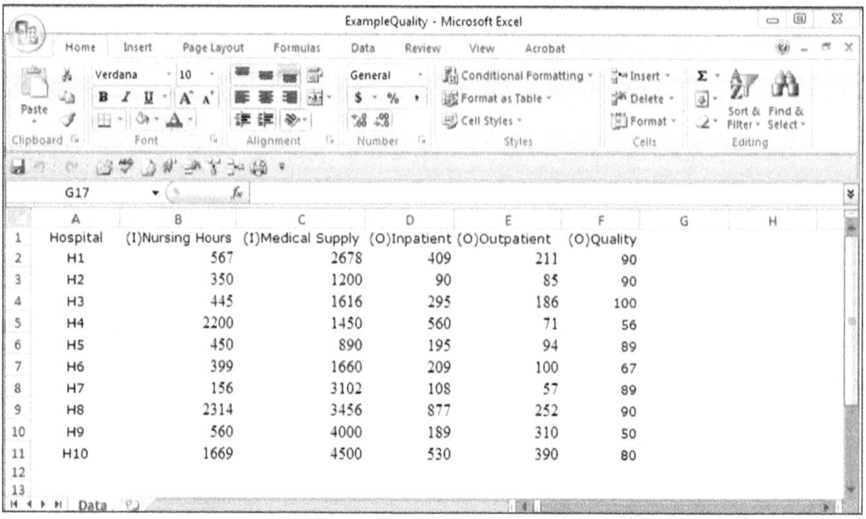

	A	B	C	D	E	F
1	Hospital	(I)Nursing Hours	(I)Medical Supply	(O)Inpatient	(O)Outpatient	(O)Quality
2	H1	567	2678	409	211	90
3	H2	350	1200	90	85	90
4	H3	445	1616	295	186	100
5	H4	2200	1450	560	71	56
6	H5	450	890	195	94	89
7	H6	399	1660	209	100	67
8	H7	156	3102	108	57	89
9	H8	2314	3456	877	252	90
10	H9	560	4000	189	310	50
11	H10	1669	4500	530	390	80

Fig. 7.1 Data setup for quality as an additional output

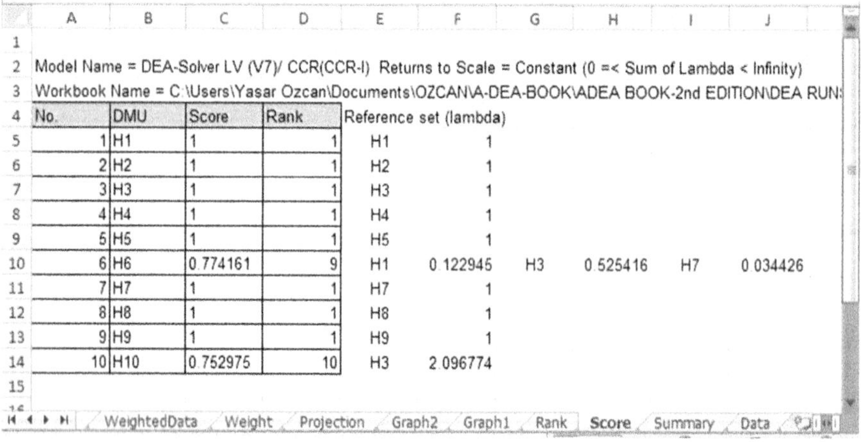

Model Name = DEA-Solver LV (V7)/ CCR(CCR-I) Returns to Scale = Constant (0 =< Sum of Lambda < Infinity)

Workbook Name = C:\Users\Yasar Ozcan\Documents\OZCAN\A-DEA-BOOK\ADEA BOOK-2nd EDITION\DEA RUN

No.	DMU	Score	Rank	Reference set (lambda)					
1	H1	1	1	H1	1				
2	H2	1	1	H2	1				
3	H3	1	1	H3	1				
4	H4	1	1	H4	1				
5	H5	1	1	H5	1				
6	H6	0.774161	9	H1	0.122945	H3	0.525416	H7	0.034426
7	H7	1	1	H7	1				
8	H8	1	1	H8	1				
9	H9	1	1	H9	1				
10	H10	0.752975	10	H3	2.096774				

Fig. 7.2 Results of CCR input-oriented model with a quality output

The setup for our ongoing hospital example with quality as an additional output is shown in Fig. 7.1. As the number of variables (one additional output) increased in this model compared to the basic CCR model, one can expect more hospitals to become efficient while keeping the number of hospitals in this evaluation the same (ten).

Figure 7.2 displays the results of the CCR input-oriented envelopment model with an additional quality variable. As expected, compared to the basic model, two more hospitals became efficient. Compared to the basic model, Hospitals 2 and

Fig. 7.3 Comparison of
DEA models and quality
score

DMU Name	Basic Model Input-Oriented CCR Efficiency	Quality as additional output Input-Oriented CCR Efficiency	Raw Quality Score
H1	1.00000	1.00000	90
H2	0.61541	1.00000	90
H3	1.00000	1.00000	100
H4	1.00000	1.00000	56
H5	1.00000	1.00000	89
H6	0.75780	0.77416	67
H7	0.96852	1.00000	89
H8	1.00000	1.00000	90
H9	1.00000	1.00000	50
H10	0.75297	0.75297	80
Average	0.90947	0.95271	80

7 are classified as best performers. In order to examine the performance of the
hospitals, it is prudent not only to compare the basic DEA model with the modified
DEA model with additional quality output, but also to compare the original raw
quality scores of the hospitals.

Figure 7.3 provides this comparison. As can be observed, the average performance of the hospitals increased from 0.909 to 0.953, as an additional variable was
introduced to the DEA model. We also may have introduced some tradeoffs
between efficiency and quality, as suggested by Sherman and Zhu (2006). However, the more important observation here is whether the additional quality variable
provides the needed performance information for managerial decision-making.

Upon closer examination of the last two columns of Fig. 7.3, we observe that the
two hospitals, H2 and H7, which are now among the best performers, have raw
quality scores of 90 and 89, respectively. This score may be acceptable, assuming
that 90 is a good raw quality score. Yet with other hospitals, such as H4 and H9,
despite their perfect DEA scores, display raw quality scores of 50 and 56, nowhere
near acceptable levels. Thus, this illustration shows one of the shortcomings for
inclusion of quality variables into the benchmark model as an additional output.

7.3   Quality as an Independent Output

In this section we examine the impact of quality as an independent output in a
separate DEA model and make comparisons between the basic DEA model,
quality-adjusted DEA model, and raw quality scores. This way we have two
independent DEA evaluations, one for efficiency and one for quality.

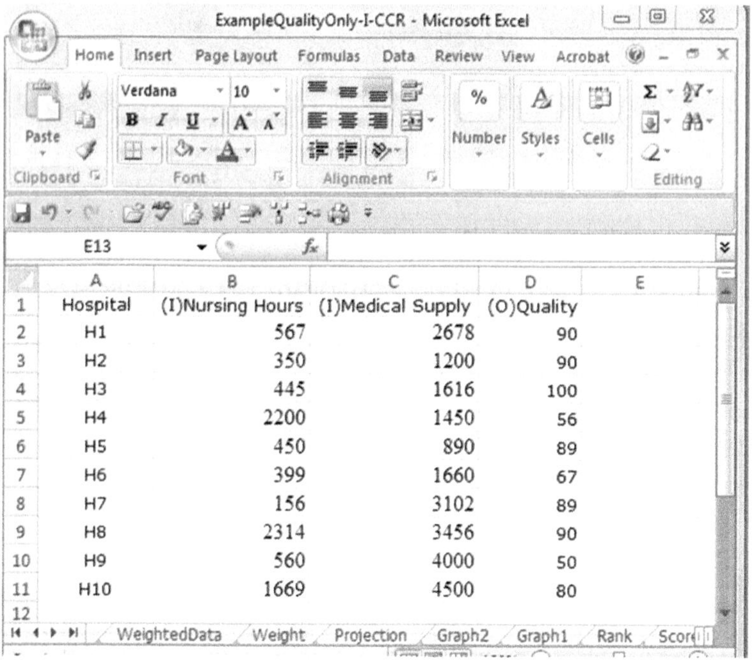

	A	B	C	D	E
1	Hospital	(I)Nursing Hours	(I)Medical Supply	(O)Quality	
2	H1	567	2678	90	
3	H2	350	1200	90	
4	H3	445	1616	100	
5	H4	2200	1450	56	
6	H5	450	890	89	
7	H6	399	1660	67	
8	H7	156	3102	89	
9	H8	2314	3456	90	
10	H9	560	4000	50	
11	H10	1669	4500	80	
12					

Fig. 7.4 Setup for quality as an independent output

Using our example again, Fig. 7.4 shows the setup for quality as an independent output DEA model. As the reader can observe, there is only one output variable, quality.

The results of the CCR input-oriented DEA model, where quality is the only output, are shown in Fig. 7.5. This model, along with the basic DEA model, will provide two independent dimensions of performance to the health care manager.

The independent quality evaluation using DEA shows that only three hospitals, H2, H5, and H7, perform well (at 1.0 level). Of course, this is an independent quality evaluation, and it should be compared to raw quality scores for validation of this model. The reader can observe that H5, which was identified as an efficient hospital in the basic DEA model, is also an excellent performer in the quality dimension. On the other hand, Hospitals 2 and 7, which were identified as inefficient in the basic DEA model, are now identified as excellent performers once quality is considered.

Figure 7.6 provides the comparison of the basic DEA, independent quality models, and the raw quality scores. While we can validate that Hospital 5 is both efficient and effective in both DEA models, it has a near-acceptable raw quality score. However, we cannot validate a quality DEA score for Hospitals 1, 3, and 8. These hospitals had good raw quality scores but the quality DEA model resulted in poor performance on quality.

	A	B	C	D	E	F	G	H	I	J
1										
2	Model Name = DEA-Solver LV (V7)/ CCR(CCR-I) Returns to Scale = Constant (0 =< Sum of Lambda < Infinity)									
3	Workbook Name = C:\Users\Yasar Ozcan\Documents\OZCAN\A-DEA-BOOK\ADEA BOOK-2nd EDITION\DEA RUN:									
4	No.	DMU	Score	Rank	Reference set (lambda)					
5	1	H1	0.563396	6	H2	0.840902	H7	0.161087		
6	2	H2	1	1	H2	1				
7	3	H3	0.861	4	H2	1.081204	H7	0.030281		
8	4	H4	0.383621	7	H5	0.625				
9	5	H5	1	1	H5	1				
10	6	H6	0.61644	5	H2	0.671489	H7	0.070117		
11	7	H7	1	1	H7	1				
12	8	H8	0.260742	9	H5	1.0125				
13	9	H9	0.272461	8	H2	0.33753	H7	0.220751		
14	10	H10	0.21111	10	H2	0.498525	H5	0.395243		
15										

H ◄ ► H | Slack / WeightedData / Weight / Projection / Graph2 / Graph1 / Rank / **Score** / Summary / Data

Fig. 7.5 Results of CCR input-oriented model with an independent quality output

Fig. 7.6 Comparison of DEA models and quality score

DMU Name	Basic Model Input-Oriented CRS Efficiency	Quality as independent Output Input-Oriented CRS Efficiency	Raw Quality Score
H1	1.00000	0.56340	90
H2	0.61541	1.00000	90
H3	1.00000	0.86100	100
H4	1.00000	0.38362	56
H5	1.00000	1.00000	89
H6	0.75780	0.61644	67
H7	0.96852	1.00000	89
H8	1.00000	0.26074	90
H9	1.00000	0.27245	50
H10	0.75297	0.21111	80
Average	0.90947	0.61688	80

This introduces the dilemma of how to incorporate quality into DEA models. In these examples we used only one quality variable. Other dimensions of the quality certainly would change the results of these evaluations. Because this is a fertile area of research in health care management, and many operations and health services researchers are examining this issue as more public data become available in quality of care, better models should be built and validated for health care managers' use.

This begs the question of how to evaluate the two dimensions of performance, efficiency and effectiveness (quality), in the meantime. Actually, this is not that problematic, as long as health care managers have access to quality data.

7.4   Combining Efficiency Benchmarks and Quality Scores

The health care managers can use the power of the DEA benchmarks from the efficiency models and the quality scores as shown in Fig. 7.7

The next step for the health care manager is to decide cut-off points for high and low efficiency and quality dimensions of the performance. For illustrative purposes, let us suppose that the manager decided to use 1.0 for high efficiency provided by the DEA score. Any hospital that did not achieve the score of one will be considered low in efficiency. Similarly, the health care manager can set the high and low values for the quality scores. Let us assume a score of 90 or above (out of 100) represents high quality. With this information we can construct the quadrants of low/high efficiency and quality, shown as combined performance in Fig. 7.8.

Best-performing hospitals are shown in the upper right quadrant of Fig. 7.8. These include H1, H3, and H8, which all had a perfect efficiency score, and 90 or better on their quality scores. The other three efficient hospitals, H4, H5, and H9, appear on the upper left quadrant, indicating that they need to improve their quality. Although H2 has a high quality score, its efficiency is low, thus causing H2 to appear in the lower right quadrant, indicating that it needs improvement on efficiency.

Poor performance on both dimensions, efficiency and quality, is identified in the lower left quadrant. Hospitals 6, 7, and 10 are identified as poor performers; hence they not only need to improve their efficiency, but also their quality at the same time.

Using these combined performance models, health care managers of the hospitals lacking performance on efficiency would have information on how to improve

DMU Name	Basic Model	
	Input-Oriented CRS Efficiency	Raw Quality Score
H1	1.00000	90
H2	0.61541	90
H3	1.00000	100
H4	1.00000	56
H5	1.00000	89
H6	0.75780	67
H7	0.96852	89
H8	1.00000	90
H9	1.00000	50
H10	0.75297	80
Average	0.90947	80

Fig. 7.7 Benchmark and quality scores

Fig. 7.8 Combined
performance

		Effectiveness (Quality)	
		Low <90	**High>=90**
Efficiency	**High = 1.0**	Improvement Need on Quality **H4, H5, H9**	Best Performance H1, H3, H8
	Low < 1.0	Poor Performance H6, H7, H10	**Improvement Need on Efficiency H2**

efficiency by examining targets provided by DEA solutions. Similarly, health care managers who know the quality scores will be able to take the necessary actions to improve that dimension.

7.5   Extended Examples of Quality Variables in DEA

7.5.1   Sensitivity Testing

We have tested the single quality variable in a larger sample with more inputs and outputs (50 DMUs) and obtained similar mixed results. A single quality variable, when included in DEA models, may generate sensitive results (often non-stable). However, if there is a sufficient number of DMUs and the intent is to measure both efficiency and quality in the single model where multiple quality variables are available, then such a performance model will yield much more reliable results. The data set with 50 hospitals, three inputs, and three outputs, is shown in Fig. 7.9. The inputs include beds, labor FTEs, and operational expenses (supplies, etc.) excluding labor. Outputs include adjusted discharges, outpatient visits, and the raw quality measure described earlier in Sect 7.2. Adjusted discharge output and input variables are further described later in Chap. 9, Hospital Applications.

Figure 7.10 depicts the results of three input-oriented CCR models, similar to comparisons in Fig. 7.6. The first model, labeled "Efficiency," includes only two output variables, "Adjusted Discharges" and "Outpatient Visits," hence it is a three-input, two-output model. The quality variable is intentionally left out of this model. The second model, labeled "Efficiency & Quality," includes the quality score as an output, thus, it is a three-input, three-output model. The last model, labeled Quality, uses quality as the only output, hence it is a three-input, one-output model. The raw

	A	B	C	D	E	F	G	H
1	Hospital	(I) Beds	(I) Labor	(I) Expenses	(O)Adj Discharges	(O)Outpatient	(O)Raw Quality	
2	H1	139	912	73615564	14615	237098	75	
3	H2	131	509	29864662	7585	101564	67	
4	H3	60	243	8079345	2152	42073	58	
5	H4	89	288	17457371	2715	35565	58	
6	H5	505	2890	196167849	42660	267854	58	
7	H6	54	315	18019962	2817	51420	58	
8	H7	23	178	17239682	2751	13561	58	
9	H8	116	519	69702193	9696	10745	58	
10	H9	230	847	46188037	21301	37787	50	
11	H10	48	141	6587447	1384	37054	50	
12	H11	80	806	30146273	5438	161489	50	
13	H12	70	220	12736398	2030	61782	50	
14	H13	533	2380	133808566	39077	355542	50	
15	H14	27	86	3775749	523	46475	50	
16	H15	41	145	5679470	1170	19596	50	
17	H16	30	182	6578127	1331	16228	50	
18	H17	116	503	25783306	5208	76016	50	
19	H18	296	1254	51244592	14604	92011	50	
20	H19	52	257	8309569	1540	97328	50	
21	H20	195	710	55682528	16112	83321	50	
22	H21	126	467	58501688	6633	65396	50	
23	H22	80	271	11747118	3435	27253	50	
24	H23	316	1456	108958000	25093	85732	42	
25	H24	150	1107	79680004	19454	108702	42	
26	H25	79	360	14830380	2963	65298	42	
27	H26	56	311	13998318	1787	83510	42	
28	H27	50	412	13800783	2610	71297	42	
29	H28	157	426	23774263	2564	199476	42	
30	H29	183	713	44404300	11424	52342	42	
31	H30	40	227	12943311	723	57121	42	
32	H31	102	157	3121301	301	16825	42	
33	H32	215	874	40527354	14576	104303	42	
34	H33	45	258	13262757	2575	108763	42	
35	H34	319	1393	136074006	26203	54387	42	
36	H35	59	280	19823347	3886	14301	42	
37	H36	55	308	27157604	5823	7073	42	
38	H37	82	408	30404442	6112	51751	42	
39	H38	39	263	9318102	1072	96899	42	
40	H39	64	218	46228851	4276	20891	42	
41	H40	146	957	84830003	10302	61598	33	
42	H41	538	1378	94314000	16721	62751	33	
43	H42	228	177	799142	1343	28551	33	
44	H43	64	211	7357059	1144	12233	33	
45	H44	49	150	6935624	808	25690	33	
46	H45	28	204	9430973	1170	32683	33	
47	H46	32	134	16184554	3466	8738	33	
48	H47	107	467	19178625	5617	88029	33	
49	H48	142	388	46566500	8548	45565	33	
50	H49	327	4949	236634000	34138	767602	33	
51	H50	297	1286	116087186	26869	241835	33	

H   ◀   ▶   H   Data   🗐

Fig. 7.9 Efficiency quality model data for sensitivity tests

Hospital	Efficiency	Efficiency & Quality	Quality	Raw Quality Score
H1	1.000	1.000	1.000	75
H2	0.844	1.000	1.000	67
H3	0.854	1.000	1.000	58
H4	0.540	0.781	0.729	58
H5	1.000	1.000	0.071	58
H6	0.717	0.907	0.731	58
H7	1.000	1.000	1.000	58
H8	0.813	0.909	0.343	58
H9	1.000	1.000	0.115	50
H10	0.836	0.839	0.610	50
H11	1.000	1.000	0.316	50
H12	0.742	0.751	0.391	50
H13	1.000	1.000	0.049	50
H14	1.000	1.000	1.000	50
H15	0.885	0.891	0.665	50
H16	1.000	1.000	0.880	50
H17	0.619	0.647	0.227	50
H18	0.736	0.747	0.090	50
H19	1.000	1.000	0.516	50
H20	0.985	1.000	0.136	50
H21	0.698	0.721	0.210	50
H22	0.808	0.817	0.337	50
H23	0.849	0.849	0.081	42
H24	1.000	1.000	0.162	42
H25	0.678	0.678	0.337	42
H26	0.680	0.680	0.467	42
H27	0.850	0.850	0.520	42
H28	1.000	1.000	0.202	42
H29	0.697	0.697	0.144	42
H30	0.741	0.741	0.641	42
H31	0.901	0.901	0.901	42
H32	0.971	0.971	0.124	42
H33	1.000	1.000	0.575	42
H34	0.898	0.910	0.081	42
H35	0.748	0.751	0.433	42
H36	0.917	0.928	0.449	42
H37	0.774	0.778	0.309	42
H38	1.000	1.000	0.673	42
H39	0.825	0.878	0.418	42
H40	0.579	0.579	0.164	33
H41	0.508	0.508	0.062	33
H42	1.000	1.000	1.000	33
H43	0.656	0.656	0.503	33
H44	0.638	0.638	0.573	33
H45	0.913	0.913	0.913	33
H46	1.000	1.000	0.813	33
H47	0.861	0.861	0.250	33
H48	0.951	0.951	0.222	33
H49	1.000	1.000	0.071	33
H50	1.000	1.000	0.087	33
Average	0.854	0.875	0.452	45.33

Fig. 7.10 Sensitivity test

	Efficiency	Efficiency & Quality	Quality	Raw Quality Score
Efficiency	1			
Efficiency & Quality	0.9338	1		
Quality	0.1377	0.2604	1	
Raw Quality Score	0.0963	0.2912	0.3189	1

Fig. 7.11 Correlation across efficiency and quality scores

quality scores are also presented in the last column to explore the concordance among models and the raw quality score.

To examine the concordance, a correlation analysis was performed among three models and the raw quality score as shown in Fig. 7.11. As expected, there is high correlation between the "Efficiency" and "Efficiency & Quality" models ($r = 0.9338$). That is, adding the quality variable into the efficiency model provides similar results with higher average efficiency, emanating from the addition of an extra variable. However, comparison between "Efficiency" and "Quality," or between "Efficiency & Quality" and "Quality" (first model to third model, and second model to third model) show very low correlations, 0.1377 and 0.2604, respectively. In addition to these, the comparison of DEA scores to raw quality scores for the second and third models show low concordance with correlation coefficients 0.2912 and 0.3189, respectively.

It would be helpful to re-examine the last two columns of Fig. 7.10 where dissimilarities between DEA-generated quality score and raw quality score are highlighted. The hospitals are sorted from highest raw quality score to lowest; among the top 25 hospitals, 11 scores are in the opposite direction between quality and raw quality scores. One would expect higher quality scores from the "Quality" model. Similarly, among the bottom 25 hospitals (discordance highlighted with different shade), ten hospitals exhibit better scores than what the raw quality scores indicate. What is interesting here is that the average scores of both the "Quality" and the "Raw Quality" models are almost similar at 0.45 (the last column average should be divided by 100 to make this comparison).

7.5.2   Efficiency and Quality Inclusive Performance Models

Mark et al. (2009) examined 226 medical, surgical nursing units in 118 randomly selected hospitals. The study employed a non-oriented BCC [VRS] slack-based model (SBM-additive model), which assumed managers can control both inputs and outputs. Some of the inputs and outputs were traditional variables used to measure technical efficiency in previous studies. The inputs included beds, three components of nursing labor, and operating expenses. The first segment of the outputs included case-mix adjusted discharges and outpatient visits. A unique contribution of this study is the three quality variables included as outputs: patient satisfaction, medication errors, and patient falls. Of course higher patient satisfaction and lower medication errors and patient falls are desired. Thus they used the reciprocal of the latter two so when the DEA model tries to augment the outputs, it would actually identify potential reduction targets for medication errors and patient falls, while trying to increase patient satisfaction for efficiency targets.

Other studies, such as Valdmanis et al. (2008) who examined 1,377 urban hospitals using DEA, found quality could be improved through an increase in labor inputs for hospitals classified as low-quality providers. A study by Nayar and Ozcan (2009) demonstrated that efficient hospitals were also performing well in the quality aspect of the delivery; they used various process quality measures for hospitalized pneumonia patients. These studies provide guidance on how quality and patient safety variables can be integrated into DEA for a more comprehensive examination of performance, namely both efficiency and effectiveness (quality of care).

7.6   Summary

This chapter examined the effectiveness (quality) dimension of performance and illustrated how different evaluations can yield unexpected scores. More specifically, DEA models with quality variables may produce results that may not be valid. Thus, it is safer to evaluate efficiency and effectiveness dimensions independently to make managerial decisions in performance assessment and devise necessary improvement strategies.

When a sufficient number of DMUs exist, one can measure both efficiency and quality in the single model, especially if multiple quality variables are available. Such models using non-oriented SBM models may provide more robust performance results.

Chapter 8
Advanced DEA Models

The DEA field has grown tremendously during the past three decades. In addition to the most frequently used models presented in this book, there are other models of DEA. These more specific models provide solutions to specific conditions and also they provide advancement to basic models. We will briefly describe them here, and the interested reader can further inquire from the following texts listed in the references: Cooper et al. (2007) and Zhu (2009). We will demonstrate super-efficiency and congestion DEA methods below, which can be applied to problems in health care organizations. We will also extend the discussion to network and dynamic DEA models that have been recently added to the DEA arsenal. We will conclude the chapter with multistage applications of DEA including bootstrapping.

8.1 Super-Efficiency DEA Models

Super-efficiency models, among other purposes, can identify super-efficient Decision Making Units (DMUs). To evaluate the super-efficiency, the DMU under evaluation is not included in the reference set (benchmarks) of the basic envelopment models. More specifically, other DMUs form the reference set of benchmarks without the focal (current) DMU in the evaluation. Super-efficiency-based DEA models provide differentiation to efficient DMUs under non-super-efficient versions of the model. This result emanates from the fact that the frontier was constructed from the other DMUs for each efficient DMU, and thus the comparison standard is different (Zhu 2009, pp. 205–209). More explanations for these models can be found in Andersen and Petersen (1993), as well as in Zhu (2009) and Cooper et al. (2007).

To illustrate the impact of the super-efficient DEA model versus a standard one, we will use our 10-hospital example data set and run the super-efficient DEA model. Figure 8.1 illustrates the model selection from DEA Solver LV.

Y.A. Ozcan, *Health Care Benchmarking and Performance Evaluation*, 121
International Series in Operations Research & Management Science 210,
DOI 10.1007/978-1-4899-7472-3_8, © Springer Science+Business Media New York 2014

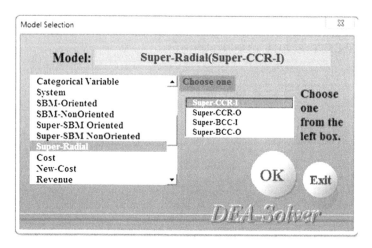

Fig. 8.1 Model selection for super-efficiency CCR-I

	A	B	C	D	E	F	G	H	I	J
1										
2	Model Name = DEA-Solver LV (V7) (Super-Radial(Super-CCR-I)) Returns to Scale = Constant (0 =< Sum of Lambda < Infinity)									
3										
4	No.	DMU	Score	Rank	Reference set	λj	Reference set	λj	Reference set	λj
5	1	H1	1.0848936	4	H3	1.2894812	H7	0.2648431		
6	2	H2	0.6154122	10	H3	0.4569892				
7	3	H3	1.3325784	2	H1	0.2925839	H5	0.7231571	H9	0.1815743
8	4	H4	1.5219282	1	H8	0.6385405				
9	5	H5	1.0136963	6	H3	0.466202	H4	0.1026257		
10	6	H6	0.7577962	8	H1	0.2583855	H3	0.3502384		
11	7	H7	0.9685221	7	H1	0.2366765	H3	0.0379637		
12	8	H8	1.0265704	5	H3	1.4985717	H4	0.7766453		
13	9	H9	1.3244048	3	H3	1.6666667				
14	10	H10	0.7529749	9	H3	2.0967742				
15										
16	Model Name = DEA-Solver LV (V7) (CCR(CCR-I)) Returns to Scale = Constant (0 =< Sum of Lambda < Infinity)									
17										
18	No.	DMU	Score	Rank	Reference set	λj	Reference set	λj		
19	1	H1	1	1	H1	1				
20	2	H2	0.6154122	10	H3	0.4569892				
21	3	H3	1	1	H3	1				
22	4	H4	1	1	H4	1				
23	5	H5	1	1	H5	1				
24	6	H6	0.7577962	8	H1	0.2583855	H3	0.3502384		
25	7	H7	0.9685221	7	H1	0.2366765	H3	0.0379637		
26	8	H8	1	1	H8	1				
27	9	H9	1	1	H9	1				
28	10	H10	0.7529749	9	H3	2.0967742				
29										
30										
31										
32										

⊢ ◂ ▸ ⊣   Projection   Graph2   Graph1   Rank   **Score**   Summary   Data

Fig. 8.2 Comparison of super-efficient and standard CCR-I models

After running the model, one is curious to know how conventional and super-efficiency models differentiate the DMUs, especially those that were efficient under the standard DEA model. Figure 8.2 displays the results of both the super-efficiency model (see rows 1–15) and the standard CCR-I model displayed in Chap. 2, Fig. 2.7 (see rows 16–28).

	A	B	C	D	E	F
4	No.	DMU	Score			
5		I/O	Data	Projection	Difference	%
6	1	H1	1.0848936			
7		Nursing Hours	567	615.13464	48.134644	8.49%
8		Medical Supply	2678	2905.3449	227.34493	8.49%
9		Inpatient	409	409	0	0.00%
10		Outpatient	211	254.93955	43.939554	20.82%
11	2	H2	0.6154122			
12		Nursing Hours	350	203.36022	-146.63978	-41.90%
13		Medical Supply	1200	738.49462	-461.50538	-38.46%
14		Inpatient	90	134.81183	44.811828	49.79%
15		Outpatient	85	85	0	0.00%
16	3	H3	1.3325784			
17		Nursing Hours	445	592.99738	147.99738	33.26%
18		Medical Supply	1616	2153.4467	537.44666	33.26%
19		Inpatient	295	295	0	0.00%
20		Outpatient	186	186	0	0.00%
21	4	H4	1.5219282			
22		Nursing Hours	2200	1477.5827	-722.41733	-32.84%
23		Medical Supply	1450	2206.7959	756.7959	52.19%
24		Inpatient	560	560	0	0.00%
25		Outpatient	71	160.9122	89.912201	126.64%
26	5	H5	1.0136963			
27		Nursing Hours	450	433.2365	-16.763504	-3.73%
28		Medical Supply	890	902.18975	12.189749	1.37%
29		Inpatient	195	195	0	0.00%
30		Outpatient	94	94	0	0.00%

Fig. 8.3 Input and output targets for a super-efficiency model

Notable differences are shown on the scores of DMUs that were efficient under the standard model. These are the hospitals H1, H3, H4, H5, H8, and H9. The reader can verify that these hospitals had the same efficiency score and ranking of 1 under the standard DEA model. However, the super-efficiency model now can differentiate these hospitals such that their scores are shown over 1, and rankings are generated based on their new efficiency scores. Hospital 4 is the most super-efficient hospital among the six efficient hospitals in standard model. It should also be noted that the efficiency scores and rankings of previously inefficient hospitals H2, H6, H7, and H10 remained the same in super-efficiency evaluation.

Super-efficiency DEA models provide more insight to health care managers with respect to benchmarking on their facilities. It is no longer that many hospitals can claim that they are providing best performance as evaluated under the standard DEA model. Thus, identifying the best of the best can lead to further improvement in performance evaluations and setting better targets for the managers. Figure 8.3, an abridged version of the projection results, demonstrates these facts where the realignment (frontier formation) in inputs and outputs for the efficient hospitals are now totally different and reflected at the target expectations.

This section demonstrated the super-efficiency model for the input-oriented CCR model and contrasted it to its standard DEA counterpart. The interested reader can also use the BCC input-oriented version as well as output-oriented versions of super-efficiency models from DEA Solver LV. Additionally, DEA Solver LV provides slack-based oriented- and non-oriented versions of the super-efficiency model. To apply these slack-based models (SBM), a refresher from Chap. 5 is suggested.

8.2 Congestion DEA

If a situation in which a reduction in one or more inputs generates an increase in one or more outputs (the reverse can also occur), congestion might be present. Fare and Grosskopf (1983) developed models to handle conditions that arise from these situations. Zhu (2009) also provides solutions using slack-based congestion models. Grosskopf et al. (2001), Ferrier et al. (2006), Clement et al. (2008), and Simoes and Marques (2011) have shown in various hospital studies how congestion can affect hospital service production.

Figure 8.4 shows conceptualization of congested and uncongested frontiers under convex production possibilities (pp) of two inputs (nursing hours and medical supplies) and one output (inpatients). In this example the congested hospital H4 is

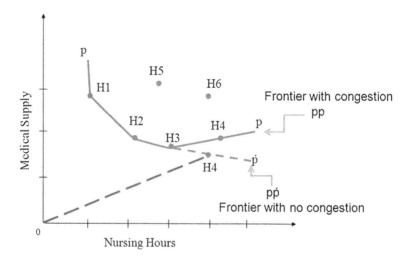

Fig. 8.4 Conceptualization of congested and non-congested frontiers [adapted from Grosskopf et al. (2001)]

	A	B	C	D	E
1	Hospital	(I)Nursing Hours	(I) Medical Supply	(O)Inpatient	(O)Oupatient
2	H1	6133920	192128922	40728	347734
3	H2	6905600	129577546	56530	291348
4	H3	6824480	434195000	42539	256498
5	H4	9563840	245534736	55310	497586
6	H5	9110400	207745824	56401	703391
7	H6	7334080	288705306	53135	497114
8	H7	4199520	108324102	30394	358117
9	H8	10928320	404115000	59396	227459
10	H9	8864960	244809382	59403	252694
11	H10	8810880	218422239	54206	508772
12					

Congestion Score Summary Data

Fig. 8.5 Data for congestion model

using more medical supplies compared to uncongested H4 (per pṕ frontier), and hence may consider reducing excess use of medical supplies.

Congestion may emanate from scale elasticity in service production, namely having too much of a particular input(s) may sometimes congest the process, creating bottlenecks and reducing the production of one or more outputs. The presence of congestion can be classified into two categories: 1) strong, and 2) weak congestion. Strong congestion, suggested by Cooper et al. (2007: p. 357), considers the presence of proportionately reduced values of input(s) and enlarged output(s) under convex production possibilities (shown in Fig. 8.7). The weak congestion on the other hand can occur when a DMU that is efficient under convex production possibilities while employing a service process that uses fewer resources in one or more inputs to produce more in one or more outputs.

To understand the congestion, we deploy DEA Solver, which utilizes the variable returns (BCC) model. To illustrate the congestion measure, we will use data from ten large hospitals, shown in Fig. 8.5 (different than those used in previous examples), where nursing hours and medical supply inputs are in a large scale and correspondingly inpatient and outpatient outputs are also reflected in the data. DEA Solver provides BCC scores, congestion measure, and scale diseconomies to illustrate the impact of the economies of scale in congestion.

Figure 8.6 shows the results of standard BCC scores, where only H1 and H10 were not efficient hospitals. One should keep in mind that congestion can occur both for efficient and inefficient hospitals. A close examination of Fig. 8.7 reveals that inefficient hospitals H1 and H10 are congested. On the other hand, H3, H4, and H8 are also exhibiting congestion despite the fact that they were BCC efficient. Figure 8.7 provides rich information to examine the congestion further and what can be done to correct the congestion. Obviously H2, H5, H6, H7, and H9 are not congested and they are efficient.

By examining improved inputs and outputs columns and comparing those to original data, one can gain perspective on what improvements are needed to eliminate congestion. In Fig. 8.7 those improved inputs and outputs that are

No.	DMU	Score	Rank	1/Score	Reference	λ	Reference	λ	Reference	λ	Reference	λ
1	H1	0.8891149	10	1.124714	H2	0.2457333	H3	0.0316439	H6	0.378478	H7	0.3441448
2	H2	1	1	1	H2	1						
3	H3	1	1	1	H3	1						
4	H4	1	1	1	H4	1						
5	H5	1	1	1	H5	1						
6	H6	1	1	1	H6	1						
7	H7	1	1	1	H7	1						
8	H8	1	1	1	H8	1						
9	H9	1	1	1	H9	1						
10	H10	0.9492064	9	1.0535116	H2	0.0589891	H5	0.5936963	H6	0.055011	H9	0.2923031

Model Name = DEA-Solver Pro8 0/ Congestion(Congestion)

Fig. 8.6 DEA scores for congestion BCC model

No.	DMU	Projected DMU VScore	Efficiency Category	Scale Diseconomies	Improved Nursing Hours	Improved Medical Supply	Improved Inpatient	Improved Outpatient	Slacks Nursing Hours	Slacks Medical Supply	Slacks Inpatient	Slacks Outpatient
1	H1	1.007715041	Congestion	-6.349840976	6133920	191110245	45808	404263	0	-10186.77	0	13167
2	H2	1	BCC-efficient		6905600	129577546	56530	291348	0	0	0	0
3	H3	1.281520401	Congestion	-0.920978822	6924480	161466928	44295	542873	0	-272728072	1756	286175
4	H4	1.041999939	Congestion	-2.152541702	9110400	207745624	56401	703391	-453440	-37786912	1092	2058805
5	H5	1	BCC-efficient		9110400	207745624	56401	703391	0	0	0	0
6	H6	1	BCC-efficient		7234080	298705306	53135	497114	0	0	0	0
7	H7	1	BCC-efficient		4199520	108324102	30394	358117	0	0	0	0
8	H8	1.000116169	Congestion	-0.396099599	8855524	244724181	59396	253730	-2062796	-159390819	0	26271
9	H9	1	BCC-efficient		8864960	244809382	59403	252694	0	0	0	0
10	H10	1.002200733	Congestion	-0.689780915	8810080	207663704	57107	554209	0	-10759535	0	18211

Fig. 8.7 DEA congestion results

different than their original values are highlighted. These values serve as target projections. Furthermore, by examining slacks of the congested hospitals one can gain information on weak or strong congestion. If a hospital exhibits slacks for all inputs and outputs, the status of congestion is defined as strong (Cooper et al. 2007: p. 363). In this example H4 exhibits a strong congestion. On the other hand, H1 and H10 exhibit weak congestion caused by medical supplies on both outputs.

8.3 Network DEA Models

In health care, services are produced by various departments that each contribute to the overall efficiency of the larger unit (e.g., hospital). This is more so for those hospital systems where the individual hospitals and other networks such as physician practices, nursing homes, ambulatory surgery centers, and diagnostic centers may be part of the whole picture.

The traditional DEA models do not take account of the internal structure of health care organizations (DMUs). In recent years, an extension to traditional DEA models, the "network DEA model" has been developed. This new model accounts for sub-unit (e.g., departments) efficiencies as well as overall efficiency in a unified framework. Through the network DEA model, one can observe not only efficiency of the health care facility but also its sub-unit efficiencies as its components. Network DEA models were first introduced by Färe and Grosskopf (2000), and

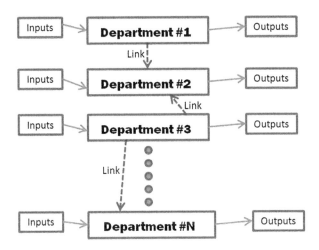

Fig. 8.8 Conceptualization of network DEA models

their models have been extended by Tone and Tsutsui (2009) and others. The network DEA model extended by Lewis and Sexton (2004) presents a multi-stage structure as an extension of the two-stage DEA model. Tone and Tsutsui (2009) developed a network model using a slack-based measure called the network slack-based measure (NSBM) approach. The NSBM is a non-radial method and is suitable for measuring efficiencies when inputs and outputs may change non-proportionally.

Figure 8.8 shows the conceptualization of network DEA where internal efficiencies are accounted for. The departments in this conceptualization are the sub-units of the health care facility; each may have their own inputs and outputs, and they can be linked to other sub-units.

8.4 Network and Dynamic DEA Models

The dynamic DEA model can measure the efficiency score obtained from long-term optimization using carryover variables. The traditional DEA model only focuses on a single period; therefore, the measurement of longitudinal efficiency change has long been a potential subject of development in DEA. As we have observed in Chap. 6, the window analysis by Klopp (1985) was the first approach to account for longitudinal efficiency change, and Färe et al. (1994) developed the Malmquist index to measure this in the DEA framework.

On the other hand, the newer dynamic DEA model developed by Färe and Grosskopf (2000) identifies the inter-connecting activities. Tone and Tsutsui (2009) extended this model within the slack-based measurement. Finally, the dynamic network DEA model takes into account the internally heterogeneous

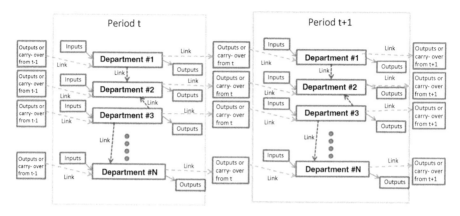

Fig. 8.9 Conceptualization of network and dynamic DEA models

organizations of DMUs, where sub-units are mutually connected by link variables and trade internal products with each other. This dynamic network model can evaluate the overall efficiency over the entire observed terms (time t, or t + 1 etc.), dynamic change in the period efficiency, and dynamic change in the divisional efficiency. Figure 8.9 shows the conceptualization of dynamic network DEA where multiple periods as well as internal efficiencies are accounted for. The departments in this conceptualization are the sub-units of the health care facility; each may have their own inputs and outputs, and they can be linked to other sub-units. In addition, each DMU has carryover variables or outputs that take into account a positive or negative factor in the previous period. This can also accommodate the desirable or undesirable outputs from previous periods in the modeling. Any longitudinal associations and carryovers or outputs from different periods are identified with the links. DEA Solver professional version has an extensive portfolio of models to evaluate network and dynamic network DEA.

8.5   Two-Stage DEA Analysis

In health care, managers and policy makers would like to know the factors that influence the performance. Thus, once the measures of efficiency through DEA are obtained, a second-stage (often multi-stage) analysis is carried out to assess the predicates of efficiency. Hence, the efficiency score obtained by DEA becomes the dependent variable in this second stage (post hoc) analysis.

Models such as ordinary least squares (OLS) regression, log or logistic regression, Tobit regression, etc. are among the popular second-stage analysis and have been widely applied to examine technical and allocative efficiency in a variety of research papers; see Chaps. 14 and 15 for examples of such studies. Again, many of these studies have used a two-stage approach, where efficiency is estimated in the first stage, and then the estimated efficiencies are regressed on covariates (different from those used in the first stage) representing patient or organizational variables and environmental control variables as shown in (8.1) (Simar and Wilson (2005)).

$$DEA\ Score = f\ (patient\ or\ organizational\ variables, environmental\ control\ variables)$$
(8.1)

As we know from earlier chapters, DEA scores can take value in the range $0 > DEA\ Score \leq 1$. Thus, they represent positive values of continuous and discrete values; inefficient health care providers have a score of less than "1," and others that are efficient have a score of "1." This situation may violate the normal and homoscedastic distribution assumptions of OLS regression, and regression estimates would be biased. DEA scores resemble truncated or censored distributions shown in the econometrics and statistical literature (Chilingerian 1995). Since DEA scores do not exclude any observations and are not truncated above the value of "1," it is more of a censoring of the efficiency scores at "1" for efficient providers. In such instances, either logistic or Tobit regression may be a helpful alternative to OLS regression in second-stage analysis. The interested reader is referred to Hosmer et al. (2013) and Chilingerian (1995) for details and justification of using logistic and Tobit regression analysis, respectively. Here, we will show the procedures that can be used to conduct logistic and Tobit regression analysis in examining predicates of efficiency (performance) for health care providers.

8.5.1 Logistic Regression

Logistic regression uses binary or dichotomous outcome (dependent) variables where the outcome is identified as "1" or "0." This outcome variable is then regressed against independent predictor variables and other covariates (control variables). Although there are additional assumptions for this parametric technique aside from linear regression (e.g., ordinary least squares, or OLS), once those are satisfied, logistic regression follows the general rules of parametric estimation. The interested reader is referred to Hosmer, Lameshow and Sturdivant (2013) for the details. Here, we introduce how DEA efficiency scores can be deployed as an outcome variable in a logistic regression model. Since the value of "1" represents efficient providers, one may choose to keep this value the same and set any efficiency score below "1" to "0" to identify inefficient providers for logistic regression. Hence,

$$Logistic\ regression\ dependent\ variable:\ g(x) = \begin{pmatrix} 1, & if\ DEA\ score\ \theta = 1 \\ 0, & if\ DEA\ score\ \theta < 1 \end{pmatrix}$$
(8.2)

Logistic regression dependent variable g(x) then can be expressed by the logit function shown in (8.3), where "x_i" represents the independent predictors for the estimated logit $\widehat{g}(x)$. The equation in (8.3) is solved using likelihood estimator methods described in Hosmer and Lameshow (2000).

$$\widehat{g}(x) = \beta_0 + \beta_1 x_1 + \beta_2 x_2 + \ldots + \beta_n x_n \qquad (8.3)$$

One of the criticisms of the creation of logistic regression dependent variables is using the approach shown in (8.2). If there are providers with θ values near "1," they will be missed since they are identified as inefficient. Thus, the cut-off point may require reevaluation, and different models can be evaluated with varying cut-off points (e.g., 0.95; 0.90 etc.) to test the sensitivity of the logistic regression model with respect to DEA score, "θ," results.

Another way to evaluate the determinants of efficiency is to create a multinomial dependent variable by setting different cut-off points to "θ." For example, while the efficient providers, $\theta = 1$, might be one outcome, those providers in the fourth quartile, $0.75 < \theta < 1$, third quartile, $0.5 < \theta \le 0.75$, and the rest, $0 < \theta \le 0.5$, may be assigned to three logit functions to estimate various levels of efficiency using multinomial logistic regression as shown in (8.4). In each logit function the reference category remains the efficient providers, $\theta = 1$. But this also can be altered by setting a value between 0.90 and 1.0.

$$\widehat{g}_1(x) \begin{pmatrix} 1, & \textit{if DEA score } \theta = 1 \\ 0, & \textit{if DEA score } .75 < \theta < 1 \end{pmatrix} = \beta_{10} + \beta_1 1 x_1 + \beta_{12} x_2 + \ldots + \beta_{1n} x_n$$
$$\widehat{g}_2(x) \begin{pmatrix} 1, & \textit{if DEA score } \theta = 1 \\ 0, & \textit{if DEA score } .50 < \theta \le .75 \end{pmatrix} = \beta_{20} + \beta_2 1 x_1 + \beta_{22} x_2 + \ldots + \beta_{2n} x_n$$
$$\widehat{g}_3(x) \begin{pmatrix} 1, & \textit{if DEA score } \theta = 1 \\ 0, & \textit{if DEA score } 0 < \theta \le .50 \end{pmatrix} = \beta_{30} + \beta_{31} 1 x_1 + \beta_{32} x_2 + \ldots + \beta_{3n} x_n$$

$$(8.4)$$

Although practical, in this approach cut-off points are arbitrary; perhaps distributional values of DEA scores can be closely examined to set cut-off points in different percentile ranges rather than quartiles.

Examples of logistic regression in second-stage analysis in health care have been demonstrated in the literature. Kazley and Ozcan (2009) used ownership, hospital system membership, and teaching status variables to investigate the impact of these variables on performance associated with electronic medical record implementation in the hospitals.

As in any method, the logistic regression approach will have its limitations regarding these cut-off points. Perhaps in employing yet another methodology, one may avoid such cut-off point selection. Tobit regression provides such opportunity.

DEA score θ	Transformed DEA score $\hat{\theta}$
1.00	0.00
0.90	0.11
0.80	0.25
0.75	0.33
0.50	1.00
0.25	3.00
0.10	9.00
0.05	19.00
0.01	99.00

Table 8.1 DEA and transformed DEA scores

8.5.2 Tobit Regression

Tobit regression overcomes the normalization issues in OLS regression and also does not need a cut-off point for varying efficiency values if DEA scores that are censored at "1" can be transformed to be censored at "0" instead. As reported by Chilingerian (1995), a transformation of DEA scores using (8.5) provides the necessary transformation.

$$Transformed\ DEA\ Score = \frac{1}{DEA\ Score} - 1 \qquad (8.5)$$

Let us call transformed DEA Score $\hat{\theta}$; then the expression in (8.5) can be rewritten as:

$$\hat{\theta} = \frac{1}{\theta} - 1 \qquad (8.6)$$

To gain understanding for this transformation, a couple of numerical examples would be helpful. Let us suppose the DEA Score θ was equal to 1; then through this transformation $\hat{\theta}$ will have a value of zero, indicating the fact that the new transformed variable $\hat{\theta}$ is censored at "0." Table 8.1 shows a few of these θ transformed to $\hat{\theta}$ using (8.6).

Now we can observe as DEA Score "θ" efficiency decreases, the transformed DEA Score increases. So, the $\hat{\theta}$ becomes an inefficiency score and has no upper bound. Hence, it can be expressed as in (8.7).

$$Tobit\ regression\ dependent\ variable: \quad y_i = \begin{pmatrix} > 0, & if\ DEA\ score\ \theta_i < 1 \\ 0, & if\ DEA\ score\ \theta_i = 1 \end{pmatrix} \qquad (8.7)$$

Y_i is now what is called a left-censored continuous variable and lends itself to use in a Tobit regression model. After settling the dependent variable, the Tobit model can be expressed as in (8.8) which contains a residual (error) term, u_i. The equation (8.8) can be solved through likelihood estimation methodology as in logistic regression.

$$Y_i = \beta_0 + \beta_1 x_1 + \beta_2 x_2 + \ldots + \beta_n x_n + u_i \tag{8.8}$$

In a Tobit regression model, however, the slope coefficients of Tobit are interpreted as if they were an ordinary least squares regression. They represent one unit change in the independent variable(s) making change in the dependent variable while holding everything else constant. The interested reader is referred to Maddala (1983) and Chilingerian (1995) for details and justification of using Tobit analysis. Here, we have explained how these procedures can be used to conduct Tobit analysis in examining predicates of efficiency (performance) for health care providers.

Recent examples of Tobit regression in second-stage analysis in health care have been demonstrated by various publications. The study by Sikka, Luke and Ozcan (2009) deployed competition, ownership, and other hospital characteristics as independent variables. Corredoira et al. (2011) assessed performance in addiction treatment where number of patients, county income per capita, clinics per square mile, and state funding were used as independent predictors of ineffectiveness. Another application by Zeng et al. (2012) considered 13 independent variables, of which ten showed significant impact on efficiency for national HIV/AIDS programs in various countries around the world. Nayar et al. (2013) applied Tobit regression on a DEA model with quality outputs and used ownership, size, location, teaching status, and affiliation variables as independents to measure the impact. Among the hospital characteristics, teaching, ownership, and size of hospital showed significant impact on performance outcomes.

This background in two-stage analysis brings us to bootstrapping, a method that may be necessary in certain instances. In the next section we will discuss and demonstrate bootstrapping methodology. The reader should keep in mind that if the research they are undertaking comprises the whole population of DMUs, bootstrapping may not be necessary. For example, if one is to evaluate the performance of teaching hospitals only and has access to data for all teaching hospitals in a country, there may be no need for bias estimate correction. However, in the two-stage analysis, if the reader would like to place confidence intervals around the second-stage analysis (i.e., Tobit, logistic regression), such confidence intervals can be built through bootstrapping by deploying the bootstrapping option in STATA.

8.6   Bootstrapping

Simar and Wilson (2005) claimed that the differences in efficiency estimates would not make the regression results sensible. They further claimed that DEA efficiency estimates are serially correlated. To overcome this problem some researchers used a naive bootstrap method based on sampling from an empirical distribution to correct the serial correlation problem (Hirschberg and Lloyd 2002). However, their method of bootstrapping has been challenged as being inconsistent and sometimes infeasible (Simar and Wilson 2005).

DEA efficiency scores may be affected by the sample, and the frontier would be underestimated if the best performers in the population are not included in the sample. To account for this, Simar and Wilson (1998, 2000) originally proposed a bootstrapping method allowing the construction of confidence intervals for DEA efficiency scores. Their method relies on smoothing the empirical distribution, where they employ simulation of a true sampling distribution by using the outputs from DEA. This way they generate a new data set, and DEA scores are re-estimated using this data set. Repeating the process many times (say, 1,000 or 2,000 times) provides an approximation of the true distribution (population) of the DMUs. Although Simar and Wilson (2005) developed this new method of bootstrapping to adjust efficiency estimates for upward bias, their new methods were criticized as well. Tziogkidis (2012) states Simar and Wilson's (2000) assumption of equality between the bootstrap and DEA biases is practically implausible, and it should be avoided by correcting twice for bootstrap bias or using the "enhanced" confidence intervals. They suggest the simple bootstrap is always consistent and has a very good performance.

As DEA is a non-parametric as well as non-stochastic approach where error due to sampling is not accounted for, efficiency scores from DEA have been treated as deterministic. Another problem arises due to serial correlations of efficiency scores due to construction of the model. In order to account for both the bias and serial correlation of efficiency scores, Simar and Wilson (2005) proposed a double bootstrap procedure. The double bootstrap approach corrects for the DEA efficiency scores for bias in the first stage of a bootstrap procedure. In the second stage, bias-corrected efficiency scores are regressed on environmental variables using a second, parametric bootstrap procedure applied to the truncated regression (generally available in STATA statistical package).

More recently Kaoru Tone proposed a bootstrap methodology which is included in DEA Solver Professional Version 11 (Tone 2013) and uses the following procedures to create the bootstraps for the DEA scores:

1. Input upside and downside percentage error of data.
2. Randomize input/output data within the bounds using the triangular distribution.
3. Solve DEA model using the randomized data.
4. Repeat the above to obtain the bootstrap estimates.
5. Obtain 97.5, 75, 50, 25, and 2.5 % confidence estimates of DEA score.

Tone's approach is based on re-sampling and use of triangular distribution. Triangular distribution is also known as beta distribution in statistical literature as well as in PERT—Program Evaluation and Review Technique—project management circles, where use of normal (Gaussian) distribution is not appropriate. Since DEA scores do not follow a normal distribution, use of triangular distribution with

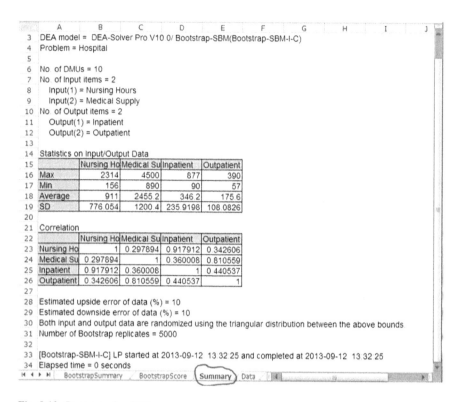

Fig. 8.10   Bootstrapping DEA scores—summary

optimistic, most likely, and pessimistic estimates to resample DEA scores to identify bootstrap and build confidence intervals may be more appropriate.

We will demonstrate bootstraps and confidence intervals with Tone's method and using DEA Solver for our ongoing 10-hospital example.

Figure 8.10 displays the bootstrap summary for the 10-hospital example using the slack-based input-oriented CCR model. The model uses 5,000 bootstrap replicates where inputs and outputs are randomized using triangular distribution. Figure 8.11 displays the summary of the bootstrap procedure where original SBM-I-C DEA score; 97.5, 75, 50, 25, and 2.5 % confidence estimates of DEA score; and their average and final ranking based on bootstrap method are displayed. The final average DEA scores are bias corrected. Figure 8.12 displays the 2.5 and 97.5 % confidence intervals for the SBM-I-C bootstrap scores.

At the beginning of this chapter, the super-efficiency model was introduced. Figures 8.13 and 8.14 depict the bootstrapping on the super-efficiency example of the ten hospitals shown in Fig. 8.2. The reader can confirm that column "C5" through "C14" in Figs. 8.2 and 8.14 are identical. However, bootstrapped values shown in column "J" of Fig. 8.14 are slightly different. Figure 8.15 displays the 2.5 and 97.5 % confidence intervals for the SBM-I-C bootstrap scores.

	A	B	C	D	E	F	G	H	I	J	K
1	DEA-Solver Pro. V10.0										
2	Model=Bootstrap-SBM-I-C										
3											
4	No.	DMU	DEA	97.50%	75%	50%	25%	2.50%		Average	Rank
5	1	H1	1	1	1	1	1	0.8364		0.9803	4
6	2	H2	0.5982	0.6857	0.6287	0.5981	0.5706	0.5226		0.6001	10
7	3	H3	1	1	1	1	1	1		1	1
8	4	H4	1	1	1	1	1	1		1	1
9	5	H5	1	1	1	1	0.9382	0.8198		0.9659	6
10	6	H6	0.7399	0.8274	0.7662	0.7321	0.7005	0.6446		0.7338	7
11	7	H7	0.5963	1	1	0.5935	0.5682	0.5242		0.7152	8
12	8	H8	1	1	1	1	0.9608	0.8747		0.9764	5
13	9	H9	1	1	1	1	1	1		1	1
14	10	H10	0.656	0.7568	0.6907	0.6581	0.6266	0.5772		0.6601	9
15											

H ◀ ▶ H BootstrapSummary BootstrapScore Summary Data

Fig. 8.11 Bootstrapping DEA scores—bootstrap summary

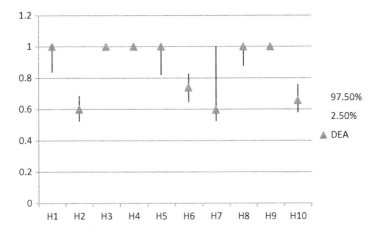

Fig. 8.12 Bootstrapping 95 % confidence interval

Once bootstraps are obtained to correct bias, if two-stage (or multiple) models are to be used to explore the determinants of bootstrapped efficiency scores to alleviate possible serial correlation, using a second-stage bootstrap can be added at this stage. This is easily done using statistical packages such as STATA.

8.7 Economies of Scope

This DEA model can be used to evaluate whether a health care organization might produce different services by spinning them off as separate organizations. Similarly, one can test whether separate organizations delivering the services might be

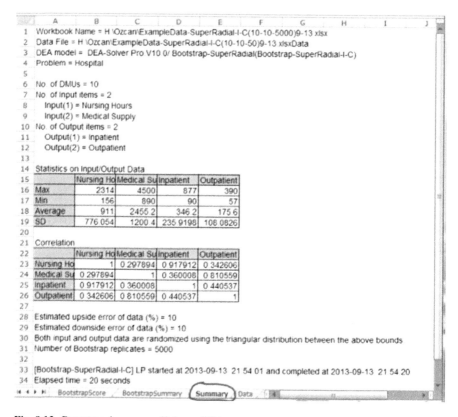

Fig. 8.13 Bootstrapping super-efficiency DEA scores—summary

No.	DMU	DEA	97.50%	75%	50%	25%	2.50%	Average	Rank
1	H1	1.0849	1.2611	1.144	1.0858	1.0281	0.927	1.0869	4
2	H2	0.6154	0.7212	0.6528	0.6194	0.5887	0.5351	0.6218	10
3	H3	1.3326	1.4844	1.3782	1.3261	1.2757	1.1869	1.3283	2
4	H4	1.5219	1.78	1.6064	1.5176	1.4376	1.2959	1.5239	1
5	H5	1.0137	1.1582	1.0685	1.0209	0.9784	0.9084	1.0248	5
6	H6	0.7578	0.8522	0.7886	0.7541	0.7223	0.6664	0.756	8
7	H7	0.9685	1.1191	1.0169	0.9705	0.9262	0.8495	0.9737	7
8	H8	1.0266	1.135	1.0514	1.0086	0.9673	0.8965	1.0104	6
9	H9	1.3244	1.5421	1.3969	1.322	1.2506	1.1338	1.326	3
10	H10	0.753	0.8789	0.7943	0.7538	0.7124	0.6442	0.7552	9

Fig. 8.14 Bootstrapping super-efficiency DEA scores—bootstrap summary

better off by consolidating under one umbrella. Economies of scope provide some answers to many capacity-related questions using DEA. For further details of effects of divestitures and mergers, the interested reader is referred to Fare et al. (1994) and Cooper et al. (2007).

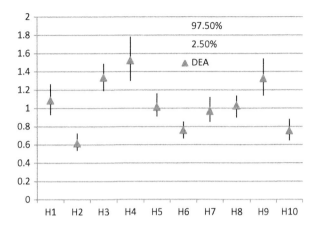

Fig. 8.15 Bootstrapping
95 % confidence interval for
super-efficiency

8.8   Summary

In this chapter, we demonstrated super-efficiency and congestion DEA methods, which can be easily applied to problems in health care organizations. We also presented network and dynamic DEA models that have been recently added to the DEA arsenal. Finally, the chapter concludes with multistage applications of DEA including bootstrapping.

Section II
Applications

The first eight chapters introduced various models of efficiency and effectiveness that can be solved using data envelopment analysis (DEA). The next eight chapters are devoted to applications of DEA. Chapter 9 develops a robust hospital DEA model based on these previous studies, while Chap. 10 provides an in-depth look at DEA-based physician evaluations. Chapter 11 specifies the DEA-based nursing home models. Chapter 12 introduces a few studies on health maintenance organizations (HMOs) and DEA models associated with them. Chapter 13 explores home health and introduces DEA models for home health agencies.

Chapter 14 examines other health care organizations including dialysis centers, community mental health centers, community-based youth services, organ procurement organizations, aging agencies, and dental providers. Chapter 15 provides insight into other DEA models designed to evaluate health care provider performance for specific treatments including stroke, mechanical ventilation, and perioperative services. This chapter also discusses DEA models for physicians at hospital settings, hospital mergers, hospital closures, hospital labor markets, and hospital services in local markets. Finally Chap. 16 surveys the country-based international health care applications of DEA.

Chapter 9
Hospital Applications

9.1 Introduction

In health care, the first application of DEA is dated to 1983 with the study of Nunamaker, measuring routine nursing service efficiency. Since then, DEA analysis has been used widely in the assessment of hospital technical efficiency in the United States as well as around the world at different levels of decision making units.

Earlier DEA studies were aimed at specific characteristics or types of hospitals, such as teaching and non-teaching hospitals, studied by O'Neill (1998) and Grosskopf et al. (2001, 2004). Harrison et al. (2004) evaluated the technical efficiency of 280 United States (US) federal hospitals in 1998 and 245 US federal hospitals in 2001 using DEA methodology. The study found that overall efficiency in federal hospitals improved from 68 % in 1998 to 79 % in 2001, while at the same time there was a potential for savings of $2.0 billion annually through more efficient management of resources. Harrison and Sexton (2006) evaluated the efficiency of religious not-for-profit hospitals using DEA and found that overall efficiency in religious hospitals improved from 72 % in 1998 to 74 % in 2001. Wang et al. (1999) evaluated trends in efficiency among 314 metropolitan American hospital markets with 6,010 hospitals. Results suggested that larger hospital size was associated with higher inefficiency. Ozcan (1995) studied the hospital industry's technical efficiency in 319 US metropolitan areas and found that at least 3 % of health care costs in the gross domestic product (GDP) are due to inefficiencies created by the excessive buildup of providers.

Changes in hospitals' technical efficiency resulting from the impact of policy, technology, and environment issues also were studied in the literature. One of the areas of application of DEA to the hospital industry was an assessment of hospital mergers (Harris et al. 2000; Ferrier and Valdmanis 2004). Lee and Wan (2004) used DEA in the study of the relationship between information system (IS) integration and efficiency of 349 urban hospitals, measured in 1997 and 1998. Chu et al. (2004)

examined the effect of capitated contracting on hospital efficiency in California and found that less efficient hospitals are more likely to participate in capitated contracting and that hospital efficiency generally increases with respect to the degree of capitation involvement. Mobley and Magnussen (2002) assessed the impact of managed care penetration and hospital quality on efficiency in hospital staffing in California using a DEA production function model, including ancillary care among the inputs and outputs. The study found that market share and market concentration were the major determinants of excess staffing and that poor quality was associated with less efficient staffing. Chirikos and Sear (1994) studied technical efficiency and the competitive behavior of 189 acute Florida hospitals and found that inefficiency ratings were systematically linked to the competitive conditions of local health care markets. A study by Brown (2002) used the Healthcare Cost and Utilization Project (HCUP) sample of hospitals for 1992–1996 to estimate hospital technical efficiency and found that increased managed care insurance is associated with higher technical efficiency.

Different studies used different levels of DMUs (Ozcan and McCue 1996; Ozcan et al. 1996a). While most researchers used the hospital level, there are also applications of DEA at the managerial level. O'Neill (2005) compared multifactor efficiency (MFE) and non-radial super-efficiency (NRSE) for operating room managers at an Iowa hospital. These techniques lead to equivalent results for unique optimal solutions and a single output. Multifactor efficiency incorporates the slack values from multiple output variables and can be easier for managers because it does not require additional steps beyond the DEA. O'Neill and Dexter (2004) developed and validated a method to measure "market capture" of inpatient elective surgery using DEA for Perioperative Services at 53 non-metropolitan Pennsylvania hospitals, demonstrating DEA's potential as a valuable tool for managers' decision-making.

Data envelopment analysis for estimation of different aspects of health care services and hospitals' technical efficiency was used in Spain (Pina and Torres 1996; Sola and Prior 2001; Dalmau-Atarrodona and Puig-Junoy 1998), Taiwan (Chang 1998), Thailand (Valdmanis et al. 2004), Turkey (Ersoy et al. 1997; Sahin and Ozcan 2000), Greece (Giokas 2001; Athanassopoulos and Gounaris 2001), Germany (Helmig and Lapsley 2001), Canada (Ouellette and Vierstraete 2004), United Kingdom (Field and Emrouznejad 2003; McCallion et al. 2000), Belgium (Creteur et al. 2003), Kenya (Kirigia et al. 2004), Botswana (Ramanathan et al. 2003), and Sweden (Gerdtham et al. 1999). Biørn et al. (2003) studied the effect of activity-based financing on hospital efficiency in Norway. DEA also was used for international comparison (Mobley and Magnussen 1998; Steinmann and Zweifel 2003). For more in-depth evaluation and a summary of health and hospital applications of DEA, the reader is referred to papers by Hollingsworth (2003) as well as O'Neill et al. (2008).

9.2 Defining Service Production Process in the Hospital Sector

The studies mentioned above defined hospital service production in varying models. Sherman and Zhu (2006) identified the variations in hospital production models and suggested that it is hard to compare outcome of efficiency studies due to a lack of standard conceptualization of inputs and outputs in this process. O'Neil et al. (2008), in a recent taxonomy of DEA hospital studies, illustrated various inputs and outputs used by different researchers in the service production process.

Ozcan et al. (1992), Ozcan (1992–1993), Ozcan and Luke (1993), O'Neill et al. (2008), and later studies by Ozcan identified three major categories of inputs as capital investment, labor, and other operating costs. Similarly, the taxonomy of O'Neill et al. (2008) provides categories of inputs and outputs and identifies three broad categories of inputs: namely capital investment, labor, and other operating expenses. These categories of inputs through the research over the years emerged as the standard for hospital service production. On the output side, Ozcan et al. (1992), and Ozcan and Luke (1993) introduced the following output measurements: case-mix adjusted discharges for inpatient side, outpatient visits for ambulatory activities, and teaching for those hospitals engaged in medical education. O'Neill and associates' taxonomy also includes outpatient visits, admissions or discharges, and teaching. Although inpatient days are also identified as another output category in this taxonomy, O'Neill and associates also provide trends that shape the usage of inputs and outputs in hospital studies. More specifically, they show that the use of "inpatient days" measuring inpatient activities is replaced by adjusted admissions or discharges as Diagnosis-Related Group (DRG)-based reimbursement took place both in the US and some European countries.

While conceptualization of service production using these input and output categories is very important for robust DEA modeling, it is equally important to operationalize these variables with available measurements from the field via existing data bases.

American Hospital Association (AHA) data, available at www.aha.org, is the main source for operationalization of the DEA input and output variables in the United States. However, the AHA database alone cannot provide all the necessary components for a robust model. Thus, other databases such as those of the Centers for Medicare and Medicaid Services (CMS), available at www.cms.hhs.gov, are necessary to identify the nature of the outputs, especially for inpatients through determination of case-mix for the hospitals. It should also be noted that data elements collected by AHA change over time. For example, until the 1990s financial data that could determine the operational costs were reported. However, in later years, researchers could only obtain such data from the CMS database. Furthermore, reporting of some variables was substituted with their variants, as is the case with the AHA, which no longer reports discharges but instead reports admissions.

These idiosyncrasies challenge practicing administrators and researchers to operationalize the inputs and outputs for a robust DEA model of hospital service production. However, culmination of the research to date demonstrates that most commonly agreed to and available variables from the mentioned databases are used to evaluate general hospital efficiency throughout the United States. Non-US examples appear to follow similar steps.

Based on this discussion, it is possible to create a nomenclature for performance evaluation and a robust DEA model that is operationalized for the hospital sector in general.

9.3 Inputs and Outputs for Acute Care General Hospitals

As it is briefly introduced in the previous section, inputs of hospitals can be categorized in three major areas as: capital investments, labor, and operating expenses. Outputs, on the other hand, should reflect both inpatient and outpatient activity. Those hospitals that provide a teaching function would be considered an extension to this model.

9.3.1 Hospital Inputs

Operationalization of three broad categories of inputs using AHA and CMS databases requires the construction of variables and proxies. For example, capital investment is a variable that is not directly available from these databases. Statewide databases or hospitals in their accounting books may report this variable as "assets;" however, the value of assets depends on their recorded or acquisition time and their depreciation. Thus, using the book values of such investments does not reflect what is on the ground as a health service facility.

9.3.1.1 Capital Investments

Ozcan and Luke (1993) showed that one can estimate capital investments in a hospital using two indicators: (1) plant size, measured by the number of operational beds, and (2) plant complexity, measured using the number of diagnostic and special services provided exclusively by the hospital. These two proxy variables were tested using Virginia data to assess their approximation to actual assets of the hospitals in the state. Their assessment found significant association between the two proxies and hospital assets, thus validating these measures for capital investment. Although we will use the same variables in defining our model, we will choose more commonly used names that correspond to current literature. For example, plant complexity will be referred to as service-mix.

Beds: The AHA database routinely provides operational beds in its annual survey reports; thus the measurement of this variable is readily available.

Service-Mix: The AHA database currently identifies up to 80 services that are offered by a hospital and provides coding that indicates whether these services are offered by the hospital or through the hospital by others. The key to the coding is whether the services are offered by the hospital, indicating appropriate investment is in place. If the service is not offered or offered by others for this hospital, then it can be coded as zero (0); otherwise the code would be one (1), indicating the service offering. By adding the number of services offered by the hospital, the service-mix variable is created. The value of this variable technically can range from 0 to 80; however, using the 2004 AHA survey report we calculated the median number of service-mix for small, medium, and large hospitals as 9, 14, and 18, respectively.

Weighted Service-Mix: As seen in these median numbers, service-mix does not provide sharp differentiation among hospitals. Furthermore, the more recent AHA data (AHA 2011) lists 151 services compared to earlier years. The highest number of services reported by large hospitals is 137 in 2011. Yet some these services are very complex and require intense financial investment compared to simpler services such as social work, clergy services, etc. Thus, the service-mix variable without any weighting for service complexity may not capture the complexity of the services adequately, especially with hospitals with great input diversity. In order to rectify this, Chou et al. (2012) developed relative weighting by ranking the services from 1 to 3. This was based on relative clinical and investment intensities, and the authors applied these weights to calculate a new service-mix index. The scoring of the services was based on two dimensions: (1) clinical intensity, and (2) investment intensity, then multiplication of these two rating scores, for which each service can receive a score from 1 to 9. Summing the weighted scores across all the services for a hospital's reported services produced a weighted service-mix score for each hospital. The maximum weighted service-mix index for a hospital reporting all services would be 683; however, the highest weighted service-mix based on reported services calculated in 2011 was 635. This measure of weighted service-mix was also used by Ozcan and Luke (2011) in evaluating Veterans Integrated Service Networks (VISNs). Appendix J at the end of this chapter displays the clinical and investment intensity scoring of the services for hospital services, and the weight that was developed for each service.

9.3.1.2   Labor

Labor is the second major category for hospital inputs. Operationalization of this variable would be different in the US and other countries, especially in those where socialized medicine is practiced and physicians are the part of the labor force for the hospitals. In the US, however, physicians generally are not hospital employees, with the exception of chiefs and department heads. Thus, in evaluating the performance, it is prudent to attribute the labor as non-MD labor or their full-time equivalents (FTEs). The number of non-physician FTEs employed by a hospital would cover all nursing, diagnostic, therapy, clerks, and technical personnel. It is also prudent to remind the reader that some of the DEA studies used labor costs to measure this variable. Depending upon the location of the hospital and the availability of skill-mix, labor salaries may not accurately reflect this input variable. Thus, the labor costs would require regional or even state- or city-based adjustments. However, using FTEs overcomes this weakness.

FTEs: The AHA database provides the total FTEs as well for various categories. Part-time labor is converted to full-time equivalent by dividing their number by 2.

9.3.1.3 Operating Expenses

Operating expenses for hospitals can be obtained from the CMS database; however, to eliminate double counting, labor expenses and expenses related to capital investments such as depreciation should be subtracted from this amount. Ozcan and Luke (1993) labeled this variable as supplies, indicating all necessary non-labor resources in the provision of patient care. We label this variable as operational expenses.

Operational Expenses: This variable provides the account for medical supplies, utilities, etc., to provide the services to patients.

9.3.2 Hospital Outputs

Inpatient and outpatient services constitute the majority of outputs for general hospitals that do not provide a teaching function. Thus, each type of service needs to be accounted for in the hospital service production with appropriate measurements.

9.3.2.1 Inpatient

Inpatient services are easy to account for through admissions or discharges. However, not all patients arriving at the hospital require the same level of attention and service. Some come for a day for a minor ailment, yet others go through major medical or surgical procedures. In order to account for this diversity in health service demand or its provision, we must account for severity for the admissions. CMS publishes case-mix indexes for hospitals each year. The case-mix index is calculated based on patient Diagnosis-Related Groups (DRGs), providing relative weight for acuity of the services provided by a hospital. For instance, if the case-mix for a hospital is equivalent to 1.2, this means the hospital served 20 % more acute patients than a standard hospital (compared to a hospital with a case-mix index value of 1). This measure is calculated based on Medicare and Medicaid

Fig. 9.1 Outputs and inputs
for a robust hospital DEA
model

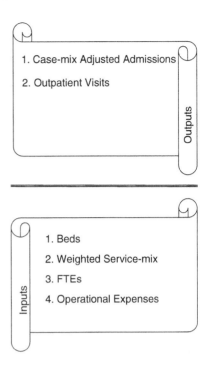

patients, and since a good portion of the hospital revenues come from these sources, we could extrapolate the case-mix index for the other patients of the hospital.

Case-mix Adjusted Admissions: This variable is created using admissions from the AHA database and multiplying them by the CMS case-mix index. This way a hospital with 10,000 admissions a year and a case-mix index of 1.2 would be reflected as 12,000 adjusted admissions. Similarly, a hospital with a case-mix index of 0.9 and 10,000 admissions would be reflected as 9,000 adjusted admissions.

9.3.2.2 Outpatient

Outpatient visits are a readily available variable from the AHA database. Unfortunately it does not have case-mix adjustments as in inpatient visits, since the payment systems are not in a similar vein. Here, health care managers and researchers have options to differentiate the visits, indicating whether these are day surgery, emergency, or routine visits. Unfortunately, most general databases do not differentiate the visits.

Outpatient Visits: This variable is available from the AHA database as described.
The ongoing identification of input and output variables for a robust hospital sector service production via the DEA model is summarized in Fig. 9.1. This model

includes two outputs and four inputs and encompasses the majority of the hospital service production processes.

In this model, hospital managers are in control of the assets of the hospital, its labor, medical supplies, and associated operational expenses. Admitted patients and visits to clinics (outpatient) constitute its final outputs. Of course, in order to produce these outputs given inputs, many intermediate processes are to occur, and these processes involve clinical decisions largely controlled by physicians or other clinicians. The aim of the proposed model is to capture the managerial performance (although often affected by clinical decisions) that can be attributed to hospital management.

Using the model and its variants described in this section, various studies were conducted to date. Most of these studies were applied to acute and general hospitals while others targeted federal government-run institutions such as Veterans Administration (VA) hospitals as well as Department of Defense (DoD) hospitals. Furthermore, hospitals with a teaching mission or academic medical centers were also considered in various studies where outputs or inputs of the model were adjusted accordingly. Ensuing sections of the chapter provide brief discussions of these studies, starting with acute and general hospitals (Sect. 9.4), large general hospitals (Sect. 9.5), government hospitals (Sect. 9.6), and academic medical centers (Sect. 9.7).

9.4 Acute Care General Hospital Applications

Acute and general hospital applications are the most frequently reported application areas in health institution performance measurement. These studies can be grouped by their profit and non-profit status, public versus private, as well as religious affiliations.

Grosskopf and Valdmanis (1987) conducted the first study comparing 82 public and not-for-profit hospitals. This study showed that public hospitals were slightly more efficient (96 %) than their not-for-profit counterparts (94 %). The results of Valdmanis' (1990) study with 41 hospitals showed 98 % efficiency for public hospitals compared to 88 % for not-for-profit hospitals. Similarly, using the 1989 AHA database, Ozcan et al. (1992) and Ozcan and Luke (1993) found public hospitals were more efficient (91 %) than church (87 %), not-for-profit (88 %), and for-profit (83 %) hospitals.

These studies also intrigued White and Ozcan (1996), who conducted further investigation of the not-for-profit hospitals further by examining ownership by church and secular dimensions. This study examined 170 California hospitals using the variant of the robust model described above, and found that church-based hospitals were more efficient (81 %) than secular (76 %) hospitals.

Using the DEA techniques learned in earlier chapters, and the robust hospital performance model presented in this chapter, we will show a hospital application example.

9.5   Large Size General Hospital Performance Evaluation

It is prudent to illustrate the robust model with recent data. This example follows the model presented in Sect. 9.3 for large acute and general hospitals in the US. The data is drawn from 2011 AHA and CMS databases. Few hospitals were deleted from consideration because of important missing information. This yielded 255 hospitals with 500 or more beds for evaluation of their efficiency. Table 9.1 summarizes the descriptive statistics for this group of hospitals.

Large US hospitals considered in this example have an average of 725 beds with an average weighted service-index of 457 based on different services offered. They employ the equivalent of 4,568 full-time employees and spend over $336 million on their operational expenses not including labor. On the output side, on average 59,585 adjusted (due to high severity) inpatient admissions and over one-half million outpatient visits occurred at each hospital.

Although these 255 large hospitals account for about 4 % of the US hospitals, the total number of beds in these hospitals represents approximately 19.3 % of all US hospital beds. Similarly, outputs of these 255 large hospitals constitute approximately 28 % of all adjusted inpatient admissions and 18.7 % of all outpatient visits in the US. Thus, evaluation of performance for large hospitals is important and may shed some light on health care performance, as well as identify excessive resources spent in this country.

Figure 9.2 displays a partial view of the data input and setup for 255 hospitals with 500 or more beds for DEA Solver Pro software. Figure 9.3 also provides a partial view of the results of the efficiency evaluations for these hospitals. The reader can note that four inputs and two outputs are shown at the top of the results spreadsheet in this figure.

The results are summarized in Table 9.2. Large hospitals' average efficiency scores were about 0.713, indicating on average 28.7 % overall inefficiency. One hospital reported score of 0.397, the worst inefficiency. Further description of efficiency is displayed in Table 9.3, where the range of efficiency, number of

Table 9.1 Descriptive statistics for US hospitals with 500 or more beds (n = 255)

	Inputs				Outputs	
Statistics	Beds	Weighted service-mix	FTEs	Operational expenses (in million $)	Adjusted admissions	Outpatient visits
Mean	725	457	4,568	336	59,585	561,434
STD	254	87	3,001	224	23,030	469,129
Min	501	219	573	35	20,613	62,373
Max	2,264	635	24,857	1,436	213,522	4,311,183
Total	184,817	116,630	1,164,824	85,605	15,194,421	143,165,755
US total[a]	957,919		5,397,648		54,427,598	767,266,951

[a]Approximate values based on AHA and CMS 2011 data (n = 6317)

	A	B	C	D	E	F	G
1	Hospital	(I)Beds	(I)Service-Mix	(I)FTEs	(I)Operational Expenses	(O)Adjusted Admissions	(O)Outpatient Visits
2	H1	789	427	2464	253780857	54572	153575
3	H2	750	530	3160	380640740	49761	306552
4	H3	645	348	1709	124530898	46172	128395
5	H4	592	447	2022	133350660	43324	158877
6	H5	592	386	2334	187023543	49890	160885
7	H6	584	332	2044	173198609	40257	171150
8	H7	537	424	1756	159730695	41958	118307
9	H8	535	391	2351	269230000	37487	211861
10	H9	524	367	1715	137097466	40753	293625
11	H10	511	380	1241	103193977	27320	119528
12	H11	1484	487	5549	532722596	130317	431528
13	H12	1342	376	5140	308300051	110368	288607
14	H13	775	330	1858	147284868	44443	92501
15	H14	655	353	2157	146163908	52684	220070
16	H15	550	317	1848	128967918	49097	243314
17	H16	506	393	2711	133684042	52061	199233
18	H17	2264	635	18433	1062860000	183267	1830183
19	H18	2170	552	14665	1425410252	213522	904759
20	H19	1763	571	14376	1199054862	111224	1189471
21	H20	1541	503	5899	390397000	110539	617000
22	H21	1491	514	12643	567749000	142081	669168
23	H22	1418	608	16012	1020751000	145237	1853618
24	H23	1407	624	10893	1079425000	99458	1035175
25	H24	1321	577	5246	501103326	108265	571064
26	H25	1305	599	8326	816690693	96217	689089
27	H26	1267	601	24857	827488000	92008	4311183
28	H27	1172	462	4184	254673387	93642	451411
29	H28	1081	431	3002	159428078	55809	482744
30	H29	1070	537	6674	548166000	96887	1298056
31	H30	1066	504	6040	563718369	99267	1217905

H ◀ ▶ H   Data

Fig. 9.2 Data input and setup for hospitals with 500 or more beds for DEA Solver Pro

hospitals, and percentage of hospitals are reported. Only 15 hospitals (5.9 % of large hospitals) achieved a perfect efficiency score of 1.00 among their peers. Another 17 hospitals achieved less than perfect efficiency, with an efficiency score above 0.9 but less than 1.00.

Figure 9.4 displays the efficient targets for the input-oriented CCR model. As the reader can observe, the target values for efficient hospitals are equivalent to their original input and output values (see hospitals H11, H12, H18, and H26 from Fig. 9.4). Calculation of targets is the same as in the CCR model, and they can be found in Chap. 2. For a detailed formulation of these calculations, the reader is referred to Appendix B, Part 3.

One of the aims of DEA evaluation of performance is to find out what quantity of unnecessary resources are used by each hospital and how much they lack in attracting patients to their facilities. Elimination of the excessive resource use and production of more health services with the given resources will improve efficiency of each hospital. In order to find the exact amount of the excess resource (input) use and lack of outputs, we can subtract the target values of each input and output variable presented in Fig. 9.4 from the original data of inputs and outputs shown in Fig. 9.2. Figure 9.5 displays a partial view of results for the inefficiencies. As the

Fig. 9.3 Efficiency results for hospitals with 500 or more beds using DEA Solver Pro

	A	B	C	D
2	Model Name = DEA-Solver Pro8.0/ CCR(CCR			
3	Workbook Name = C:\Users\Yasar Ozcan\Do			
4	No.	DMU	Score	Rank
5	1	H1	0.744391	103
6	2	H2	0.594489	204
7	3	H3	0.924008	28
8	4	H4	0.8255	52
9	5	H5	0.804044	64
10	6	H6	0.701211	129
11	7	H7	0.82226	55
12	8	H8	0.612779	192
13	9	H9	0.835109	48
14	10	H10	0.704678	126
15	11	H11	1	1
16	12	H12	1	1
17	13	H13	0.814393	59
18	14	H14	0.92498	27
19	15	H15	0.995931	16
20	16	H16	0.941303	24
21	17	H17	0.932296	25
22	18	H18	1	1
23	19	H19	0.620759	183
24	20	H20	0.836749	46
25	21	H21	0.96521	21
26	22	H22	0.823523	54
27	23	H23	0.558508	217
28	24	H24	0.838689	45
29	25	H25	0.606024	197
30	26	H26	1	1
31	27	H27	0.956626	22
32	28	H28	0.788005	77
33	29	H29	0.718131	119
34	30	H30	0.784527	80

H ◀ ▶ H / Rank / Score

Table 9.2 Summary of efficiency results

Statistic	Efficiency
Mean	0.713
St. Dev.	0.144
Min	0.397
Max	1.0

Table 9.3 Magnitude of efficiency

Efficiency level	Hospitals	Percent
1.0	15	5.9
≥0.9 to <1.0	17	6.7
≥0.8 to <0.9	37	14.6
≥0.7 to <0.8	60	23.5
≥0.6 to <0.7	72	28.2
≥0.5 to <0.6	39	15.3
≥0.4 to <0.5	13	5.1
<0.4	2	0.8
Total	255	100

Model Name = DEA-Solver Pro8 0/ CCR(CCR-I) Returns to Scale = Constant (0 =< Sum of Lambda < Infinity)

Workbook Name = C:\Users\Yasar Ozcan\Documents\OZCAN\A-DEA-BOOK\ADEA BOOK-2nd EDITION\DEA RUNS\Hospitals 500 beds.xlsx

No	DMU	Score	(I)Beds Projection	Change(%)	(I)Service-Mix Projection	Change(%)	(I)FTEs Projection	Change(%)	(I)Operational Expenses Projection	Change(%)	(O)Adjusted Admission Projection	Change(%)	(O)Outpatient Visits Projection	Change(%)
1	H1	0.744391	587.3242	-25.56%	317.6848022	-25.56%	1833.806	-25.56%	1745179276	-31.23%	6457179121	0.00%	697684.1456	354.30%
2	H2	0.594489	445.8666	-40.55%	292.3122666	-44.95%	1878.287	-40.55%	211665939.8	-44.42%	49761.28964	0.00%	862432.029	181.33%
3	H3	0.924008	595.9863	-7.60%	308.8775623	-11.24%	1578.668	-7.60%	115067565	-7.60%	46172.11614	0.00%	495978.2863	286.29%
4	H4	0.8256	498.6962	-17.45%	276.3793745	-38.17%	1668.749	-17.45%	110081014.3	-17.45%	43324.09044	0.00%	534136.0822	236.19%
5	H5	0.804044	475.9943	-19.60%	264.6785743	-31.43%	1876.238	-19.60%	150375249.8	-19.60%	49890.03363	0.00%	745053.1512	363.10%
6	H6	0.701211	409.5073	-29.88%	221.5623491	-33.27%	1432.925	-29.88%	121448801.8	-29.88%	40256.85201	0.00%	558834.2668	226.52%
7	H7	0.82226	441.5534	-17.77%	239.086093	-43.61%	1443.477	-17.77%	131340104.5	-17.77%	41958.36034	0.00%	565228.5588	369.31%
8	H8	0.612779	327.8366	-38.72%	216.7958078	-44.55%	1440.337	-38.72%	168417071.4	-41.16%	37487.11656	0.00%	665795.554	214.26%
9	H9	0.835109	437.5973	-16.49%	230.3695731	-37.23%	1431.795	-16.49%	114491369.7	-16.49%	40752.69632	0.00%	531928.7756	81.16%
10	H10	0.704678	360.0902	-29.53%	182.761789	-51.90%	874.1525	-29.53%	72718491.44	-29.53%	27319.82139	0.00%	281458.1361	135.47%
11	H11	1	1484	0.00%	487	0.00%	5548.5	0.00%	532722596	0.00%	130316.7486	0.00%	431528	0.00%
12	H12	1	1342	0.00%	376	0.00%	5139.5	0.00%	308300951	0.00%	110368.3901	0.00%	280607	0.00%
13	H13	0.814393	521.6824	-32.69%	260.7495414	-18.56%	1512.734	-18.56%	119947699.2	-18.56%	44442.77127	0.00%	533818.0346	477.09%
14	H14	0.92498	605.8619	-7.50%	326.5178439	-7.60%	1994.719	-7.50%	136198693.2	-7.50%	52684.12904	0.00%	614942.2215	179.43%
15	H15	0.995931	547.7623	-0.41%	303.3742478	-4.30%	1836.983	-0.41%	128443200.9	-0.41%	49096.69232	0.00%	613920.7302	162.32%
16	H16	0.941303	476.2992	-5.87%	340.4227642	-13.38%	2651.401	-5.87%	125837161.6	-5.87%	52061.28352	0.00%	531181.9759	166.61%
17	H17	0.932296	1651.928	-27.03%	592.0081579	-6.77%	11031.76	-40.15%	990900457.8	-6.77%	183267.0614	0.00%	1830183	0.00%
18	H18	1	2170	0.00%	552	0.00%	14664.5	0.00%	1425410252	0.00%	213621.8977	0.00%	904759	0.00%
19	H19	0.620759	1075.46	-39.06%	364.4531484	-37.92%	8923.715	-37.92%	709300586.2	-40.86%	111224.3636	0.00%	1189471	0.00%
20	H20	0.836749	1264.755	-17.93%	420.8846887	-16.33%	4935.562	-16.33%	326664176.5	-16.33%	110638.8688	0.00%	617000	0.00%
21	H21	0.96621	1439.128	-3.48%	496.1180638	-3.48%	7329.847	-42.02%	547997149	-3.48%	142081.165	0.00%	1169314.546	74.74%
22	H22	0.823623	1167.756	-17.66%	500.7017374	-17.66%	8606.142	-46.25%	779043636.3	-23.68%	145237.1323	0.00%	1951741.937	5.29%
23	H23	0.568608	786.8207	-44.15%	348.5089596	-44.15%	5831.958	-46.46%	524924614.3	-51.37%	99458.20729	0.00%	1396616.538	34.92%
24	H24	0.838689	1107.908	-16.13%	483.9234762	-16.13%	4399.342	-16.13%	389842174.3	-22.20%	108264.9917	0.00%	1060947.366	85.78%
25	H25	0.506024	790.9609	-39.40%	363.0081861	-39.40%	5045.46	-39.40%	449076824.8	-45.01%	86216.99051	0.00%	1320044.312	91.56%
26	H26	1	1267	0.00%	601	0.00%	24856.5	0.00%	827480000	0.00%	92008.45406	0.00%	4311183	0.00%
27	H27	0.956626	1121.166	-4.34%	441.9612647	-4.34%	4002.045	-4.34%	243627212.6	-4.34%	93642.11082	0.00%	588687.7297	30.41%
28	H28	0.798006	748.9261	-30.72%	339.6303003	-21.20%	2365.198	-21.20%	125630176.9	-21.20%	55808.77733	0.00%	482744	0.00%
29	H29	0.718131	768.4002	-28.19%	386.6363609	-28.19%	4792.447	-28.19%	393656012.2	-28.19%	96886.80718	0.00%	1508805.293	16.24%
30	H30	0.784627	836.3058	-21.56%	395.4016239	-21.56%	4738.151	-21.56%	416762162.6	-26.07%	99266.8311	0.00%	1351061.436	10.93%

Projection / Graph2 / Graph1 / Rank / Score / Summary / Data

Fig. 9.4 Efficient targets for hospitals with 500 or more beds using DEA Solver Pro

reader can note, the negative values in inputs indicate that they must be reduced by that amount. Shortage of outputs, on the other hand, requires augmentation of the outputs by the indicated amount.

Although Fig. 9.5 provides an excellent prescription for individual hospitals for their course of action towards efficiency, we can also study the impact of these efficiencies for a larger economy. As indicated before, these 255 large hospitals account for approximately 19.3 % of all US hospital beds, 28 % of all adjusted inpatient admissions and 18.7 % of all outpatient visits in the US. Thus, improvement of overall inefficiency for the large hospitals in the health care industry would contribute significantly to this sector. To view this from a macro perspective, we can summarize the values obtained from Fig. 9.5.

A summary of excessive inputs and lack of outputs for all 255 large hospitals is shown in Table 9.4. As the reader can note, a total value on the last row indicates the total excessive input or total shortage by all 255 hospitals.

Results show that, collectively, large hospitals can reduce beds by 53,849 from 184,817 existing beds shown in Table 9.1. Additionally, 40,450 weighted services can be curtailed while FTEs can be reduced from 1,164,824 by 416,636 (a 35.7 % reduction). Furthermore, large hospitals must reduce non-labor operational expenses by $31.6 billion dollars. These findings are similar to Ozcan (1995), who determined that at least 3 % of health care costs in the gross domestic product are due to inefficiencies created by the excessive buildup of providers.

Although there is no shortage of inpatient admissions, to achieve efficiency the large hospitals must attract 106 million more outpatient visits (augmentation of output). This way outpatient visits should increase from the current 143 million visits to 249 million visits. This means more care should shift to outpatient by some hospitals (see H1–H10, H13–H16, H21–H25 and so on in Fig. 9.5).

Hospital	Inefficiencies					
	Excessive Inputs				Shortage of Outputs	
	Beds	Service-Mix	FTEs	Operational Expenses	Adjusted Admissions	Outpatient Visits
H1	-202	-109	-630	-79262929	0	544109
H2	-304	-238	-1281	-169074800	0	555880
H3	-49	-39	-130	-9463333	0	367583
H4	-103	-171	-353	-23269646	0	375258
H5	-116	-121	-457	-36648293	0	584168
H6	-174	-110	-611	-51749807	0	387684
H7	-95	-185	-312	-28390590	0	436922
H8	-207	-174	-910	-110812929	0	453935
H9	-86	-137	-283	-22606096	0	238304
H10	-151	-197	-366	-30475496	0	161930
H11	0	0	0	0	0	0
H12	0	0	0	0	0	0
H13	-253	-61	-345	-27337169	0	441317
H14	-49	-26	-162	-10965215	0	394872
H15	-2	-14	-8	-524717	0	370607
H16	-30	-53	-159	-7846880	0	331949
H17	-612	-43	-7401	-71959542	0	0
H18	0	0	0	0	0	0
H19	-688	-217	-5452	-489754276	0	0
H20	-276	-82	-963	-63732824	0	0
H21	-52	-18	-5313	-19751851	0	500147
H22	-250	-107	-7405	-241707364	0	98124
H23	-621	-275	-5061	-554500386	0	361442
H24	-213	-93	-846	-111261152	0	489883
H25	-514	-236	-3280	-367613868	0	630955
H26	0	0	0	0	0	0
H27	-51	-20	-181	-11046174	0	137277
H28	-332	-91	-636	-33797902	0	0
H29	-302	-151	-1881	-154510988	0	210749
H30	-230	-109	-1301	-146956206	0	133156

Fig. 9.5 Calculation of inefficiencies

Table 9.4 Excessive inputs and shortage of outputs for US hospitals with 500 or more beds

	Excessive inputs				Shortage of outputs	
Statistics	Beds	Weighted service-mix	FTEs	Operational expenses (in million $)	Adjusted admissions	Outpatient visits
Mean	211	158	1,633	124	154	416,712
St. Dev.	127	90	1,720	138	1,363	347,578
Total	53,849	40,450	416,636	31,613	39,393	106,261,554

9.6 Federal Government Hospitals (VA and DOD)

A study by Burgess and Wilson (1993) evaluated 32 Veterans Administration (VA) hospitals and compared them to non-federal hospitals (n = 1,445). Ozcan and Bannick (1994) compared VA hospitals to Department of Defense (DoD) hospitals (n = 284). The Burgess and Wilson study showed that VA hospitals were more efficient (91.8 %) than their non-government counterparts (84.9–88.0 %). On the other hand, Ozcan and Bannick showed that defense hospitals (n = 126) were generally more efficient (87 %) than VA (n = 158) hospitals (78 %). Due to different size and comparison groups, it is hard to generalize the results on a comparison of government to non-government hospitals. Even within a government hospital framework, there might be idiosyncrasies that should be accounted for in the comparisons. Bannick and Ozcan (1995) provide useful discussion on the homogeneity and heterogeneity of DoD versus VA hospitals. Nevertheless, due to funding and administration differences, comparison of government acute care hospitals to other government hospitals may produce misleading results. Thus, the VA or DoD hospitals should be only compared among themselves.

Ozcan and Bannick (1994) in an earlier study used DEA to evaluate trends in DoD hospital efficiency from 1998 to 1999 using 124 military hospitals, with data from the American Hospital Association Annual Survey. This study used the model described earlier and included Army, Air Force, and Navy hospitals in the comparison. They found that average efficiency ranged from 91 to 96 % among these three service branches.

Coppola (2003) conducted a DEA study of military hospitals using 1998–2002 data. In his study, he selected the following input variables: costs, number of beds in the military facility, FTEs, and number of services offered. For output variables, he included surgical visits, Ambulatory Patient Visits (APVs), emergency visits, Case Mix Adjusted Discharges (CMAD), and live births. Data was obtained from the US DoD, and 390 facilities were included in the study. Coppola's study found that 119 (31 %) of the hospitals were efficient. Air Force hospitals were leading with 92 % efficiency while Navy hospitals were recorded at 87 %. Average efficiency gradually declined from 91 % in 1998 to 89 % in 2002.

Up to this point, the studies were conducted at the strategic level under a different operational paradigm prior to the large-scale adoption of managed care. In the most recent work in the area of military training facilities (MTF), Fulton (2005) analyzed the performance of 17 US Army Community Hospitals and seven Army Medical Centers over a 3-year period, 2001–2003. Fulton's model, however, uses a different approach than Coppola's and evaluates from the managed care perspective by including quality, patient satisfaction, readiness measure, Relative Value Units (RVUs), Relative Weighted Product (RWP), and graduate medical education (GME) training as outputs. His inputs include cost and enrollment/ population measures as a non-discretionary input. The VRS input-oriented model yielded 97.6 % efficiency while an output-oriented VRS model showed 98.9 % efficiency. According to Fulton, the results suggest that about a $10 million reduction in cost could have been achieved in 2001.

Ozcan and Luke (2011) examined whether the restructuring of hospitals within the Veterans Health Administration (VA) network through the inception of Veterans Integrated Service Networks (VISN) effected the performance of these facilities. The study uses a pre-post evaluation of VISN performance by comparing the performance of a VISN in 1994 (pre-period) with the performance of the VISN in 2004 (post-period). The data for the study came from the AHA annual survey data for the years 1994 and 2004. The study consisted of 150 VA general medical-surgical hospitals for the year 1994 as compared to 135 hospitals for the year 2004. The study variables included admissions and outpatient visits as the output variables, and labor force (FTE), operational expenses (1994 operational expenses adjusted using the Consumer Price Index to make them comparable with 2004 operational expenses), beds, and service-mix (weighted on two dimensions: clinical intensity and investment intensity) as the input variables. A t-test on the VISN hospital membership between the two study periods showed significant differences between the two groups. In addition, there was an average reduction in beds per VISN by approximately 907 beds; using the weighted service-mix per VISN, the authors found a reduction of approximately 337 weighted services per VISN with admission reduced on average by 11,228 cases per VISN between the two study periods. The results also reported an increase in FTEs (on average an increase of 669 FTEs) and expenses (on average an increase of $240 million) per VISN. To evaluate the VISN productivity change over time (1994–2004), the Malmquist Index was calculated using the input-oriented constant returns to scale (CCR) option of DEA. The results of the study showed that while the DEA efficiencies were almost identical for the years 1994 and 2004 (0.92), the change in the Malmquist scores was entirely attributable to structural or technical changes in the VISNs. There was also a strong correlation between the changes in the numbers of hospitals per VISN with the technology component of the Malmquist Index (-0.379), whereas the efficiency component of the Malmquist Index was not reported to have a significant correlation. The results showed that in order for the inefficient VISNs to become efficient they would have to reduce on average

388 beds, 97 adjusted service-mix values, 1,901 FTEs, and $81.6 million in operational costs. On the output side they would also be required to increase their outpatient visits by an average of 37,162 and annual admissions by 244. The study findings were in line with the authors' hypothesis that a decrease in the number of hospitals and functional restructuring contributed to performance improvements in the VISNs. This was in fact an effective tool to improve efficiency in the delivery of acute care services for VA hospitals.

From a policy perspective the study provides evidence on how implementing certain restructuring as well as infusing new technologies—VA implemented across–the-board electronic medical records (EMR) during the restructuring period—can help improve efficiency even in the wake of an increase in the total utilization. The limited generalizability of the study to other acute care settings can be considered as a study limitation.

Depending upon the purpose of the efficiency evaluation, models deployed by various researchers utilized the variants of the essential inputs and outputs presented in the robust model shown in Fig. 9.1.

9.7 Academic Medical Center Applications

An academic medical center application of DEA is another variant of the model presented above. The only difference in this model is capturing the training or teaching output (Morey et al. 1995). This particular variable can be captured in terms of resident MD and dentist FTEs from the AHA database. This begs the question, then, of whether this variable should be considered just as an output (teaching function of the academic medical centers). Others may also argue that these FTEs provide an immense resource for the hospitals, thus they can also be considered as an input. To test these assertions, in separate studies Ozcan (1992–1993) and Valdmanis (1992) performed sensitivity analysis to test the impact of using a teaching variable (FTEs) as input, output, or both. Both studies showed that using input, output, or both did not affect efficiency scores dramatically, other than having the effect of the additional variable. Thus, in order not to over-inflate efficiency scores, a more prudent approach would be to include the variable only one time. Since teaching is an important output for academic medical centers, using the variable as output seems a more reasonable approach. Hence, we can identify medical resident FTEs as teaching output for academic medical centers as shown in Fig. 9.6.

Another investigation by Harrison et al. (2010) addresses the question of what key factors affect quality of care among teaching hospitals, specifically examining whether improved efficiencies among teaching hospitals correspond to an improvement in the quality of care provided to patients. These authors describe how recent studies have revealed that teaching hospitals not only commonly struggle to achieve

Fig. 9.6 DEA model for
academic medical centers

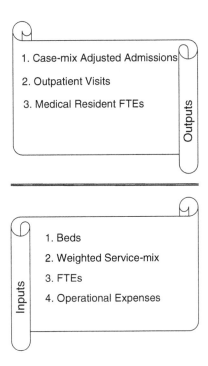

long-term financial stability, but that they also are less efficient than their local non-teaching competitors. In response, efforts to promote "benchmark" facilities that teaching hospitals may emulate have led to improved financial performance and efficiency as teaching hospitals have embraced operational transformations. However, the authors note that studies have failed to examine the impact that such changes have had on the quality of care provided to patients at teaching hospitals. By evaluating how resource utilization may lead to improved quality, the authors suggest that their study would enhance benchmarking among academic medical centers.

The authors' literature review suggests that teaching hospitals in the past were less efficient than non-teaching hospitals but had better quality of care. The authors then mention previous discussions regarding the clinical involvement, resource allocation, leadership monitoring, and collaborative work of different departments required to realize quality improvement in academic medical centers. A description of how the efficiency of teaching hospitals can be evaluated is then provided as the authors offer a summary of data envelopment analysis (DEA). They provide an example of a study among university teaching hospitals showing that the hospitalist model led to improvements in hospital efficiency without compromising the quality of care provided to patients.

The study was limited to 216 members of the Council of Teaching Hospitals (COTH), and data was taken from the AHA annual survey database as well as Joint Commission on Accreditation of Healthcare Organizations (JCAHO) evaluation scores of quality measures. Within the DEA model, the authors utilized inputs of hospital beds, the number of clinical services offered, operating expenses (less payroll), and full-time employees, and outputs included inpatient days, surgical procedures, outpatient visits, births, and graduate medical education (GME) residents trained. DEA methods were incorporated to obtain efficiency scores for each hospital, and these efficiency scores served as the independent variable in a multiple regression analysis, with the JCAHO quality scores used as the regression's dependent variable.

The DEA scores showed that teaching hospitals overall operated at 88 % efficiency. The results of the multiple regression model examining quality within teaching hospitals revealed that long-term debt to equity, HMO competition, and RN hours per inpatient day had positive and statistically significant relationships with quality, such that hospital quality increases as long-term debt to equity, HMO competition, or RN hours per inpatient day increases. In light of such findings, the authors argue that their study supports the assertion that how managers decide to allocate resources can improve the performance of their organizations, as suggested in strategic management theory. For example, in regards to the relationship between long-term debt to equity and quality, the authors explain their finding by suggesting that managers at teaching hospitals accumulate debt in order to make improvements to their facilities and enhance their technology, which in turn leads to improved quality of care. Similarly, teaching hospitals competing in markets with high HMO competition are forced to improve their quality of care so that they may capably compete with other health care providers. Finally, managers at teaching hospitals may increase their nursing hours in order to improve the quality of care that their patients may receive. To bolster their argument, the authors connect their study's findings to the results of several previous studies connecting improved performance and efficiency at hospitals to improved quality.

9.8 Summary

This chapter provided general guidance for a robust hospital performance model and its operationalization using generally available databases. Furthermore, development of these models is connected to research conducted during the past several decades. Using the robust model presented, the efficiency of large size US hospitals is also examined. Variations of the models for federal government hospitals and academic medical centers are also discussed.

Appendix J: Development of Service Weight Based on Clinical and Investment Intensity

AHA 2011 service categories	(1) Clinical intensity	(2) Investment intensity	Variable name	(1) * (2) service weight
General medical and surgical care (adult)	2	2	GENHOS	4
General medical and surgical care (pediatric)	2	2	PEDHOS	4
Obstetric care	2	3	OBHOS	6
Medical/surgical intensive care	3	3	MSICHOS	9
Cardiac intensive care	3	3	CICHOS	9
Neonatal intensive care	3	3	NICHOS	9
Neonatal intermediate care	3	3	NINTHOS	9
Pediatric intensive care	3	3	PEDICHOS	9
Burn care	3	3	BRNHOS	9
Other special care	2	2	SPCICHOS	4
Other intensive care	3	3	OTHIHOS	9
Physical rehabilitation care	2	2	REHABHOS	4
Alcohol/drug abuse or dependency inpatient care	2	1	ALCHHOS	2
Psychiatric care	2	2	PSYHOS	4
Skilled nursing care	2	2	SNHOS	4
Intermediate nursing care	1	2	ICFHOS	2
Acute long term care	1	1	ACUHOS	1
Other long term care	1	1	OTHLTHOS	1
Other care	1	1	OTHCRHOS	1
Adult day care program	1	1	ADULTHOS	1
Airborne infection isolation room	2	2	AIRBHOS	4
Alcoholism-drug abuse or dependency outpatient services	1	1	ALCOPHOS	1
Alzheimer Center	1	1	ALZHOS	1
Ambulance services	2	3	AMBHOS	6
Ambulatory surgery center	2	3	AMBSHOS	6
Arthritis treatment center	2	2	ARTHCHOS	4
Assisted living services	1	1	ASSTLHOS	1
Auxiliary services	1	1	AUXHOS	1
Bariatric/weight control service	2	2	BWHTHOS	4
Birthing room/LDR room/ LDRP room	2	2	BROOMHOS	4
Blood Donor Center	1	1	BLDOHOS	1
Breast cancer screening/ mammograms	1	1	MAMMSHOS	1
Adult cardiology services	3	3	ACARDHOS	9
Pediatric cardiology services	3	3	PCARDHOS	9
Adult diagnostic/invasive catheterization	3	3	ACLABHOS	9

(continued)

(continued)

AHA 2011 service categories	(1) Clinical intensity	(2) Investment intensity	Variable name	(1) * (2) service weight
Pediatric diagnostic/invasive catheterization	3	3	PCLABHOS	9
Adult interventional cardiac catheterization	3	3	ICLABHOS	9
Pediatric interventional cardiac catheterization	3	3	PELABHOS	9
Adult cardiac surgery	3	3	ADTCHOS	9
Pediatric cardiac surgery	3	3	PEDCSHOS	9
Adult cardiac electrophysiology	3	3	ADTEHOS	9
Pediatric cardiac electrophysiology	3	3	PEDEHOS	9
Cardiac Rehabilitation	2	2	CHABHOS	4
Case Management	2	1	CMNGTHOS	2
Chaplaincy/pastoral care services	1	1	CHAPHOS	1
Chemotherapy	2	2	CHTHHOS	4
Children wellness program	1	1	CWELLHOS	1
Chiropractic services	1	1	CHIHOS	1
Community outreach	1	1	COUTRHOS	1
Complementary medicine services	1	1	COMPHOS	1
Computer assisted orthopedic surgery	3	3	CAOSHOS	9
Crisis prevention	1	1	CPREVHOS	1
Dental Services	1	2	DENTSHOS	2
Emergency Department	3	3	EMDEPHOS	9
Pediatric emergency department	3	3	PEMERHOS	9
Freestanding/Satellite Emergency Department	2	2	FSERHOS	4
Certified trauma center	3	3	TRAUMHOS	9
Enabling services	1	1	ENBHOS	1
Optical Colonoscopy	2	2	ENDOCHOS	4
Endoscopic ultrasound	2	2	ENDOUHOS	4
Ablation of Barrett's esophagus	3	2	ENDOAHOS	6
Esophageal impedance study	2	2	ENDOEHOS	4
Endoscopic retrograde cholangiopancreatography (ECRP)	3	3	ENDORHOS	9
Enrollment assistance program	1	1	ENRHOS	1
Extracorporeal shock-wave lithotripter (ESWL)	2	3	ESWLHOS	6
Fertility Clinic	1	1	FRTCHOS	1
Fitness center	1	1	FITCHOS	1
Freestanding outpatient center	2	2	OPCENHOS	4
Geriatric services	1	1	GERSVHOS	1
Health fair	1	1	HLTHFHOS	1
Community health education	1	1	HLTHCHOS	1
Genetic testing/counseling	1	1	GNTCHOS	1

(continued)

(continued)

AHA 2011 service categories	(1) Clinical intensity	(2) Investment intensity	Variable name	(1) * (2) service weight
Health screenings	1	1	HLTHSHOS	1
Health research	1	1	HLTRHOS	1
Hemodialysis	2	2	HEMOHOS	4
HIV-AIDS services	2	1	AIDSSHOS	2
Home health services	1	1	HOMEHHOS	1
Hospice program	1	1	HOSPCHOS	1
Hospital-base outpatient care center/services	2	2	OPHOSHOS	4
Immunization program	1	1	IMPRHOS	1
Indigent care clinic	1	1	ICARHOS	1
Linguistic/translation services	1	1	LINGHOS	1
Meals on wheels	1	1	MEALSHOS	1
Mobile Health Services	1	1	MOHSHOS	1
Neurological services	2	2	NEROHOS	4
Nutrition programs	1	1	NUTRPHOS	1
Occupational health services	1	1	OCCHSHOS	1
Oncology services	2	2	ONCOLHOS	4
Orthopedic services	2	2	ORTOHOS	4
Outpatient surgery	2	2	OPSRGHOS	4
Pain management program	1	1	PAINHOS	1
Palliative care program	1	1	PALHOS	1
Inpatient palliative care unit	2	2	IPALHOS	4
Patient Controlled Analgesia (PCA)	2	2	PCAHOS	4
Patient education center	1	1	PATEDHOS	1
Patient representative services	1	1	PATRPHOS	1
Assistive technology center	1	2	RASTHOS	2
Electrodiagnostic services	1	2	REDSHOS	2
Physical rehabilitation outpatient services	2	2	RHBOPHOS	4
Prosthetic and orthotic services	2	2	RPRSHOS	4
Robot-assisted walking therapy	2	2	RBOTHOS	4
Simulated rehabilitation environment	2	2	RSIMHOS	4
Primary care department	2	2	PCDEPHOS	4
Psychiatric child/adolescent services	2	1	PSYCAHOS	2
Psychiatric consultation/liaison services	1	1	PSYLSHOS	1
Psychiatric education services	1	1	PSYEDHOS	1
Psychiatric emergency services	2	2	PSYEMHOS	4
Psychiatric geriatric services	2	2	PSYGRHOS	4
Psychiatric outpatient services	2	2	PSYOPHOS	4
Psychiatric partial hospitalization program	2	2	PSYPHHOS	4
Psychiatric residential treatment	2	2	PSTRTHOS	4
Radiology, diagnostic—Computed-tomography (CT) scanner	3	3	CTSCNHOS	9

(continued)

(continued)

AHA 2011 service categories	(1) Clinical intensity	(2) Investment intensity	Variable name	(1) * (2) service weight
Radiology, diagnostic—Diagnostic radioisotope facility	3	3	DRADFHOS	9
Radiology, diagnostic—Electron Beam Computed Tomography (EBCT)	3	3	EBCTHOS	9
Radiology, diagnostic—Full-field digital mammography	3	3	FFDMHOS	9
Radiology, diagnostic—Magnetic resonance imaging (MRI)	3	3	MRIHOS	9
Radiology, diagnostic— Intraoperative magnetic resonance imaging	3	3	IMRIHOS	9
Radiology, diagnostic—Multislice spiral computed tomography (MSCT)	3	3	MSCTHOS	9
Radiology, diagnostic—Multi-slice spiral computed tomography (64+ Slice CT)	3	3	MSCTGHOS	9
Radiology, diagnostic—Positron emission tomography (PET)	3	3	PETHOS	9
Radiology, diagnostic—Positron emission tomography/CT (PET/CT)	3	3	PETCTHOS	9
Radiology, diagnostic—Single photon emission computerized tomography (SPECT)	3	3	SPECTHOS	9
Radiology, diagnostic—Ultrasound	3	3	ULTSNHOS	9
Image-guided radiation therapy (IGRT)	3	3	IGRTHOS	9
Intensity-Modulated Radiation Therapy (IMRT)	3	3	IMRTHOS	9
Proton therapy	3	3	PTONHOS	9
Shaped beam radiation System	3	3	BEAMHOS	9
Stereotactic radiosurgery	3	3	SRADHOS	9
Retirement housing	1	1	RETIRHOS	1
Robotic surgery	3	3	ROBOHOS	9
Rural health clinic	2	2	RURLHOS	4
Sleep Center	2	2	SLEPHOS	4
Social Work services	1	1	SOCWKHOS	1
Sports medicine	2	2	SPORTHOS	4
Support groups	1	1	SUPPGHOS	1
Swing bed services	1	1	SWBDHOS	1
Teen outreach services	1	1	TEENSHOS	1
Tobacco Treatment/Cessation program	1	1	TOBHOS	1

(continued)

(continued)

AHA 2011 service categories	(1) Clinical intensity	(2) Investment intensity	Variable name	(1) * (2) service weight
Transplant, Bone marrow transplant services	3	3	OTBONHOS	9
Transplant, Heart	3	3	HARTHOS	9
Transplant, Kidney	3	3	KDNYHOS	9
Transplant, Liver	3	3	LIVRHOS	9
Transplant, Lung	3	3	LUNGHOS	9
Transplant, Tissue	3	3	TISUHOS	9
Transplant, Other	3	3	OTOTHHOS	9
Transportation to health services	1	1	TPORTHOS	1
Urgent care center	2	2	URGCCHOS	4
Virtual colonoscopy	2	2	VRCSHOS	4
Volunteer services department	1	1	VOLSVHOS	1
Women's health center/services	1	1	WOMHCHOS	1
Wound Management Services	2	2	WMGTHOS	4
Maximum Weighted Service-Mix Index				683

Chapter 10
Physician Practice and Disease-Specific Applications

10.1 Introduction

Physician practice applications to date have been limited due to the complicated nature of accounting for the performance of physicians with available data. Physician practice applications are often referred to as clinical applications or primary care physician models in the literature. Although physician practice on specific diseases is often the main focus of the applications in this area (Ozcan 1998; Ozcan et al. 2000), more generic models of physician production were also modeled (Chilingerian and Sherman 1997b).

Starting with diagnosis-related groups (DRGs) in the 1980s for the hospital payments, in the 1990s the US federal government extended the fixed pricing mechanism to physicians' services through Resource-Based Relative Value Scale (RBRVS) to achieve efficiency in health care delivery. The aim of these pricing mechanisms is to influence the utilization of services and control the payments to hospitals and professionals. However, the effective cost control must be accompanied by a greater understanding of variation in physician practice behavior and development of treatment protocols for various diseases (Ozcan 1998).

Patient outcomes research and studies of variations in clinical practice eventually resulted in the development of guidelines to disseminate information to practitioners for diseases that are common and/or costly for overall treatment of the condition (AHCPR 1994). Over the past several decades, researchers have demonstrated differences in the patterns of care being delivered for the same disease by physicians in the US. One of the most probable causes for this variation in the use of health care resources is differing physician practice styles. There is a growing concern about the efficiency in which health care services are delivered; thus inefficiencies emanating from the varying practice styles should be identified. DEA methodology helps us not only to identify the efficient practices, but also by using multiplier (weight restricted) models, one can further evaluate the impact of specific policy decisions (such as payment mechanisms to enforce utilization patterns) in health care.

Y.A. Ozcan, *Health Care Benchmarking and Performance Evaluation*,
International Series in Operations Research & Management Science 210,
DOI 10.1007/978-1-4899-7472-3_10, © Springer Science+Business Media New York 2014

DEA has also been used in health care for evaluation of physician practice patterns. Although limited research has been fielded, considerable potential is available to health care leaders. Chilingerian and Sherman (1997a) employed DEA to benchmark physician practice patterns as a potential approach for cost containment. They were able to demonstrate that some specialists practicing as primary care providers (PCPs) were more efficient than some general practitioner PCPs. In addition, Chilingerian and Sherman (1997a) were able to use DEA modeling in the identification of opportunities to manage high cost groups as a means of controlling costs. They estimated potential resource savings of about 30 % if all primary care physicians in the health maintenance organization (HMO) studied were to adopt the best practice patterns associated with the efficient primary care physicians.

As shown in the previous chapter for hospitals, conceptualization of a model for production of services needs to be identified for physician practices. This model will identify service production for this sector of providers and operationalize input and output measurements from available databases.

There are many challenges for practicing administrators and researchers to operationalize the inputs and outputs for a robust DEA model for physician practice service production. The culmination of research to date demonstrates most commonly agreed upon and available variables from claim-based databases to evaluate physician efficiency for common diseases are otitis media (Ozcan 1998), sinusitis (Ozcan et al. 2000), asthma (Ozcan et al. 1998b), cardiac surgery (Chilingerian et al. 2002), overall primary care (Chilingerian and Sherman 1997b), and diabetes (Testi et al. 2014).

10.2 Production of Services in Physician Practice

Inputs and outputs of physician practice follow the same logic used in hospital production, where patient treatments are measured as outputs and the resources used to produce these treatments as inputs. The only difference in production of the services between hospitals and physician practice is that we will be modeling the physician as the decision-making unit (DMU) rather than the organization (either solo or group practice). In addition, this model can be applied to a specific disease that is under evaluation or to a type of practice, such as primary care.

Physicians make decisions for each patient visit. These decisions include ordering various diagnostic tests, therapeutic interventions, and medications. Thus, depending upon the disease, patients' condition, and physicians' training, the magnitude of diagnostic, therapeutic, and prescription orders will vary. Hence, evaluating the performance of a physician who treats only a specific disease compared to a generalist physician should be avoided. However, this does not preclude evaluation of specific diseases treated by specialists and generalists (say primary care physicians). As long as a patient panel represents the treatment of a specific disease by different types of practitioners, one should be able to make comparisons.

When a specific disease is targeted for physician evaluation, the next step is to identify the inputs or the resources used to treat the patient. Patient treatment generally occurs over time. We may call these episodes or encounters.

In order to analyze the practice behavior of physicians, claims data must be converted to an episode base for each patient. This way, one can detect the patterns of services by each physician provider. Since episodes of patient care needs are different in terms of severity, one also has to identify those patients in various severity categories, retrospectively, at this stage. These severity categories will serve as a case-mix adjustment for the model outputs, as they will be explained later in discussion of outputs.

10.2.1   Physician Practice Inputs

An episode of a common disease starts with a visit to the physician's office, and various laboratory and radiological tests may be ordered. Some episodes of the diseases may conclude in a short time with a follow-up visit, say 3–4 weeks, yet others may take up to 3–6 months or longer. Depending upon the test findings, therapy and/or medications would be ordered. Some cases would be referred to a specialist. Again, depending upon the condition of the patient, other ambulatory clinics or hospitalization may be required. During the episode of the disease, the patient's condition may worsen, and emergency room interventions may be required. Utilization (variation) of these services also depends on the practice behavior, training, and experience of the physician, and his or her approach to risk (malpractice concerns). To simplify the unit of analysis, the physician would be identified as a DMU, and all resource consumption that occurred during an episode is attributed to his/her credit as a primary care physician (PCP).

10.2.1.1   PCP Visits

One of the main ingredients in the service production of physician practice is the patient visit to the physician's office. Depending upon the definition of the episode length of a disease, patients may have multiple visits either requested by their PCP or on their own initiative. Every visit claim made by the PCP's office to insurance companies (public or private) would register as an encounter in the claims database.

10.2.1.2   Specialists Visits

A patient referred to a specialist by a PCP or a patient-initiated specialist visit that occurred during an episode is considered as resource consumption attributable to the PCP's practice. Each of these would register as a specialist visit encounter in the database.

10.2.1.3   Ambulatory Clinic Visits

Some physicians refer their patients to ambulatory clinics, which are more technologically equipped than their offices. Thus, when this occurs, the number of ambulatory clinic visits by patients during the episode would be attributed to the PCP.

10.2.1.4   Emergency Room (ER) Visits

When medical emergency situations arise that the PCP or the PCP office is not equipped to handle, they refer the patient to the emergency room; this could happen during office hours or when a patient goes to the ER when the office is closed (nights and weekends or patient vacation/traveling). If the patient's condition is sub-acute and does not require hospitalization, the patient is discharged from the ER after appropriate care. When the patient's condition is acute and requires hospitalization after initial care in the ER, the patient is admitted. If these occurrences are connected to the ongoing disease episode, the number of ER visits would be attributed to the PCP.

10.2.1.5   Hospitalization

If the patient's condition is acute, the PCP may decide to admit the patient to a hospital for treatment, or the patient may be admitted through the ER. When such an occurrence is connected to the ongoing disease episode, the number of patient hospitalizations would be attributed to the PCP.

10.2.1.6   Laboratory Tests

The number of diagnostic tests, including various blood chemistry tests, culture tests, and so forth, ordered by the PCP connected to the ongoing episode of care would be accumulated and attributed to the PCP.

10.2.1.7   Radiology

The number of diagnostic or therapeutic radiology encounters ordered by the PCP connected to the ongoing episode of care would be accumulated and attributed to the PCP.

10.2.1.8 Medications

The cost of medications prescribed for the condition during the episode of care would be accumulated and attributed to the PCP.

10.2.1.9 Durable Medical Equipment

If the patient's condition requires durable medical equipment, such as portable oxygen units or wheelchairs, ordered by the PCP and connected to the ongoing disease episode, the cost of these would be attributed to the PCP.

10.2.2 Related Costs for Visits, ER, Hospitalizations, Lab, Radiology, Medications, and Durable Medical Equipment

Although visits, emergency room encounters, hospitalizations, and lab and radiology tests can be used as count variables in the physician performance model, having their associated costs provides more enhanced information to observe the economic differences between efficient and inefficient providers. These additional cost variables would be used in a post hoc analysis to assess the impact of efficiency. Ozcan (1998) showed that the average total cost of otitis media treatment of an episode by efficient providers amounted to $357. By contrast, for inefficient providers, the same treatment cost was $492; the cost was about 38 % higher for inefficient PCPs.

10.2.3 Physician Practice Outputs

Physician practice outputs are the patients that are in varying acuity conditions. Thus, it is prudent to differentiate the patients who seek health care for the particular disease or condition.

To accomplish this task, procedure codes for the physician claims need to be reviewed and categorized into severity groups based on categories from the Current Procedural Terminology (CPT) manual. CPT coding incorporates level of complexity in medical decision-making for outpatient and inpatient services. Based on the complexity level of decision-making, one can associate severity of the episode. A typical example of this is low, medium, and high decision-making complexity as a guide to identify the severity of each patient encounter as severity 1 through 3, respectively (Ozcan 1998). However, we must recognize that there may be a problem regarding the encounter severity scores due to CPT upcoding (CPT code creep) by physicians. Further discussion about this possibility and a suggested solution is shown in Appendix K at the end of this chapter.

Fig. 10.1 Outputs and inputs for a physician practice DEA model

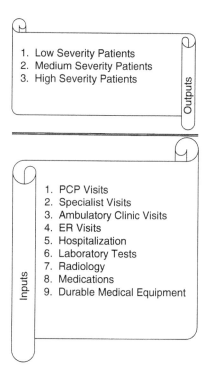

1. Low Severity Patients
2. Medium Severity Patients
3. High Severity Patients

Outputs

1. PCP Visits
2. Specialist Visits
3. Ambulatory Clinic Visits
4. ER Visits
5. Hospitalization
6. Laboratory Tests
7. Radiology
8. Medications
9. Durable Medical Equipment

Inputs

Chilingerian and Sherman (1997b) and Sherman and Zhu (2006) approached case-mix and severity adjustment using a simpler approach. They classified the patients based on gender and age groups, and the sheer counts of patients in these age-gender-based categories formed their seven outputs. In another study, Chilingerian et al. (2002) used DRG 106 and DRG 107 to identify low and high severity coronary artery bypass graft (CABG) discharges with and without catheterization in four outputs.

The ongoing identification of input and output variables for a physician practice service production via a DEA model is summarized in Fig. 10.1. This general model includes three outputs and nine inputs and encompasses the majority of the physician service production processes.

This model can be applied to various diseases to evaluate groups of physicians' performance for a particular disease. In the next section, three examples from the literature will be shown.

10.3 Physician Practice Applications

The applications of the physician practice model shown in Fig. 10.1 are applied to the specific diseases of: (1) otitis media, (2) sinusitis, and (3) asthma. Each disease's episode time and input (resource) usage may vary. Thus, for each disease, the model needs to be adjusted.

Fig. 10.2 Physician
practice styles (Source:
Ozcan 1998)

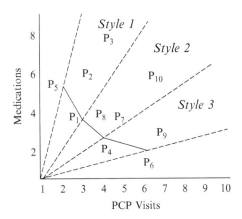

10.3.1   Measuring Physician Performance for Otitis Media

While there may be several different ways of treating patients, there is a growing emphasis on the effectiveness and efficiency of health care services, and these variation studies illustrate that there is an opportunity to identify best care practices, which optimize resource use while obtaining acceptable outcomes.

To illustrate this point, let us assume, in a very simple manner, that otitis media can be treated with a combination of primary care (PCP) visits and medications. Of course, there are many other resources (e.g., specialist visits, laboratory tests, hospitalization for severe cases) that may be needed to complete treatment. Furthermore, there may be differences in outcomes for otitis media treatment (e.g., cured cases, partially cured cases). There are multiple inputs to treatment and multiple outputs of outcome. These issues will be addressed after we introduce the concept. To assist in the conceptualization of practice styles using a combination of inpatient and primary care visits, we will first assume a uniform outcome, and we will later relax this assumption.

In order to fully explore best physician care practices, let us consider the hypothetical situation shown in Fig. 10.2, which depicts ten physicians who use varying combinations of the two resources to treat a specific disease. For example, physician P_5 utilizes five units of medications in conjunction with two primary care visits. Physician P_8 utilizes these resources in a different way, with four units of medications and four primary care visits, while physician P_6 uses two units of medications and six primary care visits. Based on each physician's preference (or practice behavior/style) of medications versus primary care visits in the treatment of this disease, one can group physician practice styles.

In this case, Fig. 10.2 displays three different possible styles based on these practice behaviors. Given a practice style, let us say style 2, we observe variation in resource utilization within the practice pattern. For example, physician P_{10} treats a condition by utilizing six units of medications and seven primary care visits, while physician P_1 achieves the same result with four units of medications combined with three primary care visits. Given practice style 2, one can argue that physician P_{10} is practicing less efficiently when compared to physician P_1 and P_4 Similar arguments can be made for physicians P_7 and P_8 for style 2. The same concept can also be extended to other styles. This conceptualization of practice styles recognizes historical variations, but it seeks reduction in inefficiencies once the style is identified. Although the reduction of inefficiencies is the primary goal when reducing the consumption of costly resources, one must identify all the efficient physicians from each practice style in order to achieve this reduction. With the physicians who are identified as efficient practitioners, we can form a "treatment possibilities frontier." Figure 10.2 illustrates such a frontier with physicians P_5, P_1, P_4, and P_6. This frontier is the efficiency frontier. Given their practice styles, there is no other physician who can practice with fewer resources than those on the frontier. The remaining physicians could change their practice behaviors in order to become more efficient.

To further develop this concept, one can challenge the more extreme or costlier practice styles. For example, from the cost perspective, style 1 would be preferred to style 2. From another perspective, style 1 and style 3 might be considered as outlier styles (one as risky, the other one as costly), and style 2 might be accepted as the standard. Thus, style 2 can be called the "quality assurance region" of practice behavior. The reader should note that reference to cost implies payments made by third-party payers (e.g., government or private insurance) for the services, not the actual cost of producing the services.

In our discussions there will be two main areas of focus. The first is simply looking at physicians involved in the treatment of otitis media and determining which physicians are indicated as efficient and inefficient in regards to input consumption and output production. The second examination will look at weight restricted DEA models and the ability to direct physician behavior towards practice styles found to be technically efficient.

10.3.1.1   Efficiency Focus

The measures for the otitis media evaluation include the number of treated patient episodes categorized to three distinct (low, medium, and high) severity levels (outcome measures) as outputs. The number of primary care physician visits, specialist visits, hospitalizations, laboratory tests, and medications (prescriptions) consist of the input measures. Separately, the costs of inputs were tracked. The unit of analysis is the physicians who treated at least 100 cases of otitis media. The DMU for the evaluation was 160 PCPs. Figure 10.3 displays the outputs and inputs for a physician practice for otitis media.

Analysis of 160 PCPs showed that indeed there is a practice variation for those PCPs with a panel of 100 or more patients. Of the 160 PCPs, 46, or 28.8 %, were classified as efficient. The remaining 114, or 71.2 %, were classified as inefficient compared to efficient PCPs. Given the levels of comparable inputs, the inefficient PCPs, on average, could have treated an additional 21.6 low severity, 4.4 medium

Fig. 10.3 Outputs and inputs for a physician practice—otitis media model

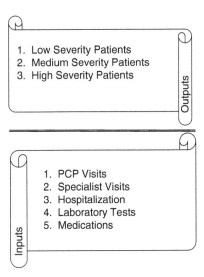

severity and 0.3 high severity otitis media episodes. Similarly, compared to efficient producers of otitis media treatment, the inefficient PCPs, on average, used excessive amount of inputs. For example, an average inefficient PCP's patients collectively use 118.2 PCP visits, 4.5 specialist visits, 94.6 hospitalizations, 324.3 prescriptions, and 91.9 lab procedures in excess of the benchmark created by efficient frontier PCPs.

Since physicians do not have control over who is going to appear in their office for diagnosis and treatment, we could set aside the issues related to outputs that could have been produced. However, it is necessary to examine the factors that the PCPs have control over, given the patient's condition of severity. For detailed discussion of these, the reader is referred to Ozcan (1998).

To gain a better understanding of efficient and inefficient practices, resources consumption per patient among efficient and inefficient PCPs was analyzed for three severity panels. The inefficient providers, irrespective of severity panel, tend to use higher amounts of PCP visits, hospitalization, and prescriptions. Inefficient PCPs with low and medium severity panels use more lab procedures per patient than efficient ones. Only one inefficient PCP with a high severity panel used fewer lab procedures per patient than comparable efficient peers.

To examine the service production differences between efficient and inefficient PCPs, overall output production and resource consumption can be analyzed. In this evaluation, efficient PCPs treated, on average, more medium and high severity patients. On the other hand, inefficient PCPs treated, on average, more low severity patients, although the difference is insignificant. In sum, there is a clear pattern in excessive resource consumption by inefficient PCPs, which suggests that their clinical practice for otitis media needs re-tooling by examining the practice patterns of the efficient providers, or by continuing education and adherence to established clinical guidelines.

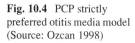

Fig. 10.4 PCP strictly preferred otitis media model (Source: Ozcan 1998)

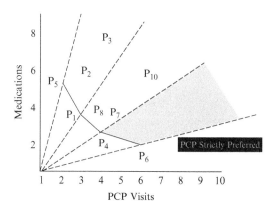

Similar to analysis of input consumption, examination of the cost of the inputs used by PCPs indicates that payments made by third-party payers (insurers) to PCPs, specialists, and pharmacies are significantly higher for inefficient PCPs. The payments made to hospitals and laboratories for those patients treated by inefficient PCPs were also higher but not significant. In general, an insurance company or network provider that is seeking cost-efficient and effective care providers for inclusion/exclusion of such providers to their panel of PCPs would generally look to total cost of treatment. In this case, average total cost of otitis media treatment of an episode by efficient providers amounted to \$357, whereas it was \$492 for inefficient providers, a \$135 (38 %) difference. With over 25 million otitis media-related visits in a year, this is not a sum that can be ignored by the health care industry.

10.3.1.2 Behavior Focus

In our previous example, illustrated in Fig. 10.2, there are ten PCPs and three practice styles. Practice style 3 can be defined as a PCP strictly preferred model (Fig. 10.4). Here primary care visits are designated as the preferred type of treatment, taking preference over everything else, especially over medications. This particular style's ratio constraints can be defined as PCP visits over specialty visits, PCP visits over hospitalization, PCP visits over medications, and PCP visits over laboratory tests. When restricted by these preferred ratio constraints, the efficiency frontier would only include that section, creating the desired practice style.

Style 2 can be defined as a balanced primary care otitis media model as shown in Fig. 10.5. This style of behavior has ratio constraints that prefer PCP visits over specialty visits, PCP visits over hospitalization, medications over specialty visits, laboratory tests over specialist visits, and specialist visits over hospitalization. Again, implementing these constraints (comparisons of physician behaviors) is done with respect to the frontier within style 2.

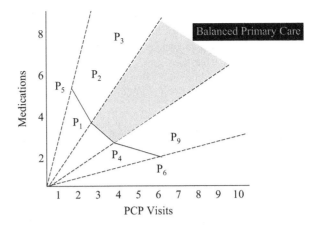

Fig. 10.5 Balanced primary care otitis media model (Source: Ozcan 1998)

To create the preferred ratio constraints that are used to define the practice styles, DEA weights (also referred to as prices or multipliers) are utilized. The desired ratio (s) are calculated using the input or output weights from each DMU. Then, for each ratio created, the minimum, first quartile, median, third quartile, and maximum values should be calculated. These values illustrate the distribution of the ratio and give the researcher options on what level to which to restrict it. How much restriction is placed on a particular ratio depends on the distribution level selected (usually median or third quartile values are selected initially); this application uses median values. These newly restricted ratios can be plugged back into the DEA model and restrict the use of those certain inputs and outputs needed to reach the efficiency frontier.

10.3.1.3   Implication of Weight Restricted Practice Styles

It is seen that the cost for treatment of an otitis media episode for both efficient and inefficient providers decreases as the models shift from practice as usual to a PCP strictly preferred style, and finally to a balanced primary care model. By restricting particular inputs and outputs, and directing all physicians to treat otitis media through a balanced primary care model, physicians would be able to provide the same quality care at an average savings of $93.10 per efficient and $21.53 per inefficient provider episode compared to the average cost incurred in the treatment of otitis media as usual.

The key is getting physicians to change their practice behavior so it falls within the output and input ratios that such a preferred style needs. This can be done by providing education to physicians on the necessary changes and creating financial incentives for those physicians that maintain ratios within practice style specifications.

Further studies can be conducted using such data sources that not only evaluate a PCP's performance on one disease category but also a majority of the PCP's practice, yielding an overall report card for the PCP in a given year. Using the

20/80 rule, one can determine for a given type of PCP 20 % of the diseases which encompass 80 % of the PCP's business. In this manner, a solid report card system generation mechanism can be established. This report card would provide a more accurate and reliable measurement of physician efficiency since the foundation of the methodology relies on optimization (Ozcan 1998).

10.3.2   Measuring Physician Performance for Sinusitis

Sinusitis, the inflammation of sinuses that often presents initially as a common cold, is another common health complaint with high treatment expenses. Thus, it is prudent to evaluate physician practice efficiency in managing patient care for this disease. Evaluations by researchers shed some light on physician practice in this area by examining the generalist versus specialist care, as well as regional variations. Past research has indicated that specialty care is more expensive, since they have adopted clinical protocols that result in higher utilization of services. In addition, specialty training has also been associated with more intensive care than generalist care.

Whether primary care physicians or specialists provide more efficient care was investigated by Ozcan and associates (Ozcan et al. 2000). Physician-level data were obtained from 1993 Medicaid claim files. Several decision rules were used to eliminate cases that did not meet study criteria (i.e., if a non-MD claim preceded an MD claim by more than 2 months, or if no MD claim was encountered during 1993). DEA was used to examine the utilization of PCP visits, specialist visits, ER visits, laboratory tests, and medications in the treatment of sinusitis. Primary care physicians were generalists, specialists were otolaryngologists, and they comprised the DMUs in this evaluation.

There were five input and three output variables as detailed in Fig. 10.6. The three output variables were organized into the three levels of severity based on CPT codes while adjustments were made for the potential for up-coding (see Appendix for details). Physician-level data were constructed from claim files, and those physicians with fewer than ten treatments of sinusitis in a year were removed from evaluation. This yielded 176 physicians (DMUs), of which 152 were generalists and 24 were otolaryngologists in the final evaluation.

Constant returns to scale (CRS) input-oriented model results showed that 38 (25 %) of the generalists were providing efficient care based on this model with an average cost of $442 per episode. Only 5 (21 %) of the 24 otolaryngologist were efficient, and cost of their treatment per episode averaged $720. More interestingly, cost per episode for inefficient generalists and otolaryngologists was much higher than their efficient counterparts. The inefficient generalists' cost of treatment per episode was $693 (57 % higher than efficient generalists) and their average efficiency score was 0.71. The inefficient otolaryngologists provided services at an average cost of $769 (only 7 % higher than efficient otolaryngologists) and their average efficiency score was 0.73. It should be noted that about two-thirds of these costs were medication costs.

Fig. 10.6 Outputs and inputs for a physician practice—sinusitis model

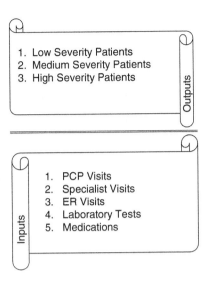

1. Low Severity Patients
2. Medium Severity Patients
3. High Severity Patients

Outputs

1. PCP Visits
2. Specialist Visits
3. ER Visits
4. Laboratory Tests
5. Medications

Inputs

The main conclusion was that there are no differences in technical efficiency between generalists and specialists in the treatment of sinusitis. However, specialists tend to use more resources and, hence, incur higher service costs. A possible explanation for the specialists using more resources was the higher acuity of their patients compared to generalists.

In a separate evaluation, using the same group of physicians (n = 176) and the same model presented in Fig. 10.6, Ozcan et al. (2000) evaluated the effect of practice variation in sinusitis treatment for metropolitan versus rural locations across the four regions of the State of Virginia. Ninety-eight (55 %) of the physician practices were in metropolitan areas, and the others were in rural locations.

Results showed that 24 (24 %) of the physicians located in metropolitan areas were providing efficient care with an average cost of $340 per episode. Only 19 (24 %) of the 78 rural physicians were efficient, and cost of their treatment per episode averaged $644. Additionally, the cost per episode for inefficient metropolitan and rural physicians was much higher than for their efficient counterparts. The inefficient metropolitan physicians' cost of treatment per episode was $603 (77 % higher than efficient metropolitan physicians) and their average efficiency score was 0.75. The inefficient rural physicians provided the services at an average cost of $830 (38 % higher than efficient metropolitan physicians) and their average efficiency score was 0.66. It should be noted that medications were 61 % of the costs for efficient metropolitan physicians, but 71 % for efficient rural physicians. The percentages of costs for medication for inefficient metropolitan and rural physicians were 69 and 73 %, higher than for their efficient counterparts.

Inefficient physicians located in the southwest region of the state were in most dire need of improved performance. The observed regional differences were attributed to lack of laboratories and competition (for medication dispensing) in rural regions of the state.

10.3.3   Measuring Physician Performance for Asthma

Community variation in treating asthma, as with many other medical conditions, has been noticed by researchers. In the Boston, Massachusetts area, evaluation of pediatric bronchitis/asthma admission rates was conducted by Payne and associates (Payne et al. 1995). They determined that approximately 4.4 % of admissions for bronchitis/asthma were inappropriate. In addition, sharp decreases in admission rates were experienced once the key hospital staff were notified of the research findings. Community variation leads many medical researchers and health care leaders to question the components of medical care and search for what constitutes the best practice of medicine. In addition, many health care leaders begin to think of potential cost savings if best practices are adopted.

Coventry et al. (1996) compared costs of treating asthma patients across different treatment settings. Using CPT codes and a database consisting of payments made under the Civilian Health and Maintenance Program for the Uniformed Services (CHAMPUS), the authors evaluated the cost of pediatric asthma care in four treatment settings: physician office, emergency room, hospital outpatient, or unknown. The cost of treating patients in each of the settings varied dramatically. For example, the amount paid for treatment of pediatric asthma was $36 in a physician office visit, $153 in a hospital outpatient setting, and $182 in the emergency room.

A study by Ozcan and associates (Ozcan et al. 1998b) using 1995 Medicaid claims from Virginia conducted an evaluation of PCP performance. The claims files contained all related visits, hospitalizations, and other resources used to treat the asthma patients. Files also contained detailed information regarding the date of service, identifier codes for provider and patient, procedure and diagnoses codes, as well as charge and payment information for each of the services provided. Descriptions of variables and measures used in this evaluation are shown in Fig. 10.7. As mentioned earlier, related costs for each of the input variables were available.

All diagnosis (ICD-9-CM) codes from 49300 to 49391 were used to extract encounters by providers who treated patients for asthma in 1995. The extraction of data generated 309,240 claims, which can be classified as follows:

- 38.43 % were for office visits,
- 1.12 % were for emergency room visits with subsequent hospitalization,
- 4.73 % were for emergency room visits without subsequent hospitalization,
- 0.90 % were for hospitalization without immediately preceding emergency room visits,
- 2.37 % were for clinic visits, and
- 52.44 % were for medications.

A Current Procedure Terminology, 1995 (CPT 1995) manual was used to categorize patient severity. CPT coding incorporates three complexity levels for the medical decision-making process. For example, low decision-making complexity occurs in a quarterly follow-up office visit for a 45-year-old male established

Fig. 10.7 Outputs and inputs for a physician practice—asthma model

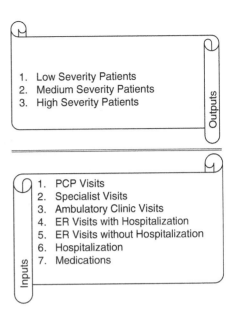

patient, with stable chronic asthma, on steroid and bronchodilator therapy. Such a visit might require 15 min of face-to-face time with the patient, whereas in moderate complexity cases 25 min of face-to-face time might be required. In contrast, high complexity decision-making typically requires 40 min of face-to-face time with the patient. Based upon the complexity of the medical decision-making process, three categories of severity were developed:

- low, with a severity score equal to 1;
- medium, with a severity score of 2; and
- high, with a severity score of 3.

The following decision rules were employed to construct an episode of asthma care:

1. The chronology of the events. If the first claim filed in 1995 was not for physician service, it was excluded from the current episode of treatment since it could be included in an earlier (1994) episode.
2. If a non-physician claim preceded a claim for a physician by more than 2 months, it was classified as the end of a previous episode.
3. If no physician claim was encountered in 1995, then such a recipient was deleted from the study database.
4. If a patient changed their PCP and was subsequently treated by a different PCP in a new time window without any referral during 1995, a new episode of care was created and subsequent claims were attributed to the second PCP.

By employing decision rules, all multiple claims to a specific provider were aggregated. The aggregated provider-based recipient claims constituted 110,209 utilization records classified as follows:

- 67.93 % for PCP visits,
- 2.65 % for specialist visits,
- 1.66 % for emergency room visits with subsequent hospitalization,
- 4.56 % for emergency room visits with no subsequent hospitalization,
- 1.02 % for hospitalization with no immediately preceding emergency room visit,
- 1.69 % for clinic visits, and
- 20.48 % for medications.

A PCP is defined as a general practice, internal medicine, and/or pediatric physician who treated asthma patients as evidenced in the data files. In addition to PCPs, a specialist might behave as a primary care physician when providing health care to asthma patients. In either case, all claims filed in chronological order for the patient were attributed to that particular physician. Reference to claims files was made previously. PCP use of a specialist referral was attributed when a specialist filed a claim for compensation subsequent to a compensation claim filed by a PCP. For the aggregated physician claims, 29.84 % were filed by general practitioners, 40.21 % by internists, 19.68 % by pediatricians, and 10.27 % by specialists.

PCPs who treated fewer than 50 asthma patients in a year were considered infrequent providers of asthma services and were deleted from the final database. The rationale for this cut-off point is simply that the performance of a physician may not be representative of physician capabilities when adequate numbers of patients are not treated. As a consequence, medical decision-making skills related to diagnosis and treatment of asthma may be sacrificed at the expense of a different practice pattern for the physician. After removing infrequent physicians from the database, 277 physicians remained for final analysis. Of the physicians remaining, 274 physicians were classified as primary care physicians (PCPs) and 3 physicians were classified as specialists. Analyses were carried out using only PCPs.

Table 10.1 presents the descriptive statistics for both outputs and inputs when treating asthma patients. On average, in 1995 PCPs in the final database were attributed with:

- treating 767 patient visits to PCPs,
- referring 49 patient visits to specialists,
- 5 patients who had emergency room visits with subsequent hospitalization,
- 16 patients who had emergency room visits only,
- 17 patients who were seen in the ambulatory clinics,
- 5 patients who were admitted to the hospital directly, and
- prescription of 1,206 medications.

These activities were for a panel of 135 patients consisting of 107 classified as low severity, 19 classified as medium severity, and 11 patients who were classified as high severity. Costs associated with treatment of asthma patients in this evaluation were higher than those identified by Coventry, Weston and Collins in their 1996 study, however, the pattern was nearly identical—the physician office treatment was least costly, followed by ambulatory clinic visits, emergency room, and

Table 10.1 Descriptive statistics for asthma episodes

Variables	Mean (Std. Dev.) N = 274
Outputs	
Low severity patients	107.36 (103.79)
Medium severity patients	19.36 (22.76)
High severity patients	10.53 (14.19)
Inputs	
Primary care physician visits	767.33 (1005.22)
Specialist visits	48.54 (94.06)
Emergency room visits followed by subsequent hospitalization	4.51 (6.98)
Emergency room visits only	15.70 (22.43)
Hospitalizations with no immediately preceding emergency room visits	4.82 (12.56)
Clinic visits	16.85 (52.69)
Prescriptions	1205.82 (1367.95)
Average costs (in $)	
Primary care physician visits	139.40 (117.76)
Specialist visits	486.00 (1658.55)
Emergency room visits followed by subsequent hospitalization	2579.03 (4076.26)
Emergency room visits only	241.80 (375.32)
Hospitalizations not immediately preceding emergency room visits	2611.47 (5267.38)
Clinic visits	228.43 (690.26)
Prescriptions	1206.03 (1417.73)
Total average cost	1070.31

admission. Within this database, the average PCP cost paid for the respective visits is broken down as follows:

- $139.40 for a PCP office consultations,
- $486.00 for specialist visits,
- $2,579.03 for emergency room visits followed by hospitalization,
- $241.80 for emergency room visits only,
- $2,611.47 for patients admitted to the hospital directly,
- $228.43 for clinic visits, and
- $1,206.03 for medications.

An input-oriented constant returns to scale (CRS) DEA model was evaluated, and the result of the average CRS efficiency score was 0.72. The model identified 156 (56.93 %) physicians as efficient, whereas 118 (43.07 %) were considered inefficient. The efficiency score for inefficient DMUs averaged 0.68 (Table 10.2).

The inefficient physicians, on average, treated 8.68 fewer low severity patients, 4.41 fewer medium severity patients, and 2.36 fewer high severity patients than their efficient physician counterparts. The inefficient physicians tended to use more resources compared to efficient physicians. For example, the excesses (in comparison to efficient physicians) included:

Table 10.2 Efficiency results

Efficient DMUs		n = 156	56.93 %
Inefficient DMUs		n = 118	43.07 %
Variables	n	Mean	Std. Dev.
Efficiency			
Efficient DMU included	274	0.861	0.232
Efficient DMU excluded	118	0.677	0.257
Output shortages			
Low severity patients	20	8.68	5.66
Medium severity patients	50	4.41	3.69
High severity patients	45	2.36	1.95
Input excess			
PCP visits	4	415.52	237.38
Specialist visits	50	62.65	88.86
ER visits with hospitalization	45	3.86	5.04
ER visits only without hospitalization	35	7.6	8.04
Hospitalization without ER visits	50	6.77	15.08
Clinic visits	34	29	54.02
Prescriptions	52	783.1	1064.1

- 415.52 PCP visits,
- 62.65 specialist visits,
- 3.86 emergency room visits followed by hospitalization,
- 7.60 emergency room visits only,
- 6.77 direct hospitalization,
- 29.00 clinic visits, and
- 783.10 prescriptions.

Table 10.3 presents the number of asthma patients in three categories of severity that the inefficient PCPs should increase in order to bring their practice to the efficiency frontier: 1,024 for low severity; 520 for medium severity; and 278 for high severity. It can be further broken down to a reduction in inputs of 49,031 PCP visits, 455 emergency room visits followed by hospitalization, and 897 emergency room only visits.

Numbers in parenthesis (from Table 10.3) show the number of inefficient PCPs for each input (from Table 10.2), and savings are the cross product of reduction column multiplied with costs (from Table 10.1).

As for the costs associated with caring for asthma patients, there were no significant differences for most input variables except for prescription payments. Inefficient PCPs tended to generate charges (payments) higher than their efficient peers. However, the use of medications was not determined to be a significant variable. This implies that inefficient PCPs tended to prescribe more expensive medicines for the patients they see. The inefficient physicians may, for example, prescribe at the same rate as their efficient peers; however, the inefficient providers may be prescribing more expensive medications when less expensive medications

Table 10.3 Total increase and reduction in outputs, inputs, and cost for inefficient PCPs

Variable	Increase	Reduction	Savings ($)
Outputs			
Low severity patients	1,024		
Medium severity patients	520		
High severity patients	278		
Inputs			
PCP visits		$(4) \times 415.52$	231,694
Specialist visits		$(50) \times 62.65$	1,522,395
ER visits with hospitalization		$(45) \times 3.86$	447,978
ER visits without hospitalization		$(35) \times 7.6$	64,319
Hospitalization without ER visits		$(50) \times 6.77$	883,983
Clinic visits		$(34) \times 29$	225,232
Prescriptions		$(52) \times 783.1$	49,110,989
Total potential savings in $			52,486,589

will afford the same outcome. One possible explanation for this is that inefficient physicians may be prescribing medications for which there are no commercially available generic substitutes, thus resulting in higher payments for brand-name medications. If the inefficient PCPs were brought to the efficiency frontier, there could be a potential saving of $52,486,589 of which $49,110,989 (93.6 %) are for prescription payments.

10.3.3.1 Limitations

A difficult issue to address in many health care studies that rely on secondary, or administrative, data is related to adjusting the data for differences in patient severity of illness. Patient severity is an important adjustment to be made due to differences in resource consumption, mortality, etc., and is generally performed on the basis of the patient mix considering age, gender, race, or other readily available methods. Typically, sicker patients consume more resources than patients who are not as severe. Asthma patient severity is clinically gauged based largely upon the patient's peak expiratory flow rate (PEFR). According to the National Institutes of Health (NIH 1991), chronic mild asthma results in PEFRs that are ≥ 80 % of the individual's personal best or individual norms. Chronic moderate asthma results of PEFRs are in the 60–80 % of patient personal best (or individual norms), and chronic severe asthma is indicated when PEFRs are <60 % of personal bests/individual norms. In consideration of resource consumption, a truly severe asthma patient, as determined by clinical indicators, may initially be seen in the emergency room and, failing satisfactory progress with treatment, might be admitted to the intensive care unit. A less clinically severe patient may be treated in the emergency room and released. Yet another patient diagnosed with asthma may be able to perform regular daily living activities or compete in world-class athletic events with only a few regular follow-up visits with their physician to discuss any problems they may have noticed and perhaps receive a medication refill. These examples of three patients with three clearly different levels of resource consumption poignantly identify the need for an accurate method of adjusting data for severity of illness when comparing resource utilization across physicians. In addition, the same patient can, on diverse occasions, present either as asymptomatic or as experiencing mild, moderate, or severe asthma attacks.

In most administrative databases, however, such as the data employed in this evaluation, clinical measures of illness severity are not readily available. As a consequence, using CPT codes as an indicator of the level of decision-making required to determine the severity of the patient may not accurately reflect physiological conditions of a patient in terms of their severity. Furthermore, it is thought that physicians may be tempted to up-code to a higher level of complexity in order to maximize reimbursement for the procedure or office visit. Consequently a patient visit coded as medium severity may actually be low severity in terms of the guidelines found in the CPT coding manual. In a case study by Robinette and Helsel, up-coding rates for 1991 were as high as 7.4 %. Specifically, they looked at situations where a 99245 consultation code was billed when a 99215 office visit would have been more appropriate (or cases where initial office visits were charged for established patients). Following review, the authors noted a precipitous drop in up-coding rates, and by the fifth quarter, found only 0.1 % up-coding (Robinette and Helsel 1992). On the other hand, a patient with a tendency to experience severe episodes of acute asthma may only require a brief (low severity) office visit (due to their past experiences with and education about asthma) to obtain expensive medications to prevent acute exasperation of the disease.

Coding visits to the emergency room for severity and coding hospital admissions for severity becomes a bit more tedious. CPT codes do not differentiate these areas as to whether or not they consist of a high degree of decision-making expertise or a low degree of decision-making expertise. The tendency to consider emergency room visits and hospitalizations as higher severity treatment than a standard office visit might initially appear logical; after all, a patient must be quite sick to present to the emergency room. In consideration of the data obtained, this may not be a valid assumption, since many Medicaid patients do not have primary care providers who follow the patient on a regular basis in a physician office setting. Instead, the Medicaid patient may have a tendency to be seen in the emergency room, even if only for a medication refill. Albeit an inefficient delivery mechanism for routine care, many Medicaid patients simply do not have the benefit of an assigned primary care provider. Admittedly, this may be changing with the implementation of capitated payment mechanisms for Medicaid patients, which require their enrollment on the practice panel of a primary care provider. Despite the difficulties associated with using CPT codes, patient severity as identified in our study did meet our expectations that the majority of patients would be classified as low severity, followed by a smaller number of medium severity patients, and even fewer numbers of high severity patients.

10.3.3.2 Summary of the Asthma Evaluation

Overall, 57 % of the physicians were efficient and 43 % were inefficient in this study. We found that inefficient PCPs in Virginia who treated 50 or more Medicaid asthma patient encounters treated fewer patient visits and more prescribed medications, which resulted in higher payment for medications than the efficient PCPs had during 1995. Moving inefficient physicians to the efficiency frontier as practiced by their peers has the potential of considerably decreasing Virginia's annual expenditure for treatment of patients diagnosed with asthma.

In order to improve their efficiency, the inefficient PCPs should increase their production function, i.e., increase the number of patient encounters they treat. In addition, all physicians should be encouraged to engage in comprehensive patient education/health education programs as an effective preventive measure. Perhaps when a system of reimbursement is fully implemented that encourages providers to educate the patient, thus reducing the need for service utilization, educational programs will play a more vital role in physician practice patterns for treatment of asthma. In addition, physicians and other practitioners who prescribe medications should always actively consider providing medications that provide the desired physiological response while considering the financial impact of their prescribing habits.

Further consideration should be given to the study of asthma treatment practice efficiency. Especially in the area of patient education, based on the amount of education provided to patients, one can assess how much practice efficiency could be achieved. It is also suggested that future studies risk adjust based upon clinically valid measures of disease severity, rather than on complexity of the medical decision-making process. In addition, an interesting area for further research would be to compare provider efficiency based how frequently they follow clinical practice guidelines (e.g., all the time, some of the time, or never).

10.3.4 Measuring Physician Performance for Diabetes Mellitus

A study by Testi et al. (2014) evaluated the physician performance in treating diabetes mellitus using general practitioner data from the Ligure region of Italy. According to Nicholoson and Hall (2011), diabetes mellitus (also known as diabetes II) affects approximately 240 million adults worldwide and is expected to increase to 380 million by year 2025. Authors examined 200,000 records of patients who were treated by 140 physicians, and were able to evaluate 96 physicians using alternative DEA models. Their model included three outputs and four inputs as shown in Fig. 10.8.

The three severity levels of the patients were determined based on a combination of age and co-morbidities as follows: (1) low severity patients were those less than

Fig. 10.8 Outputs and
inputs for a physician
practice—diabetes model

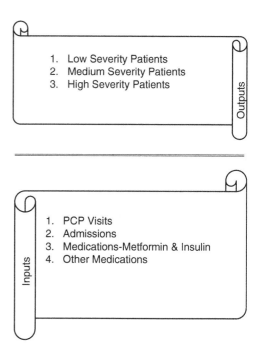

65 years old with no co-morbidity, (2) medium severity patients were 65 years or older with no co-morbidity, and (3) high severity patients were 65 years or older and had co-morbidities. The inputs consisted of primary care physician (PCP) visits, admissions to the hospital, use of diabetes medications (metformin and insulin), and other medications. The study measured not only the efficiency of practices but also evaluated the effectiveness of the treatments by what they called "appropriateness." This measure was created using a weighted score based on whether the physician checked: (1) hemoglobin and alpha 1 once every year, (2) creatinine once every 15 months, (3) microalbuminuria once every 15 months, (4) low density lipoprotein (LDL) once every 15 months, and (5) smoking. The weighted score was standardized to range between 0 and 1.

The study results using variable returns to scale model an average efficiency of 86 %. Using the bootstrap method discussed in Chap. 8, the biased corrected average efficiency score was 78 %. The authors also examined three weight restricted models (see Chap. 4) where: (1) drugs preferred over admissions, (2) visit preferred over admissions, and (3) both drugs and visits preferred over admissions. These restricted models compared to the base model had lower efficiency scores and a lower number of physicians stayed on the efficiency frontier as expected. More interestingly, the appropriateness scores (ranged between 0 and 1) averaged 0.36. The authors clustered the physicians based on efficiency scores (low <1, high $= 1$) and appropriateness scores (low <0.9, high ≥ 0.90) to group them for their performance in treating diabetes mellitus. There were only two physicians classified as best performers whose efficiency score was perfect and had higher than a 0.9 appropriateness score. There were 33 physicians who had high efficiency but less than a desirable appropriateness score. Another interesting finding of this study is that the remaining 61 inefficient physicians were also classified as ineffective with appropriateness scores of less than 0.90.

10.4   Summary

This chapter provided general guidelines for a physician practice performance model and its operationalization using generally available claims databases. Furthermore, development of these models connected to research conducted in the past. Using the presented model, several applications of disease-specific physician practice models were discussed, including otitis media, sinusitis, and asthma.

Appendix K: CPT-Based Claim Processing and Data Development (Source: Ozcan 1998)

K.1 Procedures for Development of an Episode

The development for CPT-based severity classification requires structuring multiple visits to a particular provider within the time frame (i.e., year). For example, a patient could have two visits to one provider, and 6 months later he/she can go to another provider. Thus, all multiple claims to a specific provider should be aggregated to a single-level claim file for the primary care provider (PCP).

In the subsequent stage of data structuring, claims would be sorted based on the recipient's age (in terms of calendar days) at the time of service and the claim patterns would be examined. In the chronology of events based on aggregated provider claims, different patterns would be identified to develop decision rules for the identification of episodes, hence the inclusion/exclusion of various claims to the final database. Decision rules associated in this stage include:

- In the chronology of the events, if non-physician claims were preceded by a physician claim, and they were more than the usual episode time apart (2 months for otitis media), they can be ruled out as the end of an earlier episode which the provided time window did not have sufficient information to build as part of the current episode.
- If no physician claim is encountered, then the whole claim stream for the particular recipient can be deleted.

These decision rules enabled physician claims to serve as the trigger for the start of an episode. On the next level, the decision rules assessed whether the encounter with the physician was with a PCP or a specialist. One can also observe that there could be instances when specialists are acting as PCPs.

Once the PCP is identified in the claim stream, all claims should be followed in the chronology of the claims for the recipient that were attributed to that PCP. These should include referrals to specialists, ER, inpatient hospitalization, pharmacy, and lab claims. The same patient, however, could change his/her PCP in time and go to another PCP in a different time window within the evaluation period. Claims following such instances can be attributed to those PCPs who were taking care of the new patient, hence the start of a new episode. If a claim was filed by a specialist following a claim by an internist, pediatrician, or family/general practitioner, this particular claim can be attributed to a PCP as part of specialist use in the treatment of care.

Since the unit of analysis for the evaluation is the PCP, the final aggregation of the data should be conducted by identifying a number of recipients for each physician who acted as the PCP for the patient's episode. This way, for the relevant disease, patient panels for each PCP during an evaluation period can be identified (Ozcan 1998).

K.2 CPT Code Creep

The prospective payment system (PPS) has always depended on the accurate reporting of clinical diagnoses and procedures. If errors are present in the reporting process, over-reimbursement or under-reimbursement of services can occur. Since the implementation of the PPS, there have been increases in the average case mix index. Because each percent increase in the case mix index corresponds to large growth in revenue for providers (Carter et al. 1990), this increase has been closely examined.

Payers of health care services are concerned that a majority of this change is due to upcoding. Upcoding, or code creep, is when a provider bills for services that are more extensive or intensive than the ones really performed; services are coded as higher weighted diagnoses, tests, or procedures, when there is no change in the actual resources needed or used. Payers believe that much of the case mix increase has occurred because the PPS gives providers an incentive to code more completely, and in cases of ambiguity, to assign the most highly weighted or complex diagnosis or procedure as principal. By contrast, providers have argued that most of the change in the case mix index is correct and reflects a mix of more complex cases. They believe the increase has transpired because with the implementation of managed care, the less complex, lower weight cases have been moved outside the traditional medical setting.

Recent evidence tends to illustrate that most of the rise in the case mix index is an accurate reflection of increasing complexity (Carter et al. 1990). Studies have found that, on average, only one-third of claims have coding errors (Bailey 1990; Hsia et al. 1992; Siwolop 1989; Shwartz et al. 1996) and that this number can fall below 10 % when dealing with some CPT codes (Javitt et al. 1993). Providers may have under-coded prior to PPS because it made little difference in their payment. The implementation of PPS may have incented doctors to be more accurate about diagnosing and classifying procedures in order to get the proper reimbursement. Nevertheless, in order to overcome the possibility of CPT code creep, we devised an adjustment algorithm so that the severity of the patients was close to actual occurrences.

K.3 Adjustment Algorithm

The number of PCPs identified needs to be clustered for post-hoc evaluation based on the severity weight class of the patient panels they have seen during the year. The clustering can be done using an index of severity measures that incorporates a weighted volume of patients from each severity class. More specifically, it is assumed that the PCP's workload for the patients in the second tier of severity would be three times as much, relative to the first peer. Similarly, the PCP's workload for patients in the third tier would be three times that of the second tier's severity, or nine times those of the first tier's severity. Using the following weighing formula, each PCP's volume/severity workload can be indexed (I_i), and the cluster weight (C_j) for each PCP can be calculated as follows:

$$I_i = \frac{w_i}{\sum\limits_{i=1}^{n} w_i/n} \qquad i = (1, \ldots, 3)$$

$$C_j = \sum\limits_{j=1}^{m} P_{ij} * I_i \qquad (i = 1, .., 3; \ j = 1, \ldots, m)$$

where P_{ij} represents the number patients in the ith class of severity for the jth PCP.

As an example, the index values (I_i) calculated in Ozcan (1998) using 160 PCPs were 0.23, 0.69, and 2.08 for respective severity categories. Cluster weight distribution (C_j) ranged from 0.2016 to 0.7479. Results of the adjustment algorithm showed 6 PCPs were classified in the high severity/volume cluster, 22 PCPs in the medium, and the remaining 132 PCPs were designated to the low severity/volume cluster. This representation fit reasonably well to expectations.

Chapter 11
Nursing Home Applications

11.1 Introduction

"Nursing home facilities provide care to people who can't be cared for at home or in the community. Nursing homes provide a wide range of personal care and health services. For most people, this care generally is to assist people with support services such as dressing, bathing, and using the bathroom, for people who can't take care of themselves due to physical, emotional, or mental problems." (eldercare.health-first.org).

Nursing homes are significant health care providers in developed nations. As the life expectancy of the population has increased over the years, demand for nursing home services has also increased. The population of the US over 65 years old has increased to about ten percent during the past decade. The number of people over 85 years old increased by more than one-third (36.8 %). The percentage of persons with out-of-pocket expenses was the largest in the age group of those over 65 years; more than 96 % of persons over 65 had out-of-pocket expenses that were more than $1,000.00 (National Center for Health Statistics, United States 2005).

There are over 1.5 million residents of nursing homes over 65 years old in the US, and more than half of them are over 85 years old. In US national health expenditures, nursing home care expenditures amounted to $110.8 billion in 2003. Kemper et al. (2005) noted that as the leading edge of the baby boom generation turns 65 in 2011, the country will have to deal with a retirement boom and an increasing need in long-term care for at least the next two decades. In 2005 the average time lived after age 65 was 17.8 years, while the average time of long-term care needed was 3.0 years (2.2 for men and 3.7 for women), and 69 % of people will need any type of long-term care (Kemper et al. 2005/2006). According to the Centers for Medicare and Medicaid Services (CMS) Website, in 2005 about

Content of this chapter largely supported through research conducted by Nailya DeLellis, doctoral candidate, for a class project under the supervision of the author.

nine million people over 65 years needed long-term care, and by 2020, 12 million older Americans will need long-term care.

There are many different types of long-term care, such as community-based services, home health care, in-law apartments, housing for aging and disabled individuals, board and care homes, assisted living, continuing care retirement communities, and nursing homes with different levels of costs depending on geographic location and services provided. While long-term care can be provided at home, in the community, or in assisted living facilities, Medicaid is the major purchaser of long-term services, paying for approximately 50 % of all nursing homes expenditures and 70 % of all bed days (Grabowski 2001).

Increased demand for long-term care will require higher efficiency of institutions providing such care, as well as knowledge about the particular characteristics of efficient nursing homes.

11.2   Nursing Home Performance Studies

The question of efficiency of nursing homes is studied in the US as well as around the world. Ozcan et al. (Ozcan et al. 1998c) used Data Envelopment Analysis (DEA) to determine technical efficiency of skilled nursing facilities in the United States. The study used a 10 % national sample of 324 skilled nursing facilities and led to the conclusion that not-for-profit/for-profit status affects the mode of production. The study shows that greater efficiency is associated with higher occupancy and a larger percentage of Medicaid patients, and lower efficiency is associated with a higher percentage of Medicare patients.

Other studies examined the relationship between efficiency and particular characteristics of nursing homes. Gertler and Waldman (1994) analyzed managerial efficiency and quality in for-profit and not-for-profit nursing homes and found that for-profit nursing homes have approximately 15.9 % lower costs, but not-for-profit homes provide 3.9 % higher quality. Kleinsorge and Karney (1992) examined causes of inefficiency within a nursing home chain; the authors mentioned that the inclusion of quality measures affected the evaluation of home efficiency. Hicks et al. (1997) used Missouri Medicaid cost reports for 403 nursing homes to examine contributors to cost of care. The study found that mid-sized facilities with 60–120 beds reported the lowest per resident day (PRD) costs; PRD expenses for aides and orderlies were higher in tax-exempt facilities, and investor-owned facilities showed significantly greater administrative costs PRD. Fizel and Nunnikhoven (1993) examined efficiency of nursing home chains on a sample of 163 Michigan nursing homes and found that chain nursing homes have a higher mean level of efficiency than independent facilities.

Knox et al. (2004) examined the link between compensation and performance in for-profit and not-for-profit nursing homes in Texas. To measure facility performance (resource allocation efficiency by firm management), the study used cost and profit functions. The results of the study show that the highest paid administrators allocate their firm's resources in the most efficient way, and generally compensation of management is strongly influenced by firm size and capacity utilization. Vitaliano and Toren (1994) analyzed cost and efficiency in 164 skilled nursing facilities and 443 combination skilled and health-related facilities, using a stochastic frontier approach. The study did not find a change in efficiency between 1987 and 1990 or any difference between for-profit and not-for-profit homes.

Fried et al. (1999) used a sample of nursing homes in a nonparametric, linear programming, frontier procedure study to assess managerial efficiency that controls the external operating environment.

Banks et al. (2001) studied strategic interaction among hospitals and nursing facilities, and links between payment system structure, the incentive for vertical integration, and the impact on efficiency. The study used a static profit-maximization model of the strategic interaction between hospitals and nursing facilities and proposed that a reimbursement system affects efficiency and vertical integration of nursing homes. The authors suggested that prospective payment to nursing facilities would keep the incentive to vertically integrate with transferring hospitals, and would not increase efficiency without integration. At the same time, bundled payments would stimulate efficient production if nursing facilities are reimbursed for services performed.

Chattopadhyay and Ray (1998) used the output-oriented model of DEA to assess size efficiency of nursing homes, using 140 nursing homes from Connecticut during the year 1982–83. The study suggested that in some cases, for proper analysis a nursing home may be divided into smaller decision making units (DMUs). The study also compared the efficiency levels of for-profit and not-for-profit nursing homes. Christensen (2003) noted that nursing homes vary widely by size and used quantile regression to estimate cost functions for skilled and intermediate care nursing homes in order to account for this heterogeneity. The study found a relationship between the cost functions of nursing homes and output mix and variation of cost function across the cost distribution.

There are a number of studies of relationship between quality of care and efficiency. Schnelle et al. (2004) studied nursing home staffing and quality of care of 21 California nursing homes and found that the highest-staffed facilities reported significantly lower resident care loads on all staffing reports and provided better care than all other homes. Weech-Maldonado et al. (2003) analyzed the relationship between quality of care and costs of 749 nursing homes in five states and found a non-monotonic relationship between quality (pressure ulcer and mood decline) and cost (total patient care cost). Cawley et al. (2006) studied factor substitution (materials for labor) in nursing homes. The study found that higher wages are associated with greater use of psychoactive drugs and lower quality.

Castle (2006) analyzed characteristics of 607 nursing homes that closed from 1992 to 1998. He found a list of characteristics associated with a higher likelihood of closing, such as being in a state with lower Medicaid reimbursement, high competition, low number of beds, for-profit status, lower resident census, higher

Medicaid occupancy, and a lower quality of care. Rosko et al. (1995) used 461 Pennsylvania freestanding nursing facilities to analyze ownership, operating environment, and strategic choices in terms of labor efficiency. The study found that major factors of efficiency are ownership, occupancy rate, size, wage rate, payment source, and per capita income rather than quality. Not-for-profits respond to environment by increasing efficiency; for-profits operate at high efficiency levels all time. Aaronson et al. (1994) examined behavioral differences between for-profit and not-for-profit nursing homes and found that self-pay residents and Medicaid beneficiaries received better care in not-for-profit than in for-profit facilities.

In Europe, Laine et al. (2004) examined the association between productive efficiency and clinical quality in institutional long-term care for the elderly in Finland in 2001. The study used cross-sectional data from 122 wards in health-center hospitals and residential homes using DEA to create a production frontier. In this case, technical inefficiency in the production function was specified as a function of ward characteristics and clinical quality of care. According to the authors, there was no systematic association between technical efficiency and clinical quality of care. At the same time, technical efficiency was associated with a prevalence of pressure ulcers that is one of the indicators of poor quality.

Another study of Laine et al. (2005) provided conflicting evidence. The study examined the association between quality of care and cost efficiency in institutional long-term care in Finland using a stochastic frontier cost function and found that average cost inefficiency among the wards was 22 %. The authors found an association between the clinical quality indicators and cost inefficiency. A higher prevalence of pressure ulcers was associated with higher costs, and higher preva-lence of depressants and hypnotics drugs increased inefficiency. Crivelli et al. (2002) studied a cross-sectional sample of 886 Swiss nursing homes operating in 1998 to assess the relationship between cost efficiency, the alternative institu-tional forms, and the different regulatory settings. Björkgren et al. (2001) used DEA to measure the nursing care efficiency (in terms of cost, technical, allocative, and scale efficiency) of 64 long-term care units in Finland and found large variation in efficiency between units. The study shows that larger units operated more effi-ciently than smaller units and that allocative inefficiency is the result of using too many registered nurses and aides with too few licensed practical nurses. Blank and Eggink (2001) studied 110 Dutch nursing homes to examine a quality-adjusted cost function and found that quality was (partly) endogenous and was negatively related to input prices of nurses and other personnel, as well as the number of daycare patients and market concentration. Another study of Dutch nursing homes by Kooreman (1994) assessed technical efficiency with respect to the use of labor inputs and found that 50 % of nursing homes were efficient, while the study also found some evidence of a trade-off between labor input efficiency and the quality of care. Farsi and Filippini (2004) surveyed a sample of 36 public and private not-for-profit Swiss nursing homes studying cost efficiency and found similar efficiency of public and private nursing homes.

11.3 Performance Model for Nursing Homes

DEA base nursing home studies are summarized in Table 11.1 to gain perspective on the nursing home production process. Based on these studies, as in hospital studies, labor is the main common input. Many studies also included beds as inputs of the nursing home service production (Ozcan et al. 1998a, b; Fried et al. 1998; Björkgren et al. 2001; Dervaux et al. 2006; Laine et al. 2005). Non-payroll expenses in addition to FTEs and beds were included as inputs of DEA model by two of the studies (Ozcan et al. 1998a, b; Fried et al. 1998).

Conceptualization of outputs in these studies varied based on the access and the availability of the data. Nevertheless, outputs were based on what types of patients were cared for or patient days produced based on skilled or intensive care. The latter

Table. 11.1 Measures of inputs and outputs for nursing home DEA models

Authors, year	Inputs	Outputs
Sexton et al. (1989) (in Rosko et al. 1995)	6 labor inputs	Medicaid, non-Medicaid days
Nyman and Bricker (1989) (in Rosko et al. 1995)	4: Total nursing hours, total social workers hours, total therapists hours, total other workers hours	5: skilled nursing facility (SNF) patients, Intensive care facility (ICF) patients, limited care patients, personal care patients, residential care patients
Nyman et al. (1990) (in Rosko et al. 1995)	11 labor inputs	Number of ICF patients
Fizel and Nunnikhoven (1993)	Registered nurse (RN) hours, licensed practical nurse (LPN) hours, and aides/orderlies hours	SNF patient days and ICF patient days
Kooreman (1994)	Physicians, nurses, nurse trainees, therapists, general staff, and other personnel	Patients classified as physically disabled, psychogeriatrically disabled, full-care, and daycare
Rosko et al. (1995)	RN FTE, LPN FTE, Nurse Aid (NA) FTE, rehabilitation personnel FTE, and other personnel	SNF days and ICF days
Ozcan et al. (1998a, b)	Beds, FTE, non-payroll operational expenses	Self-pay inpatient days, government-pay inpatient days
Dervaux et al. (2006)	FTE auxiliary personnel and beds	6 groups of patients, by case-mix severity (from independent to requiring full-time surveillance)
Fried et al. (1998)	FTE RN, LPN, other (OEMP), and non-payroll expenses.	Inpatient days of skilled care and inpatient days of intermediate care
Björkgren et al. (2001)	RN FTE, LPN FTE, aides FTE, beds (proxy for capital)	Case-mix adjusted patient days
Laine et al. (2005)	RN FTE, LPN FTE, aides FTE, unit size (beds)	Case-mix weighted patient days

Fig. 11.1 Outputs and
inputs for a generic nursing
home DEA model

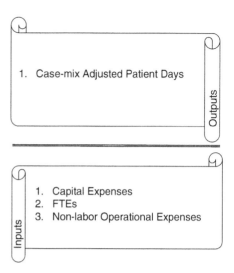

serves as a proxy for case-mix adjustment for the service outputs (Sexton
et al. 1989; Nyman and Bricker 1989; Nyman et al. 1990; Fizel and Nunnikhoven
1993; Rosko et al. 1995). On the other hand, other studies used case-mix adjusted
patient days (Björkgren et al. 2001; Dervaux et al. 2006; Laine et al. 2005), which
capture the service outputs in more appropriate way.

Based on the literature, we can define a generic nursing home service production
model to measure their performance. The inputs and outputs of this model can serve
as the guidance to develop future evaluations of nursing home performance. Based
on availability, variables in databases or their proxy measures can be used in the
evaluation. Figure 11.1 displays the generic nursing home performance model. It
should be noted that based on the intent of the evaluation, capital expenses, FTEs,
and non-labor operational expenses can be further broken down to categories for
detailed evaluation of excessive input usage for inefficient facilities. For example,
beds can be used as a proxy for a portion of the capital expenses; amortization,
depreciation, and other capital expenses can be used for the remainder of this
category. If the source of patient days is important in the evaluation, output can
also be categorized into groups for that purpose. For example, patient days can be
broken down by third-party insurance payers (government or private), or by self pay.

11.4 Data for Nursing Home Performance Evaluations

There are few sources of data to evaluate nursing home performance in the US. The
CMS database is one of these sources. Ozcan et al. (1998a, b) used this database to
evaluate skilled nursing home facilities. The CMS database contains fields to
identify the provider type, thus enabling researchers to extract appropriate information for nursing homes.

There is also state-based information available. States require periodic submission of provider information that includes patient-level-based data, as well as organizational data. Hospitals, long-term care facilities such as nursing homes, and other providers file this information with the appropriate state agency that administers these databases. For example, in the State of Virginia, Virginia Health Information (VHI) is responsible for health care data on hospitals, nursing facilities, physicians, and other health care providers (http://www.vhi.org). A Fizel and Nunnikhoven (1993) study used a comparable database from the State of Michigan; a Chattopadhyay and Ray (1998) study used the State of Connecticut database.

11.5   An Example of a Performance Model for Nursing Homes

In order to operationalize the model shown in Fig. 11.1, the example evaluation uses Virginia Health Information (VHI) data for fiscal year 2004. To obtain the efficiency score, this example uses the constant returns to scale (CRS) input-oriented DEA model, because nursing homes usually have more control over their resources (inputs), rather than outputs. As most DEA studies used beds as a proxy for capital investments, FTEs for the labor component, and the other expenses for operations, we operationalize the model with these measurements for the inputs. The choice of outputs was based on the facts that Medicaid is a major payer for long-term care and that self-paid patients are an important and valuable resource for nursing homes. Patient-days paid by other sources were included in the analysis as a third output. The detailed description of the input and output variables is provided below.

11.5.1   Inputs and Outputs of the Nursing Home Model

11.5.1.1   Inputs

Beds: Total number of Medicare, Medicaid, dual-certified beds, non-certified and adult care residence or other non-nursing facility beds.

Medical FTEs (RN and LPN): Full-time equivalents of registered nurse (RN), director of nursing, and licensed nurse practitioners (LPN) on staff.

Support FTEs (CNA): Full-time equivalents of certified nursing assistants.

Other FTEs: Full-time equivalents of administrator/assistant administrator, food service personnel, occupational therapists, dieticians, occupational therapy assistants/aides, physical therapists, physical therapy assistants/aides, speech therapists, activities personnel, social service personnel, other health professional and technical

Fig. 11.2 Outputs and
inputs for the example
nursing home evaluation

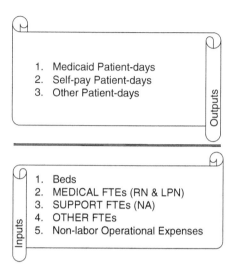

personnel, housekeeping personnel, maintenance personnel, and other non-health and
non-technical personnel.

Non-labor Operational Expenses: Contracts, home office, leases, medications,
physician fees and/or medical director, and other expenses.

11.5.1.2 Outputs

Medicaid Patient-days: Medicaid and Medicaid specialized care.

Self-pay Patient-days: Self-paid patient-days.

Other Patient-days: Medicare (Part A), HMO, PPO, other insurance, Veterans
Administration (VA) and other government not listed above, other patient days.

Figure 11.2 displays the output and inputs for the DEA model of the example
nursing evaluation.

The reader should note that the FTEs of certified nursing assistants were included
in the analysis as separate inputs. This labor category does not provide a specific
medical function for nursing home residents, but they play an important support role
for the medical personnel. This categorization of labor was also used in a number of
other studies (Rosko et al. 1995; Björkgren et al. 2001; Laine et al. 2005).

The values of the certain measures were scaled to ease the computation;
non-labor expenses were measured in millions of dollars and outputs were measured in thousands of patient-days. At the same time, full-time equivalents and the
number of beds were used without scaling.

Table 11.2 Descriptive statistics of input and output measures for nursing homes by bed size

	Nursing homes by bed size				
	<50	50–99	100–149	150–199	200>
Sample size	19	71	99	48	22
Minimum beds	8	54	100	150	200
Maximum beds	49	97	145	198	373
Not-for-profit	11	13	30	9	10
Hospital-based	12	2	2	1	0
Average beds	29	70.7	120.8	180.2	260.5
Average medical FTEs	9.0	13.5	24.1	34.1	52.2
Average support FTEs	10.0	23.0	40.1	59.0	91.8
Average other FTEs	13.2	25.9	40.0	55.3	86.6
Average medicaid patient days	3,145	14,276	24,694	38,730	55,502
Average self-paid patient days	2,935	4,260	7,115	7,499	14,913
Average other patient days	2,514	3,548	6,277	9,007	12,144

11.5.2   Homogeneous Groups and Descriptive Statistics

In order to create a robust homogeneous evaluation based on the scale of the nursing home operations, nursing homes were grouped by number of beds (Christensen 2003). Facilities were divided into groups by size (less than 50 beds, 50–99, 100–149, 150–199, 200 and more) as they were divided by the Centers for Disease Control and Prevention (CDC). Out of 259 nursing facilities in Virginia, 240 facilities have more than 50 beds and 22 have more than 200 beds, with the smallest nursing home having 8 beds and largest one having 373 beds. At the same time, all nursing homes with fewer than 26 beds are hospital-based (long-term care units).

Descriptive information on Virginia nursing homes by group and their inputs and outputs is shown in Table 11.2.

11.5.3   DEA Results

DEA results are presented in Table 11.3. It is interesting to observe that the average efficiency score increases as number of beds in a facility increases. The proportion of efficient DMUs across the size groups varies first in a decreasing pattern with the lowest percentage of efficient nursing homes in the middle groups, but then increases in the larger-size group nursing homes.

Another interesting issue in analysis of nursing homes' efficiency is the difference between for-profit and not-for-profit facilities. According to Ozcan (1998), for-profit status affects the mode of production; Rosko et al. (1995) found that not-for-profit nursing homes tended to respond to environmental changes by increasing efficiency while for-profit facilities operated at a higher level of efficiency irrespective of environment.

Table 11.3 Comparison of DEA results for nursing homes by bed size

	Nursing homes by bed size				
	<50	50–99 beds	100–149	150–199	200>
Number of efficient/ total DMU	15/19	47/71	54/99	30/48	16/22
Percent of efficient DMUs	79 %	66 %	55 %	63 %	73 %
Average efficiency St. dev	0.96 (0.092)	0.98 (0.050)	0.98 (0.040)	0.98 (0.037)	0.99 (0.013)
Minimum efficiency	0.63	0.73	0.77	0.86	0.95

Table 11.4 Excessive use of inputs and shortage of outputs by inefficient nursing homes grouped by bed size

		Excessive inputs				Shortage of outputs/ thousands of patient-days		
Nursing home groups and efficiency scores	Beds	Medical FTEs	Support FTEs	Other FTEs	Non-labor expenses	Medicaid	Self-pay	Other
Up to 50 beds, average efficiency score 0.83 (n = 4)								
Avg. inefficiency	1.298	1.420	0.924	1.668	0.181	0.074	0	0.095
50–99 beds, average efficiency score 0.98 (n = 22)								
Avg. inefficiency	1.162	0.814	1.090	2.677	0.084	0	0.458	0.037
100–149 beds, average efficiency score 0.95 (n = 45)								
Avg. inefficiency	0.279	3.336	3.193	6.265	0.082	0.319	0.239	0.250
150–199 beds, average efficiency score 0.95 (n = 18)								
Avg. inefficiency	0.740	2.803	5.790	6.399	0.114	1.672	0.979	0.189
200 or more beds, average efficiency score 0.98 (n = 6)								
Avg. inefficiency	4.299	6.187	1.844	9.352	0.318	1.677	0	0

Among Virginia nursing homes, 186 facilities are for-profit and 73 are not-for-profit. A separate DEA was run for the group of nursing homes of 100–149 beds as the group with the highest number of for-profit nursing homes. Among 99 facilities, 54 were efficient both in combined and separate analysis; 11 others were inefficient, but they had the same or similar (with a difference of 0.001–0.002) efficiency scores in both analyses. All facilities have a higher score being analyzed separately by for-profit status. An average increase in the efficiency score among for-profit nursing homes was 0.016 and among not-for-profit was 0.040.

One of the advantages of data envelopment analysis is its ability to estimate changes necessary for increasing the efficiency score for each of the inefficient DMUs. Summary information by groups is provided in Table 11.4.

Among all size groups of nursing homes, the lowest efficiency score of 0.83 is in the group with up to 50 beds. Almost all nursing homes except the group of 150–199 beds have the highest excess of labor inputs in other FTEs compared to medical FTEs and support FTEs. The average number of excessive beds ranges from a mere 0.3 beds to 4.3 beds, or from 1 to 25 in individual facilities, and can reach up to 10 % of current capacity. Excessive non-labor expenses range from $4,000 to almost $1.5 million. Shortage of patient-days as output ranges from 116 to more than 30,000 days. At the same time, the output shortage may require additional analysis, as different nursing homes may have different specialization. For instance, long-term care units of hospitals may be more involved in care for Medicare-paid patients.

11.5.4 Conclusion

The question of nursing homes' efficiency is widely discussed in the literature in its various aspects. As the population is getting older, the demand for long-term care, including care provided by nursing homes, will increase. In the situation of rapidly growing health care expenditures, it is important to use scarce resources in the most efficient way, and analysis of technical efficiency allows comparison of inputs to outputs ratios among different facilities. Analysis in this example shows that most nursing homes in Virginia operate efficiently; at the same time the average efficiency score is increasing with size of the facilities. The groups of smallest and largest nursing homes have the highest proportion of efficient facilities, while only about half of facilities are efficient in the group of nursing homes with 100–149 beds. While the efficiency score obtained through DEA estimates overall technical efficiency of decision-making units' information on inefficiency, shortage of outputs may require additional analysis on base of individual nursing homes.

This evaluation has its limitations. First of all, it is based on a sample of Virginia nursing homes only and therefore the results cannot be expanded to all nursing homes in the country. In addition, although the analysis used reports from fiscal year 2004, these reports were submitted from March to December 2004. The evaluation used only 1-year data and did not incorporate quality data.

Future evaluations of the subject may include the questions of interrelationship of quality of care and technical efficiency of nursing homes. Previous research on this issue provided mixed results. According to Schnelle et al. (2004), a higher amount of inputs (staff) used by a nursing home is associated with higher quality of care, while Weech-Maldonado et al. (2003) found a non-monotonic relationship between cost and quality. Laine et al. (2004) found no systematic association between technical efficiency and clinical quality of care. The quality models presented in Chap. 7 can be applied to nursing homes if appropriate quality data can be found. Another interesting issue relates to the changes in efficiency of nursing homes in response to changes in the environment, such as a change in demand for care, presence of substitute for care, or an increased quality requirement. This type of research would require a longitudinal study and can be carried out using the Malmquist model presented in Chap. 6.

11.6   A National Study of Nursing Homes Efficiency
and Quality Outcomes

A recent study by DeLellis and Ozcan (2013) examined the relationship between quality of care and efficiency of nursing homes to determine the characteristics of facilities that achieve higher quality and higher efficiency. The study's central objective was to examine the characteristics of efficient nursing homes as well as to determine the relationship between quality and efficiency of nursing homes. The study sample consisted of a 10 % random sample of 14,307 nursing homes in the US. The data for the study came from the 2008 Online Survey Certification and Reporting (OSCAR), the Area Resource File (ARF) database, the US Bureau of Labor Statistics and the US Bureau of Economic Analysis. The study variables included FTE of RNs, FTE of LPNs, FTE of nurses aides and trainees, FTE of others (as proxies for labor input variables), and total number of beds (as a proxy for capital input variable) as the five input variables; number of Medicare residents, number of Medicaid residents, and number of other residents (total number of residents minus Medicare and Medicaid residents) were the output variables. The study also included variables for efficiency score, quality indicators (rates of catheter use, physical restraints, bowel and bladder incontinence, pneumonia and influenza vaccinations, depression, unplanned weight change, pressure sores, and bedridden residents), market and facility characteristics (competition, system membership, ownership, and location), as well as acuity and activity of daily living indexes. The study used the input-oriented variable returns to scale DEA model.

Results of the DEA analysis showed 258 facilities (18 %) to be efficient, and 522 nursing homes had an efficiency score lower than the mean value of the sample. Results also showed that the average efficiency score was higher for nursing homes located in urban areas, for not-for-profit and governmental facilities, and for nursing homes located in counties with higher than average per capita personal income.

Additionally, nursing homes had higher average efficiency scores if they were located in counties with increased competition. Similarly, presence of a higher number of home health agencies in the county (15 or more) was associated with a higher efficiency score. System membership was shown to have no effect on nursing home efficiency scores. After transforming the DEA scores into dichotomous values (efficient and inefficient), a number of quality indicators (as simple proportions) were used to compare the quality of care in efficient and inefficient nursing homes. Results of the t-test showed that the quality measures associated with a high efficiency score were the use of physical restraints, the Pneumococcal vaccination rate, the percentage of bedridden residents, the use of catheters, and unplanned or significant weight change. Only one of the analyzed quality indicators (bladder incontinence) was lower in efficient nursing homes. The percentage of residents with clinical signs of depression and the percentage of residents with pressure sores were both lower in efficient nursing homes, although the difference was not statistically significant.

From a policy perspective, the study highlights the fact that higher efficiency in nursing homes does necessarily have to be attained by sacrificing high quality.

The results of the study also showed that some environmental factors such as a higher level of competition are positively associated with the efficiency of nursing homes. The authors noted the cross-sectional nature of the study, potential staff reporting inaccuracies in OSCAR reports, and variability of Medicaid payment rates between states as the study limitations.

11.7 Summary

This chapter provided general guidance for a nursing home performance model, and its operationalization is based on extensive literature review. Using generally available databases from either federal (CMS) or state databases, nursing home or other long-term care provider performance can be evaluated. An example nursing home performance model was presented using the database from the State of Virginia. Limitations of the past studies and suggestions for future evaluations are also provided. Lastly, a more recent study of nursing homes using a national sample is also featured. This study explored both efficiency and effectiveness (quality) dimensions of nursing home performance.

Chapter 12
Health Maintenance Organization (HMO) Applications

12.1 Introduction

Health maintenance organizations (HMOs) are a form of health insurance combining a range of coverage in a group basis. Physician groups and other medical professionals offer care through the HMO for a flat monthly rate with no deductibles. HMOs influenced financing and delivery of health care in the United States during the past several decades. By 1999, there were 643 HMO plans covering over 80 million people throughout the US (US Census 2000 on www.Allcountries.org).

There are very few empirical evaluations of HMO performance. Most of the studies in this area are concerned with whether hospitalization rates decreased, increased ambulatory-preventive services, or lowered health care costs. A significant study by Wholey et al. (1996) examined the scope of economies among various HMO types over a 4-year period (1988–1991) using the Health Care Investment Analysts (HCIA) database. The HCIA database includes all HMOs operating in the US. Similarly, Given (1996) conducted an evaluation of a sample of California HMOs. Both evaluations found that as enrollment increased, scale economies decreased due to labor intensiveness of the services. The Wholey study used a translog multi-product cost function to explain divestitures and mergers of HMOs. They used the number of commercial, Medicare, and Medi-Cal enrollees as outputs. Inputs consisted of costs related to hospitalizations, physician visits, clerical, and facility costs. Rosenman et al. (1997) evaluated the output efficiency of 28 health maintenance organizations in Florida.

12.2 HMO Performance Studies

The initial HMO efficiency study by Rosenman et al. (1997) showed clearly the reasons why studying the efficiency of HMOs is important. As indicated, managed care played a key role in health care financing and delivery of health care.

Y.A. Ozcan, *Health Care Benchmarking and Performance Evaluation*,
International Series in Operations Research & Management Science 210,
DOI 10.1007/978-1-4899-7472-3_12, © Springer Science+Business Media New York 2014

Compared to other insurance plans, HMOs provided relatively cheap and cost-saving products for the enrollees. The study explored the efficiency of HMOs and investigated whether efficiency varies across types of plans and ownership status.

Through existing literature review, several factors associated with HMO efficiency were discussed, including ownership (i.e., hospital, physician, and insurance company), an HMO's model type (i.e., staff model, group/network model, independent provider associations (IPAs)), tax status (for profit and not-for-profit) and market power.

The study was a cross-sectional design using 1994 HMO report data from the Florida Department of Insurance. A total of 28 HMOs were samples as decision making units (DMUs). Output variables included the total number of enrollees in the plan. This study further disaggregated enrollees by three kinds of payer-mix: Medicare, Medicaid, and Commercial. The reason for doing this was to crudely adjust for the differences associated with the age and income of enrollees in order to control for variations in health care utilization patterns among enrollee types. Input variables included total assets as a proxy for capital input, and total administrative and medical care expenses as a proxy for labor inputs.

Factors that may influence input efficiency included structure (model type), profit status, ownership, mix of enrollees (age, acuity level), and external market characteristics (competition, available physicians, and excess hospital capacity). The functional form used in this study is different from others, but the concept is the same.

Overall, 67 % of the HMOs were efficient. There were few differences among HMO type or ownership. Staffed models are most efficient. For-profit HMOs appear to be more efficient. Large HMOs are more efficient in terms of economies of scale. Plans with more homogeneous enrollment were more efficient with respect to economic scope. The number of Medicaid patients enrolled in the HMOs may be associated with inefficiency.

The first nationwide DEA evaluation of HMOs was conducted by Draper et al. (2000) using a stratified random sample of 249 HMOs that were operating in the US in 1995. The study used HCIA data and employed three outputs: physician ambulatory encounters, non-physician ambulatory encounters, and hospital patient days. Inputs of their model captured major group expenses for the HMOs including hospitalization, physician visits, other health care services, and administrative. They also divided HMOs into three different sizes based on enrollment. Those HMOs that had fewer than 40,000 enrollees consisted of the low enrollee group; the HMOs with 40,000–59,999 enrollees were identified as the mid-size group; and those with 60,000 or more enrollees consisted of the high enrollee group.

There were significant differences in efficiency scores between the HMO size groups. The low enrollee group ($n = 115$) and high enrollee group ($n = 102$) efficiency scores averaged 0.46 and 0.43, respectively. However, the mid-size enrollee group ($n = 32$) had an efficiency score of 0.31. Furthermore, those HMOs with no Medicaid enrollees ($n = 47$) had the lowest average efficiency score of 0.31.

Rollins et al. (2001) conducted a multi-year follow-up evaluation to Draper and associates' study. This study used the same inputs and outputs and the HCIA database over 5 years. The study evaluated 36 HMOs that were in business from 1993 to 1997.

The number of efficient HMOs increased from 21 (58 %) in 1993 to 29 (81 %) in 1997. The average efficiency score increased from 0.80 in 1993 to 0.94 in 1997. IPA type HMOs were the best performers followed by other types of HMOs. Of the 36 HMOs, 10 were the IPA type, and all of them achieved perfect efficiency by 1996 and sustained that in 1997.

12.3 Performance Model for HMOs

Based on Given (1996) and Wholey and associates (1996), one can discern that HMOs produce both health care services and health insurance coverage. On the other hand, evaluation of the production of the services provided by HMOs should capture the health care services. These health services include physician ambulatory encounters, non-physician ambulatory encounters, and the inverse of the hospital inpatient days. As HMOs tried to contain the costs, they encouraged the use of ambulatory encounters but discourage hospitalization by emphasizing preventive care. Thus, high-performing HMOs would like to reduce inpatient days. Hence, to reflect this goal in the DEA model, the inverse of the patient days is included as an output variable. When the DEA model attempts to optimize this variable by increasing this output, due to the inverse nature of the variable, it will be reduced. Consequently, those HMOs with less inpatient hospitalization would be considered efficient.

There are different categories of HMOs. The most common categories of HMOs are staff, independent provider association (IPA), network, group, and mixed. Depending upon the type of HMO, data availability may differ. For example staff HMOs employ their own physicians and may even have their own hospitals and clinics. Under such circumstances more specific input schemes shown for hospitals (Chap. 9) and physician practices (Chap. 10) can be considered. However, for a general evaluation of all type of HMOs, one should only rely on the common inputs for these organizations. The Draper et al. (2000) and Rollins et al. (2001) studies provide such common inputs by examining expenses of different resources consumed to produce HMO services.

Based on limited HMO studies one can conceptualize the outputs and inputs of the DEA model for HMOs as shown in Fig. 12.1.

HMO evaluation can be conducted by using various databases. Another data source would be the Centers for Medicare and Medicaid Services (CMS). In using the CMS database, patient-level data needs to be organized at the HMO organizational level. Furthermore, encounters need to be constructed by the evaluators.

Fig. 12.1 Outputs and inputs for an HMO DEA model

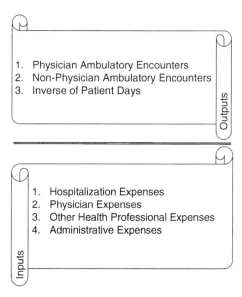

12.4 Summary

This chapter provided general guidance for an HMO performance model and its operationalization based on available literature. Using generally available databases from either federal (CMS) or other propriety databases, HMO performance can be evaluated.

Chapter 13
Home Health Agency Applications

13.1 Introduction

The home health care industry has been growing steadily in the United States. Home health care is defined as "skilled nursing, therapy, aide service, or medical social work provided to beneficiaries in their homes" (Medicare Payment Advisory Committee (MedPAC) 2005a, p. 106). The beneficiaries must be confined to the home and need intermittent, part-time home health care services. In the early- to mid-1980s, the Centers for Medicare and Medicaid Services (CMS), then Health Care Financing Administration (HCFA), had very strict eligibility criteria and annual limits on coverage for home health care. Annual spending only increased at a rate of 1 % from 1985 to 1988. A court decision broadened the guidelines for home health coverage in 1989, and it was transformed from a benefit primarily for short-term post acute hospital care to longer-term chronic disease care. Afterward, home health care spending grew at an annual rate of 30 % from 1989 to 1997 (Government Accountability Office (GAO) 2000).

A few factors contributed to this growth. Hospitals were discharging patients earlier and more surgeries were being done on an outpatient basis, requiring professional assistance at home. HCFA reviewed fewer claims for medical appropriateness, and since home health agencies were paid fee-for-service, they increased the services provided to maximize revenues. Finally, many patients preferred to remain in their home instead of being institutionalized (GAO 2000; Han et al. 2004).

In 1997, home health agencies were paid through an interim payment system (IPS) while CMS determined the prospective payment system (PPS) appropriate for home health reimbursements. The IPS had more stringent per-visit costs, and it initiated a Medicare revenue cap per beneficiary served. In order to make sure that their revenues covered their costs, the home health agencies had to become more

Content of this chapter is largely supported through research conducted by Cynthia Childress, doctoral candidate, for a class project under the supervision of the author.

Table 13.1 Medicare
home health care use
1997 and 2002

Measure	1997	2002
Number of beneficiaries served	3,558,000	2,550,000
Average visits per person served	73	31
Average visits per episode	36	19
Average minutes per episode	1,500	940
Average length of stay	106	56
Percent therapy visits	9 %	26 %

Source: *A Data Book: Healthcare Spending and the Medi-care Program,* MedPAC (MedPAC 2005b)

efficient. After the IPS, spending for home health dropped dramatically from 1997 ($12.8 billion) to 1999 ($8.4 billion), which was an annual rate of decrease of 32 %. In 2000, the PPS for home health was implemented, which changed the per-visit limits to a 60-day episode of care payment. Home health agencies that were able to provide appropriate care efficiently with fewer visits became more profitable. After PPS, Medicare spending for home health care slowly increased from 2001 ($8.7 billion) to 2004 ($11.2 billion) (GAO 2000; MedPAC 2005b).

The number of Medicare certified home health agencies dropped markedly after the introduction of the IPS in 1997, going from a high of about 9,800 in 1996 to a low of about 6,900 in 2002. Since 2002, the number of home health agencies has steadily increased to about 7,900 in 2005 (MedPAC 2005b). One-third of Medicare beneficiaries discharged from a hospital use post-acute care, and home health care is the second most common care after hospitalization, accounting for 11 % of hospital discharges.

Table 13.1 displays the changes IPS and PPS have induced in home health care use. The number of beneficiaries served, visits per person served, visits per episode, average minutes per episode, and average length of stay all decreased from 1997 to 2002. The mix of visits has changed toward more therapy (physical therapy, occupational therapy, and speech pathology) and less home health aide services because the system rewards therapy services.

13.2 Home Health Agency Performance Studies

Research on home health agencies has existed for a little over a decade, and most research focused largely on the impact of the Balanced Budget Act (1997) on utilization. McCall and colleagues (2003) found that the percentage of the eligible Medicare population utilizing home health services declined 22 % from 10.1 % in 1997 to 7.9 % in 1999. They also found that beneficiaries aged 85 and older were less likely to use home health services after the Balanced Budget Act (1997). Many other studies have examined the impact of ownership status on home health care agencies' performance relative to cost, quality, access to care, and charity care, and they found that either there was no difference between for-profit and not-for-profit home health agencies, or they found that not-for-profit home health agencies performed better (Rosenau and Linder 2001). Not-for-profit home health agencies tend to have lower average visits per patient and shorter length of stay, thereby using resources more efficiently. No plausible research to date has attempted to measure relative efficiency of home health agencies using data envelopment analysis.

13.3   Performance Model for Home Health Agencies

Although the performance (efficiency) of many other health care organizations (e.g., hospitals, dialysis centers, and nursing homes) has been evaluated using DEA, no researcher has tackled home health agencies' efficiency. One of the issues with home health agencies is the variability of the organization. Capacity cannot be measured in the traditional way of employee FTEs because the home health agencies expand or reduce their services to meet demand by contracting with other entities for skilled nursing or physical therapy.

Home health agencies do not have many capital investments to take into account.

Most of the activities for home health agencies are based on visits; one can adapt a performance model similar to one in physician practice. This means visits from various professionals involved in home care of the patient during an episode of disease. These professionals include nurses, therapists, nutritionists, speech pathologists, social workers, aides, and so on. Visits by these professionals then would constitute the resources used by a home health agency to produce the services for a variety of patients with various needs of post-hospitalization care. Although inputs can be accounted for this way, outputs of the model require the patient episode of home health care; however, these episodes would vary from patient to patient. Hence, depending upon the complexity of the post–hospitalization care, case-mixes will vary and need to be accounted for.

Based on these conceptualizations, a generic home health agency performance model can be constructed as shown in Fig. 13.1.

Depending upon available data, variables or their proxies may be used to operationalize the model.

13.4   Data for Home Health Agency
       Performance Evaluations

The CMS database is the main data source for home health agency data. As discussed in previous chapters, CMS keeps track of patient-level data by provider in the United States, thus enabling evaluations of home health agencies as a unit of analysis, or as the decision making unit (DMU). Another data source for these evaluations would come from State based systems. For example, the Office of Statewide Health Planning and Development (OSHPD) collects annual utilization data for all home health agencies and hospices in California, and the data are available on its website.

Fig. 13.1 Outputs and
inputs for home health
agency DEA model

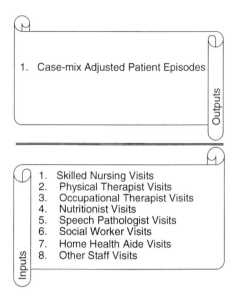

13.5   An Example of a Performance Model
for Home Health Agencies

In order to operationalize the model shown in Fig. 13.1, the example evaluation uses
Office of Statewide Health Planning and Development annual utilization data for all
home health agencies and hospices for the year 2004 (OSHPD 2006). The 2004
home health and hospice utilization file from OSHPD contained 1,035 organizations.
The analysis was limited to organizations that categorized themselves as offering
only home health services. Organizations that offered hospice only or home health
and hospice were removed from the sample. The sample was further whittled down
by removing home health agencies that closed during the year or had zero patients in
all age groups. The final sample consisted of 727 home health agencies.

13.5.1   Inputs and Outputs of the Home Health Agency Model

13.5.1.1   Inputs

The production of the services depends on resource utilization. For home health
agencies in this evaluation, the inputs, or resource utilization, are visits by different
staff members. Most common visits for various patient episodes in OSPHD were as
follows:

• Skilled Nursing Visits
• Physical Therapist Visits

- Occupational Therapist Visits
- Nutritionist Visits
- Speech Pathologist Visits
- Social Worker Visits
- Home Health Aide Visits
- Other Staff Visits

13.5.1.2 Outputs

There is no clear way of adjusting the case-mix for home health episodes. Chilingerian and Sherman (1997b), in their primary care physician evaluation, used gender and age groups to account for the case-mix of the patients. It is known that as age increases, so does the severity of the cases. Thus, the outputs of this model consist of the age group of the patient requiring home health care. Ten-year intervals of age were used to create age-grouped patient outputs as follows:

- Patients Age < 10 Years
- Patients Age 11–20 Years
- Patients Age 21–30 Years
- Patients Age 31–40 Years
- Patients Age 41–50 Years
- Patients Age 51–60 Years
- Patients Age 61–70 Years
- Patients Age 71–80 Years
- Patients Age 81–90 Years
- Patients Age >90 Years

Figure 13.2 displays the outputs and inputs for the DEA model of the example home health agency evaluation.

This evaluation uses a variable returns to scale input-oriented DEA model since home health agencies have more control over their inputs versus their outputs.

13.5.2 Homogeneous Groups and Descriptive Statistics

Only eight counties out of 58 did not have a home health agency, but the majority of home health agencies, 51 %, were clustered in Los Angeles County. More than half of the recipients of home health services were over 70 years old, and the average number of visits per individual was 25 (Harrington and O'Meara 2004).

Since DEA analysis measures relative efficiency, the development of a peer group is very important. By limiting the analysis to one state, some variation is

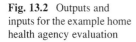

Fig. 13.2 Outputs and
inputs for the example home
health agency evaluation

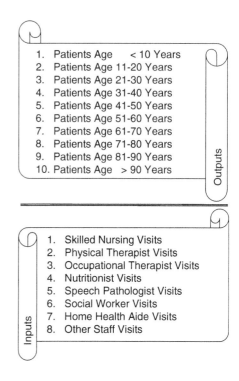

reduced because Medicaid eligibility for home health services differs from state to state. In 2003, more than half of the home health agencies were in Los Angeles County. These home health agencies would be exposed to more competition than agencies located in rural counties. Also, the larger the population and smaller the service area, the more patients home health agencies could possibly service. Use of peer groups based on local markets follows previous research (Ozcan et al. 1992; White and Ozcan 1996); however, due to many counties having only one or two home health agencies, pure local markets would have produced too few DMUs for comparison. Therefore, based on the population of the county of the home health agency, the California home health agencies were divided into three peer groups. Peer group 1 consists of all home health agencies located in Los Angeles County. Peer group 2 consists of all home health agencies located in large counties with populations over one million: Alameda, Contra Costa, Orange, Riverside, Sacramento, San Bernardino, San Diego, and Santa Clara. Peer group 3 consists of home health agencies located in small counties with populations less than one million. The descriptive statistics for input and output variables by peer group are displayed in Table 13.2.

Table 13.2 Descriptive statistics of DEA model variables by peer group

	Los Angeles county n = 342		Large counties n = 211		Small counties n = 174	
	Mean	St. dev.	Mean	St. dev.	Mean	St. dev.
Output variables						
Patients age <10 years	10.43	58.09	68.12	321.49	45.05	166.65
Patients age 11–20 years	4.27	16.07	21.19	64.21	16.95	47.47
Patients age 21–30 years	8.44	39.39	39.57	148.80	41.22	151.31
Patients age 31–40 years	12.57	41.65	46.73	135.85	34.30	79.17
Patients age 41–50 years	21.49	50.79	58.49	84.64	45.63	57.86
Patients age 51–60 years	34.38	84.38	88.50	134.68	74.47	78.26
Patients age 61–70 years	63.19	133.64	122.67	193.60	100.99	99.63
Patients age 71–80 years	109.11	170.22	190.28	306.97	159.55	160.41
Patients age 81–90 years	105.30	167.09	180.66	283.05	160.91	167.72
Patients age >90 years	29.23	43.74	42.72	65.78	41.58	44.33
Input variables						
Skilled nursing visits	10,674.39	17,075.57	8,162.36	9,826.83	6,470.35	10,251.71
Physical therapist visits	1,436.39	2,129.00	2,536.23	4,143.25	2,287.52	2,419.43
Occupational therapist visits	156.51	380.38	466.09	759.66	448.99	623.00
Speech pathologist visits	27.59	75.81	100.08	193.88	115.28	163.49
Nutritionist visits	0.93	10.46	5.88	29.45	3.25	16.21
Social worker visits	92.85	253.90	176.09	316.30	180.78	285.80
Home health aide visits	901.40	1,691.08	843.81	1,685.99	986.56	1,842.88
Other staff visits	5.91	52.40	52.03	474.77	91.44	704.39

Table 13.3 Performance by efficient and inefficient home health agencies by peer group

	Los Angeles county		Large counties		Small counties	
Mean efficiency score	0.665		0.691		0.872	
	Efficient	Inefficient	Efficient	Inefficient	Efficient	Inefficient
	n = 105	n = 237	n = 78	n = 133	n = 105	n = 69

13.5.3   DEA Results

The results of the DEA analysis are presented in Table 13.3. There were 105 efficient home health agencies in Los Angeles County with a mean efficiency score of 0.665. The inefficient home health agencies in Los Angeles County should have been able to use 33.5 % fewer inputs to create the same outputs. Among large counties, there were 78 efficient home health agencies with a mean efficiency score of 0.691. Among small counties, there were more efficient (n = 105) home health agencies than inefficient (n = 69) ones. The mean efficiency score for home health agencies in the small county peer group was 0.872.

The average inefficiency in resource utilization by peer group is presented in Table 13.4. The mean inefficiency for utilization or service production can identify how inefficient hospitals may decrease excess inputs or increase shortfall outputs to move to the efficiency frontier. The fewest number of home health agencies were inefficient in skilled nursing inputs across all three peer groups, but they would have to decrease skilled nursing visits by huge amounts to become efficient. For example, among small-county home health agencies, only one home health agency is inefficient in skilled nursing visits, but it would have to decrease skilled nursing inputs by 2,090 visits in order to reach the efficiency frontier.

Table 13.4 Magnitude of inefficiencies for home health agencies

	Los Angeles county			Large counties			Small counties		
	Number inefficient	Mean slack	St dev slack	Number inefficient	Mean slack	St dev slack	Number inefficient	Mean slack	St dev slack
Output shortages									
Patients of age group <10 years	223	10.62	10.55	105	26.65	55.69	48	13.18	15.84
Patients of age group 11–20 years	224	9.95	12.38	87	17.30	41.68	34	4.23	8.24
Patients of age group 21–30 years	227	18.50	24.31	101	32.13	92.69	67	27.02	37.64
Patients of age group 31–40 years	223	26.71	33.20	122	28.30	49.76	50	19.40	23.65
Patients of age group 41–50 years	217	35.68	45.63	101	18.59	25.71	62	22.80	21.47
Patients of age group 51–60 years	194	39.10	45.86	101	23.53	27.57	40	17.83	17.73
Patients of age group 61–70 years	150	22.58	23.51	99	21.43	25.91	41	16.87	20.48
Patients of age group 71–80 years	153	22.99	25.98	59	13.72	26.19	46	17.76	17.86
Patients of age group 81–90 years	128	15.37	17.31	63	18.74	28.50	39	16.98	18.36
Patients of age group >90 years	88	4.25	6.11	73	5.72	8.59	36	6.51	7.42
Excessive inputs									
Skilled nursing visits	11	11,372.39	14,302.22	16	3,138.51	4,159.09	1	2,090.42	N/A
Physical therapist visits	52	249.81	370.62	35	580.12	665.39	17	428.04	906.13
Occupational therapist visits	99	62.03	138.14	81	141.73	258.79	40	170.50	249.30
Speech pathologist visits	84	12.35	35.92	39	30.80	63.48	39	71.59	84.58
Nutritionist visits	70	0.41	1.76	45	12.90	43.51	16	8.92	18.05
Social worker visits	138	24.26	43.94	72	60.02	105.32	36	63.81	68.13
Home health aide visits	124	475.92	862.75	100	234.51	349.17	37	563.59	636.43
Other staff visits	62	7.15	28.85	16	190.68	723.16	3	0.28	0.48

13.5.4   Conclusion

This evaluation measured technical efficiency of home health agencies in serving different age groups. There are other measures of resource utilization in home health besides number of visits, such as length of stay and direct care time (Adams and Michel 2001). However, one limitation of the study was that the data set used in this study did not have length of stay and direct care time. Another limitation is that this evaluation only assessed efficiency of Californian home health agencies. These results might not be generalizable outside California. This evaluation also measured efficiency by peer groups based on population and competition. These peer groups might not have created desired homogeneous groups. A final limitation is the lack of case-mix information to adjust for patient severity. As insurers demand more return for their investments, efficiency in health care production will become more salient.

Since Medicare provides rewards for therapy services, weights can be considered for preferring physical therapy, occupational therapy, and speech pathology over home health aide services using weight restricted (multiplier) models presented in Chap. 4.

13.6   Summary

This chapter provided a general guidance for a home health agency performance model and its operationalization. Using generally available databases from either federal (CMS) or state databases, home health agency provider performance can be evaluated. An example of a home health agency performance model was presented using the database from the State of California. Limitations of the past studies, and suggestions for future evaluations, are also provided.

Chapter 14
Applications for Other Health Care Organizations

14.1 Introduction

In earlier chapters, models of performance evaluation for major health care providers were presented. These included hospitals, physician offices, nursing homes, health maintenance organizations, and home health care. There are many other health care providers that serve patient needs, sometimes in conjunction with major providers and sometimes independently. The literature shows that a variety of performance models were developed for providers such as dialysis centers, community mental health centers, community-based youth services, organ procurement organizations, aging agencies, dental providers, pharmacies, ophthalmology centers, diagnostic and screening centers, and so on (Hollingsworth 2003, 2008). In this chapter, performance models for selected health service providers are presented.

14.2 Dialysis Centers

End-stage renal disease (ESRD), a life threatening disease, cost $2.3 billion in 2000 for 378,862 people. The Medicare ESRD program provides coverage of over 93 % of the costs regardless of the patient's age. Due to the scope of this problem, evaluation of performance for dialysis centers, the organizations that provide treatments for ESRD, is a significant issue. Ozgen and Ozcan (2002) evaluated dialysis centers in a cross-sectional analysis using data envelopment analysis (DEA). Their study was focused on freestanding dialysis facilities that operated in 1997. The data from Independent Renal Facility Cost Report Data (IRFCRD) was utilized to obtain information on the output and input variables and market and facility features for the 791 renal dialysis centers analyzed in this evaluation. IRFCRD is a national data and maintained by the Centers for Medicare and Medicaid Services (CMS). This study, interestingly, combined both DEA and logistic regression. Technical efficiency scores were determined using DEA.

Y.A. Ozcan, *Health Care Benchmarking and Performance Evaluation*,
International Series in Operations Research & Management Science 210,
DOI 10.1007/978-1-4899-7472-3_14, © Springer Science+Business Media New York 2014

Fig. 14.1 DEA Model
for Dialysis Centers

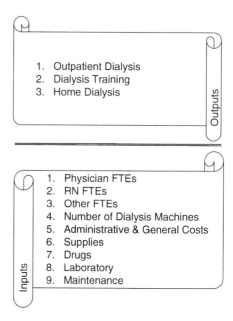

The binary variable of efficiency was then regressed against its market and facility characteristics and the control factors in a multivariate logistic regression analysis.

The output variables included outpatient dialysis, dialysis training, and home dialysis treatments. The input variables included labor inputs (FTEs of physicians, RNs, and other medical staff), capital inputs (i.e., total number of dialysis machines), and dialysis costs (i.e., administrative and general, supplies, drugs, laboratory, and machine maintenance), as shown in Fig. 14.1.

Overall, it was found that the majority of the dialysis centers are functionally inefficient. The intensity of market competition or a policy of dialyzer reuse did not impact the facilities' efficiency. However, technical efficiency was found to be significantly associated with the type of ownership, the interaction between the market concentration of for-profits and ownership type, and the affiliations with chains of different sizes. In terms of ownership, for-profit counterparts were less likely than not-for-profit and government-owned facilities to become inefficient producers of renal dialysis outputs.

A follow-up evaluation of dialysis centers was also conducted by Ozgen and Ozcan (2004). This evaluation used a longitudinal approach to analyze the efficiency because a previous cross-sectional study provided limited information to answer whether and how influences from the payer and from the provider sides may affect provider efficiency over time. Thus, the Malmquist Index based DEA model was used to analyze the dialysis centers.

Data were derived again from Independent Renal Facility Cost Report Data files from 1994 to 2000. A total of 140 facilities were selected based on those operating throughout the study years and with nonzero inputs. Malmquist Index was calculated to compare pairs of 6-year periods including: 1994–1995, 1995–1996, 1996–1997, 1997–1998, 1998–1999, 1999–2000, plus a 7-year period of 1994–2000.

The mean efficiency score for the 7 years was 0.92 and an average of 41 % of freestanding facilities were efficient. Mean efficiency scores were the lowest in 1995 (0.89) and increased to a high of 0.94 in 2000. Technical efficiency improved by 6 %.

The DEA Malmquist Index (MI) is a product of technical efficiency and technology change. Using a constant returns to scale (CRS) input-oriented model, one can observe that dialysis centers over time were progressive if $MI < 1$; had no change if $MI = 1$; and regressive if $MI > 1$. The overall 1994–2000 Malmquist Index was 1.07, meaning that the productivity regressed over time. Some of the interesting results of this evaluation are noted as:

- Outpatient outputs increased but training and home dialyses outputs decreased. Overall output averages fluctuated, resulting in an 11 % increase. Inputs use has been conservative. For operating costs there was a total average increase of 9 %.
- Comparing three cost items, supply cost declined (33–9 %), and drug costs steadily increased by 13 %, representing 43 % of total average costs in 2000. Administrative and general costs fluctuated from 29 to 25 % in 1994 and 2000 respectively.
- The overall MI and its components (efficiency change and technology change) showed loss of productivity (MI) influenced by technological change (TC). Technical efficiency was slightly positive with very little regression.

This study further examined whether system affiliation and size of dialysis organizations would have different outcomes. From the results, chain affiliations have a positive difference in technical efficiency. The size of a dialysis chain did not have a significant role in technical efficiency. Freestanding dialysis facilities improved their technical efficiency over time, but may have regressed in technology, thus having the potential to improve the quality of care.

14.3 Community Mental Health Centers

While the cost of health care in the United States was approaching $1 trillion in 1996, approximately 10 % of that money ($99 billion) was spent on behavioral health care. Mental health disorders consumed 7 % of the health care costs, with Alzheimer's disease/dementias and addiction disorders consuming 2 and 1 % of total costs, respectively (US Department of Health and Human services 1999). About 18 % of the expenditures on mental health went to multi-service mental health clinics, which include community mental health centers. From 1986 to 1996, mental health costs rose 1 % less than overall health costs did. Twelve percent of the United States population is covered under Medicaid for their health care. Medicaid's cost for behavioral health amounts to 19 % of its expenditures; per capita Medicaid mental health expenditure is approximately $481 (US Department of Health and Human services 1999). These costs justify examination of efficiency in the provision of the mental health services by community mental health organizations.

One of the early evaluations of DEA in mental health programs was by Schinnar et al. (1990), who assessed the efficiency and effectiveness of 54 of the 80 mental health partial care programs operating in New Jersey during the fiscal year 1984/1985. Schinnar and associates, using DEA, created various productivity, efficiency, and effectiveness indices. These indices included service-mix, client-mix, fiscal intensity, fiscal distribution, and program effectiveness. Depending upon the purpose and the nature of the index, various inputs and outputs were employed. Staff hours or salaries and other costs were part of the inputs for productivity and efficiency indices. Outputs in many indices constituted the young and old high; high-and-low functioning clients categorized in four groups. Mean efficiency scores for the indices ranged between 0.62 and 0.67.

Tyler et al. (1995) assessed the technical efficiency of community mental health centers (CMHC) in the production of case management services. They compared 39 CMHC programs in Virginia using data from fiscal year 1992/1993 annual statistical reports. Two outputs of the evaluation were case management clients with serious mental illness (SMI) and case management clients without SMI. Thus, SMI designation served as a case-mix for the patient outputs. The inputs were FTEs of direct service staff, FTEs of support staff, and non-labor operating expenses. An average efficiency score was 0.44. Only six (15 %) of the CMHCs were efficient.

A more recent study by Ozcan et al. (2004) used DEA to study technical efficiency of community mental health providers to improve their productivity. This was essentially a pilot investigation using DEA to examine 12 community mental health centers, all receiving traditional fee-for-service (FFS) Medicaid reimbursement in years 1–2 and switching to mandatory, capitated Medicaid managed care in years 3–5. The measures of efficiency were longitudinal patterns of provider efficiency over 5 years before and after implementation of the mandatory Medicaid managed care plan.

In 1996, a mandatory Medicaid managed care program was implemented in the Tidewater region of Virginia. The Ozcan et al. (2004) evaluation focused on care provided by these CMHCs in Virginia to patients with SMI. The care was limited to those reimbursed by Medicaid between 1994 and 1998. The CMHCs that treated fewer than 100 SMI cases were excluded to ensure proficiency. The CMHCs were located in two different regions: four in Richmond (control group) and eight in Tidewater (experimental group). The SMI patients were identified using diagnosis codes ranging from 295.00 to 298.99 (schizophrenia, major affective psychosis, paranoid states, and other non-organic psychoses).

The output variables included the number of SMI patients with supplemental security income (SSI), considered as more severe, and the number of SMI patients without SSI (less severe). The six input variables were use of non-emergency crisis support, use of outpatient assessment, use of outpatient therapy, use of outpatient medication management, use of clubhouse, and use of case management. The DEA model for this evaluation is shown in Fig. 14.2.

Fig. 14.2 DEA Model
for Community
Mental Health Centers

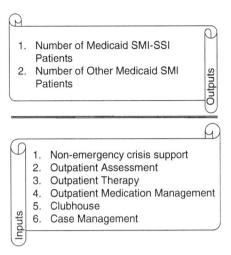

Over the 5 years, from 1994 to 1998, 31 out of the 60 ($12 \times 5 = 60$) decision making units (DMUs) were efficient. The DMUs in the Tidewater region had a higher average efficiency score of 0.895 compared to Richmond's score of 0.753. The differences in the efficiency score of the two regions were statistically significant after managed care was implemented. An increasing trend in scores over time for the Tidewater area, the region for implementation of Medicaid managed care programs, was observed. On the other hand, the Richmond area CMHCs' scores remained level.

Ozcan and associates (2004) extended their evaluation using a multiplier model (weight restricted) with preferred ratio constraints. The preferred ratio was designated as case management over non-emergency crisis support. This restriction based on this ratio constraint creates an efficiency frontier that only includes the section creating the preferred practice style. The authors added an additional preferred ratio of outpatient medication management over outpatient therapy. The number of efficient DMUs decreased in both the Richmond and Tidewater regions when a more stringent efficiency outcome was utilized.

The results of the multiplier model showed that the efficiency of CMHCs in Richmond is significantly less than in the base model. The Tidewater CMHCs' efficiency scores were reduced during the pre-managed care era and they were significantly higher after managed care. A perfect efficiency score is a score of 1.0. Richmond had only three perfectly efficient CMHCs in the multiplier model, as compared to seven in the base model, yielding a 57.1 % reduction in perfect efficiency. By contrast, the number of instances of perfectly efficient CMHCs in Tidewater dropped to 20 in the multiplier model from 24 in the base model. This model extension showed the power of the multiplier model, which produces more stringent efficiency outcomes (Ozcan et al. 2004).

The methods shown in this evaluation offer a replicable, objective methodology that can be used to compare the operational efficiency of different types of providers who care for similar populations of clients. The methodology identifies consistent measures for comparison—numbers of patients treated—and provides a means of aggregating information on different numbers of patients to serve as a measure of organizational performance.

This methodology could be useful to public mental health systems as well as to private and public managed care companies, because it can identify the combinations of services that result in the most efficient care. That information can be used to change the mix of services that a managed care company will reimburse and/or those that a provider chooses to use (Ozcan et al. 2005).

14.4   Community-Based Youth Services

Providing comprehensive mental health services to children is another important issue. Community-based youth services are a fully integrated, less expensive alternative for children and adolescents as a substitute for hospitalization. Many states, including Virginia, have established comprehensive community-based youth services (CBYS). Virginia's program started in July 1993.

Yeh et al. (1997) evaluated CBYS using DEA among 40 Virginia communities that reported their data on a regular basis to the Virginia Department of Mental Health, Mental Retardation, and Substance Abuse Services (DMHMRSAS). Financial data for the same fiscal year 1993/1994 was obtained from the Virginia Department of Education, the agency that handles the financial aspects of the CBYS program.

The CBYS model considered two outputs based on services provided, namely residential and non-residential services. Inputs included a budget for the services and a budget for the administration of the programs. In addition, the number of youths who received the services and the percentage of youth in poverty were the other inputs. Figure 14.3 illustrates this model. Analyses were carried out to

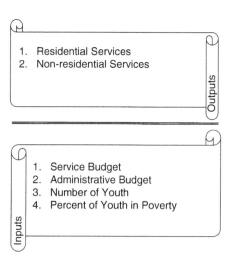

Fig. 14.3 DEA Model for Community-Based Youth Services

evaluate the effect of the size of CBYS (large if 15,000 or more youth population, small otherwise), location (urban vs. rural), and community type (poor if poverty >8 %, rich otherwise).

Output-oriented DEA model results showed that ten (25 %) of the CBYSs were efficient. CBYS programs in large communities, in rich communities, and in urban communities were more efficient than their counterparts. The inefficient CBYSs, with their current level of inputs, could have served 164 more youths for residential services and 487 more youths for non-residential services.

14.5   Organ Procurement Organizations

The United Network for Organ Sharing (UNOS) lists about 97,000 individuals on the waiting list for organs as of July 2007, and there were over 9,000 transplants during the period of January–April 2007 (www.unos.org). On average, several patients die daily while waiting for organs. UNOS coordinates the placement and distribution of donated organs, collects, analyzes, and publishes transplant data, and educates health professionals about the donation process. Organ procurement organizations (OPOs) coordinate the organ procurement and transplantation process in designated service areas (Ozcan et al. 1999). Thus, evaluation of OPO performance is an important issue, especially when many thousands of individuals are waiting for appropriate organs to be recovered and hoping one matches to save their lives.

Ozcan et al. (1999) developed a DEA model to evaluate the performance of OPOs. They indicated that the usual measure of performance by ratios, such as kidneys recovered per million population, is limited by itself due to the existence of multiple inputs and outputs related to different resources, activities, and other factors. Their evaluation assumes that OPOs would want to know how much shortfall in outputs they have with given resources as compared to other OPOs, and so an output-oriented DEA model was used.

The researchers surveyed the Executive Directors of the 66 OPOs in the US who were asked to provide information on OPO hospital development activities, expenditures, and staffing for the 1994 calendar year (McKinney et al. 1998). Sixty-four of the OPO questionnaires were useful for the analysis. Secondary data from the Association of Organ Procurement Organizations (AOPO) and UNOS were also utilized for this evaluation.

The most recognized output of OPOs is organs recovered, and the DEA-OPO model employs kidneys and extra-renal organs recovered as outputs. On the input side, the measure of hospital development formalization index (a 0–3 scale accounts for whether an OPO has a hospital development director, department, and written standards for effectiveness) developed in this study provides a proxy for the capital/structure dimension of the input resources, as it reflects the degree

Fig. 14.4 DEA Model
for Organ Procurement
Organizations

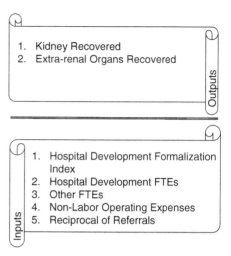

1. Kidney Recovered
2. Extra-renal Organs Recovered

Outputs

1. Hospital Development Formalization
   Index
2. Hospital Development FTEs
3. Other FTEs
4. Non-Labor Operating Expenses
5. Reciprocal of Referrals

Inputs

to which the OPO has formal structures in place to produce outputs. The other categories of inputs include hospital development labor FTEs, hospital development personnel FTEs, other labor FTEs, and operating expenses not devoted to hospital development (measured by non-FTE operating expenses). One additional nondiscretionary input is used, referrals, which are classified as nondiscretionary because OPO managers do not have control over this input. Outputs and inputs of the DEA model for OPO performance are illustrated in Fig. 14.4 (Ozcan et al. 1999).

Based on a two-output, five-input, variable returns to scale, output-oriented model, they estimated two peer-grouped (larger and smaller OPOs) DEA models with measures calculated from the survey data obtained from OPOs and secondary data mentioned above. Overall, 55 % of the OPOs (n = 35) were classified as efficient in comparison to their peers in the two-frontier (larger versus smaller) approach. In the smaller OPO frontier, the average efficiency of the 42 OPOs was 0.79, whereas in the larger OPO frontier the average efficiency score of the 22 OPOs was 0.95. The authors found that OPOs classified as efficient recover significantly more kidneys and extra-renal organs, have higher operating expenses, and have more referrals, donors, extra-renal transplants, and kidney transplants. Furthermore, it is noted that efficient OPO hospital development FTEs, other FTEs, and hospital development formalization indices do not significantly differ.

The role of referrals is interesting in this model; for the large group, none of the inefficient facilities had a lower quantity of referrals than the efficient facilities. But for the small group, inefficient facilities need approximately 92 more referrals to be classified as efficient. These findings indicate that the OPOs in the larger group have greater technical efficiency.

14.6   Aging Agencies

After the passage of the Older Americans Act of 1965, states have designed local area agencies to provide aging service for older persons. There are diverse structures and programs among different states, including not-for-profit corporations, governmental units, and regional authority of local governments. These agencies, based on their governmental types, may receive funding from different sources, such as the Older Americans Act Funds, non-federal resources, client donations, and other federal funds. These agencies provide aging services, including accurate needs assessment (i.e., nutrition services, supportive services, community-based services) and planning and leadership in service development.

Little evaluation of the efficiency of area agencies on aging exists. Researchers often found some difficulties when evaluating these organizations. Those difficulties included an ambiguous focus, wide-ranging goals, provision of multiple services, and lack of uniform input and outcome data. Specifically, the data collection included bias and inaccuracy problems. Regarding this issue, it is inappropriate to use cost-effectiveness or ratio analysis to evaluate the performance among agencies. Hence, the evaluation of these agencies by Ozcan and Cotter (1994) using DEA allowed the full considerations of multiple outputs and multiple inputs.

The Ozcan and Cotter (1994) evaluation was a cross-sectional design using 25 Area Agencies on Aging's reports for 1991 in Virginia. The annual performance report data by these agencies was used and these reports received accounting audits. Therefore, the quality of the data was satisfactory and consistent.

The outputs of the evaluation consisted of meal services and support and community-based services. Meals, however, could be delivered either in congregate settings such as at senior centers, or directly delivered to homes of the seniors. In Virginia, the scope of supportive services could amount to 26 different services, including case management, dental services, home care, geriatric day care, residential repair and renovation, etc. Since not all agencies provide all services, using these services as individual outputs would be prohibitive in any model. Thus, a support service index was developed by determining the proportional value of the unit cost of each service relative to the average of unit costs for all services. The support services index score was then used to make adjustments. This provided a combination of the intensity of the service with the total amount of production (Ozcan and Cotter 1994). The index assigns a lower intensity to telephone-based services compared to legal services; however, magnitude (number) of telephone services might be far larger than legal services. Outputs and inputs for aging agency evaluation are shown in Fig. 14.5.

This evaluation employed an output-orientation DEA model, since inputs are modestly determined by external factors and decisions often occur with output variables. This study expected that the area agencies with more control over their operations would perform at a higher level of provision of service. Three factors were also considered to affect the results of inputs into outputs, including size (i.e., small, medium, and large), organizational type (i.e., governmental, joint exercise, and private not-for-profit), and geographic (i.e., rural and urban).

Fig. 14.5 DEA Model
for Aging Agencies

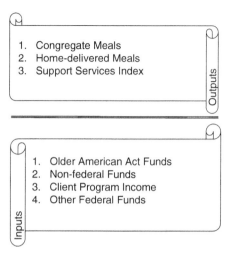

Fifteen (60 %) out of twenty-five area agencies were found to be efficient. Governmental units had the highest proportion (80 %) of efficient operations. Area agencies in large-size areas were more likely to be efficient. Area agencies covering urban areas were also more likely to be efficient. For inefficient agencies, using the benchmark targets, the analysis indicated the variety of changes needed to improve efficiency and provided information on where intervention efforts offer the most potential.

14.7   Dental Providers

There are very few evaluations of dental services using DEA. A study by Buck (2000) evaluated the efficiency of the community dental service in England where he evaluated 100 dental services and found that the average efficiency of community dental services was 0.64. Another study by Linna et al. (2003) examined the technical efficiency of oral health provision in 228 Finnish health centers. The average efficiency score ranged from 0.72 to 0.81, depending upon type of facility.

In a more recent study by Coppola et al. (2003), performance of dental providers was evaluated on posterior restorations. Dental evaluations focus on the survivability of amalgam and composite materials. However, the experience of the provider in restoration longevity must be factored into these evaluations.

Data for this evaluation was obtained from the Washington Dental Service (insurance claims database) with 650,000 subscribers, 1.5 million patients (updated monthly), and 23,103 total dentists. Dentists who provided more than 100 encounters of dental restoration services from 1993 to 1999, inclusively, were included in the evaluation, hence there were 1,240 such dental providers.

Fig. 14.6 DEA Model
for Dental Providers
Performance on
Restorations

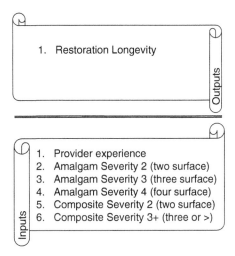

The evaluation employed severity of amalgam or composite restoration (two, three, or four surface) and provider experience as inputs. The single output was restoration longevity. Figure 14.6 displays the DEA model inputs and output for dental provider performance on restoration.

The result showed that only 122 (9.8 %) dental providers were efficient in their restoration work with an average longevity of 46.5 months. The longevity of restorations by inefficient dental providers was only 41.8 months. An average efficiency score for all dental providers was 0.79. The evaluation also found that the efficient dentists have more experience, as efficiency peaks at 14 years of provider experience and begins to decrease after the 15th year of practice. Efficient providers have amalgams or composites that last 4.7 months longer. The average age for efficient providers is 40.4 years, and the average age for inefficient providers is 46.8 years. Providers who work on amalgams are less likely to be efficient than providers who work on composites.

This study showed how DEA can be used creatively to evaluate not only performance of providers, but also the quality of the service provided as measured by the longevity of the service product.

14.8   Radiology Providers

Radiology services may be located in hospitals or complex medical centers, and also provide care as freestanding radiology centers. These providers employ a variety of capital-intensive technologies for patient diagnosis, treatment, and management. Although there are many performance evaluation studies for hospitals or health care systems, performance evaluation for radiology departments or freestanding radiology centers is very limited. Ozcan and Legg (2014) report the

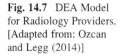

Fig. 14.7 DEA Model for Radiology Providers. [Adapted from: Ozcan and Legg (2014)]

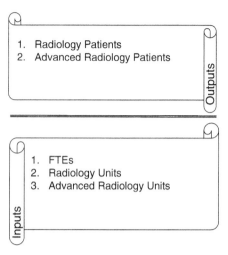

performance of these entities and illustrate how performance can be improved for the underachievers. Data were acquired through an annual Radiologic Workplace survey of 2011 conducted by the American Society of Radiologic Technologists.

The authors considered radiology services and advanced radiology services as outputs. The input resources used to produce these outputs included staff measured by full-time equivalents (FTEs), number of radiology units, and number of advanced radiology units such as computed tomography (CT), computed tomography, cardiovascular (CV) imaging, mammography, magnetic resonance (MR), sonography, and nuclear medicine.

Since individual providers do not engage in all of the advanced radiology services, the second input represents the sum of the available advanced radiology services. The conceptualization of this DEA model is displayed in Fig. 14.7. The study deploys an alteration to this general model for those providers not providing both services. For such an instance, only a one-output, two-input model is deployed. Output is the service category (either radiology services or advanced radiology services), and two inputs were included: FTEs and units in the service category (either radiology units or advanced radiology units). Based on survey results, the radiology-only group (ROG) type of facilities tend to be smaller compared to the radiology and advanced radiology group (RARG) type of facilities. Hence they evaluate these two groups of facilities independently in their evaluations using a variable returns to scale model.

Results showed that efficiency for 195 ROG type of facilities was 0.82 and for 428 RARG type of facilities the efficiency score was only 0.62. There were 133 ROG facilities with a perfect efficiency score of "1," whereas there were 145 perfectly efficient RARG facilities. The authors suggest that the higher concentration of efficiencies in ROG facilities may emanate from the simplicity of operations in these facilities compared to RARG.

The challenge for managers depends on those facilities that are not efficient and what the managers of these inefficient facilities need to do. The prescriptive information shown by targets calculated through DEA would bring some actionable decisions for managers to have their facilities reach higher efficiency levels. The authors show that the percent of reduction in FTEs as well as radiology units (excess capacity) for inefficient RARG and ROG facilities are very similar. On the other hand, to reach efficient levels ROG facilities must increase radiology service output by 61 %, which is three times more than their RARG counterparts. It is also mentioned that the unique nature of radiology technologies and the referral nature of the profession may impact the manager's ability to influence significantly these efficiency parameters.

14.9   Substance Abuse Treatment Providers

Addiction treatment is provided by clinics spread across communities in the US. These organizations are generally funded by state and federal governments, and public officials administering the funding to these organizations must justify the use of these funds by tracking the performance of these clinics. The research conducted by Corredoira et al. (2011) analyzes the performance in addiction treatment facilities using DEA in the State of Maryland system. The authors examined 161 substance abuse treatment facilities in Maryland that provide Level I care as defined by the American Society of Addiction Medicine (ASAM). More specifically, ASAM Level I care (outpatient treatment) is defined as "nonresidential, structured treatment services for less than 9 h a week per patient. Examples might include office practice, health clinic, primary care clinics, mental health clinics, and "Step Down" programs that provide individual, group and family counseling services." (Maryland Alcohol and Drug Abuse Administration 2006, p. 29).

First, the authors utilized DEA to obtain a dependent variable for an ad hoc Tobit analysis. As shown in Fig. 14.8, DEA inputs included the number of patients in three severity categories of treatment Level I to account for addiction severity. Outputs included the number of patients achieving successful treatment outcomes including the number of clients that completed the program and the number of clients with no drug use at discharge. The authors recognized that other variables would be of interest to this model, but due to data limitations additional variables were not possible.

Tobit analysis included two variables to account for environmental factors impacting clinic effectiveness (number of patients and patient support networks) and two variables to account for factors within managerial control (clinic accessibility and state funding). The county's income per capita was used as a proxy for measuring patient support networks, and the number of clinics per square mile was used as a proxy for clinic accessibility. These proxy variables were discussed to be suboptimal, but the best the authors could do given data availability.

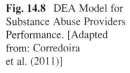

Fig. 14.8 DEA Model for
Substance Abuse Providers
Performance. [Adapted
from: Corredoira
et al. (2011)]

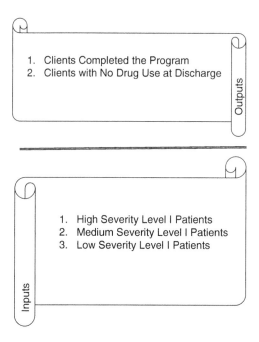

An initial DEA, constant returns to scale output-oriented model, found that 23 of
the 161 clinics were operating effectively. Ineffective clinics had DEA scores
ranging from 0.24 to 0.999. Tobit analysis assessing the ineffectiveness (effectiveness scores were transformed into ineffectiveness score, see Chap. 8, Sect. 8.5.1) of
the clinics found that only the number of clinics per square mile and state funding
were significantly associated with clinic ineffectiveness. The authors stated that the
lack of significance among other variables is unlikely due to a lack of association
between the variables, but rather an inadequate proxy to get at the core of the
variable meaning.

14.10 Health Clinics

Primary care clinics are other organizational forms that have had recent DEA
studies on performance evaluation. Rahman and Capitman (2012) examined
whether use of supporting primary care health practitioners would increase efficiency of health clinics. The study examined primary care clinics from California's
San Joaquin Valley. The main purpose of this research was to examine the relative
efficiency of health clinics that employ relatively more supporting health care
practitioners (unlicensed and licensed dependent practitioners) compared to those
that do not in California's San Joaquin Valley (SJV). The data for the study came
from the Automated Licensing Information and Report Tracking System (ALIRTS)

Fig. 14.9 DEA Model for
Health Clinics. [Adapted
from: Rahman and
Capitman (2012)]

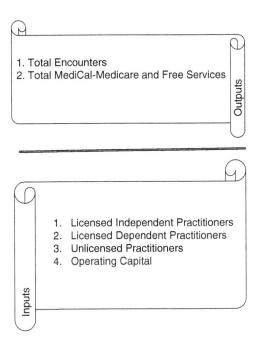

of the California Office of Statewide Health Planning and Development (OSHPD)
for the year 2006. The study sample consisted of 67 health clinics (Federally
qualified health centers [FQHCs] and rural health clinics [RHCs]) within the
Central Valley Health Network in the SJV region.

Figure 14.9 depicts the study variables for the DEA model, which included
total encounters and total MediCal-Medicare and free care services as the output
variables, licensed independent practitioners, licensed dependent practitioners,
unlicensed practitioners, and operating capital as the input variables. The study
analysis was carried out in two steps. While the variable returns to scale (BCC)
DEA model was used to measure the technical efficiency, results of the Tobit
regression analysis were used to understand the factors affecting the technical
efficiency of the health clinics. Their second-stage analysis included transportation, location, clinic type, Hispanic/total patients and MediCal-Medicare/total
patients as the control variables. The results of the study showed that while only
22 % of the clinics were found to be efficient, the average health clinic in SJV was
operating at 78.7 % of its capacity; this number was even lower for inefficient
clinics (72.6 %).

Results of the Tobit analysis showed that both a higher number of non-licensed
practitioners compared to licensed practitioners in a clinic and a lower number of
physicians relative to total licensed practitioners were correlated with higher
efficiency. While the variables transportation and Hispanic/total patients were
found to be significant, the variables location and clinic type were shown to be

statistically insignificant. A major strength of the study is that the results of the study can be easily compared with the results of the studies that looked at the technical efficiency of hospitals and health clinics due to the presence of the same payment mechanism, similar production technologies, and patient case mix. The authors also noted as study limitation that the analysis was only of health clinics in central California and did not consider the quality or appropriateness of care or staffing patterns for measuring efficiency. From a policy perspective, the study provides evidence on how a change from the existing physician-based practice models to a team-based model that better utilizes the services from non-physicians and non-licensed primary care practitioners can be used to increase the efficiency of the rural health clinics.

14.11 Free Clinics

Another form of health care organization, free clinics in the United States annually provide medical care to approximately 1.8 million poor and uninsured patients. A study by VanderWielen and Ozcan (2014) examined the performance of free clinics that provide a variety of services to meet the needs of their respective communities. Earlier studies of free clinic performance were limited to those outcome variables that focus on patient satisfaction, quality of care, and adherence to clinical guidelines. The VanderWielen and Ozcan (2014) study used DEA to evaluate free clinic performance with an objective of identifying the best free clinic performers and informing free clinics of potential performance improvement measures.

Data came from the Virginia Association of Free and Charitable Clinics (VAFCC) which had 60 member organizations in 2010. These free clinics and/or clinical support organizations provide care in the form of general medical visits, specialty visits, dental visits, health education visits, mental health visits, and prescriptions. Due to sparse data, dental visits, health education visits, and mental health visits were combined into other visits as an output variable. Only 48 of the 60 member clinics in the data set met the inclusion criteria for the model shown in Fig. 14.10.

The authors used an output-oriented variable returns to scales (BCC) model. DEA results rendered 30 of the free clinics as efficient and 18 as inefficient. Those inefficient clinics (37.5 %) lacked additional outputs needed to maximize performance. Free clinic managers using their clinic efficiency performance could assess how to improve the performance in the future. The authors indicate that "additional data is sorely needed to fully utilize DEA methodology to understand free clinic efficiency." The future studies may also look at these organizations in multi-periods using Windows analysis or Malmquist methods to shed light on performance trends for these organizations.

Fig. 14.10 DEA Model
for Free Clinics.
[Adapted from:
VanderWielen
and Ozcan (2014)]

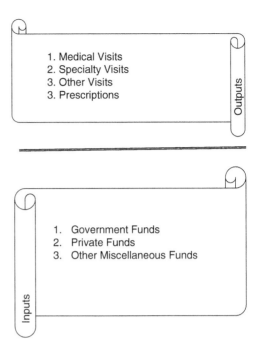

14.12 Rehabilitation Providers

Inpatient rehabilitation facilities provide specialized care to patients with limited functionality due to various impairments and ailments. These facilities are all over the US in about 1,200 locations. This sector of health care represents a significant expense to Medicare, approximately $55 billion in 2009. A study by Shay and Ozcan (2013) evaluated the freestanding inpatient rehabilitation facility performance. The purpose of this study was to examine how the operational performance of freestanding independent rehabilitation facilities (IRF) changed since the "60 % rule" has been revised and enforced in 2004. The 60 % rule requires 60 % of an IRF's admissions to meet one of ten conditions (e.g., stroke, traumatic brain injury, hip fracture). Providers not meeting the requirement risk losing their IRF designation and qualifications for IRF prospective payment system (PPS).

Annual data were taken from the American Hospital Association (AHA) annual surveys for years 2003–2008. The total sample consisted of 148 IRFs across the study period of 6 years. County-level data were obtained from the 2003 ARF file. The Malmquist Index was used to examine freestanding IRF performance before and after the revised 60 % rule's enforcement.

For the DEA model and the Malmquist Index, an input-oriented variable returns to scale (BCC) DEA model was used. Figure 14.11 depicts the model, where input variables were number of staffed beds, FTE of registered nurses, FTE of licensed practice nurses, FTE of other personnel, and operational expenses (non-labor expenses). Output variables were outpatient visits, Medicare patient days, and non-Medicare patient days. Independent variables to be included in the linear regression were system

Fig. 14.11 DEA Model for
Rehabilitation Facilities.
[Adapted from: Shay and
Ozcan (2013)]

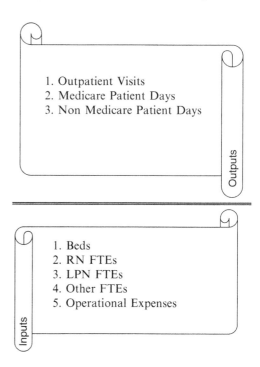

1. Outpatient Visits
2. Medicare Patient Days
3. Non Medicare Patient Days

Outputs

1. Beds
2. RN FTEs
3. LPN FTEs
4. Other FTEs
5. Operational Expenses

Inputs

membership, system size, number of system-operated IRFs, system services (i.e., with/ without acute care facilities), presence of skilled nursing unit, and composite fit (i.e., low, medium, high fit). Other control variables included ownership status, region, and market size. The log transformation of the Malmquist Index was used as a dependent variable in the linear regression in a second-stage analysis.

The results from the Malmquist analysis showed that average performance declined over the 6-year period. In particular, 52 facilities showed increased performance, while the remaining 96 facilities (65 %) experienced a decline in performance. From a policy perspective, the results indicate that the 60 % rule may have negative consequences for operational performance of freestanding IRFs.

Possible study limitations include omitted variable bias (e.g., service mix, case-mix adjusted discharges), inclusion of freestanding facilities only, and the operationalization of the fit measure.

14.13 Ambulatory Surgery Centers

Technological advances in surgery and surgery protocols fueled an upsurge in ambulatory surgery centers during the past few decades. A study by Iyengar and Ozcan (2009) evaluates the performance of 198 ambulatory surgery centers (ASCs) operating in the State of Pennsylvania in 2006.

Fig. 14.12 DEA Model
for Ambulatory Surgery
Center. [Adapted from:
Iyengar and Ozcan (2009)]

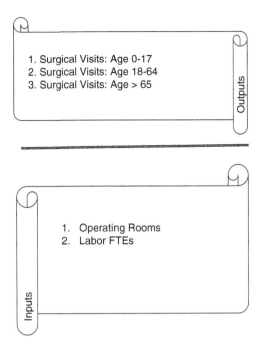

Performance was assessed with a model that included two inputs: number of operating rooms and labor FTEs. The three outputs consisted of patient surgical visits differentiated by age groups: 0–17, 18–64, 65+. Input-oriented models were employed to assess various DEA efficiency models (i.e., CCR, BCC, and scale efficiency). Results showed that about 48 (24 %) ASCs were efficient with a mean efficiency score of 0.60. The results also indicated that appropriate utilization of operating rooms and labor inputs are the main determinants of ASC efficiency.

Additionally, the results also indicated that inefficient ASCs on average have to reduce the usage of their operating rooms by two and decrease the number of staff by 13 FTEs. Similarly, inefficient ASCs must increase their surgery visits, especially for the age group 18–64 (Fig. 14.12).

14.14 Oncology Care

Oncology services have been a growing area of specialized health care centers; there are over 1,400 approved hospital-based programs as well as outpatient and group practice oncology services. A study by Langabeer and Ozcan (2009) evaluated using a longitudinal Malmquist Index over a 5-year period (2002–2006) for specialized DRG-exempt inpatient cancer centers to determine whether specialized centers achieve higher productivity over time.

Data sources included American Hospital Association survey, Ingenix benchmarks, the American Hospital Directory (AHD), and Medical Expenditure Survey (MEPS) from the Agency for Healthcare Research and Quality (AHRQ). Evaluation of ten DRG-exempt oncology centers over 5 years included the following inputs: beds, FTEs, and adjusted operational expenses less personnel costs, adjusted with both case mix and geographical wage indices. The outputs were adjusted discharges and outpatient visits as in previously discussed hospital studies (see Chap. 9).

The authors explored the efficiency change over time with quality rankings of these centers. Among the ten oncology hospitals, four of them were consistently ranked in the top four during the study period, while three of them ranked in the 30–50 range out of 100, and the remaining were not ranked as high quality. Five top-ranked oncology hospitals showed a 0.94 mean efficiency score over the 5-year period, significantly higher than the 0.83 score for the unranked group of oncology hospitals. Poor performers were both efficiency- and quality-deficient.

14.15   Summary

This chapter provided an overview of performance models for other health care providers that serve the patient needs, including dialysis centers, community mental health centers, community-based youth services, organ procurement organizations, aging centers, dental providers, radiology providers, substance abuse providers, health clinics, free clinics, rehabilitation providers, ambulatory surgery centers, and oncology centers. The evaluation of each provider type is unique, and variables and databases are also unique. We hope these examples serve as guidance to evaluate other traditional and non-traditional health provider services in the future.

Chapter 15
Other DEA Applications in Hospital Settings

15.1 Introduction

Chapter 14 introduced various performance models for other health care providers that serve the patient needs including dialysis centers, community mental health centers, community-based youth services, organ procurement organizations, aging agencies, dental providers, radiology providers, substance abuse treatment providers, free clinics, rehabilitation providers, ambulatory surgery centers, and oncology care. In addition to those, there are other DEA models designed to evaluate health care provider performance from both efficiency and effectiveness (quality) perspectives for specific treatments, including stroke, mechanical ventilation, perioperative services, physicians in hospital settings, hospital-acquired infections, hospital mergers, hospital closures, hospital labor, hospital services in local markets, geographic hospital clusters, critical care hospitals, faith-based hospitals and so forth (Hollingsworth 2003, 2008). These additional models are presented below.

15.2 Efficiency and Effectiveness Studies

There have been a few studies that explored the performance of hospitals by examining both efficiency and effectiveness (quality) as they were introduced in Chap. 1. These studies have been made possible because of the availability of limited quality data in a nationwide database that provides a set of process measures, which allow for the comparison of a large group of hospitals based on the large number of respondent organizations involved with the Hospital Quality Alliance (HQA).

Nayar and Ozcan (2009) used a cross-sectional design to examine 53 non-federal acute care hospitals in Virginia. The data for these hospitals contained input and output variables extracted from the American Hospital Association (AHA) and quality data measures from HQA as reported in 2003. This research is one of the

Y.A. Ozcan, *Health Care Benchmarking and Performance Evaluation*,
International Series in Operations Research & Management Science 210,
DOI 10.1007/978-1-4899-7472-3_15, © Springer Science+Business Media New York 2014

Fig. 15.1 DEA model
for efficiency and
effectiveness using
pneumonia [adapted
from Nayar and
Ozcan (2009)]

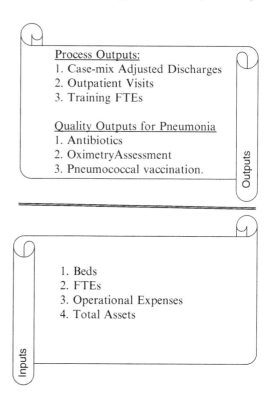

Process Outputs:
1. Case-mix Adjusted Discharges
2. Outpatient Visits
3. Training FTEs

Quality Outputs for Pneumonia
1. Antibiotics
2. OximetryAssessment
3. Pneumococcal vaccination.

Outputs

1. Beds
2. FTEs
3. Operational Expenses
4. Total Assets

Inputs

early studies that used both efficiency and quality metrics to evaluate performance. The inputs measures included beds, staff FTE, operational expenses, and total assets. The outputs included case-mix adjusted discharges, outpatient visits, and training FTEs. Three quality variables were assessed for pneumonia patients: (1) percent of patients receiving antibiotics within 4 h of arrival, (2) percent of patients given oxygenation assessment or pulse oximetry within 24 h prior to or after arrival to the hospital, and (3) percent of patients given pneumococcal vaccination. Figure 15.1 illustrates the model variables.

The study used the constant returns to scale (CCR) model using two different models. The first model tested technical efficiency using three output variables and four input variables (three outputs, four inputs). The second model additionally used the three quality variables as outputs (for a total of outputs and four inputs). The authors found that, using both models, 16 hospitals produced high efficiency and quality results and were labeled as star performers. On the other hand 32 hospitals were poor performers where both quality and efficiency were below the benchmark score of 1. The remaining five hospitals were producing high quality but lacking efficiency.

A more recent efficiency quality study by Nayar et al. (2013) extends the evaluation using a national sample of 371 urban acute care hospitals reported in AHA 2008 data. The inputs and outputs of the efficiency model were similar to the

Fig. 15.2 DEA model
for efficiency and
effectiveness using survival
rates [adapted from
Nayar et al. (2013)]

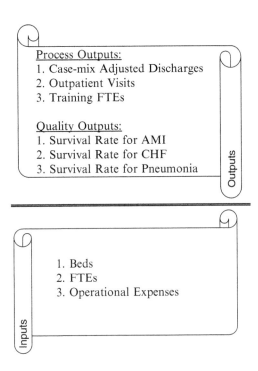

earlier Nayar and Ozcan (2009) study. However, the inpatient quality indicator (IQI) variables were obtained from the nationwide inpatient sample of the same year. The quality measures were: (1) survival rates for acute myocardial infarction (AMI), (2) chronic heart failure (CHF), and (3) pneumonia. The mortality rates were converted to survival rates to maximize survival as an output in the DEA models. Both input-oriented variable returns to scale and non-oriented (additive) slack-based (SBM) DEA models were examined with and without quality variables. Figure 15.2 depicts the model variables for this assessment.

Additionally, a second-stage analysis was performed using Tobit regression where ownership, hospital size group, metropolitan location, Joint Commission on the Accreditation of Healthcare Organizations (JCAHO) accreditation, medical school affiliation, and graduate medical education consisted of the independent control variables.

The survival rates as quality measurements appropriately serve as output variables in the DEA model since SBM DEA tries to improve outputs and inputs and at the same time to achieve higher performance levels. Nayar and associates (2013) report that 62 out of 371 urban hospitals were identified as best performers.

The two studies discussed above evaluated the quality dimension based on availability of the quality adherence data from a nationally available database (HQA), but these do not necessarily give the complete picture on quality. Quality has many dimensions depending upon the constituents of those providing and receiving the care. Hence, using more process-oriented quality variables as well as patient satisfaction may render a more complete picture of assessment of quality. The process variables may include infection rates, patient falls, medication errors, and other errors committed during the care process. Unfortunately there is no systematic reporting system or national data basis for these type metrics from the providers. Patient satisfaction and staff satisfaction with care are measured through surveys and are also not reported to national databases. Evaluations using process variables and satisfaction surveys may be conducted within hospital systems (chain and chain affiliated) where this type of data may be readily available; however, the results of these may not be generalizable beyond the evaluated system.

A study by Mark et al. (2009) partially fulfilled the assessment need for process and patient satisfaction dimensions of quality by examining the performance of 226 medical, surgical, and medical–surgical nursing units in 118 randomly selected acute care hospitals in the US. They used both SBM (see Chap. 5) and variable returns to scale (BCC) DEA models.

Authors used data from the Outcomes Research in Nursing Administration II (ORNA-II) were used. ORNA-II collected data in 2003 and 2004 on two nursing units 146 US acute care hospitals respectively. These hospitals were randomly selected from the 2002 AHA Guide to Hospitals. Overall, 226 units are analyzed in this study. Three input and four output variables were selected. Input variables included number of hours of care per patient day provided by RNs, LPNs, and unlicensed assistive personnel (AUP), the unit's wage- and inflation-adjusted operating expenses, and capital assets (i.e., the unit's number of beds as a proxy). Output variables were captured by case-mix adjusted discharges from the unit and quality of care. The latter consisted of both patient and process dimensions where patient satisfaction and patient safety metrics were deployed using the number of reported medication errors and patient falls. The authors report that to operationalize patient satisfaction, ORNA-II randomly selected ten patients per hospital who were 18+ years of age, were in the hospital for more than 48 h, could speak and read English, and were not selected for immediate discharge to fill out a questionnaire about their satisfaction. A response rate of 93 % was reached (2,213 patients in total). Figure 15.3 depicts the variables for the nursing unit based performance evaluation model.

The SBM DEA results identified 161 inefficient nursing units (59.6 %) and 65 efficient nursing units (40.4 %). Among inefficient units, the average efficiency score was 0.23. The overall efficiency averaged out at 0.45. The results suggested that inefficient nursing units needed to reduce all input variables and improve patient safety and quality of care to reach the efficiency benchmark. More specifically, the results show that both medication errors and patient falls needed to be drastically reduced to achieve better performance, as well as slight increases in adjusted discharges and patient satisfaction.

The authors did not find statistically significant differences between efficient and inefficient nursing units concerning location (i.e., urban and rural), number of hospital beds, Magnet status, Medicare Case Mix Index, availability of support services, percentage of RNs with a bachelor's degree, or length of experience of RNs.

Fig. 15.3 Nursing unit
based DEA model for
efficiency and effectiveness
[adapted from Mark
et al. (2009)]

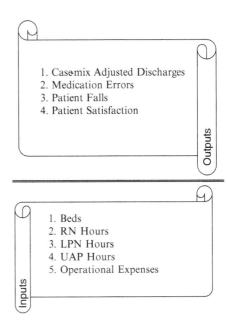

The general impact of this study was the use of quality measurements including patient satisfaction and patient safety. The two measurements of patient safety (medication errors and patient falls) were the two variables that needed to be impacted the most by inefficient nursing units to reach the efficiency frontier. This demonstrates how important it is to include such measurements in overall performance assessment, and if such measurements are available, researchers should strongly consider using them in their models.

Even though it is one of the more comprehensive studies to date evaluating the quality dimension of the performance, there were some limitations of the study including omitted variable bias related to unavailable data on unit-level processes, such as model of care delivery, staffing patterns, architectural design, and availability and use of electronic medical records.

In another study, Mutter et al. (2010) investigate high- versus lower-quality hospitals with a comparison of environmental characteristics and technical efficiency. The authors apply congestion analysis methods (see Chap. 8) to determine if differences exist between hospitals with high quality and lower quality of care. By comparing the technical efficiency and frontiers of hospitals associated with high quality to those providing lower quality of care, the authors identify characteristics that are associated with organizations exhibiting the highest performance.

The study identifies goals of efficiency and quality that commonly elude hospitals, noting that previous studies have yielded mixed results regarding the relationship between efficiency and quality and raise doubts about whether the two goals can be simultaneously realized. As it discusses previous attempts to examine the relationship between quality and efficiency, the article points to the difficulty that prior studies have experienced in accounting for hospitals' quality of care, primarily due to a lack of available data on hospital quality. The authors express their intent to contribute to existing literature on the relationship between quality and efficiency by determining whether high-quality hospitals exhibit common characteristics associated with efficiency in comparison to facilities with medium and low levels of quality. To accomplish their objective, the authors employ a methodological approach known as congestion analysis that assumes a weak disposability of outputs. The authors define high-quality hospitals as "those without output congestion due to patient safety events," and their analysis allows them to ascertain whether hospitals incurring different levels of patient safety events offset this deficit through the more efficient use of resources.

The study's model is introduced in which total technical efficiency (CCR) is the product of pure technical efficiency (BCC), scale efficiency, and congestion. It is noted that congestion measures the impact that bad outputs have on total productivity and is similar to the concept of pollution emitted by industrial production. The authors are able to create three samples of hospitals based upon their congestion levels, including those without congestion (high-quality hospitals), those with congestion levels below the median (medium-quality hospitals), and those with congestion levels above the median (low-quality hospitals). The study results suggest that employing DEA methods across these three groups identifies whether different groups operate on different best-practice frontiers. By employing these steps collectively, the authors are able to eliminate the inefficiency in the lower-quality hospitals and directly measure two quality-based frontiers where the lower-quality frontiers are not confounded by the inefficiency of the medium- or low-quality hospitals.

The study data sources include the American Hospital Association Annual Survey of Hospitals, the Medicare Hospital Cost Reports, the Agency for Healthcare Research and Quality, and Solucient, Inc., providing statistics from 2004. Short-term, community hospitals were the units included in the study, with a total of 1,371 hospitals from 34 participating states. The inputs utilized include bassinets, acute beds, beds in non-acute units, RNs, LPNs, interns and residents, and other personnel. Outputs used include the Medicare Case Mix Index, adjusted admissions (calculated as the product of MCMI and admissions), total surgeries, outpatient visits, births, and patient days in non-acute care units. The adverse outcomes that were included in the study were "failure to rescue, infection due to medical care, postoperative respiratory failure, and postoperative sepsis." Second-stage analyses were conducted using organizational characteristics that were employed for comparison purposes including ownership status, teaching status, system membership, high-technology services, capital expenditures per bed, FTE personnel to adjusted admissions, FTE personnel to beds, births to total admissions, ER visits to total outpatient visits, outpatient surgeries to total outpatient visits, Medicaid and Medicare admissions to total admissions, average length of stay, county-level Hirschman-Herfindahl Index of hospital competition, HMO penetration, and county-level uninsured population percentage. The authors provide justification for their inclusion of each of these organizational characteristics.

The authors find that both pure technical inefficiency and overall technical inefficiency increase from high-quality hospitals to medium-quality hospitals, as well as from medium-quality hospitals to low-quality hospitals. Next, they examine performance results of medium-quality hospitals after completing frontier adjustments, specifically comparing the characteristics among medium-quality hospitals that outperform hospitals defined as high-quality to those whose performance is still below the high-quality organizations. The authors suggest that medium-quality hospitals shown to outperform high-quality hospitals after correcting for input inefficiency had "higher total expenditures, a higher birth rate percentage, a lower percent of total patients covered by Medicaid, [were] less likely to be government owned, and [were] more likely" to maintain not-for-profit ownership status.

A similar comparison was made between high-quality and low-quality hospitals, and the authors found that low-quality hospitals failed to outperform high-quality hospitals in any respect even after correction for inefficiencies. After dividing the low-quality hospitals into two groups based upon a median value of low-quality organizations, the authors' comparison noted that the higher performing hospitals within the low-quality group "had lower total expenditures, a lower proportion of total admissions that were births, a higher share of Medicare patients, a lower occupancy rate, spent less capital per bed, and were less likely" to maintain teaching hospital status.

The comparison of different hospital group frontiers found an association between high-quality hospitals and measures of technical efficiency such that the high-quality hospitals experienced higher efficiency levels. Their findings suggest that quality and efficiency can indeed be achieved simultaneously. Reiterating the ways in which some medium-quality hospitals outperformed the high-quality group after correcting for inefficiencies, the article also concludes that medium-quality hospitals "can improve both their efficiency and their quality" by eliminating technical inefficiencies and approaching the best practice frontier through a balance of quality and resource utilization. The authors provide a similar conclusion for low-quality hospitals, noting that their examination of low-quality hospitals found that those closer to the high-quality frontier had lower expenditures and a higher proportion of Medicare patients, and they suggest that these findings offer support for low-quality hospitals to "mitigate poor quality/inefficiency outcomes" by "reducing their range of services."

15.3 Efficiency of Treatment for Stroke Patients

Stroke is the number one cause of adult disability and the third leading cause of death in the United States. Stroke kills 137,000 people a year. Stroke is also a leading cause of serious, long-term disability in the US. Although stroke affects people of all ages, genders, and races, people over 55, males, and African-Americans are at higher risk for stroke (www.strokeassociation.org). At the writing

Fig. 15.4 DEA model for
stroke treatment

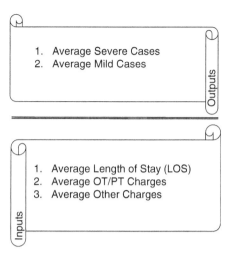

of this book, there are over 5.5 million stroke survivors alive, and 795,000 people suffer a new or recurrent stroke each year. Thus, it is important to evaluate performance of providers in treatment of stroke.

The study by Ozcan et al. (1998a) used DEA to examine the relationships between provider experience and technical efficiency in treatment of stroke patients. The evaluation further examined the volume-efficiency relationship and showed that provider experience and high volume practice improve performance.

Ozcan and associates analyzed the relative technical efficiency among experience-based peer groups using data envelopment analysis within the input-oriented DEA model. The unit of analysis was hospitals that provide stroke treatment. This evaluation used Centers for Medicare and Medicaid (CMS) data from 1989. The final sample contained 214 hospitals. Of these 214 hospitals, 124 are in the low volume category for stroke cases (25–49 cases), 73 are in the medium volume category (50–99 cases), and 17 are in the high volume category (100+ cases). Thus, the evaluation uses DEA to test for technical efficiency in stroke treatments based on the average number of cases that the facility treats.

The input variables were an average length of stay (ALOS), average occupational and physical therapy charges, and average all other charges. The output variables were average mild and severe stroke cases per provider. Figure 15.4 displays the DEA model for the stroke treatment.

Results suggest that efficiency scores increase from low to high experience hospitals. The efficiency score for low stroke volume hospitals was 0.59, medium volume hospitals 0.61, and high volume hospitals 0.81. Upon further analysis, it was determined that the efficient hospitals tend to use lesser inputs to produce a similar number of outputs. The findings of this study also show that high experience providers also have higher charges, which are also associated with higher severity of cases.

15.4   Benchmarking Mechanical Ventilation Services

Mechanical ventilation provides external breathing support to patients who might have ineffective ventilation due to respiratory failure, chest trauma, pneumonia, etc. Mechanical ventilation could be needed for the short term (2 days or less) or longer term (3 or more days). Depending upon the patient's condition and severity, the outcomes of mechanical ventilation could be recovery, morbidity, or mortality. This technology requires multiple resource use and drives hospitalization costs higher. Thus, it is prudent to identify efficient practices related to mechanical ventilation use.

O'Neal et al. (2002) provided an evaluation of mechanical ventilation services in teaching hospitals. The data were obtained from the University Hospital Consortium (UHC), a national university hospital consortium that keeps a detailed patient-level database. The data included 62 UHC hospitals (out of 69) that had non-missing data for 1997. Using diagnosis-related group (DRG) 475, for mechanical ventilation, outputs and inputs of the service production were identified. Patient-level data was converted to hospital level; thus 62 UHC hospitals were the decision-making units (DMUs). An input-oriented DEA model was employed.

Outputs included adjusted discharges to home, the reciprocal of patients transferred, and the reciprocal of patients expired. The last two outputs indicate morbidity and mortality, thus, as outputs, hospitals would want less of them. Hence, using the reciprocal of the measured values, DEA model converts them to be less. The authors also tested ventilator patient days as an alternative output to adjusted discharges and conducted sensitivity analyses. Their findings showed that an adjusted discharge variable was more robust.

Inputs included charges occurring from the departments of respiratory therapy, pharmacy, laboratory, and radiology. These are the most common charge centers for the mechanical ventilation patients in addition to other common charges. Figure 15.5 shows the DEA model for mechanical ventilation.

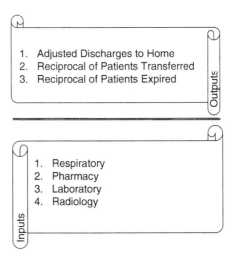

Fig. 15.5 DEA model
for mechanical ventilation

Results showed that practice variation (resource utilization) existed among 62 UHC hospitals in the use of mechanical ventilation. Only seven hospitals achieved perfect efficiency. The average efficiency score was 0.49. Inefficient hospitals transferred more patients to other hospitals and more patients expired in them. Examining the efficiency targets for 55 inefficient hospitals, the authors found that the excessive charges (overutilization of inputs) amounted to $530,000 for respiratory therapy, $150,000 for pharmacy, $570,000 for laboratory, and $630,000 for radiology services (O'Neal et al. 2002).

This model provides guidance for administrators and researchers who would like to examine utilization or efficiency of a particular service product in the hospital, and could provide strategies for where to look for cost reductions or streamlining the operations.

15.5 Market Capture of Inpatient Perioperative Services

Preoperative care, elective surgery, and post-operative care define Perioperative Services (POS). According to O'Neill and Dexter (2004), the assessment of efficiency of POS can be used to estimate how many more cases can be accomplished by each specialty hospital.

The O'Neill and Dexter evaluation used an output-oriented DEA CRS and super-efficient model. Output orientation promotes the increase o surgical procedures. The outputs were eight different surgical procedures, most of them with high DRG intensity weights. These outputs included the following surgical procedures: abdominal aortic aneurysm (AAA), coronary artery bypass graft (CABG), colorectal resection, craniotomy not for trauma, hip replacement, hysterectomy, lobectomy of lungs or pneumonectomy, and nephrectomy. Selection reasons for these particular surgeries were justified by their frequency and availability in many hospitals.

As shown in Fig. 15.6, inputs of the model were beds, technology measured by high-tech services offered by the hospital, number of surgeons, weighted hospital discharges for the eight surgical outputs into the county where the hospital is located (regardless of where the care is received), and weighted hospital discharges for the eight surgical procedures into the surrounding region regardless of where the care was received.

Twenty-nine of the 53 hospitals were identified as efficient performers by DEA. The DEA benchmark targets in inefficient hospitals, specifically for output shortages in various surgery types, provide rich information to their hospital managers for strategic initiatives. This way, hospital managers can design strategic initiatives to market more surgery time on specific surgical procedures to reach efficiency in perioperative services (O'Neill and Dexter 2004).

Fig. 15.6 DEA model for
perioperative services

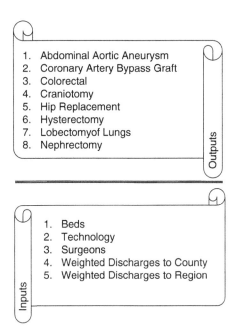

15.6   **Electronic Medical Records (EMR) and Efficiency**

Health care providers in the US are under immense pressure to adopt information technologies, especially electronic medical records (EMRs). These pressures come not only from the federal government through meaningful use goals of these technologies but also immense competition as well as ever-changing reimbursement claim processes. Additionally, there are potential penalties by the government in reimbursement from Medicare and Medicaid if the certifications on meaningful use standards are not achieved by 2015 (Ford et al. 2013). The adaptation of EMR and other health technologies are projected to improve efficiency and quality of health care delivery. Despite the initial cost of these systems and the learning curve during adaptation periods, the impact of these technologies hopefully will render its promise in the near future. In the interim period of these adaptations, a few researchers have been exploring the EMR adaptation and its impact on efficiency. We present a few of these investigations to shed some light on further assessments in this vast area of research.

15.6.1   EMR and Efficiency

One of the early studies evaluating the impact of EMR use and efficiency was conducted by Kazley and Ozcan (2009) using DEA Windows analysis of hospitals. They examined the impact of EMR use on the technical efficiency of 4,606 US non-federal acute care hospitals. Data were taken from the Health Information Management Systems Society (HIMSS) and the American Hospital Association (AHA) annual surveys. Two research designs were employed. First, a cross-sectional retrospective with a non-equivalent control group (i.e., 4,127 hospitals not using EMR in 2004) was used to test the hypothesis that hospitals with EMRs are more efficient than hospitals without EMRs.

An input-oriented CRS DEA model was used to generate efficiency scores for small, medium, and large hospitals separately. Small hospitals were defined as facilities with 6–100 beds, medium hospitals as facilities with 101–349, and large hospitals as facilities with 350 and more beds. DEA model variables were adopted from the robust hospital DEA model discussed in Chap. 9. Hence, input variables were non-physician FTEs, beds set up and staffed, service-mix, and non-labor operating expenses. Output variables were case-mix-adjusted admissions and out-patient visits. Hospitals within the 75th percentile were considered technically efficient in this study. Three logistic regressions (i.e., for small, medium, and large hospitals) were then employed to estimate the likelihood of being technically efficient predicted by EMR use, teaching status, ownership, system affiliation, and bed size. While the authors hypothesized that EMR use would increase efficiency through the relationship between systems and outcomes, they found that this was only true for small hospitals in the years of early EMR adaptation.

Windows analysis using data from 2001 to 2004 was used to test another hypothesis: "hospitals with EMRs will increase in efficiency over time more than hospitals without EMRs." The logistic regressions for medium and large hospitals generated no significant differences in efficiency performance based on EMR use. The authors concluded that EMR use did not improve efficiency over time for hospitals with EMRs any more than the hospitals that did not have EMRs during this period.

15.6.2   EMR Adaptation Strategies

A later study by Fareed et al. (2012) examined hospital EMR enterprise application strategies using DEA. The main purpose of this study was to identify which of the three possible types of EMR enterprise application strategies—single vendor (SV), best of breed (BOB), and best of suite (BOS)—was associated with hospitals' greater likelihood of being efficient. The authors used the central tenets of Struc-tural Contingency theory to develop two major hypotheses: (1) hospitals pursuing an SV strategy are more likely to be efficient than hospitals that have a BOB strategy; and (2) hospitals pursuing a BOS strategy are more likely to be efficient than hospitals that have an SV or a BOB strategy.

The study sample consisted of 2,171 non-federal, general acute care hospitals. The data for the study came from the AHA 2008 Annual Survey of Hospitals, the

2008 CMS Case Mix Index, the 2008 Area Resource Files (ARF), and the 2008 HIMSS Analytics database. The study used the input-oriented variable returns to scale (BCC) DEA model again following the robust hospital model from Chap. 9. The study input variables consisted of hospital bed size, service mix, labor force (FTE), and operational expenses; case-mix-adjusted admissions and outpatient visits were the output measures. In a second-stage analysis, DEA scores were transformed before being analyzed by Tobit regression. The analysis used the hospital's EMR enterprise application strategy as the primary independent variable and EMR implementation status as a moderating variable.

The analysis controlled for various hospital characteristics such as: a hospital's ownership type, system affiliation, teaching status, bed size, Joint Commission on Accreditation of Healthcare Organizations (JCAHO) accreditation status, and payer mix. The analysis also controlled for some market characteristics such as hospital services area (HSA) competition, county population (a proxy for market size), county unemployment rate (a proxy for the percentage of uninsured), county percentage of the population over 65 years of age, county percentage of African-Americans in the population, and geographical location.

Results of the DEA analysis showed only 32 hospitals to be efficient with an average efficiency score of 0.55. Results of the Tobit analysis showed no support for Hypothesis 1 and provided partial support for Hypothesis 2 (BOS EMR enterprise application strategy may be significantly more likely to be efficient than hospitals with an SV strategy, whereas there was no significant differences between hospitals that had BOS and BOB strategies). Results showed that hospitals that were teaching, had system membership, or were in larger markets were more likely to be efficient. On the other hand, hospitals that were not-for-profit, had more beds, were JCAHO accredited, had a greater share of Medicare or Medicaid patients, were in an urban market, or were situated in the Northeast or Midwest (versus the South) were found to be less likely to be efficient across both the models (BOS and BOB strategies). Results showed that hospitals with an SV strategy and an EMR status of "not automated" or had "contracted with a vendor or not yet installed their EMR" were likely to be more efficient than hospitals with an SV strategy and an EMR status of "fully automated." By contrast, hospitals with an SV strategy and an EMR status of "not yet contracted" or those with a BOS strategy and an EMR status of "not automated" were likely to be less efficient than their respective, fully automated counterparts. From a policy perspective, the study provided insights into which Health Information Technology strategies work and how hospitals can effectively achieve "meaningful use" of their EMRs.

The authors noted the inconsistency in the features of various EMRs, the possibility of discrepancy between a hospital's current stated strategy and its current application portfolio, the inability of the study to be certain if the stated strategy was actually carried out in a hospital or not, and the cross-sectional nature of the study as some of the study's limitations.

15.6.3   EMR Adaptation Strategy—Longitudinal

A similar study using the same vendor strategies as in Fareed et al. (2012) was conducted by Ford et al (2013). This study used the Malmquist method to evaluate vendor strategies. This article used three input variables and five output variables from the American Hospital Association's Annual Survey of Hospitals for a 6-year period of assessment, 2002 through 2007. Three input variables consisted of beds, nursing FTEs (RN and LPNs), and other FTEs. Five output variables consisted of outpatient surgeries, adjusted admissions, patient days, emergency room visits, and outpatient visits. Although the authors argue that "the number of patient-days beyond the admission day provided a measure of length of stay and, together with the adjusted admission variable, can be used to capture the average daily census," use of patient days in any form duplicates the outputs and introduces upward bias to DEA scores.

The study had a total of 1,716 hospitals for the 6 years. The second stage of the analyses was conducted using three ordinal logistic regression analyses with Malmquist, and its components efficiency and technology change (see Chap. 6) were deployed as dependent variables. Results showed only the technology change component of the Malmquist Index was the significantly related factor to the vendor selection strategy of the hospitals. Compared with the single vendor strategy, both the best of breed and best of suite were associated with relatively higher levels of technical change. The authors claimed lack of significant differences in the Malmquist Index and could not discern the role of technical change in driving productivity increase. They conclude that large costs of adopting one of the vendor selection strategies, much of it in the form of process redesign, impacted the technical change component of the Malmquist Index.

15.7   Physicians at Hospital Setting

Chilingerian (1995) provided an extensive analysis and discussion of a clinical efficiency study involving 36 physicians at a single major teaching hospital. The aim of this evaluation was to determine the various levels of efficiency practiced by physicians. He identified the variance in resources utilized (i.e., diagnostic procedures) between physicians practicing within the same hospital and identified variance in physician decision making. This evaluation using DEA and the multi-variant Tobit model analyzed physician efficiency and identified key factors associated with the efficient use of clinical resources in the provision of hospital services.

Chilingerian concluded that inefficient physician decision making may be one of the root causes of runaway costs and low hospital productivity. The deficiencies of prior studies are that most of the prior studies did not look at the nature of efficient relationships inside health care organizations. Prior research on physician utilization of hospital services is reliant on a single-input, single-output analysis, not multiple-input, multiple-output analysis. Also, analytic methods were at the central tendencies rather than identifying the best results.

The physicians included in this study were any physician who treated more than 35 cases during the 3 months as active attending physicians. This sampling rule was generated by a pilot testing result. The data were collected through MedisGroups. To minimize the influence of case mix complexity, the study was conducted using a pair of DEA models. Both a CRS and VRS model were established and partitioned by internists and surgeons, with a 2:1 ratio between them. The second CRS and VRS evaluation models included a relative weight for case mix. The purpose of the two models was to minimize any extraneous variables.

The output variables were the number of high severity discharges and the number of low severity discharges. The input variables were the total length of each patient's stay and the total charges for all ancillary services.

The result indicated that physician practice characteristics are more important factors associated with efficient care than patient illness characteristics. Most of the HMO physicians practiced in regions of constant returns to scale, and most of the fee-for-service physicians practiced in regions of increasing returns to scale. Physicians affiliated with the group-practice HMO increased their likelihood of being efficient. The proportion of very high severity cases had a strong negative effect on inefficiency scores while specialization by DRG and the size of a physician's caseload were also found to improve the likelihood of physician efficiency (Chilingerian 1995). One of the major limitations of this evaluation was that the study was only conducted in one hospital with physicians admitting at least a certain number of patients, so the generalizability of the study result is difficult.

The results indicated a potential savings impact of $1,000,000 if the lesser two-thirds could perform at the level of the more efficient physicians. This value may not be fully rational. A Post-hoc Tobit analysis demonstrated that HMO affiliation was a significant factor (Chilingerian 1995).

15.8   Hospital-Acquired Infections

Health care associated infections are a result of both inefficiency and ineffectiveness for hospital providers. In a recent study, Pakyz and Ozcan (2014) investigated the clostridium difficile infection (CDI) to create a benchmarking strategy for targeting high-risk antibacterial drugs causing CDI. They used University Hospital Consortium (UHC) data with 58 hospitals that subscribe to the Clinical Resource Manager (CRM) program, which provides procedure-and-diagnosis-specific data. The input-oriented CCR model included a single output, which was CDI, and five input variables. The input variables were the commonly used antibacterial drug classes that are particularly associated with CDI risk: (1) clindamycin, (2) β-lactam/β-lactamase combinations (piperacillin/tazobactam, ticarcillin/clavulanate), (3) fluoroquinolones (moxifloxacin, ciprofloxacin, levofloxacin), (4) third- and fourth-generation cephalosporins (ceftriaxone, cefotaxime, ceftazidime, cefepime), and (5) carbapenems (doripenem, imipenem, meropenem, ertapenem).

Their results showed that 17 hospitals were 'best-practice hospitals.' More specifically, these hospitals are considered the benchmark hospitals in regard to low occurrence of health care associated CDI. They also showed the necessary reductions in use needed for clindamycin, carbapenems, and β-lactam/β-lactamase combinations for the non-benchmark hospitals.

15.9 Hospital Mergers

Harris et al. (2000) conducted a retrospective longitudinal study of hospital mergers and the relationship to enhanced efficiency as a possible result. DEA CRS and VRS models were used to investigate the impact of horizontal hospital mergers on technical efficiency. Multi-period analysis was used to study efficiency levels before and after the merger year. Two research questions focused on how mergers enhance efficiency and how soon mergers impact efficiency levels. The unit of analysis was a new hospital created by a merger.

The sample size was 20 hospitals that had been created from mergers in 1992. The sample size was increased to 60 hospitals using the multi-period analysis that considered prior and post merger years (3 years × 20 hospitals). Data included survey data for 1991, 1992, and 1993 from the American Hospital Association and the CMS Case Mix Index. Inputs and outputs were the same as shown in the robust DEA model in Chap. 9 (see Fig. 9.1). Both CRS and VRS models were used for an input-oriented model.

Of the 20 hospitals under the CRS model, 11 hospitals (55 %) stayed the same or improved efficiency in the merger year and 12 (60 %) in the post merger year. One hospital (Hospital B) had the greatest improvement and another (Hospital O) had the largest decrease in efficiency. Average efficiency scores were 0.812, 0.803, and 0.852 for years 1991, 1992, and 1993. The total efficiency change was 1.51 % and 8.46 % from 1991 to years 1992 and 1993, respectively.

Under the BCC model, of the 20 hospitals, 13 (65 %) had similar scores or improved in the merger year and 13 (65 %) in the post merger year. Hospital B had the greatest improvement and Hospital K had the largest decrease in efficiency. Average efficiency scores were 0.862, 0.894, and 0.889 in years 1991, 1992, and 1993, respectively. The total efficiency change was 6.42 % and 5.42 % in years 1992 and 1993. For all inefficient hospitals, more post-merger work needs to be performed to achieve efficiency levels.

This study used data from 1991 to 1993 to access efficiency changes. Since 1993, the rate of mergers has increased, especially during the mid to late 1990s. The reasons for this change to a market system include but are not limited to government policies. As a result, some mergers were due to offensive efficiency-seeking behavior, while others were due to defensive strategies. Replication of this study for more recent years and in a larger time span would be prudent.

15.10   Hospital Closures

Hospital closures in rural and inner city locations became epidemic in the late 1980s mainly as the effect of implementation of the Prospective Payment System (PPS) through DRGs. Ozcan and Lynch (1992) examined hospital closures in rural locations. This study used 1988 AHA survey files and similar inputs and outputs to the DEA model presented in Fig. 8.1, although they added a training FTE variable as an additional output. The sample contained 1,535 hospitals of which 726 were located in rural areas and 809 in urban areas. There were 66 hospitals that closed and 1,469 remained open. The average efficiency score for closed rural hospitals was 0.75, and for those that remained open was 0.80. In urban locations, the average efficiency for closed hospitals was 0.72 and for those that remained open was 0.76. The efficiency differences between closed and open hospitals were not significant, but closed hospitals experienced lower efficiencies.

Later in a separate study with the same data, Lynch and Ozcan (1994) used a combination of DEA and logistic regression to determine if inefficient hospitals were more likely to experience closures. They also investigated the relationship between high Medicaid payer shares and closures. Results showed that hospitals providing larger proportions of Medicaid paid days of care were being driven from the market. They also found that small hospitals that do not experience a demand for their services were found to be at greater risk for closure.

15.11   Labor Efficiency in Hospital Markets

Many hospital cost containment initiatives were introduced in the early 1980s, especially Medicare's Prospective Payment System and actions by managed care organizations, and a big portion of hospital budgets is labor costs. Thus, examination of hospital labor markets and labor efficiency became an important issue.

Ozcan et al. (1996b) used AHA Annual Survey of Hospitals for 1989 and 1993 for all non-federal acute care general hospitals to evaluate hospital labor efficiency in major markets. The hospitals' data were aggregated at Metropolitan Statistical Areas (MSAs) markets and designated as the DMU. A total of 633 MSAs in two time periods (319 in 1989, 314 in 1993) were analyzed. The MSAs were divided into four market groups based on population size to control for the effect of market size on efficiency.

The two outputs were case-mix adjusted discharges and outpatient visits as in the model in Chap. 8. The seven inputs were FTEs in nursing, allied health, administration, salaried physicians and trainees, physician extenders, nonprofessional assistants, and nonprofessional technicians. The study used the input-oriented DEA CRS model.

The descriptive statistics show an increase in outpatient visits, especially dramatic in the small population MSAs (12 million to 160 million), between 1989 and

1993, reflecting the industry trend toward increased outpatient procedures. Clinical labor inputs increased in all categories except large market nursing assistants from 1989 to 1993. Administrative labor inputs increased substantially from 1989 to 1993.

The DEA analysis showed that MSAs in the medium market category significantly decreased in their efficiency score between 1989 and 1993. The percentage of inefficient hospital markets increased over time in every market category. The excessive use of inputs by inefficient labor markets on RN, allied health, and administrative FTEs for medium MSAs also significantly increased. The changes in administrative FTEs were significant for large MSAs.

Why is it that hospital labor markets did not improve their efficiency? Among the potential explanations are: (1) hospitals focusing on capital efficiency, not labor efficiency (institutional stronghold delaying significant labor transitions; concerns for quality not allowing cutbacks and substitution; uncertainty of job redesign and the effect on efficiency becoming evident later than the study period), (2) hospitals focusing on quality instead of efficiency (Total Quality Management adoptions), and (3) the turbulent environment in the early 1990s.

The evaluation also provided recommendations for potential hospital market savings. Inefficient medium MSAs utilized an average of 605 more FTEs than the efficient MSAs, totaling $24 million in excess human resources per inefficient MSA.

15.12   Excess Hospital Service Capacity in Local Markets

Evaluation of labor efficiency in hospital markets also led to another study by Ozcan (1995). This evaluation focuses on hospital-generated inefficiencies in local markets as one of three major sources of health care inefficiency. The aim of the study was to provide a preliminary assessment of hospital service delivery performance at the local market level and to assess the degree of duplication and redundancy in capital resources in health care markets. More specifically, the aim was to assess the variation in efficiency of hospital resources allocation across metropolitan areas in the nation.

The Ozcan (1995) study analyzed 319 metropolitan areas (less than 250,000, 250,000–1,000,000, 1,000,000–2,500,000, more than 2,500,000), and the primary source of data was the AHA survey for 1990.

Inputs and outputs of the input-oriented DEA model were similar to the model presented in Fig. 8.1. Outputs were adjusted discharges and outpatient visits; inputs were capital (service complexity and hospital size), labor (non-physician FTEs) and operating expenses.

Findings of this evaluation can be summarized as:

– Average technical efficiency ranges between 0.79 and 0.92 across the different sizes of metropolitan areas,

- Increase in average efficiency with size (except medium market size), which may be attributed to economy of scale,
- Analysis of efficient targets showed that (except for very large markets), production of adjusted discharges is appropriate. For large markets, there was an average shortage of 427 discharges (0.4 %); in very large markets an average of an additional 152,940 outpatient visits could have been handled with available resources,
- Inefficiency contributes to approximately 23 % of the increase in health care costs, and that
- Certificate of Need and regulatory environment showed no significant correlation to waste in local markets (Ozcan 1995)

A more recent study by Valdmanis et al. (2010) offers a unique application of DEA methods in order to determine whether hospitals in the state of Florida maintain the collective capacity and economic capability to meet patient demand for medical services in response to a major disaster or a state of emergency. The authors emphasize the importance of excess capacity, which is defined as "a failure to reach potential output." Citing several studies, the article notes that as hospitals have sought to decrease excess capacity and improve upon efficient practices to ensure financial stability, access to valuable health services has decreased. However, it is also explained that a decrease in access does not take place uniformly across the entire market; for example, the article provides the example of a decrease in services at one hospital leading to another hospital increasing access to meet the communities' unmet needs. Valdmanis and colleagues state their intent to "explore whether one hospital *market* could absorb unmet need if another hospital market was compromised" using the example of a hurricane disaster in Miami, Florida.

The analysis of hospital capacities and capabilities in the face of disaster is conducted through multiple stages: (1) Johansen's (1968) definition of plant capacity is employed to "determine how much output can be substituted among markets;" (2) the concept of capacity is extended to medical and economic considerations to address whether "hospitals outside of the disaster area have the ability to care for patients with specific medical needs" and "what levels of compensation will be required to allow for hospitals to absorb these additional cases in an economically feasible manner; and (3) the relative economic tradeoffs of moving patients varying distances over varying time frames" are examined in light of the disastrous outcomes of patients that were not moved in advance of Hurricane Katrina in New Orleans. The existence of sufficient capacity to absorb additional patients in the event of an emergency specifically occurs when specific patient care needs are met—including the provision of specialized services—and when hospitals are adequately compensated for the care they provide so that neither patients or receiving facilities "incur a real loss." The authors choose to focus on the hypothetical situation of a hurricane disaster in Miami, Florida, noting that Miami represents a major market and that its geographic positioning minimizes the likelihood of out-of-state evacuations.

A DEA approach toward measuring capacity and capability of hospitals in an emergency situation is applied within the study, and the authors explain the advantages and benefits of utilizing DEA methods, including consideration of multiple outputs and variable inputs as well as an emphasis on overall performance. The analysis first uses a "constant returns to scale output-based measure of technical efficiency" and then determines output-based efficiency and capacity utilization by holding the variable of beds as a fixed input while allowing labor inputs such as nurses and FTE staff to vary. To determine plant capacity utilization, which the authors define as the amount of output that can be produced given some fixed inputs and some variable inputs, the output-based efficiency measure is divided by the fixed-input technical efficiency measure. A similar approach is employed to determine medical capability, with fixed and variable inputs denoted for specialty care as well as general care, and hospital service units (general and specialty segments) are summed across hospital markets to determine market area capacity. The data source for hospital capacity and discharges is the Florida Agency for Health Care Administration, providing financial and operating statistics for "all general, short term hospitals and non-specialty or long term care facilities" in the state of Florida. The model of 13 inputs (Total FTE residents, Total FTE staff, Total FTE nursing hours, Total beds, Cardiac care FTE residents, Cardiac care FTE staff, Cardiac care beds, Medical/surgical intensive care FTE residents, Medical/surgical intensive care FTE staff, Medical/surgical intensive care beds, Pediatric intensive care FTE residents, Pediatric intensive care FTE staff, Pediatric intensive care beds) and 5 outputs (Total inpatient days, Cardiac care inpatient days, Medical/surgical inpatient days, Pediatric intensive care inpatient days, Case mix index) is applied to a sample of 162 facilities (the entire population of hospitals in Florida).

The study's results show that "Florida hospitals were utilizing available resources at high capacity," with particularly high utilization rates for medical/surgical intensive care and pediatric intensive care services. Four separate analyses for plant capacity according to each service line were performed and "aggregated to measure medical capability by market," and the authors identify designated beds as "the excess capacity that could be available for potential patient evacuees multiplied by the number of staffed beds per service," holding efficiency constant. The findings of the analysis indicate that the state of Florida is not capable of providing adequate capacity for medical/surgical intensive care patients in the event that patients from Miami would have to evacuate to other cities within the state. The authors suggest that even if other hospitals upgraded general beds to intensive care beds to bolster available supply in the event of an emergency, the transition would require increased expenses that would be undesirable and unsustainable given reduced efficiency and quality. Cardiac intensive care beds outside of Miami also lack adequate supply, and the pediatric intensive care beds were the only service line that maintained sufficient capacity to meet increased demand if Miami patients were to evacuate to other Florida hospitals.

Given the findings of their DEA model, the article concludes that, in the event of a major disaster such as a hurricane event in Miami, hospitals in the state of Florida would fail to adequately absorb the excess patient flow of patient evacuees from Miami given considerations of available capacity, medical capability, and economic capability.

15.13 Geographic Hospital Clusters

Sikka et al. (2009) investigated an interesting phenomenon that has unfolded across the US health care system over the past several decades: the formation of hospitals into geographic clusters. Further, they noted that very few studies had examined the efficiency with which services are distributed across cluster members. Thus, they set out to empirically explore cluster efficiencies with two techniques: (1) the use of DEA to measure cluster configuration efficiencies, and (2) a Tobit regression to test relationships between selected indicators of cluster configuration and the DEA scores.

Having provided a historical basis for why hierarchical configurations (i.e., clusters with large hospitals at their centers) may be theorized to be more efficient clusters, the authors listed the aforementioned characteristics as a key hypothesis of their study along with several others. These included: cluster efficiency would be positively associated with hospitals that are closer together spatially, with a greater number of hospitals in the cluster, and higher percentages of cluster hospitals located in urban areas, while the presence of academic medical centers (AMCs) would be negatively associated with cluster efficiency.

The authors defined a cluster as "two or more same-system hospitals located in the same local market or region" and also used clusters as the DMU for DEA. Using a modified version of 2004 AHA data, they initially identified 638 clusters. However, data reporting conventions, small cluster sizes, and other limitations restricted the final sample size to 343 clusters. With the help of the AHA and Medicare Cost Reports data, the authors operationalized four inputs—number of beds, services mix, non-physician FTEs, and non-labor expenses—and two outputs—case-mix-adjusted admissions and outpatient visits—in their DEA model similar to one presented in Chap. 9. Data were summed to the cluster level from the hospital level, when needed. An input-oriented, constant returns to scale model was used, and the ability for cluster managers to have greater control of inputs was the basis for their selection of an input-oriented model. Interestingly, they also provided a discussion around the perplexity of using teaching status in DEA models, and, as a compromise, included it in their Tobit analysis.

Results of the DEA demonstrated that 20, or 5.8 %, of the 343 clusters were efficient. The average level of efficiency was 75 % across the clusters. Service mix seemed to be the most important contributor to the inefficiency, which was a finding that ran against conventional notions of clusters being rationalized distributors of service capacity. The aforementioned finding with service mix may have also been a result of the use of a raw service mix variable versus an index, which would have properly weighted the use of certain types of services over others.

The Tobit analysis contained seven dimensions of clusters—those with AMC hospitals, their center hospital's size, percentage of urban hospitals, dispersion, number of hospitals within a cluster, ownership, and competition—as predictors of cluster efficiency. The authors found that, consistent with their hypothesis, hierarchical clusters were significantly more efficient. Further, urban clusters were also significantly more efficient. However, cluster dispersion, AMC presence, ownership, number of hospitals, and competition were not significant.

In conclusion, the authors provided evidence that cluster configuration could affect efficiency of service capacity distributions across clustered members. The findings on hierarchical configurations from the Tobit analysis supported historical claims that such a means of organizing is ideal for health care systems. They noted that the clusters in their analysis may not have had sufficient time to effectively reorganize their service configurations in ways that would produce higher efficiencies. Thus, a longitudinal analysis, to complement their study, was provided as a recommendation. Another important recommendation was to delineate the DEA analyses by urban/rural clusters in an effort to obtain more in-depth assessments of clusters.

15.14   Critical Care Hospitals

Certain hospitals are certified as Critical Access Hospitals (CAH) under a set of Medicare Conditions of Participation (CoP), which are structured differently than the acute care hospital CoP. The requirements for CAH certification include: (1) 25 inpatient beds or less, (2) annual average length of stay of 96 h or less for acute inpatient care, (3) offering 24/7 emergency care, and (4) located in a rural area that is about a 35-mile drive to another hospital or CAH. The aforementioned conditions for certification allow CAHs to focus on common care conditions and outpatient care. The CAH certification provides cost-based reimbursement from Medicare, rather than the standard DRG-based reimbursement rates. This restructuring of rural hospital payments enhanced the financial performance of many that were losing money prior to CAH designation. This also helped to reduce rural hospital closures (Health Resources and Services Administration 2013).

Gautam et al. (2013) analyzed the relative efficiency of CAHs in the state of Missouri and compared their performances with other rural acute care hospitals in the same state. The study used the input-oriented variable returns to scale (BCC) DEA model to estimate technical efficiency (TE), allocative efficiency (AE), and cost efficiency (CE). The data for the study came from the Missouri Hospital Association (for input and output variables), Missouri Department of Health and Senior Services (information on number of beds and inpatients), and Hospital Compare data from the Centers for Medicare and Medicaid Services (quality variable; 30-day readmission rates). The study variables included Case Mix Index adjusted inpatient days, total emergency room visits, and total nonemergency outpatient visits as the three output variables; total full-time equivalent employees and number of staffed beds as the input variables; price of labor and price of capital as the two input prices; and 30-day readmission rates for pneumonia and congestive heart failure as the hospital quality indicators. DEA results showed that there was a slight improvement in the mean cost efficiency (CE) of the Missouri CAHs, but a marginal loss in technical efficiency (TE) in 2009 compared to 2006.

The results of the study showed that while the mean DEA efficiencies (both technical and cost) were good for the state CAHs, there was a large variability in these CAHs. The majority of the CAHs were inefficient (60 % technically inefficient and 66 % cost inefficient) in 2009, 30 % were below the mean TE, and 42 % of the hospitals were below the mean CE in 2009. While 39 % of hospitals were technically efficient, and 33 % were cost efficient in 2009, only 9 (28 %) of the hospitals were shown to be consistently efficient (TE and CE) in both years, and 17 (52 %) of the hospitals are neither technically nor cost efficient in both years. Most of the hospitals that were inefficient in 2006 remained inefficient in 2009. Results on the quality indicator showed that only 3 (11 %) out of 28 CAHs included were benchmark CAHs (high quality and high efficiency), 8 (29 %) CAHs were poor performers (on both CE and quality) and 25 (89 %) CAHs needed improvement in either CE or quality or both. Banker's F-test results confirmed that CAHs were significantly more inefficient than other rural acute care hospitals in the state. From a policy perspective the study highlights the tradeoff that the states have to make between providing access and efficiency of the CAHs. The article also points to the relative disadvantage that the other higher efficiency rural hospitals face relative to the CAHs as a policy implication. The authors note small sample size, use of a single quality indicator, possibility of omitted variable bias, and limited generalizability of the study to other acute care settings as study limitations.

Another study by Nadela and Fannin (2013) used a two-stage approach to evaluate CAH rural hospitals in which the data sample consisted of 186 rural CAHs in 2005 and 229 rural CAHs in 2006. Their model used number of outpatient visits, number of admissions, post-admission days (inpatient days—admissions), emergency room visits, outpatient surgeries, and total births as outputs. They also used two quality variables as outputs following Nayar and Ozcan (2009): (1) percent of patients given pneumococcal vaccination, and (2) percent of patients given initial antibiotics within four hours after arrival. The labor component of the inputs included RN FTEs, LPN FTEs, and other FTEs. The capital input was total staffed and licensed hospital beds.

The first stage assessment was conducted through DEA with bootstrapped methodology to obtain bias corrected technical efficiency scores. In the second stage they employed a bootstrapped truncated regression model to evaluate environmental variables' effect on double bootstrapped efficiency scores. The authors showed that their model with quality variables included as outputs showed a more clear significant relationship with environmental variables using a double bootstrap methodology.

15.15 Faith-Based Hospitals

Faith-based or religious hospitals have significant market share in many hospital markets. Thus, efficiency of these hospitals within their own religious domain is an interesting phenomenon to assess. Chou et al. (2012) examined the relationships between the technical and scale efficiency of Catholic system-affiliated hospitals and relevant organizational and market characteristics using a combined approach of data envelopment analysis and multivariate regression analyses. In particular, the study aims to determine whether stewardship is positively related to efficiency. Among Catholic health systems, stewardship is commonly selected to be representative of responsible use of material, human, and financial resources, which is ultimately hypothesized to lead to higher efficiency and quality of care.

The study focused on Catholic short-term, acute general hospitals that had an affiliation with Catholic multiple-hospital systems. The three primary data sources were the AHA Annual Survey of Hospitals files, CMS Case Mix Index files, and Area Resource Files (ARF). Finally, information about the value of stewardship of Catholic health systems was taken from the systems' websites. The study utilized longitudinal data from 2005, 2006, and 2007. The data analysis took place in a two-stage process, which is commonly applied in health care efficiency research using data envelopment analysis. First, efficiency scores for each system-affiliated Catholic hospital in the 3 years were generated using data envelopment analysis. To do so, an input-oriented, variable returns to scale (BCC) model was employed. Then, multivariate regressions were applied to examine the association between the efficiency scores and the variable of interest (health system's value of stewardship). In particular, independently pooled cross-sections across the study period were employed. The dependent variable of interest was a measure of inefficiency, generated by applying DEA. The DEA input variables were hospital size (number of operational beds in a hospital in a given year), service complexity (weighted service-mix index), labor (number of non-physician FTE employed in a hospital in a given year), and supplies (operating expenses minus payroll and capital expenses). The DEA output variables are outpatient surgeries (number of a hospital's outpatient operations in a given year), outpatient visits (visits to outpatient facilities minus outpatient surgeries and ER visits), emergency visits, medical education activities (weighted sum of trainees), and treated cases (inpatient admissions multiplied by the hospital's case-mix index in a given year).

The second stage analysis used a key independent variable, health systems' value of stewardship, which was operationalized as a binary variable. In the subsequent multivariate regression analyses (i.e., Tobit model, a logit model, and a two-limit Tobit model), the following organizational and market characteristics were included: hospital and system size, system sponsorship, hospital payer-mix, rural location, market competition, proportion of Medicare and Medicaid patients in the market, and for-profit hospital prevalence in the market. The study did not find a significant relationship between technical and scale efficiencies and Catholic health system value of stewardship. Furthermore, Catholic system-affiliated hospitals did not increase their efficiency over the study period of 3 years. The diocesan governance model was found to be more efficient compared to religious congregation models of governance. Lastly, the study was able to identify significant predictors of hospital efficiency, including proportion of Medicaid patients, rural location, market competition, and prevalence of for-profit hospitals in a given market.

The study shed light on what Catholic hospitals can do to reduce inefficiencies by reducing inputs and how many slack resources they have to provide charity care as an example.

15.16   Performance Evaluation of Nursing Staff

An interesting study by Osman et al. (2011) pursued a rather unconventional application of DEA analysis. In their article, the authors evaluate the utility of a DEA model for the appraisal and relative performance evaluation of nurses. They argued that existing human resource (HR) assessment tools were ineffective, narrow, and led to undesirable consequences among employees. Using DEA, they noted that "the weight of criteria (i.e., same inputs and outputs) are re-optimized in the best interest of each nurse rather than using a single set of fixed weights as in traditional approaches."

Having conducted an extensive review of the performance appraisal literature, the authors compiled potential inputs and outputs for their DEA study. Using the performance evaluation tool used at an HR department in a single Lebanese hospital, the authors identified the performance dimensions used by the hospital that best fit with the measures used by the leading studies in the performance evaluation field. The authors identified 45 such criteria that were scored by managers using a five-point scale. These 45 criteria were averaged (but with different sets of managerial weights) and classified into sets of inputs and outputs for DEA analyses.

The 2008 performance of 32 nurses from the hospital's critical care units was analyzed. Before a DEA was conducted, the authors used several means of ensuring robust results: (1) ensuring homogeneity of sample; (2) using different "rules of thumb" for ensuring sufficient sample sizes were used for the number of input and output variables; and (3) converting any variables in the wrong direction to ensure "isotonic data properties." Using 14 models, with different combinations of CCR, BCC, orientation, inputs, outputs, and/or samples, the authors obtained anywhere between only one to six efficient nurses. Their best model, based on two criteria (i.e., attaining normal distribution of efficiency scores and at least 10 % efficient DMUs), was CCR input-oriented and had a combination of eight input and output variables; that model had two efficient nurses. Their BCC model produced three efficient nurses. The authors suggested that the BCC model was more appropriate for the evaluation of nurses, since workload, stress, and pressure may prevent a nurse from operating at an optimal scale.

In their second-stage analyses, the authors found that a number of nurses, ranked higher in the DEA, were in fact unfairly ranked lower by the managerial assessment tool. However, the overall results between the DEA and managerial tool showed striking similarities, which demonstrated that managers could trust such an approach for HR purposes. Finally, the authors created a grid to identify nurses who were

Superstars, To Be Trained, Question Marks, and Potential Stars. The Question Mark group members were those nurses who were not efficient based on either input-oriented CCR or output-oriented BCC models.

15.17   Sensitivity Analysis for Hospital Service Production

A paper by Ozcan (1992–1993) presents a review of hospitals' technical efficiency using DEA and analyzes how sensitive the efficiency to choice of output and inputs as well as peer grouping is. In order to analyze sensitivity for the type of variables, 17 models were tested with different output/input variables. A stratified (by size, location, and ownership) random sample of 40 acute care general hospitals was obtained from AHA 1989 survey data, and another 90-hospital sample (30 from each category) was obtained for Los Angeles MSA.

The models were tested in the largest bed-size category because of the presence of teaching or training variables (most of teaching hospitals have more than 300 beds). The models included analysis of impact of assets, training, patient days, labor and breaking up labor FTE, DRG-weighted category groups, and size effect.

The results showed that some variables may be substituted without significant effect on the average efficiency score (assets for case-mix/bed), while others can significantly increase (three DRG weight category discharges for adjusted discharges) or lower (patient days for adjusted discharges) the scores. In terms of size effect, models compare pooled with non-pooled categories and analysis shows that pooling categories creates bias toward higher efficiency scores. In summary:

– Choice of variables for DEA may affect results, and
– Peer-grouping is very important (size effect in DMU); thus the use of the VRS model or scaling the data logarithmically would be a prudent action (Ozcan, 1992–1993).

15.18   Summary

This chapter introduced other DEA studies that do not fit into either traditional or non-traditional service provider evaluations discussed in Chaps. 9 through Chap. 14. However, these evaluations provide insight and solutions to many contemporary health care policy and delivery problems.

Chapter 16
International Country-Based DEA Health Studies

In this chapter we focus on specific data envelopment analysis (DEA) studies that considered either unique evaluations for a country or applied new methods to evaluate performance outcomes after dramatic health care reforms. Of the 17 countries we examine below, almost half of them had significant health care reforms during the past decade. These countries include: Austria, Brazil, Germany, Norway, Portugal, Thailand, and Turkey. There are many DEA studies being conducted in these and other various countries; some represent replication of already known methodologies, yet others provide a unique perspective in their evaluations. We will summarize the key aspects of these DEA country-based applications in alphabetical order by country. The reader should keep in mind that these are an interesting sample of studies among other DEA studies conducted in selected countries, and the discussions below does not represent an exhaustive set of either the studies or the countries.

16.1 Austria

One of the early DEA-based studies assessing the impact of health care reform in a country was conducted by Sommersguter-Reichmann (2000), who investigated the impact of the Austrian hospital financing reform on hospital productivity using constant returns to scale and variable scales to return (CCR and BCC) models of the Malmquist approach. The study covered the years from 1994 to 1998; the reform, similar to the diagnosis-related group (DRG) system, started implementation in 1997. The input-oriented Malmquist model included two output variables: (1) number of patients treated in the outpatient care unit, and (2) total number of credit points according to the crucial sector multiplied by a steering factor (in billions); and three input variables: (1) full-time-equivalent (FTE) labor, (2) total number of hospital beds, and (3) total expenses for external medical services. The results of the model showed a decrease in efficiency from 1994 to 1995, and a non-significant increase in the ensuing years. A notable change was in the technology change component of the Malmquist Index, which increased by 9.3 % from 1996 to 1997 and continued at same rate from 1997 to 1998. The study also showed steady increases in scale efficiency.

Another DEA-based efficiency study by Hofmarcher et al. (2002) investigated the Austrian health care system before DRG implementation covering the periods 1994 through 1996. However, this study was restricted to one Austrian province, and decision-making units (DMUs) were wards (hospital units) with no fewer than 25–30 beds for inpatient services. The study separates these wards as operative (n = 16) and non-operative (n = 15) medical fields and conducts two different models of evaluation. In their first model, they used the number of case mix-adjusted discharges and inpatient days as outputs; medical, paramedical, and administrative staff and number of beds consisted of the inputs. The second model used credit points, DRG-based payment points (LDF points), as outputs with the same inputs. These two models found different results: the first model with two output measurements provides 96 % average efficiency, while the second model with DRG payment points as the output measurement results in an average efficiency of 70 %. They reported that the average efficiency in the first model did not change over the 3-year period while in the second model it increased modestly during this time period.

A more recent Austrian study by Czypionka and colleagues (2015) investigated 128 public and private not-for-profit fund system hospitals from the year 2010. The hospitals ranged from specialty hospitals to secondary care, tertiary care, and academic medical centers (university hospitals). The study deploys two different models with different input and output schemes. The first model uses two outputs—DRG points (as in Hofmarcher et al. 2002) and outpatient visits—and six inputs: physician FTEs, registered nurse FTEs, other medical staff FTEs, administrative FTEs, operating expenses, and investment/capital costs. The second model uses DRG points as the only output, while using six inputs of different combinations. These are: physician FTEs, registered nurse FTEs, medical and non-medical staff FTEs, operating expenses, investment/capital costs, and medical costs/non-medical costs/administrative/other related costs.

The study investigates scale efficiencies by examining CCR and BCC in both models and finds smaller and medium-sized hospitals with a bed capacity from 200 to 400 to be most scale efficient. Overall, their results show that private not-for-profit hospitals are better performers compared to public hospitals within the Austrian fund system hospitals.

16.2   Botswana

The study by Tlotlego et al. (2010) examined 21 Botswana non-teaching hospitals using DEA including CCR, BCC, and Malmquist approaches. The 21 hospitals were randomly selected from 31 district and primary hospitals, and each hospital was visited to collect necessary data. Inputs for the study included the number of clinical staff (including physicians, nursing and midwifery personnel, dentistry personnel, and other technical health service providers) and hospital beds. Outputs included the number of outpatient department visits and number of inpatient days. The authors acknowledged the other important roles that the hospitals play (including training, coordination, and public health services such as water sanitation) but were unable to include variables to capture these key roles.

The results demonstrate that a majority of hospitals were inefficient in each of the models. A Malmquist model was also used for the years 2006, 2007, and 2008. They found that a majority of the hospitals' units had a Malmquist Index of total factor productivity change less than one. When the scores were presented by components of scale efficiency change and technical change it was evident that technical change scores were lower, on average, than pure efficiency scores.

The most interesting message of the article is their conclusion about excess clinical staff and beds. They conclude that among the inefficient hospitals 264 clinical staff and 39 beds should be transferred to posts outside of the hospital to maximize efficiency. The clinical staff was an aggregation of many types of providers (as described above), so perhaps additional information would have been understood if these provider types were entered as separate inputs. Also, this offers insight into the overall health system in the country, which is much different than in the United States.

16.3 Brazil

During the last decade Brazil went through various health reforms, especially in payment systems. Brazil has a Unified Health System (SUS) where the current legal provisions governing the operation of the health system were instituted in 1996. The SUS system created a patient-based data reporting system which can be queried at the hospital or organizational level. There is also an Information System of the Federal University Hospitals—Sistema de Informações dos Hospitais Universitários Federais (SIHUF). Here we report a few studies using DEA techniques to evaluate Brazilian teaching and for-profit hospitals.

A study conducted by Ozcan and associates (2010) examined the performance of Brazilian university hospitals in a cross-sectional evaluation. The performance of university models was evaluated from medical care (Medical Model), and teaching and research (Teaching Research Model) perspectives. SIHUF includes data on students, professors, medical residents, workforce, expenses, incomes, physical area, service production, service complexity, and administrative hospital indices. The study considered all 30 university acute general hospitals.

In the Medical Model (MM), the study employed three outputs: (1) adjusted surgeries, (2) adjusted admissions, and (3) adjusted outpatient visits; and five inputs: (1) physician FTEs, (2) non-physician FTEs, (3) operational expenses, (4) beds, and (5) service-mix. The Teaching Research Model (TRM) used three outputs: (1) undergraduate students, (2) residents, and (3) graduate students; and three inputs: (1) physician FTEs, (2) professors with a PhD, and (3) other professors.

DEA evaluation used the BCC (VRS) model using the interactive Data Envelopment Analysis Laboratory (IDEAL) software package which provides three-dimensional graphic solutions in addition to conventional reporting. The MM showed that among the 30 hospitals, 11 were considered efficient (35 %) and the proportion of efficient units was greater for the hospitals with size greater than 300 beds. In the TRM, 15 (50 %) of the teaching hospitals were considered efficient. After removing four hospitals that did not have research activity from evaluation, among the 11 remaining efficient hospitals, six hospitals had more than 300 beds. It is also noted that physicians, the only variable present in both models, shows similar numbers for excess usage indicating that these physicians could not work in an alternative activity to enhance the efficiency of the teaching hospital output.

A follow-up study by Lobo et al. (2010) investigated the impact of financing reform and productivity changes in Brazilian teaching hospitals using the Malmquist approach for the years 2003 and 2006. In Brazil, the 2004 financial reform provided an average budget increase of 51 %. This was associated with adjustments in the proportional composition of the different types of assistance (surgeries, admissions, outpatient visits) as a consequence of administrative changes and settlements with the local health authorities. Thus, this study selected 2003 as the marker year as pre-reform, and 2006 to allow enough time to observe the impact of the changes.

The outputs and inputs of the study were similar to the cross-sectional study reported above. More specifically, the outputs of the study included: adjusted admissions, adjusted inpatient surgeries, and adjusted outpatient visits. Inputs consisted of labor force (physicians and full-time equivalent non-physicians), operational expenses (not including payroll), beds, and service-mix. The study summarized the hospital teaching functions using two proxy variables: (1) teaching dedication (the number of residents per physician), and (2) teaching intensity (the number of residents per bed).

The results showed that the average efficiency of all hospitals increased from 58.6 % in 2003 to 67.3 % in 2006. Despite the observed increase in the efficiency change component, the catching-up component of the hospitals to the frontier, the Malmquist Index had shown a regress for the majority of the hospitals (93.3 %). This was due to a frontier contraction. Hence, the financial reform gave a chance for these hospitals to make managerial adjustments to reach economic balance after the budget augmentation (gaining efficiency); however, the intended technological change for the frontier as a whole did not occur as of 2006. Finally, concerning the association between the medical care efficiency and the teaching intensity, the study suggests that there was no impairment of the teaching activities after the reform.

A more recent study from Brazil by Araújo et al. (2014) evaluated the efficiency determinants and capacity issues in Brazilian for-profit hospitals. The study considers an interesting set of nine inputs and nine outputs which would overwhelm the DEA model if deployed on a small set of hospitals. Thus, a factor analytic approach was utilized to reduce the variables into two dimensions for both inputs and outputs. The final constructed input variables were: (1) a hospital infrastructure and supporting staff index, and (2) a hospital doctor and office index. Similarly outputs were reduced to two dimensions: (1) longer-term medical procedures (represented by number of intensive care unit (ICU) inpatients), and (2) shorter-term medical procedures (represented by outpatient treatments).

The study engages both CCR and BCC models and uses a bootstrapping method for bias-correction as suggested by Simar and Wilson (2007), and deploys a second-stage analysis using a truncated bootstrapped regression analysis to investigate determinants of efficiency. The study concludes that private sector hospitals have severe constraints in increasing their outputs, especially for ICU inpatients. Thus, the study suggests capacity issues for these hospitals must be further explored by policy makers and managers.

16.4 Canada

In their study, Chowdhury et al. (2011) examined efficiency change and technological change among health care services in Ontario, Canada, using recent advances in productivity analysis, including kernel-based statistical analysis of productivity changes determined through Malmquist and bootstrapped DEA methods.

The data set employed in the study consists of panel data from 113 private, not-for-profit, acute care hospitals in Ontario, Canada, spanning the periods 2002–2003 to 2005–2006. Data sources include the Health Care Indicator Tool from the Ministry of Health and Long-Term Care, providing financial and statistical reports on Canadian hospitals. A discussion of common input and output variables incorporated into DEA-based hospital efficiency studies is provided, and the authors identify several input and output "subcategories" that common input and output variables may be assigned to throughout the literature.

The study utilizes DEA techniques to estimate the Malmquist Productivity Index (MPI), where output measures include total inpatient days and outpatient visits, with neither measure adjusted for case mix, and the input variables include staff hours, nursing hours, staffed beds, medical surgical supply costs, non-medical surgical supply costs, and total equipment expenses. The variables of staff hours and nursing hours are utilized to measure human resources inputs; medical and non-medical surgical supply costs are employed to measure purchased services and supplies; and staffed beds and total equipment expenses are utilized to measure capital. Descriptive statistics of the variables are provided, and the authors note that nursing hours increased while staff hours decreased during the study's time period. Both inpatient and outpatient volume increased—with outpatient volume exhibiting substantial gains—as the number of staffed beds decreased on average during the same time. Medical and non-medical surgical supply costs as well as equipment expenses also increased, which the authors suggested was due to increased investments in medical technologies.

The distribution of Malmquist productivity scores (estimated through DEA methods) employs kernel density estimator techniques. A Li-test, based on bootstrap techniques adapted for DEA methods, is used to test "equality of distributions of productivity scores from MPI and its components."

A summary of the study's MPI estimates is provided, including descriptions of productivity and efficiency changes across the different time periods (2002–2003, 2003–2004, 2004–2005, and 2005–2006). The authors found technological progress overall during the examined time period, yet no significant increase in average productivity was observed. This finding together with an observed negative efficiency change on average led to the suggestion that any growth in productivity was "largely due to a progressive shift in the best practice frontier over the sample period rather than by improvement in the technical efficiency of hospitals." The authors explained that Ontario hospitals commonly increased their investments in capital equipment and clinical information technology over the study's time period, while at the same time experiencing increased patient complexity and staff compensation rates, leading to growth in technological efficiency coupled with declines in technical efficiency.

Malmquist productivity score distributions were not shown to be significantly different across time periods, while hospital efficiency as well as the overall efficiency distribution were shown to decline each year, indicating widespread negative efficiency changes. In contrast, the overall distribution of technological change improved across the study's time periods as the large group of hospitals showed technological improvements. Statistically significant differences were observed between urban and rural hospitals for productivity and efficiency distributions, yet distributions in technological change were not significantly different between urban and rural hospitals except for the period between 2004 and 2005. The authors noted that urban hospitals experienced more deterioration in efficiency over time in comparison to rural facilities that often consume lesser amounts of resources, and productivity for both types of hospitals in the study was overwhelmed by positive technological changes. Similar comparisons were made between small and large hospitals, as productivity, efficiency, and technological change distributions were significantly different between hospital size groups for the majority of the study's time periods. For the most part, small hospitals were found to exhibit efficiency decreases and technological regress.

Based upon their analysis results, the authors found significant and persistent inefficiencies in the delivery of health care services among Ontario hospitals. Rural hospitals were found to exhibit higher technical efficiency than urban facilities, yet they also maintained higher lengths of stay. In addition, small hospitals exhibited increasing technological regress and deterioration in technical efficiency while larger hospitals received medical technology investments as policy makers sought to establish centers of excellence. The study suggests greater emphasis on managerial and organizational efforts to improve hospital efficiency. As hospitals realize managerial improvements, they may enjoy desirable long-term productivity and performance levels in the face of technological advancements.

16.5   Chile

Ramírez-Valdivia et al. (2011) used DEA with a multiple-stage approach for performance improvement of primary health care practices in Chile. The objective of their study was to identify the factors that affect performance (technical efficiency) of the primary health care centers (PHCs) managed by each municipality.

The authors accessed the Chilean Ministry of Health database and other publicly available databases between July and October 2008. The data set includes 345 municipalities as of 2006. The majority of financial resources are provided by the central government. Due to different funding formulas (for size reasons), 52 municipalities were excluded in addition to those with missing information on key variables. The final number of municipalities for the DEA study was 259.

The study justifies the use of the following three variables as inputs: (1) the annual medical staff cost, (2) the annual general service cost, and (3) the annual pharmacy cost. The outputs of the model included: (1) the annual number of medical visits, and (2) the annual number of medical check-up visits. Both CCR (CRS) and BCC (VRS) models with output orientation were run under four different model specifications with urban and rural groups. Model I includes the input variable annual medical staff cost; Model II uses annual medical staff cost and annual general service cost; Model III uses the variables annual medical staff cost and annual pharmacy cost; and Model IV uses annual medical staff cost, annual general service cost, and annual pharmacy cost as input variables. Both output variables—annual number of medical visits and annual number of medical check-up visits—stays the same for all four models.

A second-stage Tobit analysis was also performed using bootstrapping to correct potential bias. The study results indicate that urban municipalities are more efficient than rural ones. The authors suggest that annual medical staff cost is the most influential input variable in estimating the efficiency scores and ranking of municipalities.

16.6   Germany

1. The study by Staat (2006) was influenced by the rising health-related expenditures in Germany over the past two decades. The author noted that improved efficiency is a key issue in "stabilizing health related expenditures at a sustainable level." In terms of prior literature, the study indicated that only a few studies had explored the efficiency of German hospitals, but these had samples that were either unrepresentative or too heterogonous (leading to downward biased DEA estimates). Thus, his article set out to derive accurate DEA results from a more representative sample.

   Using 1994 data on 160 German hospitals from the old federal states, the author specifically looked at two categories of hospitals: type I (i.e., hospitals of only local importance providing basic care without any large-scale technical facilities) and type II (i.e., basic care hospitals with some facilities that are of regional importance), in an effort to ensure general comparability of hospitals. To further enhance the specification of the hospitals within each group, the author restricted the hospitals to those that "provide basic care... [and] have two main departments: one for medicine and one for surgery." Using the aforementioned strategies, the author was able to attain almost identical input-output structures, which allowed DEA results to reflect differences in efficiency of service productions only.

A traditional input-oriented CRS DEA and bootstrapped DEA were performed by the author. For both DEAs, inputs (per diem rate and number of beds) and outputs (number of cases per year, reciprocal of length of stay (LOS), case mix, heterogeneous case mix indicator, and number of fields of specialization) were included. The reciprocal of LOS was used in an effort not to allow hospitals with a low per diem rate but high LOS, or vice versa, to appear efficient. Nonetheless, this study's DEA inputs and outputs varied in relation to the more conventional variables used in other hospital DEA studies (such as O'Neill et al. 2008; Ozcan 2008).

Citing Simar and Wilson (1998), the author noted the upward bias of conventional DEA estimates as a consequence of the model's assumptions. Further, as a result of the inability to account for efficient DMUs that are not in the sample, the efficiency estimates of inefficient DMUs in the sample are inflated; hence bootstrapped DEA estimates need to be obtained.

Using the traditional DEA, the study found type I institutions 0.87 efficient on average, while their bootstrapped mean efficiency was 0.75. For type II institutions, traditional DEA estimates were 0.94 versus 0.89 using bootstrapped estimates. More importantly, the author noted that the bias-corrected scores indicated the degree of inefficiency as being much higher than suggested in prior literature. The bigger spread between the conventional DEA score and the bootstrapped estimates for type I hospitals was attributed to the greater heterogeneity in this larger sample group. That is, given the same case mix, type I hospitals had more inconsistent input-output structures, which the author surmised may have been a result of varying quality of staff or different learning rates.

The main finding of the analyses demonstrated that significant productivity differences existed between identical hospitals. Further, the bias-corrected efficiency estimates underscored the true problem faced by German hospitals: the fact that the biased estimates were still low among a relatively homogenous set of hospitals exasperated notions, among policy makers, of inefficiency present within German hospitals.

2. A more recent study by Tiemann and Schreyogg (2012) investigated the changes in hospital efficiency after privatization. This study assessed the effects of privatization on technical efficiency among German hospitals. These German hospitals changed from public status to either private not-for-profit or private for-profit status. A movement of privatization occurred in Germany in the

mid-1990s, and the authors wanted to study the changes in hospital performance (technical efficiency) following privatization.

The authors used DEA methodology, which allowed them the use of multiple inputs and outputs; the authors assumed variable returns to scale. Input variables were: (1) supplies, (2) physicians, (3) nursing staff, (4) other clinical staff, (5) administrative staff, and (6) other nonclinical staff members (full-time equivalents). Only one output variable was included: inpatients. However, average in-hospital mortality rate per year for each hospital was deployed in a second model, where the number 1 minus the average in-hospital mortality rate per year was used as a metric (1 − mortality rate).

DEA efficiency scores were generated and bias-corrected scores were generated from 500 bootstrap iterations. A regression analysis was conducted with the DEA scores as the dependent variable. A difference-in-difference interaction was incorporated to assess the effect of privatization on efficiency compared to the control group (non-privatized hospitals). With this method they controlled for patient heterogeneity and hospital organizational and environmental characteristics. Follow-up sensitivity analyses included use of mortality as a quality indicator in the model, among others. The authors also constructed propensity scores in order to find appropriate control groups based on the estimated probability for being privatized.

There was a significant increase in efficiency in private for-profit status hospitals compared to the control group beginning in the second year after privatization in the unmatched sample and beginning in the first year for the matched sample. The score increased with the number of years after privatization. There were less significant increases in efficiency for the private not-for-profit group. Upon further analyses, it was found that for-profit private hospitals had reduced all labor inputs except for physicians and administrative staff. Additional analyses also revealed that efficiency gains were more difficult when the DRG time-period was considered in the regression.

When in-hospital mortality was added to the model, small efficiency gains were not seen. Thus the authors state that efficiency gains were not at the expense of quality (based on mortality rates). Other methods to test for robustness of results included multi-way clustered regression including time and firm fixed effects, a change in the pre-privatization period from 1 to 2 years, and a model that excluded inputs that had a strong correlation. None of these sensitivity analyses changed overall results.

16.7 Greece

Tsekouras and associates (2010) investigated intensive care unit (ICU) systems in Greece to explore whether the adoption of new technology boosts productive efficiency in the public sector. They used a bootstrapped DEA approach using data through a survey conducted among the 39 ICUs of the Greek Public Healthcare

System. They acquired additional data from annual hospital reports and the Ministry of Health and through face-to-face interviews with hospital managers. Output was measured as treatment days. The inputs consisted of two groups of medical equipment (old and new (after 1993)), beds, doctors, and nurses. Constant and variable returns model and scale efficiencies were calculated.

In a second-stage analysis, the determinants of ICUs' technical and scale efficiency were investigated using a bootstrapped truncated regression approach. They have found that new technology equipment has a positive effect on efficiency of ICUs. The authors also suggested that "ICUs that are located in the greater Athens area suffer the least productive size inefficiencies, which arise from specific political choices by the Greek Ministry of Health."

16.8   Italy

Garavaglia and colleagues (2011) describe the growing concern for efficiency and quality in nursing homes throughout industrialized countries given an aging population and an increased demand for long-term care services. Noting the recent applications of DEA and Stochastic Frontier Analysis (SFA) methods to examine factors determining efficiency and quality of care in nursing homes, the authors identify two aspects of nursing home performance that have yet to be fully settled. First, questions remain as to the specific measures that are best suited to measure quality of care in the nursing home setting. Second, information regarding nursing home efficiency has proven difficult to obtain due to the lack of routine assessments of nursing home efficiency. The authors seek to address these two issues in their study of the efficiency and quality of care of nursing homes in a specific area of Italy known as the Lombardy Region.

The article proceeds with a review of the literature examining efficiency and quality of care in nursing homes through DEA methods, specifically evaluating the use of Donabedian's Structure-Process-Outcome framework (Ozcan 2009) to develop quality indicators. A total of six DEA studies of nursing homes that employed quality of care measures were identified, illustrating the considerable focus of past studies on efficiency analysis. From their review, the authors conclude that "the number of DEA studies in nursing homes that included measures of quality of care is very limited," and within these studies process measures have primarily been employed as indicators of quality while "the role that residential services may play on quality of care and customer satisfaction" has been overlooked in favor of nursing activities.

The study examines the efficiency and quality of care provided to patients in 40 nursing homes operating in the Lombardy Region of Italy from the period of 2005 to 2007. Within this region, "nursing homes deliver their services in a quasi market" due to the implementation of managed competition. A description of the elderly care system in the Lombardy Region is provided to help explain the selection of input and output measures, and the SOSIA reports and Nursing

Home Reports that serve as data sources are also described. The input measures included health and nursing costs at each nursing home as well as the accommodation costs at nursing homes, providing consideration of both nursing and care-coordination activities as well as the provision of residential services. Health and nursing costs were defined as "the yearly amount of money employed by the nursing homes for care and nursing activities," with the vast majority of these costs consisting of labor expenses. Accommodation costs were related to the yearly expenses for residential or hotel activities, including "meals, laundry and cleaning of rooms," which the authors noted "accounted for more than 18 % of total costs" among the nursing homes. The output measures included patient case-mix, extra nursing hours, and out-of-pocket charges for residential services. In addition, two measures of quality—extra nursing hours and residential charges—were incorporated within the study. The authors argue that extra nursing hours served as "a proxy of higher quality of care" rather than an indicator of inefficiency, citing various studies to support their assertion. Furthermore, residential charges were argued to be a "proxy of patients' satisfaction" as it could "capture the quantity and the quality" of the nursing homes' residential services. The authors also note that due to incomplete and partially reliable data, they were unable to utilize data of nursing home deficiencies and had to strictly employ measures related to Structure aspects. In the study's second stage, explanatory variables included the number of nursing home beds, ownership type (public or private), and "percentage of patients relative to lower severity SOSIA classes" to examine the relationship between patient complexity and efficiency.

A CCR input-oriented model was employed in the study's first-stage analysis using Frontier Efficiency Analysis with R (FEAR) software. A bootstrap procedure was also incorporated to generate confidence intervals for the DEA's efficiency scores. Using the bootstrapped DEA scores as efficiency measures, a Tobit regression was then performed in the study's second-stage analysis with the previously mentioned explanatory variables. In the first stage, the study found a slight decline in the mean efficiency scores for nursing homes across the 3-year period (0.85–0.84 for traditional DEA scores, and 0.80–0.79 for bootstrapped scores). Traditional DEA scores were used to classify "best" and "worst" nursing homes according to efficiency measures, and the bootstrapped scores were employed as efficiency measures in the Tobit regression and hypothesis tests. The best group included six nursing homes (with each of the three for-profit facilities) that tended to be "medium sized, host higher severity patients and have higher residential charges" while maintaining below-average residential costs and above-average quality. In contrast, the worst group included eight nursing homes that varied in size, exhibited higher patient severity and extra nursing hours, maintained low levels of residential charges, and displayed above-average accommodation costs. The Tobit regression found ownership type to maintain a significant relationship with efficiency scores, such that "private facilities are more efficient than the public ones." No significant relationships were identified, however, between efficiency scores and either size or lower-severity SOSIA classes.

The authors employ Kruskal-Wallis tests to examine three hypotheses. First, they find that extra nursing hours have a negligible impact on efficiency scores, leading them to suggest that quality of care measures should not be incorporated directly into DEA models but should be utilized as explanatory variables in second-stage regression analyses. With respect to residential charges, the authors conclude that inefficient nursing homes increase residential charges in addition to reducing previously identified inputs. A test of facilities with above-average residential charges versus those with below-average residential charges found that, for two of the 3 years examined, there are significant differences between nursing home groups such that "residential charges may depend on the profit orientation of each facility." Finally, test results indicate that, in a fixed reimbursement system, a nursing home's efficiency is dependent upon its ability to contain health and nursing service costs—particularly labor costs—to meet established reimbursement rates. Also, public facilities are shown to exhibit greater difficulty in reducing labor expenses in comparison to for-profit and private not-for-profit facilities. The article concludes with the promotion of efficiency studies among nursing homes, seeking to understand the factors determining quality of care and efficiency in a critical component of the health care industry.

16.9   Japan

There are two recent studies from Japan, the first one examining the visiting nurse service agencies (see Chap. 13—Home Health Agency Applications for earlier work in the U.S.), and the second study examining hospitals using new dynamic and network DEA model (see Chap. 8 for discussion of this model).

1. Kuwahara and associates (2013) investigated the efficiencies of visiting nurse (VN) service agencies using data envelopment analysis. The authors examined 108 VN agencies, using five inputs consisting of various staff, and three outputs identifying types of visits. Japan has approximately 54,000 VN services in operation. The VN service agencies considered in the study are all located in one prefecture in southern Japan. Despite there being 240 VN services in this area as of 2009, only 108 responded to study data requirements. More specifically, the input variables consisted of nursing staff (nurses, assistant nurses, and public health nurses), rehabilitation staff (physical, occupational, and speech therapists), and office staff (clerks). Three output variables were organized by visits which were paid through medical insurance, long-term care insurance, or by others.

   Both CCR and BCC models were deployed, and average efficiency scores were 0.78 and 0.80, respectively, for these models. The authors investigated the relationship between VN efficiency and VN agency characteristics such as ownership type, whether the VN was part of a vertical link of the hospital, average travel time to client homes, etc., but found no significant relationships.

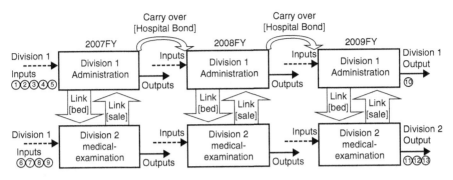

Fig. 16.1 Structure of DN-DEA model for Japanese hospitals. Source: Kawaguchi et al. (2014)

2. The second study by Kawaguchi et al. (2014) uses dynamic and network data envelopment analysis model to estimate the efficiency of Japanese hospitals. This study is the first empirical application of the dynamic and network model in the health care field.

The authors estimated the efficiency of Japanese municipal hospitals in two divisions: (1) administration division for financial management, and (2) the medical-examination division. As the authors explain, "there are two links between the divisions. The number of beds is a link from Division 1 to Division 2. The average revenue per inpatient per day is a link from Division 2 to Division 1. The dynamic-network data envelopment analysis (DN-DEA) model also indicates the relationship between the two divisions in terms of efficiency improvement from 1 year to the next. The carry-over variable is used to represent the inter-temporal relationship. Figure 16.1 depicts a visual for these relationships" (Kawaguchi et al. 2014).

As one may observe, there are a number of inputs and outputs in each division carried over the years with links between the divisions. More specifically, the administrative division has five inputs: (1) administration staff, (2) maintenance staff, (3) interest cost, (4) subsidies from municipality, and (5) medical expenses. The single output is medical income. These inputs and outputs are replicated each year for the three study fiscal years (2007, 2008, and 2009). The medical-care division has four inputs: (1) doctors, (2) nurses, (3) assistant nurses, and 4) medical technologists. The outputs of the medical-care division include: (1) inpatients per operations day, (2) outpatients per operations day, and (3) emergency unit beds. These inputs and outputs are the same for all 3 years for the division. However, administrative and medical-care divisions are linked through the variable "beds" and the medical-care division is linked to the administrative division with the variable "average revenue per inpatient day." To complete the model, a carryover variable "balance account of the public enterprise bond" is deployed, as the value of this account would change from year to year.

DMUs consisted of 112 municipal hospitals from 2007 to 2009 which were selected from hospitals with more than 300 beds among approximately 1,000 municipal hospitals. DN-DEA was evaluated using input-oriented CCR and BCC models. Key findings were summarized as: (1) the BCC-I model for 2007 yielded 0.85 overall efficiency score (which was less than estimates of earlier studies), (2) dynamic change in efficiency scores from 2007 to 2009 was 0.862 and 0.860, respectively, and (3) network structure allowed observation of efficiency for divisions, while administrative division efficiency decreased to 0.851 in 2009 from 0.867 in 2007; medical-care division efficiency increased from 0.858 in 2007 to 0.870 in 2009.

16.10 The Netherlands

Blank and Valdmanis (2010) investigated the policy implications of hospital budget allocations in the Dutch health care system. They conducted their analysis in an attempt to tease out cost inefficiencies that are specific consequences of hospital managers' control of resources, and thus should not be reimbursed by the Dutch government. The authors used a standard DEA approach along with several post hoc techniques to obtain robust study results. The authors provided important rationale behind the use of their statistical techniques. For DEA, they argued that "methodological approaches that require assumptions of cost minimization or profit maximization may not be appropriate since hospital managers may not adhere to strict economic criteria."

The study used 69 general hospitals that had data in 2000. There were 11 inputs (5 under resources and 6 under operating costs) and 5 outputs (number of first-time visits that were not admissions and four categories of case-mix groups) in a CCR input-oriented, standard cost DEA model.

Authors performed second-stage analysis to examine determinants of efficiency using Tobit and truncated regressions. The authors separately regressed raw efficiency scores and biased-corrected efficiency scores on four environmental variables: part-time personnel, seniority personnel, composition of capital, and physicians' intensity. Unlike U.S. studies that typically include the aforementioned variables in the DEA analysis, the authors in this study noted that these variables were not under the control of managers in Dutch hospitals. From their secondary statistical modeling, the authors used an inverse of the efficiency scores as the dependent variable. In this way, they were able to truncate the distribution of CE scores at 1. They failed to describe the approaches taken to develop their efficiency variable for the Tobit analysis.

The authors found that, on average, the cost efficiency of general hospitals was 87 %. Before conducting their secondary analyses, the authors conducted a nice array of statistical diagnostic tests. The results from the ordinary least squares (OLS) without bootstrap and with bootstrap were statistically different. Also, differences in coefficients were present for the same parameters across models. Overall, the authors found that the number of part-time personnel significantly contributed to lower cost efficiency and that the composition of capital had a positive effect on cost efficiency. Also, physician intensity was statistically significant and positive; thus, it contributed to poor cost efficiencies.

In conclusion, the authors demonstrated that the methods used in measuring efficiency mattered. The findings of their analysis also proved that environmental factors affect efficiency scores, which may not be accounted for in budgetary allocations by the government. In their case, such an oversight may have led to an underpayment of almost three million Euros to Dutch general hospitals.

16.11 Norway

1. Biørn and colleagues (2010) address hospitals' responses to financial reforms, noting that previous studies often find increased variation in efficiency among hospitals following reform in Norway. In these instances, "policy-makers will consider the reform as less attractive" because geographic access to hospital services is affected, even if reforms yield improvements on average efficiency. The authors seek to study whether and why such variation in hospital responses to financial reforms may exist by examining Norwegian financial reforms implemented in 1997.

   The financial reform studied consists of the replacement of a global budgeting system with an activity-based financing (ABF) system. After providing background information on the Norwegian health care system and the ABF reforms implemented in 1997, the authors examine previous studies related to their subject and conclude that a lack of studies exists on response heterogeneity to financial reform. They proceed to provide a brief examination of hospital efficiency studies that include "analyses examining average effects of latent variables."

   The data set employed in the study consists of a 10-year panel data set, spanning the 5 years before and after financial reform (1992–2001), among 47 publicly owned hospitals in Norway. The authors are careful to note that adoption of ABF reforms was staggered to a degree among the 47 hospitals due to their county governments: 30 hospitals (in 15 of 19 county governments) implemented ABF in 1997, 12 hospitals (in two counties) followed in 1998, two hospitals (from one county) followed in 1999, and the final three hospitals (from the remaining county) followed in 2000.

   The authors utilize DEA methods to examine variations in hospital efficiency as well as OLS and GLS regression to assess "the heterogeneity in the impact of introducing ABF on hospital-specific efficiency." Hospital input measures utilized include: physician FTEs, other labor FTEs, medical expenses, and operating expenses. The authors explain that they are unable to include capital costs as input measures, although they also choose not to use number of beds as a proxy for capital input. They suggest that a lack of consideration for capital expenses is a limitation in the instance that "medical equipment has been substituted for labor over the study period," which would cause the results to "overstate efficiency growth."

The hospital output measures include number of discharges (adjusted for case-mix), number of outpatient visits ("weighed by the fee paid by the state for each visit"), and outpatient revenues, which is described as a "value-related measure" that accounts "for the number of outpatients." Bootstrapping methods are applied to the DEA measures given the authors' uncertainty of their estimates. They also describe their study model, predicting that hospital efficiency is "higher under ABF than under fixed budget" because "managers are willing to exert higher effort under ABF than under fixed budget" to generate income through patient services.

Given the authors' assumption that "efficiency is positively related to effort," explanatory variables are described to be included in the regression, including "standardized budget per hospital bed" (which accounts for hospital resource variation), an ABF dummy variable (accounting for financing system changes), "share of patient-days with irregularly long lengths of stay," and "number of beds." The regression's dependent variables include cost efficiency and technical efficiency measures previously obtained by DEA methods.

The study's results indicate that the ABF dummy variable on average has a positive relationship on both technical and cost efficiency measures. However, examination of hospital-specific effects reveals considerable standard deviations for hospital-specific ABF-coefficient estimates, providing "evidence of strong response heterogeneity." The authors then examine whether a pattern exists between "year-specific efficiencies and the ABF coefficients" as well as whether "hospitals with the lowest pre-ABF efficiency experienced the strongest effect of the reform." Results indicate that practically no correlation exists between pre-ABF efficiency levels and the estimated ABF dummy variable coefficient related to efficiency, yielding evidence contrary to the hypothesis that inefficient hospitals realized a strong ABF effect. However, a strong correlation was observed between post-ABF efficiency levels and the estimated ABF dummy variable coefficient, suggesting that "hospitals which 'benefited' from the ABF were generally grouped among the most efficient post-reform hospitals." A Mann-Whitney test was employed to verify these results, finding non-significant differences between "high-performing" and "low-performing" hospitals before the ABF while finding strongly significant differences between these groups after the ABF's implementation.

The authors conclude from these results that "whereas pre-ABF efficiency did not play any role in how hospitals responded to ABF, those responding generally ended up as better-performing hospitals." An additional conclusion is that efficiency improvements following the ABF's implementation were most visible among technical efficiency measures. The authors suggest that, in light of their findings, "policy-makers need not worry about increased geographical variation in accessibility" in the event of health finance reform, "since the reform did not seem to favor the initially most efficient hospitals."

2. Another study by Linna and associates (2010) investigated the performance of hospital care in four Nordic countries using national discharge registries and cost data from 2002 for 184 public hospitals from Norway (43), Finland (38), Sweden (49), and Denmark (54). The authors explain that "in the Nordic countries, health care has been decentralized to local or regional authorities who usually purchase and also provide the health services. In all Nordic countries the funding of hospital care is a mixture of global budgeting and activity-based funding (ABF)" (Linna et al. 2010).

The study includes a single input: "adjusted operating costs (ADJ_COST)." Several outputs were considered, using a set of them in three different models that were deployed both in CCR and BCC. These outputs included: (1) - DRG-weighted inpatient surgical cases (IS), (2) DRG-weighted inpatient medical cases (IM), (3) DRG-weighted surgical day-care cases (DS), (4) DRG-weighted medical day-care cases (DM), (5) other DRGs (ODRG), (6) all DRGs, and (7) outpatient visits (OV). The three models were organized by using the same input (ADJ_COST) but varying outputs. The first model (M1) used summation of the first four outputs (IS + IM + DS + DM), namely, grouping all DRGs as one output and outpatient visits (OV), hence resulting in a one-input, two-output model. The second model (M2) was a variant of the first where inpatient surgical care, day care, and other DRGs were separated (IS + IM + ODRG), (DS + DM) and OV, thus consisted of three outputs. The third model (M3) separated all medical and surgical cases in the DRGs IS, IM, DS, DM, ODRG, and OV, and hence contained six outputs.

Results showed that depending upon the model used in all countries there were fully efficient hospitals. The lowest number of efficient units was in M1 (CCR), which estimated only one Danish and Finnish hospital to be fully efficient. When BCC models were used in conjunction with M2 and M3, where model variables increased, so did the efficiency scores and number of efficient hospitals. The authors bootstrapped the scores for bias correction.

16.12   Portugal

The study by Simões and Marques (2011) demonstrates an application of congestion DEA (see Chap. 8 for details) for the Portuguese hospitals. Authors indicate that the health sector in Portugal is a bit unstable as they went through successive reforms implemented by different governments (political sides) over the past few years. With each new government body, the policies may change with the respect to health care inducing lack of coordination and strategy. This study evaluates the efficiency of Portuguese hospitals to determine the importance of congestion effect. Double bootstrap procedure is deployed to investigate the influence of the operational and institutional environment on the efficiency to test the effect of the reforms implemented in health care. Authors explain that congestion in hospitals surface when the capacities of the inputs they employ may not be sufficient and bring up a risk for the future, hence render bad quality of service; conversely, if capacity is excessive it may create inefficiency and sometimes congestion.

The study uses three inputs and three outputs. The inputs are: (1) capital expenses, (2) staff FTEs, and (3) operational expenses. The three outputs are: (1) treated patients (discharges), (2) emergency visits, and (3) outpatient visits. The study examines efficiencies through both CCR and BCC models on 68 Portuguese hospitals using 2005 data.

An interesting part of this study is the report on congestion, which is measured through the ratio between strong efficiency and weak efficiency. The authors explain that 29 of the 68 hospitals show signs of congestion, or that on average the Portuguese hospitals are 3.6 % congested. When they consider those only those 29 congested hospitals, congestion increases to 8.1 %. They suggest that if these hospitals were congestion efficient (equal to 1, or 100 %), they could reduce 8.1 % of their inputs while producing the same outputs (Simões and Marques 2011).

16.13   Spain

The Sola and Prior (2001) study provides an assessment of effectiveness, efficiency, and quality among Spanish hospitals in Catalan region. Specifically, the efficiency and quality levels determine the effectiveness level. The trade-off between productivity and technical quality are examined.

DEA methodology is used, incorporating the Malmquist Index. The occurrence of nosocomial infections was used for measuring technical quality in the Spanish hospitals. Infections affect both quality (increase morbidity and mortality) and also efficiency (increase costs). Implementation of measures to reduce infections represents a greater use of resources. There were 20 hospitals used in the analysis. Infections were measured by the prevalence of nosocomial infections both in 1990 and in 1993. The following were outputs: inpatient days spent in different services; long-stay days; intensive care unit days; visits; and infections. A hospital improves in quality if it increases its outputs and maintains the infection prevalence or if it reduces infections while maintaining outputs at the same level. Inputs were: health staff; other staff; beds; and materials.

On average, between the two study years, hospital efficiency improved. Without considering the restriction of quality maintenance, hospitals needed to reduce inputs by 6.62 %. When considering the quality maintenance restriction, the potential efficiency improvement decreased to 6.46 %. The Malmquist Index revealed that there was a drop in the technical change (vs. quality), showing that they used more resources in 1993 than 1990 given the input-output correspondence. In the discussion, the authors expand on this finding. Given that new technology is more expensive, efficient hospitals would use more resources to give greater service provision. This reflects a fall in productivity. In conclusion, technical quality increased over the time period with an increase in the use of resources.

16.14   Thailand

The Puenpatom and Rosenman (2008) study investigated the impact of implementation of capitation-based universal health coverage in Thailand. More specifically, efficiency analysis of 92 Thai provincial public hospitals (excluding Bangkok hospitals) was carried out with a data set covering 2 years prior to reform (October 1999–September 2001) and 1 year after the reform (October 2001–September 2002).

The DEA model included five inputs and five outputs. Inputs consisted of four categories of labor and one category of capital as follows: full-time equivalent (FTEs) of primary care physicians, ancillary professional care providers (dentists and pharmacists), nurses, and other personnel. The number of beds was used as a proxy for the capital input. There were three output variables measuring inpatient and outpatient activity; all were adjusted for hospital-wide severity. Inpatient variables include: (1) the number of adjusted inpatient visits in acute surgery (e.g., general surgery and orthopedic surgery), (2) the number of adjusted inpatient visits in primary care (pediatrics, medical, and obstetrics and gynecology), and (3) the number of adjusted inpatient visits in others (dental, ear-nose-throat, ophthalmology, rehabilitation medicine, and others). The outpatient outputs are: (1) the number of surgical outpatient visits, and (2) the number of non-surgical outpatient visits (Puenpatom and Rosenman 2008).

Because revenue generation is not part of a hospital's performance criteria, the authors focused on production efficiency and input-oriented DEA. They also deployed bootstrap methodology to DEA estimates and found that universal coverage (UC) improved efficiency across the country. Additionally, truncated regression analysis was conducted to investigate the effects of environmental factors such as location, competition, and other characteristics and resources on efficiency.

Their results showed that provinces with munificence, more referrals, higher bed utilization, and competition from private hospitals were more efficient after UC implementation. They also found that the efficiency change depended on geographical locations. Hospitals in the east of the country become less efficient compared to the west after the reform (Puenpatom and Rosenman 2008).

16.15   Turkey

In Turkey, the efficiency issue mainly concerns the state because the majority of the hospitals are owned by the state and, again, the majority of the people having health insurance are under the umbrella of public programs. Thus, hospitals have the lion's share of the expenditures directed to the health sector. On the other hand, any information about how much of the hospital expenditures are derived from inefficiency is not known. Increasing efficiency is part of major reforms done both in provision and in financing of health care through the Health Transformation

Program (HTP) during the past decade. Changes made in this context are expected to influence, both directly and indirectly, the efficiency of the hospitals, which are the primary consumers of the resources allocated to the health care sector.

There are more than a few efficiency studies conducted by various researchers in Turkey during the past 15 years. We will show a snapshot of the pre-reform and post-reform investigations which tend to evaluate the impact of the HTP program undertaken by Ministry of Health in Turkey (MHT).

1. One of the earlier papers by Ersoy et al. (1997) is the first evaluation of Turkish hospital efficiency. Using the MHT data from the year 1994, the authors evaluated 573 hospitals with reliable data. The three outputs of the CCR-input oriented model were discharges, outpatient visits, and surgical operations. Inputs of the model comprised size (measured by beds), specialist FTEs, and primary care physician FTEs. Physicians are salaried staff of the hospitals and their salaries are paid by government.

   The authors identified 90.6 % of the hospitals as inefficient, pointed out the sources of these inefficiencies, and made suggestions about how these inefficient hospitals' performance can be improved.
2. The ensuing study a few years later was conducted by Sahin and Ozcan (2000) where they have concentrated the assessment to market-based evaluations, namely 80 provinces of Turkey in 1996 when 535,623 patient discharges occurred. Thus there were 80 DMUs, and all hospital data in the given provincial market area were aggregated to measure efficiency in provincial markets. This evaluation had more enhanced data compared to the earlier study; a quality variable was added to outputs of the model making three outputs (discharges, outpatient visits, and the inverse of hospital mortality rate). Inputs of the study consisted of five measures: beds, specialist FTEs, general practitioner FTEs, nurse FTEs, other allied health professional FTEs, and expenditures (e.g., operational costs). Input-oriented CCR model results showed that 44 of the 80 provinces were operating inefficiently and there was maldistribution of resources among the provinces.
3. Evaluation of the HTP program from an efficiency perspective was conducted by Sahin et al. (2011). The goal of this research was to test whether HTP made an impact on the operating efficiency of the public hospitals. Hence, they used a Malmquist approach to evaluate pre-HTP and post-HTP efficiency. Their data covered years 2005–2008 for 352 public hospitals owned and operated by the Ministry of Health (MoH) and Social Security Institution (SSI) hospitals.

   Four inputs of the study consisted of beds, physician FTEs (including specialists and general practitioners), nurse FTEs, other FTEs, and operational expenses. Study outputs included outpatient visits, inpatients, and adjusted surgeries (a case-mix index was created for major (1), moderate (1/3), and minor (1/7) surgeries to reflect appropriate volume). They used both CCR and BCC input-oriented models. The results indicate that over the 4-year period efficiency (Malmquist Index) has increased by 12.5 %, mainly improvements on technological change (innovation). The authors detailed their analysis on

Malmquist results by region of the country, by bed size, and within public ownership. According to the authors, MoH hospitals regressed in efficiency but progressed in technology, but overall improved in efficiency. Part of HTP was the transfer of SSI hospitals to MoH. Thus examining performance of previous SSI ownership would be of interest to public officials. The results showed that the SSI hospitals actually improved their efficiencies in 2008, and this was achieved by increased efficiency, rather than technology change. Overall SSI hospitals transferred to the MoH showed constantly greater total efficiency than their MoH counterparts.

4. A newer examination of hospital performance after health care reform in Turkey was conducted by Kacak et al. (2014). This study tested sensitivity of new variables that became available in the progression of HTP. Using the same variables as in Sahin et al. (2011), the authors built Model 1 and generated another model. The second model used the same input variables, but replaced outputs with two new output variables consisting of examination scores and surgery-intervention scores. These output variables were individual performance scores calculated for each physician, and they were aggregated as a total performance score for the hospitals (Kacak et al. 2014). Sensitivity testing between models did not show significant differences. Another contribution of this study was inclusion of a quality variable into both models as an additional output. The quality variable was created as an index of "service quality standards" reported by public hospitals. The combined performance model of efficiency and quality indicated no sensitivity between two models; however, the study identified four groups of hospitals based on efficiency and quality dimensions (where 90 % of the quality index was used as a cut-off point). The efficient and high-quality hospitals represented 11 % of the study hospitals, however, another 11 % of the hospitals were efficient but classified as poor quality. Inefficient but high-quality hospitals consisted of 32 %, while inefficient and poor quality was the highest category with 45 %. Even after reform, it seems that more work needs to be done to improve performance in both efficiency and quality directions.

16.16 Ukraine

In this study, Pilyavsky and associates (2006) ascertained differences in hospital efficiency between Western and Eastern hospitals in the Ukraine. Western Ukrainians are more independent and are anti-communist and anti-soviet. These cultural differences may have led to differing organizational responses in changes in efficiency after independence from the Soviet Union. The authors hypothesize that hospitals in the West of Ukraine are more likely to be influence by Western-style training programs in health care management and are more likely to take action that would lead to increased efficiency during the study period than Eastern Ukraine hospitals.

Data from Eastern Ukrainian hospitals (42) and Western Ukrainian hospitals (19) were compared from the time period of 1997 to 2001. DEA methods were used to evaluate efficiencies. Input variables included beds, physicians, and nurses. The two outputs were medical admissions and surgical admissions. Case-mix data were not available, but the average length of stay and percent of surgeries did not differ across the groups of hospitals. Two-stage analyses using bootstrapping methodology were deployed. A Tobit analysis was conducted to evaluate environmental and organizational factors related to efficiency. The primary variables were time and location (East vs. West), and also an interaction variable of time by location. Control variables included percent of elderly population, surgical population, outpatient utilization, number of physicians per capita, the average salary, and the proportion of the area's budget related to health.

The overall score of efficiency using an output-oriented CCR model was 1.29. Among the two regions, only hospitals in the Western region had a decreased relative inefficiency over time. The results from the Tobit analysis showed that there were no baseline differences in efficiency between the two groups of hospitals. Also, the inefficiency across all hospitals did not change from 1997 to 2001. Hospitals located in the West had efficiency and the difference increased over time.

Hospitals in the West were shown to improve in efficiency over time as compared to hospitals in the East. Western-style influences in management may have led to these results. The increase in efficiency may have been due to informal payments to physicians resulting in more expensive care.

16.17   OECD and Multi-country Studies

1. Adang and Borm (2007) evaluated the association between changes in satisfaction with health care systems and their economic performance. The DMUs used in their paper were 15 European Union countries. The authors utilized CRS, output-oriented Malmquist Index analyses over the periods 1995–2000 and 1995–2002. Rather than conduct the conventional between-countries comparison, they proceeded to apply a "within-countries" comparison; the authors reasoned that satisfaction was a relative notion and each country should be used as its own reference (i.e., based on changes over time).

   The authors provided a nice introduction to the Malmquist Index DEA analysis and discussed the sources of their data, which included: information on countries' health production function obtained from the Organisation for Economic Co-operation and Development (OECD) and citizens' responses on their satisfaction with their national health care system provided by the Eurobarometer health survey. For the health production function, the authors used three inputs: the country's share of GDP allocated to health care (as a measure of health care expenditures), the number of practicing physicians per 1,000 inhabitants, and percentage of daily smokers among the adult population. The output measures were life expectancy at birth and infant mortality. Since they only had a sample of

15 countries, the authors were forced to restrict the total variables included in their model in an effort to ensure its robustness. Nevertheless, they cited prior literature for the validity of their inputs and outputs.

Before their DEA was conducted, the authors first measured the change in satisfaction scores for the two time periods of their study. Unfortunately, the authors were forced to measure changes in satisfaction responses for questions that were dissimilar to each other for the two time periods, since the survey did not use the same question for the two time periods. Also, for their DEA, the authors applied a linear decreasing transformation to their input (infant mortality) and their output (number of practicing physicians), since they were pointed in the wrong direction for their DEA model. The results of the Malmquist Index showed that the total factor productivity had increased in all 15 of the countries over both time periods—almost solely due to technological progress (frontier shifts).

Spearman correlation coefficients between the changes in public satisfaction and Malmquist economic performance were tested for their significance, using bootstrapped confidence intervals, in both time periods. No significant bi-variate correlation was found to be significant. In a secondary analysis, the authors found that there was a significant correlation between total health expenditures and change in infant mortality.

In conclusion, the authors found that there was no association between health care systems' economic performance and change in satisfaction with the health care system. They reasoned that varying aspiration levels among the public may lead to downward adjustments in satisfaction that may cloud the true perceptions individuals have about their health systems. Further, they also noted that individuals may not be sufficiently exposed to the domains of the production function used in this study, the technological shifts, and efficiency gains to consequently form a reliable perception of their health care system. The authors end their article with a discussion around the limitations of their sample, the inputs and outputs used, and the measurements of the variables.

2. The purpose of Zeng and associates' (2012) study was to quantitatively evaluate the efficiency of countries' use of funding for HIV/AIDS programs and to explore the impact of some social and economic determinants on the efficiency of such programs. The study sample consisted of 68 countries with 151 observations, for the years 2002 through 2007. The data for the study came from the Joint United Nations Program on HIV/AIDS (UNAIDS) (direct inputs and direct outputs of the programs), World Bank, and the World Health Organization (contextual factors affecting the efficiency). The study used the output-oriented DEA with an assurance region (AR) (setting weight boundaries for outputs) to calculate the technical efficiency of national HIV/AIDS programs. The study uses expenditures (2007 international dollars (I$) after adjusting for purchasing power parity (PPP) and inflation) as the input variables; the number of people receiving voluntary counseling and testing (VCT), the number of HIV-positive pregnant women receiving HIV/AIDS treatment for prevention of mother-to-child transmission (PMTCT), and the number of patients receiving antiretroviral treatment (ART) are program outputs.

Indicators on economic and demographic characteristics, health financing mechanisms, and governance were used as key potential determinants of the technical efficiency. Two sets of efficiency score estimates were created using DEA models. The first set was obtained by running the DEA model on separate years (each country was compared to its peers in the same year) ('separate DEA'). The second set was calculated by pooling all countries over years with one DEA model (each country was compared to the best performers among the 6 years) ('pooled DEA'). The results from pooled DEA were used to examine the evolution of the performance of national HIV/AIDS programs over time and were used to conduct the regression analysis.

As part of the second stage of the efficiency analysis, efficiency scores from the pooled DEA model were used to construct a random-effects Tobit regression model with finite population adjustment. Results from the separate DEA showed that 18 % (27 out of 151) of the countries were on the production frontier with efficiency scores of 100 %. The overall average output-oriented efficiency was 49.8 % while this number was even lower for inefficient countries (the average efficiency score was 38.6 %). Results from the random-effects Tobit model suggested that the efficiency would increase by 40.8 % if the countries achieved an increase in two factors of governance, "voice and accountability" and "government effectiveness." Furthermore, the results showed support for the belief that fighting corruption and a higher share of expenditure from external sources would significantly improve the efficiency of using external funds and strengthen the impact of policy implementation on delivering HIV/AIDS services. Greater external shares had a higher impact on efficiency in a country with lower levels of corruption. The random-effects Tobit model also showed that the relationship between per capita gross national income (GNI) and efficiency followed an inverted U-shape.

From a policy perspective the results of the analysis have considerable social worth. Study results show that donors' financial commitments to HIV/AIDS programs cover only part (54 %) of the resources needed to meet the goal of universal access. The rest of the resources needed to run such programs are being threatened by the weak economic conditions; hence, evaluating ways in which the efficiency of such programs can be increased is important. The study results also showed that the success of such programs is not solely dependent on the funding of these programs but also on enhanced procurement, better management of human resources, and other advances of management and technical interventions.

The authors noted the selection of inputs and outputs as being limited by data availability, unconditional efficiency scores favoring countries focusing on medical activities (since all three outputs, (VCT, PMTCT, and ARV) were services in health facilities), the possibility that the assumption that the outputs for the year result entirely from inputs in the same year in the DEA model might not hold for HIV/AIDS programs, the absence of quality of the outputs in the DEA, and the possibility of country-level data having serious measurement problems as some of the study's limitations.

16.18   Summary

In this chapter we focus on specific DEA studies from 17 countries, some with multiple studies. These evaluations for a country or group of countries provide unique perspectives on cultural or programmatic organization of health care and reforms. Evaluation of health care performance using various DEA methods facilitates enriched understanding of the health care delivery around the world. Again, these are a sample of studies among other DEA studies conducted in these countries, and do not provide an exhaustive set of either the studies or the countries.

References

Aaronson WE, Zinn JS, Rosko MD (1994) Do for-profit and not-for-profit nursing homes behave differently? Gerontologist 34(6):775–777

ADAA (2006) Outlook and outcomes: 2005 annual report. Alcohol and Drug Abuse Administration, Catonsville, MD

Adams CE, Michel Y (2001) Correlation between home health resource utilization measures. Home Health Care Serv Q 20(3):45–56

Adang E, Borm G (2007) Is there an association between economic performance and public satisfaction in health care? Eur J Health Econ 08:279–285

AHA (2011) American Hospital Association (AHA) Annual Survey Database. Chicago, IL, http://www.AHADataViewer.com

AHCPR (1994) Clinical Practice Guideline No. 12: otitis media with effusion in young children, Agency for Health Care Policy and Research, US department of Health and Human Services Publication No. 94-0622

Andersen P, Petersen PC (1993) A procedure for ranking efficient units in data envelopment analysis. Manag Sci 39:1261–1264

Araújo C, Carlos P, Barros CP, Wanke P (2014) Efficiency determinants and capacity issues in Brazilian for-profit hospitals. Health Care Manag Sci 17(2):126–138. doi:10.1007/s10729-013-9249-8

Athanassopoulos A, Gounaris C (2001) Assessing the technical and allocative efficiency of hospital operations in Greece and its resource allocation implications. Eur J Oper Res 133 (2):416–432

Bailey NC (1990) How to control overcharging by physicians. Bus Health 8(8):13–18

Balance Budget Act (1997) Public law 105-33 August 5, 1997, 105th Congress. Government Printing Office. http://www.gpo.gov/fdsys/pkg/PLAW-105publ33/pdf/PLAW-105publ33.pdf. Accessed 4 Dec 2013

Banker RD, Charnes A, Cooper WW (1984) Some models for estimating technical and scale efficiencies in data envelopment analysis. Manag Sci 30:1078–1092

Banks D, Parker E, Wendel J (2001) Strategic interaction among hospitals and nursing facilities: the efficiency effects of payment systems and vertical integration. Health Econ 10(2):119–134

Bannick RR, Ozcan YA (1995) Efficiency analysis of federally funded hospitals: comparison of DoD and VA hospitals using data envelopment analysis. Health Serv Manage Res 8(2):73–85

Biørn E, Hagen TP, Iversen T, Magnussen J (2003) The effect of activity-based financing on hospital efficiency: a panel data analysis of DEA efficiency scores 1992-2000. Health Care Manag Sci 6(4):271–284

Biørn E, Hagen T, Iversen T, Magnussen J (2010) How different are hospitals' responses to a financial reform? The impact on efficiency of activity-based financing. Health Care Manag Sci 13(1):1–16

Björkgren MA, Häkkinen U, Linna M (2001) Measuring efficiency of long-term care units in Finland. Health Care Manag Sci 4(3):193–200

Blank JLT, Eggink E (2001) A quality-adjusted cost function in a regulated industry: the case of Dutch nursing homes. Health Care Manag Sci 4(3):201–211

Blank J, Valdmanis VG (2010) Environmental factors and productivity on Dutch hospitals: a semi-parametric approach. Health Care Manag Sci 13:27–34

Bowling WF (1986) Evaluating performance in governmental organizations. Gov Acc J 35(2):50–57

Brown HS III (2002) Managed care and technical efficiency. Health Econ 12(2):149–158

Buck D (2000) The efficiency of the community dental services in England: a data envelopment analysis. Community Dent Oral Epidemiol 28:274–280

Burgess JF, Wilson PW (1993) Technical efficiency in Veterans Administration Hospitals. In: Fried HO, Knox-Lovell CA, Schmidt SS (eds) The measurement of productive efficiency. Oxford University Press, New York, NY

Carter GM, Newhouse JP, Relles DA (1990) How much change in the case mix index is DRG creep? J Health Econ 9(4):411–428

Castle NG (2006) Characteristics of nursing homes that close. Health Care Manage Rev 31(1):78–89

Caves DW, Christensen LR, Diewart WE (1982) The econometric theory of index numbers and the measurement of input, and output productivity. Econometrica 50(6):1393–1414

Cawley J, Grabowski DG, Hirth RA (2006) Factor substitution in nursing homes. J Health Econ 25 (2):234–247

Chang HH (1998) Determinants of hospital efficiency: the case of central government-owned hospitals in Taiwan. Omega 26(2):307–318

Charnes A, Cooper WW, Rhodes E (1978) Measuring the efficiency of decision making units. Eur J Oper Res 2(6):429–444

Charnes A, Cooper WW, Li S (1989) Using data envelopment analysis to evaluate efficiency in the economic performance of Chinese cities. Socioecon Plann Sci 23(6):325–344

Charnes A, Cooper WW, Huang ZM, Sun DB (1990) Polyhedral cone-ratio DEA models with illustrative application to large commercial banks. J Econ 46:73–91

Chattopadhyay S, Ray SC (1998) Technical, scale, and size efficiency in nursing home care: a nonparametric analysis of Connecticut homes. Health Econ 5(4):363–373

Chilingerian JA (1995) Evaluating physician efficiency in hospitals: a multivariate analysis of best practices. Eur J Oper Res 8(3):548–574

Chilingerian JA, Sherman HD (1997a) Benchmarking physician practice patterns with DEA: a multi-stage approach for cost containment. Ann Oper Res 67:83–116

Chilingerian JA, Sherman HD (1997b) DEA and primary care physician report cards: deriving preferred practice cones from managed care service concepts and operating strategies. Ann Oper Res 73:35–66

Chilingerian JA, Glavin M, Bhalotra S (2002) Using DEA to profile cardiac surgeon efficiency. Draft of technical report to AHRQ, Heller School, Brandeis University

Chirikos TN, Sear AM (1994) Technical efficiency and the competitive behavior of hospitals. Socioecon Plann Sci 28(4):219–227

Chou T-H, Ozcan YA, White KR (2012) Technical and scale efficiencies of catholic hospitals: does a system value of stewardship matter? In: Tànfani E, Testi A (eds) Advanced decision making methods applied to health care, vol 173, International series in operations research & management science. Springer Science Publishers, New York, NY, pp 83–101, Chapter 6

Chowdhury H, Wodchis W, Laporte A (2011) Efficiency and technological change in health care services in Ontario: an application of Malmquist productivity index with bootstrapping. Int J Product Perform Manag 60(7):721–745

Christensen EW (2003) Scale and scope economies in nursing homes: a quantile regression approach. Health Econ 13(4):363–377

Chu HL, Liu SZ, Romeis JC (2004) Does capitated contracting improve efficiency? Evidence from California hospitals. Health Care Manage Rev 29(4):344–352

Clement JP, Valdmanis VG, Bazzoli GJ, Zhao M, Chukmaitov A (2008) Is more better? An analysis of hospital outcomes and efficiency with a DEA model of output congestion. Health Care Manag Sci 11(1):67–77

Cooper WW, Seiford LM, Tone K (2007) Data envelopment analysis: a comprehensive text with models, applications. References and DEA-solver software. Springer, Boston, MA

Coppola MN (2003) Correlates of military medical treatment facility (MTF) performance: measuring technical efficiency with the structural adaptation to regain fit (SARFIT) model and data envelopment analysis (DEA). Ph.D. thesis, Virginia Commonwealth University, Richmond, VA. University Microfilms Inc., Ann Arbor MI

Coppola MN, Ozcan YA, Bogacki R (2003) Evaluation of performance of dental providers on posterior restorations: does experience matter? a data envelopment analysis (DEA) approach. J Med Syst 27(5):447–458

Corredoira RA, Chilingerian JA, Kimberly JR (2011) Analyzing performance in addiction treatment: an application of data envelopment analysis to the state of Maryland system. J Subst Abuse Treat 41(1):1–13

Coventry JA, Weston MS, Collins PM (1996) Emergency room encounters of pediatric patients with asthma: cost comparisons with other treatment settings. J Ambulat Care Manag 19(2):9–21

CPT (1995) Current procedural terminology manual. American Medical Association, Chicago, IL

Creteur M, Pochet Y, Pouplier I, Closon MC (2003) Organisational performance evaluation: application to Belgian hospitals. Int J Health Care Technol Manag 1(1/2):148

Crivelli L, Filippini M, Lunati D (2002) Regulation, ownership and efficiency in the Swiss nursing home industry. Int J Health Care Finance Econ 2(2):79–97

Czypionka T, Kraus M, Mayer S, Röhrling G (2015) Efficiency, ownership, and financing of hospitals: the case of Austria. Health Care Manag Sci 18(1). doi: 10.1007/s10729-013-9256-9

Dalmau-Atarrodona E, Puig-Junoy J (1998) Market structure and hospital efficiency: evaluating potential effects of deregulation in a national health service. Rev Ind Organ 13(4):447–466

Delellis NO, Ozcan YA (2013) Quality outcomes among efficient and inefficient nursing homes: a national study. Health Care Manage Rev 38–2:156–165

Dervaux B, Leleu H, Nogues H, Valdmanis V (2006) Assessing French nursing home efficiency: an indirect approach via budget constrained DEA models. Socioecon Plann Sci 40:70–91

Draper DA, Solti I, Ozcan YA (2000) Characteristics of health maintenance organizations and their influence on efficiency. Health Serv Manage Res 13(1):40–56

eldercare.health-first.org/Resource_Detail.aspx?ID=54&ChildID=178. Accessed on December 4, 2013

Ersoy K, Kavuncubasi S, Ozcan YA, Harris JM (1997) Technical efficiencies of Turkish hospitals: DEA approach. J Med Syst 21(2):67–74

Fare R, Grosskopf S (1983) Measuring output efficiency. Eur J Oper Res 13:173–179

Färe R, Grosskopf S (1996) Intertemporal production frontiers: with dynamic DEA. Kluwer, Norwell, MA

Färe R, Grosskopf S (2000) Network DEA. Socio-Econ Plan Sci 34:35–49

Fare R, Grosskopf S, Knox-Lovell CA (1994) Production frontiers. Cambridge University Press, London

Färe R, Grosskopf S, Norris S, Zhang Z (1994) Productivity growth, technical progress, and efficiency change in industrialized countries. Am Econ Rev 84(1):66–83

Fare R, Grosskopf S, Lindgren B, Roos P (1994) Productivity developments in Swedish hospitals: a Malmquist output index approach. In: Charnes A, Cooper WW, Lewin AY, Seiford LM (eds) Data envelopment analysis: theory, methodology, and applications. Kluwer Academic Publishers, Boston, MA

Fareed N, Ozcan YA, DeShazo JP (2012) Hospital electronic medical record enterprise application strategies: do they matter? Health Care Manage Rev 37(1):4–11

Farrel MJ (1957) The measurement of productive efficiency. J R Stat Soc 120:253–281

Farsi M, Filippini M (2004) An empirical analysis of cost efficiency in non-profit and public nursing homes. Ann Publ Cooper Econ 75(3):339–366

Ferrando A, Ivaldi C, Buttiglieri A, Pagano E, Bonetto C, Arione R, Scaglione L, Gelormino E, Merletti F, Ciccone G (2005) Guidelines for preoperative assessment: impact on clinical practice and costs. Int J Qual Health Care 17(4):323–329

Ferrier GD, Valdmanis V (2004) Do mergers improve hospital productivity? J Oper Res Soc 55 (10):1071–1080

Ferrier GD, Rosko MD, Valdmanis VG (2006) Analysis of uncompensated hospital care using a DEA model of output congestion. Health Care Manag Sci 9(2):181–188

Field K, Emrouznejad A (2003) Measuring the performance of neonatal care units in Scotland. J Med Syst 27(4):315–324

Fizel JL, Nunnikhoven TS (1993) The efficiency of nursing home chains. Appl Econ 25(1):49–55

Ford EW, Huerta TR, Menachemi N, Thompson MA, Yu F (2013) Health information technology vendor selection strategies and total factor productivity. Health Care Manage Rev 38-3:177–187

Fried HO, Schmidt SS, Yaisawarng S (1998) Productive, scale and scope efficiencies in U.S. hospital-based nursing homes. INFOR Sp Iss Eval Perform Publ Serv Sect Organ 36 (3):103–119

Fried HO, Schmidt SS, Yaisawarng S (1999) Incorporating the operating environment into a nonparametric measure of technical efficiency. J Prod Anal 12(3):249–267

Fulton L (2005) Performance of army medical department health delivery components, 2001-2003: a multi model approach, Ph.D. thesis, University of Texas, Austin, TX. University Microfilms Inc., Ann Arbor MI

Garavaglia G, Lettieri E, Agasisti T, Lopez S (2011) Efficiency and quality of care in nursing homes: an Italian case study. Health Care Manag Sci 14(1):22–35

Gautam S, Hicks L, Johnson T, Mishra B (2013) Measuring the performance of critical access hospitals in Missouri using data envelopment analysis. J Rural Health 29(2):150–158

Gerdtham UG, Rehnberg C, Tambour M (1999) The impact of internal markets on health care efficiency: evidence from health care reforms in Sweden. Appl Econ 31(8):935

Gertler PJ, Waldman DM (1994) Why are not-for-profit nursing homes more costly? DRU-723-NIA. http://www.rand.org/cgi-bin/health/hilite.pl?key=1994DRU-723-NIA&hi

Giokas DI (2001) Greek hospitals: how well their resources are used. Omega 29(1):73–83

Given R (1996) Economies of scale and scope as an explanation of merger and output diversification activities in the health maintenance organization industry. J Health Econ 15(6):685–713

Government Accounting Office (2000) Medicare home health care: prospective payment system could reverse recent declines in spending. Washington, DC. Document GAO-HEHS-00-176. http://www.gao.gov/new.items/he00176.pdf

Grabowski DC (2001) Medicaid reimbursement and the quality of nursing home care. J Health Econ 20(4):549–569

Grosskopf S, Valdmanis VG (1987) Measuring hospital performance: a non-parametric approach. J Health Econ 6:89–107

Grosskopf S, Margaritis D, Valdmanis VG (2001) The effects of teaching on hospital productivity. Socioecon Plann Sci 35(3):189–204

Grosskopf S, Margaritis D, Valdmanis VG (2004) Competitive effects on teaching hospitals. Eur J Oper Res 154(2):515–525

Han B, Remsburg RE, Lubitz J, Goulding M (2004) Payment source and length of use among home health agency discharges. Med Care 42(11):1081–1090

Harrington C, O'Meara J (2004) Report on California's nursing homes, home health agencies, and hospice programs. California HealthCare Foundation. http://www.chcf.org/documents/hospitals/ReportOnNursingHomeHealthHospice.pdf

Harris JM, Ozgen H, Ozcan YA (2000) Do mergers enhance the performance of hospital efficiency? J Oper Res Soc 51:801–811

Harrison JP, Sexton C (2006) The improving efficiency frontier of religious not-for-profit hospitals. Hosp Top 84(1):2–10

Harrison JP, Coppola MN, Wakefield M (2004) Efficiency of federal hospitals in the United States. J Med Syst 28(5):411–422

Harrison JP, Lambiase LR, Zhao M (2010) Organizational factors associated with quality of care in US teaching hospitals. J Health Care Finance 36(3):1–12

Health, United States (2005) Chartbook on trends in the health of Americans. National Center for Health Statistics. Hyattsville, MD. http://www.cdc.gov/nchs/

Helling DK, Nelson KM, Ramirez JE, Humphries TL (2006) Kaiser Permanente Colorado region pharmacy department: innovative leader in pharmacy practice. J Am Pharm Assoc 46(1):67–76

Helmig B, Lapsley L (2001) On the efficiency of public, welfare and private hospitals in Germany over time: a sectoral data envelopment analysis study. Health Serv Manage Res 14(4):263–274

Hicks LL, Rantz MJ, Petroski GF, Madsen RW, Conn VS, Mehr DR, Porter R (1997) Assessing contributors to cost of care in nursing homes. Nurs Econ 15(4):205–212

Hirschberg JG, Lloyd PJ (2002) Does the technology of foreign-invested enterprises spill over to other enterprises in China? An application of post-DEA bootstrap regression analysis. In: Lloyd PJ, Zang XG (eds) Modelling the Chinese economy. Edward Elgar, London

Hofmarcher MM, Paterson I, Riedel M (2002) Measuring hospital efficiency in Austria – a DEA approach. Health Care Manag Sci 5(1):7–14

Hollingsworth B (2003) Non-parametric and parametric applications measuring efficiency in health care. Health Care Manag Sci 6(4):203–218

Hollingsworth B (2008) The measurement of efficiency and productivity of health care delivery. Health Econ 17(10):1107–1128

Hollingsworth B, Dawson PJ, Manidakis N (1999) Efficiency measurement of health care: a review of non-parametric methods and applications. Health Care Manag Sci 2(3):161–172

Hosmer DW, Lemeshow S, Sturdivant RX (2013) Applied logistic regression, 3rd edn. Wiley, New York, NY

Hospital quality alliance overview summary (2005) Accessed March 4, 2006, from www.cms.hhs.gov/HospitalQualityInits/

Hsia DC, Ahern CA, Ritchie BP, Moscoe LM, Krushat WM (1992) Medicare reimbursement accuracy under the prospective payment system, 1985 to 1988. JAMA 268:896–899

Iyengar RI, Ozcan YA (2009) Performance evaluation of ambulatory surgery centers: an efficiency approach. Health Serv Manage Res 22(4):184–190

Javitt DC, Doneshka P, Zylberman I, Ritter W, Vaughan HG Jr (1993) Impairment of early cortical processing in schizophrenia: an event-related potential replication study. Biol Psychiatry 33:513–519

Johansen L (1968) Production functions and the concept of capacity. In: Fø'rsund FR (ed) Collected works of Leif Johansen. North-Holland Press, Amsterdam, p 987

Kacak H, Ozcan YA, Kavuncubasi S (2014) A new examination of hospital performance after healthcare reform in Turkey: sensitivity and quality comparisons. Int J Publ Pol 10(4/5):178

Kawaguchi H, Tone K, Tsutsui M (2014) Estimation of the efficiency of Japanese hospitals using a dynamic and network data envelopment analysis model. Health Care Manag Sci 17(2):101–112. doi:10.1007/s10729-013-9248-9

Kazley AS, Ozcan YA (2009) Electronic medical record use and efficiency: a DEA and windows analysis of hospitals. Socioecon Plann Sci 43(3):209–216

Kemper P, Komisar HL, Alecxih L (2005/2006) Long-term care over an uncertain future: what can current retirees expect? Inquiry 42(4):333–350

Kirigia JM, Emrouznejad A, Sambo LG, Munguti N, Liambila W (2004) Using data envelopment analysis to measure the technical efficiency of public health centers in Kenya. J Med Syst 28(2):155–166

Kleinsorge IK, Karney DF (1992) Management of nursing homes using data envelopment analysis. Socioecon Plann Sci 26(1):57–71

Klopp GA (1985) The analysis of the efficiency of production system with multiple inputs and outputs, Ph.D. dissertation. University of Illinois at Chicago, Industrial and System Engineering College

Knox KJ, Blankmeyer EC, Stutzman JR (2004) Administrative compensation and organizational performance in Texas nursing facilities. Small Bus Econ 22(1):33–49

Kooreman P (1994) Nursing home care in the Netherlands: a nonparametric efficiency analysis. J Health Econ 13(3):301–316

Kuwahara Y, Nagata S, Taguchi A, Naruse T, Kawaguchi H, Murashima S (2013) Measuring the efficiencies of visiting nurse service agencies using data envelopment analysis. Health Care Manag Sci 16(3):228–235

Laine J, Linna M, Häkkinen U, Noro A (2004) Measuring the productive efficiency and clinical quality of institutional long-term care for the elderly. Health Econ 14(3):245–256

Laine J, Linna M, Noro A, Häkkinen U (2005) The cost efficiency and clinical quality of institutional long-term care for the elderly. Health Care Manag Sci 8(2):149–156

Langabeer JR II, Ozcan YA (2009) The economics of cancer care: longitudinal changes in provider efficiency. Health Care Manag Sci 12(2):192–200

Lee K, Wan TTH (2004) Information system integration and technical efficiency in Urban hospitals. Int J Health Care Technol Manag 1(3/4):452

Lewis HF, Sexton TR (2004) Network DEA: efficiency analysis of organizations with complex internal structure. Comput Oper Res 31:1365–1410

Linna M, Nordblad A, Koivu M (2003) Technical and cost efficiency of oral health care provision in Finnish health centres. Soc Sci Med 56(2):343

Linna M, Häkkinen U, Peltola M, Magnussen J, Anthun KS, Kittelsen S, Roed A, Olsen K, Medin E, Rehnberg C (2010) Measuring cost efficiency in the Nordic hospitals - a cross-sectional comparison of public hospitals in 2002. Health Care Manag Sci 13(4):346–357

Lobo CMS, Ozcan YA, da Silva ACM, Lins MPE, Fiszman R (2010) Financing reform and productivity change in Brazilian teaching hospitals: Malmquist approach. CEJOR 18(2):141–152

Lynch JR, Ozcan YA (1994) U.S. hospital closures: an efficiency analysis. Hospital Health Serv Admin 39(2):205–220

Maddala GS (1983) Limited-dependent and qualitative variables in economics. Cambridge University Press, New York, NY, pp 257–291

Malmquist S (1953) Index numbers and indifference surfaces. Trabajos de Estatistica 4:209–242

Mark BA, Jones CB, Lindley L, Ozcan YA (2009) An examination of technical efficiency, quality and patient safety on acute care nursing units. Policy Polit Nurs Pract 10(3):180–186

McCall N, Petersons A, Moore S, Korb J (2003) Utilization of home health services before and after the balanced budget act of 1997: what were the initial effects? Health Serv Res 38(1):85–106

McCallion G, Glass JC, Jackson R, Kerr CA, McKilliop DG (2000) Investigating productivity change and hospital size: a nonparametric frontier approach. Appl Econ 32:161–174

McKinney MM, Begun JW, Ozcan YA (1998) Hospital development and OPO performance. J Transpl Coord 8(2):74–80

MedPAC (2005a) Report to the congress: Medicare payment policy. http://www.medpac.gov/publications/congressional_reports/Mar05_Ch02D.pdf

MedPAC (2005b) A data book: healthcare spending and the Medicare program. http://www.medpac.gov/publications/chapters/Jun05DataBookSec10.pdf

Mobley LR, Magnussen J (1998) An international comparison of hospital efficiency: does institutional environment matter? Appl Econ 30(8):1089–1100

Mobley LR, Magnussen J (2002) The impact of managed care penetration and hospital quality on efficiency in hospital staffing. J Health Care Finance 28(4):24–43

Morey RC, Ozcan YA, Retzlaff-Roberts DL, Fine DJ (1995) Estimating the hospital-wide cost differentials warranted for teaching hospitals: an alternative to regression approaches. Med Care 33(5):531–552

Mutter R, Valdmanis VG, Rosko MD (2010) High versus lower quality hospitals: a comparison of environmental characteristics and technical efficiency. Health Serv Outcom Res Methodol 10 (3):134–153

Nadela IC, Fannin JM (2013) Technical efficiency of critical access hospitals: an application of the two-stage approach with double bootstrap. Health Care Manag Sci 16(1):27–36

National Institutes of Health (NIH) (1991) Report on asthma. U.S. Department of Health and Human Services, Bethesda, MD, http://www.hhs.gov/

Nayar P, Ozcan YA (2009) Data envelopment analysis comparison of hospital efficiency and quality. J Med Syst 32(3):193–199

Nayar P, Ozcan YA, Yu F, Nguyen AT (2013) Benchmarking urban acute care hospitals: efficiency and quality perspectives. Health Care Manage Rev 38(2):137–145

Nicholoson G, Hall M (2011) Diabetes mellitus: new drugs for a new epidemic. Br J Anaesth 107:65–73

Nunamaker TR, Lewin AY (1983) Measuring routine nursing service efficiency: a comparison of cost per patient day and data envelopment analysis models/comment. Health Serv Res 18 (2 (Part 1)):183–208

Nyman JA, Bricker DL (1989) Profit incentives and technical efficiency in the production of nursing home care. Rev Econ Stat 71(4):586–594

Nyman JA, Bricker DL, Link D (1990) Technical efficiency in nursing homes. Med Care 28 (6):541–551

Office of Statewide Health Planning and Development (2006) Find data – HHA and hospices annual utilization data. http://www.oshpd.state.ca.us/HQAD/HHA/hhautil.htm

O'Neal PV, Ozcan YA, Ma Y (2002) Benchmarking mechanical ventilation services in teaching hospitals. J Med Syst 26(3):227–239

O'Neill L (1998) Multifactor efficiency in data envelopment analysis with an application to Urban hospitals. Health Care Manag Sci 1(1):19–27

O'Neill L (2005) Methods for understanding super-efficient data envelopment analysis results with an application to hospital inpatient surgery. Health Care Manag Sci 8(4):291–298

O'Neill L, Dexter F (2004) Market capture of inpatient perioperative services using DEA. Health Care Manag Sci 7(4):263–273

O'Neill L, Rauner M, Heidenberger K, Kraus M (2008) A cross-national comparison and taxonomy of DEA-based hospital efficiency studies. Socioecon Plann Sci 42(3):158–189

Osman IH, Berbary LN, Sidani Y, Al-Ayoubi B, Emrouznejad A (2011) Data envelopment analysis model for the appraisal and relative performance evaluation of nurses at an intensive care unit. J Med Syst 35(5):1039–1062

Ouellette P, Vierstraete V (2004) Technological change and efficiency in the presence of quasi-fixed inputs: a DEA application to the hospital sector. Eur J Oper Res 154(3):755–763

Ozcan YA (1992–1993) Sensitivity analysis of hospital efficiency under alternative output/input and peer groups: a review. Knowl Pol 5(4):1–29

Ozcan YA (1995) Efficiency of hospital service production in local markets: the balance sheet of U.S. medical armament. Socioecon Plann Sci 29(2):139–150

Ozcan YA (1998) Physician benchmarking: measuring variation in practice behavior in treatment of otitis media. Health Care Manag Sci 1(1):5–17

Ozcan YA (2008) Health care benchmarking and performance evaluation: an assessment using data envelopment, analysis (DEA). Springer, New York, NY

Ozcan YA (2009) Quantitative methods in health care management: techniques and applications, 2nd edn. Jossey-Bass, San Francisco, CA

Ozcan YA, Bannick RR (1994) Trends in department of defense hospital efficiency. J Med Syst 18 (2):69–83

Ozcan YA, Cotter JJ (1994) An assessment of area agencies on aging in Virginia through data envelopment analysis. Gerontologist 34(3):363–370

Ozcan YA, Legg JS (2014) Performance measurement for radiology providers: a national study. Int J Health Tech Manag (in press)

Ozcan YA, Luke RD (1993) A national study of the efficiency of hospitals in Urban markets. Health Serv Res 28(6):719–739

Ozcan YA, Luke RD (2011) Health care delivery restructuring and productivity change: assessing the veterans integrated service networks (VISNs) using the Malmquist approach. Med Care Res Rev 68(1 suppl):20S–35S

Ozcan YA, Lynch J (1992) Rural hospital closures: an inquiry to efficiency. In: Scheffler RM, Rossiter LF (eds) Advances in health economics and health services research, vol 13. JAI Press, Greenwich, CT, pp 205–224

Ozcan YA, McCue MJ (1996) Financial performance index for hospitals. J Oper Res Soc 47:18–26

Ozcan YA, Luke RD, Haksever C (1992) Ownership and organizational performance: a comparison of technical efficiency across hospital types. Med Care 30(9):781–794

Ozcan YA, McCue MJ, Okasha AA (1996a) Measuring the technical efficiency of psychiatric hospitals. J Med Syst 20(3):141–150

Ozcan YA, Yeh S-C, McCollum D, Begun JW (1996b) Trends in labor efficiency among American hospital markets. Ann Oper Res 67:61–82

Ozcan YA, Watts J, Harris JM, Wogen SE (1998a) Provider experience and technical efficiency in the treatment of stroke patients: DEA approach. J Oper Res Soc 49(6):573–582

Ozcan YA, Luu SK, Glass KW, Shasky, Rossiter LF (1998) Physician benchmarking for asthma cases with, INFORMS meeting, Montreal, Canada, April 25–27, 1998

Ozcan YA, Wogen SE, Mau LW (1998c) Efficiency evaluation of skilled nursing facilities. J Med Syst 22(4):211–224

Ozcan YA, Begun JW, McKinney MM (1999) Benchmarking organ procurement organizations (OPOs): a national study. Health Serv Res 34(4):853–872

Ozcan YA, Jiang HJ, Pai C-W (2000) Physician efficiency in treatment of sinusitis: do primary care physicians or specialist provide more efficient care? Health Serv Manage Res 13(2):90–96

Ozcan YA, Merwin E, Lee K, Morrisey JP (2004) Benchmarking using DEA: the case of mental health organizations. In: Brandeau ML, Sainfort F, Pierskalla WP (eds) Operations research and health care: a handbook of methods and applications. Kluwer Academic Publishers, Boston, MA

Ozcan YA, Lins MPE, Lobo MSC, da Silva ACM, Fiszman R, Pereira BB (2010) Evaluating the performance of Brazilian university hospitals. Ann Oper Res 178(1):247–261

Ozgen H, Ozcan YA (2002) A national study of efficiency for dialysis centers: an examination of market competition and facility characteristics for production of multiple dialysis outputs. Health Serv Res 37(3):711–732

Ozgen H, Ozcan YA (2004) Longitudinal analysis of efficiency in multiple output dialysis markets. Health Care Manag Sci 7(4):253–261

Pai C-W, Ozcan YA, Jiang HJ (2000) Regional variation in physician practice pattern: an examination of technical and cost efficiency for treating sinusitis. J Med Syst 24(2):103–117

Pakyz AL, Ozcan YA (2014) Use of data envelopment analysis to quantify opportunities for antibacterial targets for reduction of health care–associated clostridium difficile infection. Am J Med Q. Doi:1062860613502520

Pastor JT, Ruiz JL, Sirvent I (1999) An enhanced DEA Russell graph efficiency measure. Eur J Oper Res 115(3):596–607

Payne SM, Donahue C, Rappo P et al (1995) Variations in pediatric pneumonia and bronchitis/asthma admission rates. Is appropriateness a factor? Arch Pediatr Adolesc Med 149(2):162–169

Pilyavsky AI, Aaronson WE, Bernet PM, Rosko MD, Valdmanis VG, Golubchikov MV (2006) East-west: does it make a difference to hospital efficiencies in Ukraine? Health Econ 15 (11):1173–1186

Pina V, Torres L (1996) Methodological aspects in efficiency evaluation of public hospitals. Finan Acc Manag 12(1):21–35

Puenpatom RA, Rosenman R (2008) Efficiency of Thai provincial public hospitals during the introduction of universal health coverage using capitation. Health Care Manag Sci 11(4):319–338

Rahman MA, Capitman JA (2012) Can more use of supporting primary care health practitioners increase efficiency of health clinics? Evidence from California's San Joaquin Valley. J Health Care Finance 38(3):78–92

Ramanathan TV, Chandra KS, Thupeng WM (2003) A comparison of the technical efficiencies of health districts and hospitals in Botswana. Dev South Afr 20(2):307–320

Ramírez-valdivia MT, Maturana S, Salvo-garrido S (2011) A multiple stage approach for performance improvement of primary healthcare practice. J Med Syst 35(5):1015–1028

Robinette BA, Helsel EV (1992) Ambulatory care review: utilization management illustrated. Am J Med Qual 7(1):21–23

Rollins J, Lee K, Xu Y, Ozcan YA (2001) Longitudinal study of health maintenance organization efficiency. Health Serv Manage Res 14(4):249–262

Rosenau PV, Linder SH (2001) The comparative performance of for-profit and nonprofit home health care services in the US. Home Health Care Serv Q 20(2):47–59

Rosenman R, Siddharthan K, Ahern M (1997) Output efficiency of health maintenance organizations in Florida. Health Econ 6(3):295–302

Rosko MD, Chilingerian JA, Zinn JS, Aaronson WE (1995) The effect of ownership, operating environment and strategic choices on nursing homes efficiency. Med Care 33(10):1001–1021

Sahin I, Ozcan YA (2000) Public sector hospital efficiency for provincial markets in Turkey. J Med Syst 24(6):307–320

Sahin I, Ozcan YA, Ozgen H (2011) Assessment of hospital efficiency under health transformation program in Turkey. CEJOR 19(1):19–37

Schinnar AP, Kamis-Gould E, Delucia N, Rothbard AB (1990) Organizational determinants of efficiency and effectiveness in mental health partial care programs. Health Serv Res 25 (2):387–420

Schnelle JF, Simmons SF, Harrington C, Cadogan M, Garcia E, Bates-Jensen BM (2004) Relationship of nursing home staffing to quality of care. Health Serv Res 39(2):225–250

Sexton TR, Lewis HF (2003) Two-stage DEA: an application to major league baseball. J Prod Anal 19:227–249

Sexton TR, Leiken AM, Sleeper S, Coburn AF (1989) The impact of prospective reimbursement on nursing home efficiency. Med Care 27(2):154–163

Shay PD, Ozcan YA (2013) Freestanding inpatient rehabilitation facility performance following the 60 percent rule a matter of fit. Med Care Res Rev 70(1):46–67

Sherman HD (1984) Hospital efficiency measurement and evaluation: empirical test of a new technique. Med Care 22(10):922–938

Sherman HD, Zhu J (2006) Service productivity management: improving service performance using data envelopment analysis (DEA). Springer, Boston, MA

Shwartz M, Iezzoni LI, Ash AS, Payne SMC, Restuccia JD (1996) Health care databases, diagnostic coding, severity adjustment systems and improved parameter estimation. Ann Oper Res 67:23

Sikka V, Luke RD, Ozcan YA (2009) The efficiency of hospital-based clusters: evaluating system performance using data envelopment analysis. Health Care Manage Rev 34(3):251–261

Simar L, Wilson WP (1998) Sensitivity analysis of efficiency scores: how to bootstrap in nonparametric frontier models. Manag Sci 44(1):49–61

Simar L, Wilson WP (2000) Statistical inference in nonparametric frontier models: the state of the art. J Prod Anal 13:49–78

Simar L, Wilson WP (2005) Estimation and inference in two-stage, semi-parametric models of production processes. J Econ 136(1):31–64

Simar L, Wilson PW (2007) Estimation and inference in two-stage, semi-parametric models of production processes. J Econ 136:31–64

Simões P, Marques R (2011) Performance and congestion analysis of the Portuguese hospital services. CEJOR 19(1):39–63

Singaroyan R, Seed CA, Egdell RM (2006) Is a target culture in health care always compatible with efficient use of resources? A cost-effectiveness analysis of an intervention to achieve thrombolysis targets. J Public Health 28(1):31–34

Siwolop S (1989) Doctored fees. Finan World 158:64

Sola M, Prior D (2001) Measuring productivity and quality changes using data envelopment analysis: an application to Catalan hospitals. Finan Acc Manag 17(3):219–246

Sommersguter-Reichmann M (2000) The impact of the Austrian hospital financing reform on hospital productivity: empirical evidence on efficiency and technology changes using a non-parametric input-based Malmquist approach. Health Care Manag Sci 3(4):309–321

Staat M (2006) Efficiency of hospitals in Germany: a DEA-bootstrap approach. Appl Econ 38:2255–2263

Steinmann L, Zweifel P (2003) On the (in)efficiency of Swiss hospitals. Appl Econ 35(3):361–370

Testi AA, Fareed N, Ozcan YA, Tanfani E (2014) Assessment of physician performance for diabetes: a bias-corrected DEA model. Qual Prim Care 21(6):345–357

Thompson RG, Langemeir LN, Lee C, Lee E, Thrall RM (1990) The role of multiplier bounds in efficiency analysis with application to Kansas farming. J Econ 46:93–108

Tiemann O, Schreyogg J (2012) Changes in hospital efficiency after privatization. Health Care Manag Sci 15(4):310–326

Tlotlego N, Nonvignon J, Sambo L, Asbu E, Kirigia J (2010) Assessment of productivity of hospitals in Botswana: a DEA application. Int Arch Med 3(1):27

Tone KA (2002) A slacks-based measure of super-efficiency in data envelopment analysis. Eur J Oper Res 143(1):32–41

Tone K (2013) Resampling in DEA. National Graduate Institute for Policy Studies, Japan

Tone K, Tsutsui M (2009) Network DEA: a slacks based measurement approach. Eur J Operational Res 197:243–252

Tone K, Tsutsui M (2014) Dynamic DEA with network structure: a slacks-based measure approach. Omega 42(1):124–131

Tsekouras K, Papathanassopoulos F, Kounetas K, Pappous G (2010) Does the adoption of new technology boost productive efficiency in the public sector? The case of ICUs system. Int J Prod Econ 128:427–433

Tyler LH, Ozcan YA, Wogen SE (1995) Technical efficiency of community mental health centers. J Med Syst 19(5):413–423

Tziogkidis P (2012) The Simar and Wilsons bootstrap DEA approach: a critique, Cardiff economics working paper series, Paper E2012/19

U.S. Census 2000, www.Allcountries.org

U.S. Department of Health and Human services (1999) Mental health: a report of the surgeon general. Substance abuse and mental health services administration center for mental health services. National Institute of Mental Health, Bethesda, MD

USDHHS-HSRA (2013) http://www.hrsa.gov/healthit/toolbox/RuralHealthITtoolbox/Introduc tion/critical.html. Accessed on October 16, 2013

Valdmanis V (1990) Ownership and technical efficiency of hospitals. Med Care 28(6):552–561

Valdmanis V (1992) Sensitivity analysis for DEA models: an empirical example using public vs. NFP hospitals. J Publ Econ 48(2):185–205

Valdmanis VG, Kumanarayake L, Lertiendumrong J (2004) Capacity in Thai public hospitals and the production of care for poor and non-poor patients. Health Serv Res 39(6):S2117–S2135

Valdmanis VG, Rosko MD, Mutter R (2008) Hospital quality, efficiency, and input slack differentials. Health Serv Res 43:1830–1848

Valdmanis VG, Bernet P, Moises J (2010) Hospital capacity, capability, and emergency preparedness. Eur J Oper Res 207:1628–1634

VanderWielen LM, Ozcan YA (2014) An assessment of the healthcare safety net: performance evaluation of free clinics. Nonprof Volunt Sec Q. doi:10.1177/0899764013520235

Vitaliano DF, Toren M (1994) Cost and efficiency in nursing homes: a stochastic frontier approach. J Health Econ 13(3):281–300

Wang BB, Ozcan YA, Wan TTH, Harrison J (1999) Trends in hospital efficiency among metropolitan markets. J Med Syst 23(2):83–97

Weech-Maldonado R, Neff G, Mor V (2003) Does quality of care lead to better financial performance? The case of the nursing home industry. Health Care Manage Rev 28(3):201–216

White KR, Ozcan YA (1996) Church ownership and hospital efficiency. Hospital Health Serv Admin 41(3):297–310

Wholey D, Feldman R, Christianson J, Engberg J (1996) Scale and scope economies among health maintenance organizations. J Health Econ 15(6):657–684

Yeh J, White RK, Ozcan YA (1997) Efficiency evaluation of community-based youth services in Virginia. Commun Mental Health J 33(6):487–499

Zeng W, Shepard DS, Chilingerian JA, Avila-Figueroa C (2012) How much can we gain from improved efficiency? An examination of performance of national HIV/AIDS programs and its determinants in low- and middle-income countries et al. BMC Health Serv Res 12:74

Zhu J (2009) Quantitative models for performance evaluation and benchmarking: data envelopment analysis with spreadsheets, 2nd edn, International series in operations research and management science. Springer, New York, NY

User's Guide to DEA-Solver-Learning Version (LV 8.0)

Preface to DEA-Solver

This is an introduction and manual for the attached DEA-Solver-LV. There are two versions of DEA-Solver, the "Learning Version" (called DEA-Solver-LV), in the attached CD, and the "Professional Version" (called DEA-Solver-PRO). DEA-Solver-PRO can be viewed in website at: http://www.saitech-inc.com/. DEA-Solver-LV 8.0 includes 28 clusters of DEA models and can solve up to 50 DMUs, while DEA-Solver-PRO 10.0 includes 45 clusters and can deal with large-scale problems within the capacity of Excel worksheet. DEA-Solver was developed by Kaoru Tone. All responsibility and intellectual property rights are attributed to Tone, but not to others in any dimension.

We can classify all DEA models into three types: (1) Radial, (2) NonRadial and Oriented, (3) and NonRadial and NonOriented. 'Radial' means that a proportionate change of input/output values is the main concern and hence it neglects the existence of slacks (input excesses and output shortfalls remaining in the model) as secondary or freely disposable, whereas 'NonRadial' deals with slacks directly and does not stick to a proportionate change of input/output. 'Oriented' indicates the input or output orientation in evaluating efficiency, i.e., the main target of evaluation is either input reduction or output expansion. For example, input oriented models first aim to reduce input resources to the efficient frontier as far as possible, and then to enlarge output products as the second objective. 'NonOriented' models deal with input reduction and output expansion at the same time. We can classify them into the three categories as displayed below.

Category	Cluster or model
Radial	CCR, BCC, IRS, DRS, AR, ARG, NCN, NDSC, BND, CAT, SYS, Bilateral, Window, Malmquist-Radial, FDH
NonRadial and Oriented	SBM-Oriented, Super-efficiency-Oriented
NonRadial and NonOriented	Cost, New-Cost, Revenue, New-Revenue, Profit, New-Profit, Ratio, SBM-NonOriented, Super-SBM-NonOriented, Weighted SBM

Y.A. Ozcan, *Health Care Benchmarking and Performance Evaluation*, 301
International Series in Operations Research & Management Science 210,
DOI 10.1007/978-1-4899-7472-3, © Springer Science+Business Media New York 2014

1. Platform

The platform for this software is Microsoft Excel 97 (a trademark of Microsoft Corporation) or later. If DEA-Solver does not work correctly on your PC, please try to change the Regional Settings of your PC through the Windows Control Panel. This manual is for use of English (United States) Regional Settings.

2. Notation of DEA Models

DEA-Solver applies the following notation to describe DEA models.

Model Name—I or O—C, V or GRS

where I or O corresponds to "Input"- or "Output"-orientation, and C or V to "Constant" or "Variable" returns to scale, respectively. For example, "AR-I-C" means the Input-oriented Assurance Region model under Constant returns-to-scale assumption. In some cases, "I or O" and/or "C or V" are omitted. For example, "CCR-I" indicates the Input oriented CCR model that is naturally under constant returns-to-scale. "GRS" indicates the "General" returns to scale model. Models with the GRS extension demand to input two parameters through keyboard. The one is the lower bound L of the sum of lambdas (λ) and the other its upper bound U. "Bilateral" and "FDH" have no extensions. The abbreviated model names correspond to the following models.

1. CCR = Charnes-Cooper-Rhodes model
2. BCC = Banker-Charnes-Cooper model
3. IRS = Increasing Returns-to-Scale model
4. DRS = Decreasing Returns-to-Scale model
5. GRS = Generalized Returns-to-Scale model
6. AR = Assurance Region model
7. NCN = Non-controllable variable model
8. NDSC = Non-discretionary variable model
9. BND = Bounded variable model
10. CAT = Categorical variable model
11. SYS = Different Systems model
12. SBM-Oriented = Slacks-Based Measure model in input/output orientation
13. SBM-NonOriented = Slacks-Based Measure without orientation
14. Supper-SBM-Oriented = Super-efficiency model in input/output orientation
15. Super-SBM-NonOriented = Super-efficiency model without orientation.
16. Super-Radial = Super-efficiency model using Radial inputs and outputs.
17. Cost = Cost efficiency model
18. New-Cost = New cost efficiency model
19. Revenue = Revenue efficiency model
20. New-Revenue = New revenue model

21. Profit = Profit efficiency model
22. New-Profit = New profit model
23. Ratio = Ratio efficiency model
24. Bilateral = Bilateral comparison model
25. Window = Window Analysis
26. FDH = Free Disposal Hull model
27. Malmquist-Radial = Malmquist productivity index model under the radial scheme
28. Weighted SBM = Weighted Slacks-Based Measure model

3. DEA Models Included

Version 8.0 consists of 28 clusters.

No.	Cluster	Model
1	CCR	CCR-I, CCR-O
2	BCC	BCC-I, BCC-O
3	IRS	IRS-I, IRS-O
4	DRS	DRS-I, DRS-O
5	GRS	GRS-I, GRS-O
6	AR (Assurance Region)	AR-I-C, AR-I-V, AR-I-GRS, AR-O-C, AR-O-V, AR-O-GRS
7	NCN (Non-Controllable)	NCN-I-C, NCN-I-V, NCN-O-C, NCN-O-V
8	NDSC (Non-Discretionary)	NDSC-I-C, NDSC-I-V, NDSC-I-GRS, NDSC-O-C, NDSC-O-V, NDSC-O-GRS
9	BND (Bounded Variable)	BND-I-C, BND-I-V, BND-I-GRS, BND-O-C, BND-O-V, BND-O-GRS
10	CAT (Categorical Variable)	CAT-I-C, CAT-I-V, CAT-O-C, CAT-O-V
11	SYS (Different Systems)	SYS-I-C, SYS-I-V, SYS-O-C, SYS-O-V
12	SBM-Oriented (Slacks-based Measure)	SBM-I-C, SBM-I-V, SBM-I-GRS, SBM-O-C, SBM-O-V, SBM-O-GRS, SBM-AR-I-C, SBM-AR-I-V, SBM-AR-O-C, SBM-AR-O-V
13	SBM-NonOriented	SBM-C, SBM-V, SBM-GRS, SBM-AR-C, SBM-AR-V
14	Weighted SBM	WeightedSBM-C, WeightedSBM-V, WeightedSBM-I-C, WeightedSBM-I-V, WeightedSBM-O-C, WeightedSBM-O-V
15	Super-SBM-Oriented	Super-SBM-I-C, Super-SBM-I-V, Super-SBM-I-GRS, Super-SBM-O-C, Super-SBM-O-V, Super-SBM-O-GRS
16	Super-SBM-NonOriented	Super-SBM-C, Super-SBM-V, Super-SBM-GRS
17	Super-Radial	Super-CCR-I, Super-CCR-O, Super-BCC-I, Super-BCC-O
18	Cost	Cost-C, Cost-V, Cost-GRS
19	New-Cost	New-Cost-C, New-Cost-V, New-Cost-GRS
20	Revenue	Revenue-C, Revenue-V, Revenue-GRS
21	New-Revenue	New-Revenue-C, New-Revenue-V, New-Revenue-GRS
22	Profit	Profit-C, Profit-V, Profit-GRS
23	New-Profit	New-Profit-C, New-Profit-V, New-Profit-GRS

(continued)

(continued)

No.	Cluster	Model
24	Ratio (Revenue/Cost)	Ratio-C, Ratio-V
25	Bilateral	Bilateral-CCR-I, Bilateral-BCC-I, Bilateral-SBM-C, Bilateral-SBM-V
26	Window	Window-I-C, Window-I-V, Window-I-GRS, Window-O-C, Window-O-V, Window-O-GRS
27	FDH	FDH
28	Malmquist-Radial	Malmquist-Radial-I-C, Malmquist-Radial-I-V, Malmquist-Radial-I-GRS, Malmquist-Radial-O-C, Malmquist-Radial-O-V, Malmquist-Radial-O-GRS

The meanings of the extensions -C, -V and -GRS are as follows. Every DEA model assumes a returns to scale (RTS) characteristics that is represented by the ranges of the sum of the intensity vector λ, i.e., $L \leq \lambda_1 + \lambda_2 + \cdots + \lambda_n \leq U$. The *constant* RTS (-C) corresponds to $(L = 0, U = \infty)$, and the variable RTS (-V) to $(L = 1, U = 1)$, respectively. In the models with the extension GRS, we have to supply L and U through keyboard, the defaults being $L = 0.8$ and $U = 1.2$. The *increasing* RTS corresponds to $(L = 1, U = \infty)$ and the *decreasing* RTS to $(L = 0, U = 1)$, respectively. It is recommended to try several sets of (L, U) in order to identify how the RTS characteristics exerts an influence on the efficiency score.

4. Preparation of Data File

The data file should be prepared in an Excel Workbook prior to execution of DEA-Solver. The formats are as follows:

(1) **The CCR, BCC, IRS, DRS, GRS, SBM and FDH Models**
   Figure 1 shows an example of data file for these models.

   (a) **The first row (Row 1)**
      The first row (Row 1) contains Names of the problem and Input/Output Items, i.e.,
      Cell (A1) = Problem Name
      Cell (B1), (C1), ... = Names of I/O items.
      The heading (I) or (O), showing them as being input or output, should head the names of I/O items. The items without an (I) or (O) heading will not be considered as inputs and outputs. The ordering of (I) and (O) items is arbitrary.

   (b) **The second and subsequent rows**
      The second row contains the name of the first DMU and I/O values for the corresponding I/O items. This continues up to the last DMU.

   (c) **The scope of data area**
      A data set must have at least by one blank column at right and one blank row at bottom. This is a necessity for knowing the end of the data area. The data set should start from the top-left cell (A1).

	A	B	C	D	E	F
1	Hospital	(I)Doctor	(I)Nurse	(O)Outpatient	(O)Inpatient	
2	A	20	151	100	90	
3	B	19	131	150	50	
4	C	25	160	160	55	
5	D	27	168	180	72	
6	E	22	158	94	66	
7	F	55	255	230	90	
8	G	33	235	220	88	
9	H	31	206	152	80	
10	I	30	244	190	100	
11	J	50	268	250	100	
12	K	53	306	260	147	
13	L	38	284	250	120	
14						

Fig. 1 Sample.xls in excel sheet

(d) **Data sheet name**

A preferable sheet name is "DAT" (not "Sheet 1"). Never use names "Summary," "Score," "Projection," "Weight," "WeightedData," "Slack," "RTS," "Window," "Malmquist," "Rank" and "Graph" for the data sheet. They are reserved for this software.

The above sample problem "Hospital" has 12 DMUs with two inputs "(I) Doctor" and "(I)Nurse" and two outputs "(O)Outpatient" and "(O)Inpatient." The data set is bordered by one blank column (F) and by one blank row (14). The GRS model has the constraint $L \leq \lambda_1 + \lambda_2 + \ldots + \lambda_n \leq U$. The values of L ($\leq 1$) and U ($\geq 1$) must be supplied through the Message-Box on the display by request. Defaults are $L = 0.8$ and $U = 1.2$.

(2) **The AR Model**

Figure 2 exhibits an example of data for the AR (Assurance Region) model. This problem has the same inputs and outputs as in Fig. 1. The constraints for the assurance region should be denoted in rows 15 and 16 after "one blank row" at 14. This blank row is necessary for separating the data set and the assurance region constraints. These rows read as follows: the ratio of weights "(I)Doctor" vs. "(I)Nurse" is not less than 1 and not greater than 5 and that for "(O)Outpatient" vs. "(O)Inpatient" is not less than 0.2 and not greater than 0.5. Let the weights for Doctor and Nurse be v(1) and v(2), respectively. Then the first constraint implies

$$1 \leq v(1)/v(2) \leq 5.$$

Similarly, the second constraint means that the weights u(1) (for Outpatient) and u(2) (for Inpatient) satisfies the relationship

$$0.2 \leq u(1)/u(2) \leq 0.5.$$

	A	B	C	D	E	F
1	Hospital	(I)Doctor	(I)Nurse	(O)Outpatient	(O)Inpatient	
2	A	20	151	100	90	
3	B	19	131	150	50	
4	C	25	160	160	55	
5	D	27	168	180	72	
6	E	22	158	94	66	
7	F	55	255	230	90	
8	G	33	235	220	88	
9	H	31	206	152	80	
10	I	30	244	190	100	
11	J	50	268	250	100	
12	K	53	306	260	147	
13	L	38	284	250	120	
14						
15	1	(I)Doctor	(I)Nurse	5		
16	0.2	(O)Outpatient	(O)Inpatient	0.5		
17	1	(I)Doctor	(O)Inpatient	5		
18						

Fig. 2 Sample-AR.xls in excel sheet

Notice that the weight constraints can be applied between inputs and outputs, e.g.,

$$1 \le v(1)/u(2) \le 5.$$

(3) **The Super-efficiency Model**

In most DEA models, the best performers have the full efficient status denoted by unity (1), and from experience, we know that plural DMUs usually have this "efficient status." The "Super-efficiency models" rank these efficient DMUs by assigning an efficiency score greater than 1. The larger the efficiency score, the more efficient the DMU is judged to be. For this, we have two clusters: nonradial and radial. NonRadial model bases on the slacks-based measure (SBM) of efficiency. This SBM type model has nine variations. The first six: Super-SBM-I-C, Super-SBM-I-V, Super-SBM-I-GRS, Super-SBM-O-C, Super-SBM-O-V and Super-SBM-O-GRS are "Oriented," while the other three: Super-SBM-C, Super-SBM-V and Super-SBM-GRS, are "NonOriented." They have the same data format as the CCR model. We also include four radial type super-efficiency models; Super-CCR-I, Super-CCR-O, Super-BCC-I and Super-BCC-O.

(4) **The NCN and NDSC Models**

The non-controllable variable (NCN) and non-discretionary variable (NDSC) models have basically the same data format as the CCR model. However, the non-controllable/non-discretionary inputs or outputs must have the headings (IN) or (ON), respectively. Figure 3 exhibits the case where 'Doctor' is a non-controllable/non-discretionary input and 'Inpatient' is a non-controllable/non-discretionary output.

	A	B	C	D	E	F
1	Hospital	(IN)Doctor	(I)Nurse	(O)Outpatient	(O)Inpatient	
2	A	20	151	100	90	
3	B	19	131	150	50	
4	C	25	160	160	55	
5	D	27	168	180	72	
6	E	22	158	94	66	
7	F	55	255	230	90	
8	G	33	235	220	88	
9	H	31	206	152	80	
10	I	30	244	190	100	
11	J	50	268	250	100	
12	K	53	306	260	147	
13	L	38	284	250	120	
14						

Fig. 3 Sample-NCN.xls in excel sheet

Here, we describe the difference between the NCN and NDSC models. In the **NCN** (non-controllable variable) model, Non-controllable input/output = A nonnegative combination of non-controllable inputs/outputs of all DMUs.

However, if other situations (constraints) are preferred, i.e., 'greater than or equal (≥)' constraints in input and 'less than or equal (≤)' constraints in output, the **NDSC** (non-discretionary variable) model can be utilized. Thus, in this model, we assume the following inequality constraints:

Non-discretionary input ≥ A nonnegative combination of non-discretionary input of all DMUs.

Non-discretionary output ≤ A nonnegative combination of non-discretionary output of all DMUs.

(5) **The BND Model**

The bounded inputs or outputs must have the headings (IB) or (OB). The columns headed by (LB) and (UB) supply the lower and upper bounds, respectively. Also, these (LB) and (UB) columns must be inserted immediately after the corresponding (IB) or (OB) column. Figure 4 implies that 'Doctor' and 'Inpatient' are bounded variables and their lower and upper bounds are given by the columns (LB)Doc., (UB)Doc., (LB)Inpat., and (UB) Inpat, respectively.

(6) **The CAT, SYS and Bilateral Models**

These models have basically the same data format as the CCR model. However, in the last column they must have an integer showing their category, system or bilateral group, as follows.

For the CAT model, the number starts from 1 (DMUs under the most difficult environment or with the most severe competition), 2 (in the second group of difficulty) and so on. It is recommended that the numbers are continuously assigned starting from 1.

	A	B	C	D	E	F	G	H	I	J
1	Hospital	(IB)Doc.	(LB)Doc.	(UB)Doc.	(I)Nurse	(O)Outpat.	(OB)Inpat.	(LB)Inpat.	(UB)Inpat.	
2	A	20	15	22	151	100	90	80	100	
3	B	19	15	23	131	150	50	45	55	
4	C	25	20	25	160	160	55	50	60	
5	D	27	21	27	168	180	72	70	76	
6	E	22	20	25	158	94	66	60	80	
7	F	55	45	56	255	230	90	80	100	
8	G	33	31	36	235	220	88	80	95	
9	H	31	29	33	206	152	80	70	90	
10	I	30	28	31	244	190	100	90	110	
11	J	50	45	50	268	250	100	90	120	
12	K	53	45	54	306	260	147	130	160	
13	L	38	30	40	284	250	120	110	130	
14										

Fig. 4 Sample-BND.xls in excel sheet

	A	B	C	D	E	F	G
1	Hospital	(I)Doctor	(I)Nurse	(O)Outpatient	(O)Inpatient	Cat.	
2	A	20	151	100	90	1	
3	B	19	131	150	50	2	
4	C	25	160	160	55	2	
5	D	27	168	180	72	2	
6	E	22	158	94	66	1	
7	F	55	255	230	90	1	
8	G	33	235	220	88	2	
9	H	31	206	152	80	1	
10	I	30	244	190	100	1	
11	J	50	268	250	100	2	
12	K	53	306	260	147	2	
13	L	38	284	250	120	2	
14							

Fig. 5 Sample-CAT.xls in excel sheet

For the SYS model, DMUs in the same system should have the same integer starting from 1.

For the Bilateral model, DMUs must be divided into two groups, denoted by 1 or 2.

Figure 5 exhibits a sample data format for the CAT model.

(7) **The Cost and New-Cost Models**

The unit cost columns must have the heading (C) followed by the *input* name. The ordering of columns is arbitrary. If an input item has no cost column, its cost is regarded as zero. Figure 6 is a sample.

Attention:

Using the optimal solution x^* of this LP, the cost efficiency of DMUo is defined as

$$E_C = c_o x^*/c_o x_o.$$

	A	B	C	D	E	F	G	H
1	Hospital	(I)Doctor	(C)Doctor	(I)Nurse	(C)Nurse	(O)Outpat.	(O)Inpat.	
2	A	20	500	151	100	100	90	
3	B	19	350	131	80	150	50	
4	C	25	450	160	90	160	55	
5	D	27	600	168	120	180	72	
6	E	22	300	158	70	94	66	
7	F	55	450	255	80	230	90	
8	G	33	500	235	100	220	88	
9	H	31	450	206	85	152	80	
10	I	30	380	244	76	190	100	
11	J	50	410	268	75	250	100	
12	K	53	440	306	80	260	147	
13	L	38	400	284	70	250	120	
14								

Fig. 6 Sample-Cost.xls/-New-Cost.xls in excel sheet

	A	B	C	D	E	F	G	H
1	Hospital	(I)Doctor	(I)Nurse	(O)Outpat.	(P)Outpat.	(O)Inpat.	(P)Inpat.	
2	A	20	151	100	550	90	2010	
3	B	19	131	150	400	50	1800	
4	C	25	160	160	480	55	2200	
5	D	27	168	180	600	72	3500	
6	E	22	158	94	400	66	3050	
7	F	55	255	230	430	90	3900	
8	G	33	235	220	540	88	3300	
9	H	31	206	152	420	80	3500	
10	I	30	244	190	350	100	2900	
11	J	50	268	250	410	100	2600	
12	K	53	306	260	540	147	2450	
13	L	38	284	250	295	120	3000	
14								

Fig. 7 Sample-Revenue.xls/-New-Revenue.xls in excel sheet

This implies that if we double the unit costs c_o to $2 c_o$, the cost efficiency E_C still remains invariant. If you feel that this is strange and wish to modify the model in such a way that the magnitude of unit costs directly influences the cost efficiency, you can utilize the New-Cost model. The input data format for this model is the same as the Cost model.

(8) **The Revenue and New-Revenue Models**
The unit price columns must have the heading (P) followed by the *output* name. The ordering of columns is arbitrary. If an output has no price column, its price is regarded as zero. See Fig. 7 for an example.

Attention:
Using the optimal solution y^* of this LP, the revenue efficiency of DMUo is defined as

	A	B	C	D	E	F	G	H	I	J	K	L
1	Car	89		90		91		92		93		
2	DMU	(I)Sales	(O)Profit	Sales	Profit	Sales	Profit	Sales	Profit	Sales	Profit	
3	Toyota	719	400	800	539	850	339	894	125	903	103	
4	Nissan	358	92	401	139	418	120	427	34	390	0	
5	Honda	264	74	275	100	280	65	291	54	269	33	
6	Mitsubishi	190	44	203	49	231	66	255	56	262	57	
7												

Fig. 8 Sample-Window.xls/-Malmquist.xls/Malmquist-Radial.xls in excel sheet

$$E_R = p_o\, y_o / p_o y^*$$

This implies that if we double the unit prices p_o to $2\, p_o$, the revenue efficiency E_R still remains invariant. If you feel that this is strange and you wish to modify the model in such a way that the magnitude of unit prices directly influences the revenue efficiency, you can utilize the New-Revenue model. The input data format is the same as the Revenue model.

(9) **The Profit, New-Profit and Ratio Models**

As a combination of *Cost* and *Revenue* models, these models have cost columns headed by (C) for inputs and price columns headed by (P) for outputs.

Attention:

Using the optimal solution (x^*, y^*) of this LP, the profit efficiency of DMUo is defined as

$$E_P = (p_o y_o - c_o x_o)/(p_o y^* - c_o x^*)$$

This implies that if we double the unit prices p_o to $2\, p_o$, and the unit costs c_o to $2\, c_o$, the profit efficiency E_P still remains invariant. If you feel that this is strange and wish to modify the model in such a way that the magnitude of unit prices and unit costs directly influences the profit efficiency, you can utilize the New-Profit model.

(10) **The Window and Malmquist-Radial Models**

Figure 8 exhibits an example of the data format for the Window and Malmquist models. The top-left corner (A1) contains the problem name, e.g., "Car" as shown below. The next right cell (B1) must include the first time period, e.g., "89." The second row beginning from column B exhibits "(I)/(O) items," e.g., "(I)Sales" and "(O)Profit." The names of the DMUs appear from the third row in column A. The contents (observed data) follow in the third and subsequent rows. This style is repeated until the last time period. Note that each time period is placed at the top-left corner of the corresponding frame and (I)/(O) items have the same names throughout the time period. It is not necessary to insert headings (I)/(O) to the I/O names of the second and subsequent time periods. I/O items are determined as desig-nated in the first time period. Figure 8 demonstrates performance of four

	A	B	C	D	E	F
1	WSBM	(I)Doctor	(I)Nurse	(O)Outpatient	(O)Inpatient	
2	A	20	151	100	90	
3	B	19	131	150	50	
4	C	25	160	160	55	
5	D	27	168	180	72	
6	E	22	158	94	66	
7	F	55	255	230	90	
8	G	33	235	220	88	
9						
10	WeightI	10	1			
11	WeightO	1	5			
12						

Fig. 9 Sample WeightedSBM.xls in excel sheet

car-manufacturers, i.e., Toyota, Nissan, Honda and Mitsubishi, during five time periods, i.e., from (19)89 to (19)93, in terms of the input "Sales" and the output "Profit."

(11) **The Weighted SBM Model**

This model requires weights to inputs/outputs as data. They should be given at the rows below the main body of data set with one inserted blank row. See Fig. 9. The first column (A) has **WeightI** or **WeightO** designating input or output, respectively, and the weights to inputs or outputs follow consecutively in the order of input (output) items recorded at the top row. In this example, the weights to Doctor and Nurse are 10:1, and those to Outpatient and Inpatient are 1:5. The values are relative, since the software normalizes them properly. If they are vacant, weights are regarded as even.

5. Starting DEA-Solver

After completion of the data file in an Excel worksheet on an Excel workbook as mentioned above, save the data file and click the file "DEA-Solver-LV(V7)". This starts DEA-Solver. Then follow the instructions on the window.

This Solver proceeds as follows,

(1) **Selection of a DEA model**
(2) **Selection of a data set in Excel Worksheet**
(3) **Selection of a Workbook for saving the results of computation and**
(4) **DEA computation**

6. Results

The results of computation are stored in the selected Excel workbook. The following worksheets contain the results, although some models lack some of them.

(1) **Worksheet "Summary"**
    This worksheet shows statistics on data and a summary report of results obtained.

(2) **Worksheet "Score"**
    This worksheet contains the DEA-score, reference set, λ-value for each DMU in the reference set, and ranking of efficiency scores.
    A part of a sample Worksheet "Score" is displayed in Fig. 10, where it is shown that DMUs A, B and D are efficient (Score $= 1$) and DMU C is inefficient (Score $= 0.8827083$) with the reference set composed of B ($\lambda_B = 0.9$) and D ($\lambda_D = 0.13888889$) and so on.
    The ranking of DMUs in the descending order of efficiency scores is listed in the worksheet "Rank."

(3) **Worksheet "Projection"**
    This worksheet contains projections of each DMU onto the efficient frontier analyzed by the chosen model.

(4) **Worksheet "Weight"**
    Optimal weights v(i) and u(i) for inputs and outputs are exhibited in this worksheet. v(0) corresponds to the constraints $\lambda_1 + \lambda_2 + \ldots + \lambda_n \geq L$ and u(0) to $\lambda_1 + \lambda_2 + \ldots + \lambda_n \leq U$. In the BCC model where $L = U = 1$ holds, u(0) stands for the value of the dual variable for this constraint.

(5) **Worksheet "WeightedData"**
    This worksheet shows the optimal weighted I/O values, $x_{ij}v(i)$ and $y_{rj}u(r)$ for each DMU$_j$ (for $j = 1, \ldots, n$).

(6) **Worksheet "Slack"**

No.	DMU	Score	Rank	Reference set (lambda)					
1	A	1	1	A	1				
2	B	1	1	B	1				
3	C	0.8827083	8	B	0.9	D	0.13888889		
4	D	1	1	D	1				
5	E	0.7634995	12	A	0.5794409	B	5.72E-02	D	0.1526401
6	F	0.8347712	10	B	0.2	D	1.11111111		
7	G	0.9019608	7	A	0.2588235	B	1.29411765		
8	H	0.7963338	11	A	0.3866921	B	1.35E-02	D	0.6183983
9	I	0.9603922	4	A	0.6470588	B	0.83529412		
10	J	0.8706468	9	D	1.3888889				
11	K	0.955098	6	A	0.86	D	0.96666667		
12	L	0.9582043	5	A	0.6470588	B	1.23529412		

Fig. 10 A sample score sheet

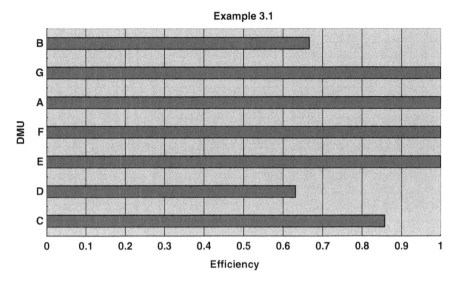

Fig. 11 A sample Graph2

This worksheet contains the input excesses s^- and output shortfalls s^+ for each DMU.

(7) **Worksheet "RTS"**

In case of the BCC, AR-I-V and AR-O-V models, the returns-to-scale characteristics are recorded in this worksheet. For BCC inefficient DMUs, returns-to-scale characteristics are those of the (input or output) projected DMUs on the frontier.

(8) **Graphsheet "Graph1"**

This graphsheet exhibits the bar chart of the DEA scores. You can redesign this graph using the Graph functions of Excel.

(9) **Graphsheet "Graph2"**

This graphsheet exhibits the bar chart of the DEA scores in the ascending order. Figure 11 shows a sample Graph2.

(10) **Worksheets "Window$k$"**

These sheets are only for Window models and k ranges from 1 to L (the length of the time periods in the data). They also include two graphs, 'Variations through Window' and 'Variations by Term'.

Let $k = 3$ (so we deal with three adjacent years, for example). The results of computation in the case of "Window-I-C" are summarized in Fig. 12.

From this table we can see row-wise averages of scores for each maker, which we call "Average through Window." The graph "Variations through Window" exhibits these averages. See Fig. 13.

We can also evaluate column-wise averages of scores for each maker, which we call "Average by Term." The graph "Variations by Term" exhibits these averages. See Fig. 14.

	89	90	91	92	93	Average	C-Average
Toyota	0.8257	1	0.5919			0.8059	
		1	0.5919	0.2075		0.5998	
			1	0.3506	0.286	0.5455	0.6504
Nissan	0.3814	0.514	0.4261			0.4407	
		0.514	0.4261	0.1182		0.3529	
			0.7198	0.1997	0	0.3065	0.3667
Honda	0.416	0.54	0.3446			0.4334	
		0.54	0.3446	0.2754		0.3866	
			0.5821	0.4653	0.3076	0.4517	0.4239
Mitsubishi	0.3437	0.358	0.4241			0.3753	
		0.358	0.4241	0.3259		0.3694	
			0.7164	0.5506	0.5455	0.6042	0.4497

Fig. 12 Window analysis by three adjacent years

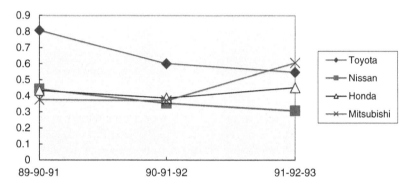

Fig. 13 Variations through Window

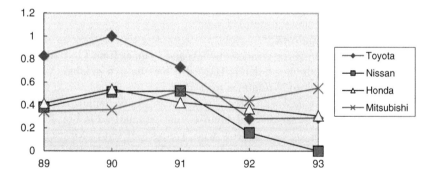

Fig. 14 Variations by Term

Malmquist	89=>90	90=>91	91=>92	92=>93	Average
Toyota	1.170124	0.512571	0.297443	0.815787	0.698981
Nissan	1.348856	0.828199	0.277361	2.75E-08	0.613604
Honda	1.297297	0.638393	0.799366	0.66109	0.849037
Mitsubishi	1.04232	1.183673	0.83616	1.212713	1.068717
Average	1.214649	0.790709	0.552583	0.672398	0.807585

Fig. 15 Sample Malmquist index

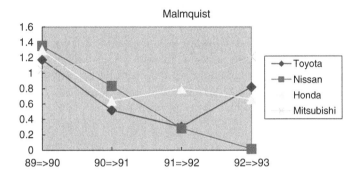

Fig. 16 Malmquist index

(11) **Worksheets "Malmquist$k$"**

These sheets are only for Malmquist models and k ranges from 1 to L (the length of the time periods in the data). The worksheet "Malmquist$k$" exhibits the results regarding the Malmquist index with the time interval k. For example, for the data set in Fig. 8, the worksheet "Malmquist1" contains the three indices: "Catch-up," "Frontier-shift" and "Malmquist," with respect to the time period pairs: $(89 \geq 90)$, $(90 \geq 91)$, $(91 \geq 92)$ and $(92 \geq 93)$ (Time interval = 1). The worksheet "Malmquist2" includes the above indices with the time period pairs: $(89 \geq 91)$, $(90 \geq 92)$ and $(91 \geq 93)$ (Time interval = 2). Figure 15 shows the Malmquist index ("Malmquist1") for the data set in Fig. 8 as evaluated by the Malmquist-I-C (input-oriented and constant returns-to-scale) model.

This worksheet also contains the graph of the above table. See Fig. 16. The graphs for the "Catch-up" and "Frontier-shift" tables are also exhibited in each worksheet.

Note. The BCC, AR-I-V and AR-O-V models contain all the worksheets except "Window" and "Malmquist." The CCR, IRS, DRS, GRS, AR-I-C, AR-O-C, SBM and Super-efficiency models contain all sheets except "RTS," "Window" and "Malmquist." The NCN, NDSC, BND, CAT, SYS, Cost, Revenue, Profit, Ratio and FDH models produce "Summary," "Score,"

"Projection," "Graph1" and "Graph2." The Bilateral model shows "Summary" and "Score" sheets. The Window (Malmquist) model contains "Window (Malmquist)" and "Summary" sheets.

7. Data Limitations

(1) **Problem size**
    The number of DMUs must be less than or equal to 50.
(2) **For the sake of numerical accuracy**
    Comparing an extremely large scale DMU with an extremely small scale DMU within a data set may result in the loss of numerical accuracy in the score obtained. In some cases, this leads to infeasible or unbounded LP solutions. We recommend that, within an input or output item, the ratio min/max of data is greater than 10^{-4} on average. In order to avoid such troubles, grouping DMUs within a comparable size and analyzing each group separately will be helpful.

8. Inappropriate Data for Each Model

DMUs with the following irregular data are excluded from the comparison group as "inappropriate" DMUs. They are listed in the Worksheet "Summary." We will adopt the following notations for this purpose.

xmax (*xmin*) = the max (min) input value of the DMU concerned
ymax (*ymin*) = the max (min) output value of the DMU concerned
costmax (*costmin*) = the max (min) unit cost of the DMU concerned
pricemax (*pricemin*) = the max (min) unit price of the DMU concerned

(1) **For the CCR, BCC-I, IRS, DRS, GRS, CAT, SYS and Adjusted Projection models**
    DMUs with no positive value in inputs, i.e., $xmax \leq 0$, will be excluded from computation. Zero or minus values are permitted if there is at least one positive value in the inputs of the DMU concerned.
(2) **For the BCC-O model**
    DMUs with no positive value in outputs, i.e., $ymax \leq 0$, will be excluded from computation.
(3) **For the AR and ARG models**
    DMUs with a non-positive value in inputs/outputs regarding AR-constraints are excluded from the comparison group.
(4) **For the FDH model**
    DMUs with no positive input value, i.e., $xmax \leq 0$, or a negative input value, i.e., $xmin < 0$, will be excluded from computation.

(5) **For the Cost and New-Cost models**

DMUs with $xmax \leq 0$, $xmin < 0$, $costmax \leq 0$, or $costmin < 0$ will be excluded. DMUs with non-positive current input cost (≤ 0) will also be excluded.

(6) **For the Revenue, New-Revenue, Profit, New-Profit and Ratio models**

DMUs with no positive input value, i.e., $xmax \leq 0$, no positive output value, i.e., $ymax \leq 0$, or with a negative output value, i.e., $ymin < 0$, will be excluded from computation. Furthermore, in the **Revenue** and **New-Revenue** models, DMUs with $pricemax \leq 0$, or $pricemin < 0$ will be excluded from the comparison group. In the **Profit** and **New-Profit** models, DMUs with $costmax \leq 0$ or $costmin < 0$ will be excluded. Finally, in the **Ratio** model, DMUs with $pricemax \leq 0$, $pricemin < 0$, $costmax \leq 0$ or $costmin < 0$ will be excluded.

(7) **For the NCN, NDSC and BND models**

Negative input and output values are set to zero by the program. DMUs with $xmax \leq 0$ in the controllable (discretionary) input variables will be excluded from the comparison group as "inappropriate" DMUs. In the BND model, the lower bound and the upper bound must enclose the given (observed) values; otherwise these values will be adjusted to the given data.

(8) **For the Window model**

For the Window-I-C, Window-I-V and Window-O-C models, no restriction exists for output data, i.e., positive, zero or negative values for outputs are permitted. However, DMUs with $xmax \leq 0$ will be characterized as being zero efficiency. For the Window-O-V model, no restriction exists for input data, i.e., positive, zero or negative values for inputs are permitted. However, DMUs with $ymax \leq 0$ will be characterized as being zero efficiency. This is for the purpose of completing the score matrix. So, you must take care in interpreting the results in this case.

(9) **For the SBM and Super-efficiency models**

We exclude DMUs with no positive input value, i.e., $xmax \leq 0$ from computation.

(10) **For the Bilateral model**

We cannot compare two groups if there is an input item in which one group has all zero-value while the other group has positive values for the corresponding input items.

(11) **For the Malmquist model**

We insert a small positive number (10^{-8}) to any non-positive value in inputs or in outputs.

9. Sample Problems and Results

This version includes sample problems and results for all clusters in the folder "Sample-DEA-Solver-LV(V8)."

About the Author

Dr. Ozcan is a professor of Health Administration at Virginia Commonwealth University and the Editor-in-Chief of the journal, *Health Care Management Science*. He has written a book that will have wide use in the academic and practitioner health care communities. It is a book that will be particularly influential in the application and utility of performance measures in the health care systems worldwide.

Y.A. Ozcan, *Health Care Benchmarking and Performance Evaluation*, 319
International Series in Operations Research & Management Science 210,
DOI 10.1007/978-1-4899-7472-3, © Springer Science+Business Media New York 2014

Index

A

Activity-based financing (ABF), 142, 279–281
Acute care general hospitals
  applications, 148
  CAH, 260–261
  capital investments
    beds, 145
    plant complexity, 144
    service-mix, 145
    weighted service-mix, 145
  EMR and efficiency, 249–250
  inpatient services, 146–147
  labor, 145–146
  operating expenses, 146
  outpatient visits, 147–148
Advanced DEA models
  bootstrapping method
    empirical distribution, 132–133
    SBM-I-C bootstrap scores, 134, 135
    slack-based input-oriented CCR model, 134
    STATA statistical package, 133, 135
    super-efficiency DEA scores, 134, 136–137
    triangular distribution, 133
  congestion DEA, 124–126
  health care organization, 135
  network and dynamic, 126–128
  super-efficiency evaluation
    input and output targets, 123
    input-oriented CCR model, 124
    model selection, CCR-I, 121, 122
    SBM, 124
    vs. standard CCR-I models, 122
    super-efficiency models, 121–124
    two-stage analysis, 128–132

Allocative efficiency
  description, 19, 20
  group input practices, 19
  physicians, 21
Ambulatory surgery centers (ASCs)
  DEA, 236–237
  inefficient, 237
Assurance region (AR) models *See* Weight restricted (multiplier) models
Asthma
  clinical practice guidelines, 185
  community variation, 178
  decision rules, 179
  descriptive statistics, 180, 181
  diagnosis (ICD-9-CM) codes, 178
  efficiency score, DMU, 181, 182
  generic substitutes, 183
  input-oriented constant returns to scale (CRS), 181
  limitations, 183–184
  medical decision-making process, 178
  outputs, inputs and cost increase and reduction, 182, 183
  patient severity, 178, 179
  patient treatment, 185
  steroid and bronchodilator therapy, 178–179
  treatment practice, 185

C

CABG *See* Coronary artery bypass graft (CABG)
CAH *See* Critical Access Hospitals (CAH)
Categorical models
  data setup, 86, 87
  "difference" column, 86, 88
  summary, 86, 88

CPSIA information can be obtained
at www.ICGtesting.com
Printed in the USA
LVOW05*2004090817

544398LV00001B/21/P